Theatre Spaces
1920–2020

RELATED TITLES AVAILABLE FROM METHUEN DRAMA

The Art of Making Theatre
Pamela Howard with Pavel Drábek
ISBN 978-1-3502-7798-4

The Art of Scenic Design
Robert Mark Morgan
ISBN 978-1-3501-3954-1

Consuming Scenography: The Shopping Mall as Theatrical Experience
Nebojša Tabački
ISBN 978-1-3501-1089-2

Contemporary Scenography: Practices and Aesthetics in German Theatre, Arts and Design
Edited by Birgit E. Wiens
ISBN 978-1-3500-6447-8

The Development of the English Playhouse
Richard Leacroft
ISBN 978-0-4136-0600-6

Performing Architectures: Projects, Practices, Pedagogies
Edited by Andrew Filmer and Juliet Rufford
ISBN 978-1-4742-4798-6

Scenography Expanded: An Introduction to Contemporary Performance Design
Edited by Joslin McKinney and Scott Palmer
ISBN 978-1-4742-4439-8

Theatre Spaces 1920–2020
Finding the Fun in Functionalism

A memoir by Iain Mackintosh

methuen | drama
LONDON · NEW YORK · OXFORD · NEW DELHI · SYDNEY

METHUEN DRAMA
Bloomsbury Publishing Plc
50 Bedford Square, London, WC1B 3DP, UK
1385 Broadway, New York, NY 10018, USA
29 Earlsfort Terrace, Dublin 2, Ireland

BLOOMSBURY, METHUEN DRAMA and the Methuen Drama logo are trademarks of
Bloomsbury Publishing Plc

First published in Great Britain 2023
Reprinted 2023

Copyright © Iain Mackintosh, 2023

Iain Mackintosh has asserted his right under the Copyright, Designs and Patents Act 1988
to be identified as author of this work.

For legal purposes the Acknowledgements on pp. 228–230 constitute an extension of this copyright page.

Published in association with The Society for Theatre Research

Cover design: Ben Anslow
Cover image: Jerwood Theatre with audience, Royal Court Theatre, London (Photo © Stephen Cummiskey)

All rights reserved. No part of this publication may be reproduced or transmitted in any form or
by any means, electronic or mechanical, including photocopying, recording, or any information
storage or retrieval system, without prior permission in writing from the publishers.

Bloomsbury Publishing Plc does not have any control over, or responsibility for, any third-party websites
referred to or in this book. All internet addresses given in this book were correct at the time of going
to press. The author and publisher regret any inconvenience caused if addresses have changed or
sites have ceased to exist, but can accept no responsibility for any such changes.

A catalogue record for this book is available from the British Library.

Library of Congress Cataloging-in-Publication Data
Names: Mackintosh, Iain, author. | Society for Theatre Research.
Title: Theatre spaces 1920-2020 : finding the fun in functionalism / Iain
   Mackintosh.
Description: London ; New York : Methuen|Drama, 2023. | "Society fo
   Theatre Research." | Includes bibliographical references and index.
Identifiers: LCCN 2022025618 (print) | LCCN 2022025619 (ebook) |
   ISBN 9781350056244 (paperback) | ISBN 9781350056251 (hardback) |
   ISBN 9781350056268 (epub) | ISBN 9781350056275 (ebook)
Subjects: LCSH: Theater architecture–History–20th century. | Theater
   architecture–History–21st century. | Theaters–Designs and plans.
Classification: LCC NA6821 .M26 2023 (print) | LCC NA6821 (ebook) |
   DDC 725/.822—dc23/eng/20220720
LC record available at https://lccn.loc.gov/2022025618
LC ebook record available at https://lccn.loc.gov/2022025619

ISBN:	HB:	978-1-3500-5625-1
	PB:	978-1-3500-5624-4
	ePDF:	978-1-3500-5627-5
	eBook:	978-1-3500-5626-8

Typeset by RefineCatch Limited, Bungay, Suffolk
Printed and bound in India

To find out more about our authors and books visit www.bloomsbury.com
and sign up for our newsletters.

CONTENTS

List of illustrations vii
Foreword by Sir Richard Eyre xi

An introduction and a summary 1

Act I Pre-1920: Setting the scene and some early pioneers 3

1. Theatre is ephemeral while buildings endure. Some necessary background 5
2. Richard Wagner, Adolphe Appia and the spreading of the fan 17

Act II 1920–1976: The march of modernism 25

3. The Festival Cambridge, Stratford-upon-Avon and early days of the National 27
4. Guthrie's thrust stages 40
5. Germany's building boom and Anglo-American Shakespeare 53
6. The Olivier, the Lyttelton and the Barbican theatres 59

Act III 1976–2020: The past informs the present 81

7. The Cottesloe and other courtyards 83
8. Worthy scaffolds: Brook's empty space and spaces found by others 102
9. Regenerating the old offers an antidote to modernism. Part One: English theatres of the eighteenth and nineteenth centuries 117
10. Regenerating the old offers an antidote to modernism. Part Two: A couple of twentieth-century Scottish theatres reborn – one in Edinburgh and the other in Florida 134
11. New opera houses from Glyndebourne to Dallas. Elsewhere some starchitects upstage the performers 144

12 Learning from the Netherlands, Berlin, Brazil, Australia and from Indian and Chinese cultures 163

13 2010–2020: Some new builds, two renovations – one at Stratford-upon-Avon and one in London – and diversions on in-the-round and the open air 179

Act IV 2021: The future 207

14 Unforeseen consequences of seventeenth-century plagues, of the arrival of the talkies and the more recent dangers of the pandemic and of 'virtual theatre'. Some central themes restated 209

Bibliographies 221
Acknowledgements 228
Theatre index 231
Person index 235

ILLUSTRATIONS

Cover: Since 1952 the Royal Court Theatre London has been the home of new drama. In 2000 architect Steve Tompkins stripped out many layers of paint and plasterwork from successive versions of the original 1888 auditorium to reveal purposeful structural steel thus giving the whole a contemporary character. Photo Stephen Cummiskey

1.1	Plan of the Old Vic overlaid on that of the Olivier Theatre	6
1.2	'Cheek by jowl', 1894 engraving of poorer pit patrons immediately behind expensive front stalls	13
2.1	Bayreuth interior as built in 1896 before level inserted over boxes and below gallery	18
2.2	Two isometrics by Richard Leacroft: *Hellerau* over *Le Vieux-Colombier*	22
3.1	Two isometrics by Richard Leacroft: Wilkins' Barnwell Theatre Cambridge of 1814 over Gray's Festival Theatre of 1926	28
3.2	Cambridge Festival Theatre auditorium 1926 over map of Norwich company circuit	29
3.3	Cambridge Festival Theatre section over plan 1926	31
3.4	Cambridge Festival Theatre: *Oresteia* 1926 over *The Provok'd Wife* 1927	33
3.5	Drawings by Richard Leacoft of *Künstler Theater* Munich 1908 over Stratford-on-Avon 1932	37
4.1	*The Thrie Estaitis* at the Assembly Hall Edinburgh 1948 drawn by Richard Leacroft	41
4.2	Festival Theatre Stratford Ontario 1957 over Guthrie Theatre Minneapolis, *The Three Sisters* 1963	43
4.3	Same-scale comparisons of six thrust stages. Capacities: Assembly Hall 1,350; Stratford Ontario 2,250; Chichester 1,350; Minneapolis 1,400; Crucible 1,000; Olivier 1,150	45
4.4	Opening production of *Amadeus*, Chichester Festival Theatre after 2014 renovation by Haworth Tompkins	47
4.5	*Life of Galileo* at Young Vic 2017	50
5.1	*Antony & Cleopatra* at Shakespeare's Globe 1999	55
5.2	Two plans of Shakespeare's Globe yard level: as built in 1997 over proposal of 2015	56
6.1	Two Lasdun sketches for the Olivier: Scheme A over Scheme B	66
6.2	Lasdun's model for the Olivier with setting envisaged by Jocelyn Herbert over photo of Olivier set up for *Small Island* 2020	67

6.3	Epidaurus sketch by Onno Greiner 1959	70
6.4	Eden Court Theatre Inverness 1976 taken in 2009	73
6.5	Two Barbican sketches – Richard Southern 1959 and Elizabeth Bury 1968	75
6.6	Full auditorium at the Barbican Theatre	77
7.1	Four sketches of Cottesloe layouts: *Half Life* 1977, *The Beggar's Opera* 1982, *Fuente Ovejuna* 1992 and *The Voysey Inheritance* 1989	84
7.2	In *The Mysteries* at the Cottesloe, God on top of a fork-lift creates a world lit only by candles.	85
7.3	Opening performance at the Wilde Theatre Bracknell 1984	91
7.4	The flexible Martha Cohen Theatre Calgary 1985: *Angels in America* over *Candide*	92
7.5	Westminster School Connecticut Theatre 1988	93
7.6	Edward Alleyn Hall Dulwich College 1983: Tim Foster's axonometric over-audience photo	94
7.7	Iain Mackintosh sacred geometry overlay on plan originally supposed by Inigo Jones himself	95
7.8	Pair of supposed Inigo Jones drawings once known as 7b and 7c and now as H&T 10 and H&T 11. Worcester College, Oxford	96
7.9	Sam Wanamaker Playhouse 2014 adjacent to Shakespeare's Globe 1997	97
7.10	Hall Two Sage Gateshead: 2004: TPC proposal over in-the-round performance	99
8.1	Audiences in the Tricycle Theatre Kilburn 1980 and Georgian Theatre Royal Richmond Yorkshire 1766 restored 1963	104
8.2	*The Bacchae* at the *Teatro Oficina* São Paulo Brazil in 1996	106
8.3	Royal Court Theatre 1888 renovated 2000: long section of extension to Sloane Square over auditorium	108
8.4	Tina Packer Playhouse Lenox Massachusetts 2001. Architects' drawings over auditorium	109
8.5	*Théâtre des Bouffes du Nord* Paris 1878 acquired by Peter Brook 1974. Photo by Jean-Guy Lecat, a key member of Brook's team	111
8.6	*Théâtre des Bouffes du Nord*, long section, as adapted for Peter Brook and drawn by Jean-Guy Lecat	113
8.7	Majestic Theatre New York 1904 as adapted for Peter Brook 1987 by Jean-Guy Lecat and Hardy Holzman Pfeiffer Associates architects	114
9.1	First night Lawrence Batley Theatre Huddersfield 1994 within already gutted chapel	118
9.2	Bristol Old Vic auditorium renovated 2012 by Andrzej Blonski architect over studio by Haworth Tompkins Architects 2018	123
9.3	Theatre Royal Bury St Edmunds: a 1906 full house over auditorium renovated in 2007	125
9.4	Theatre Royal Bury St Edmunds 1819, William Wilkins' geometry explained by Axel Burrough of Levitt Bernstein	127
9.5	Newcastle Theatre Royal 1837 over interior by Frank Matcham 1897	129
9.6	Nottingham Theatre Royal: 1837 auditorium renovated 1978 by architects RHWL	131

ILLUSTRATIONS

10.1	Opening in 1990 of Dunfermline Opera House, now the Mertz Theatre in Sarasota Florida, over same when derelict in Dunfermline, Scotland	135
10.2	Lyric Theatre Hammersmith 1895 as translated to new site 1979	136
10.3	Festival Theatre Edinburgh built as Empire Theatre 1928 renovated 1994	141
10.4	New facade of Festival Theatre Edinburgh 1994	142
11.1	Glyndebourne: TPC's concept design July 1990	146
11.2	'Iain's mumbo jumbo' received by architect Michael Hopkins from TPC April 1990	147
11.3	Glyndebourne auditoriums: new opened in 1994 over old theatre demolished in 1992	149
11.4	Longborough Festival Opera 1998	152
11.5	New Garsington Opera 2011. Architects Robin Snell and Partners advised by Iain Mackintosh. Interior over exterior	153
11.6	New Garsington. Robin Snell's sketch for positioning the opera house	155
11.7	Grange Park Opera: design and illustration by Tim Ronalds over photo as built by others	156
11.8	Dallas Opera House 2010. Architects Foster + Partners advised by TPC	159
11.9	Oslo Opera House 2008. Architects Snøhetta advised by TPC	161
12.1	Onno Greiner's *De Tamboer* at Hoogeveen 1990	163
12.2	*De Maagd* Theatre within deconsecrated church, Bergen op zoom 1990 over Greiner drawing of renovation at *Enschede Schouwburg* 1988. Both advised by TPC	165
12.3	Interiors of Ouro Preto theatre 1770 over Manaus Opera House 1897	169
12.4	*Theatro José de Alencar* Fortaleza 1910	171
12.5	Two temple *kuttampalams* in Kerala India at Haripad 1769 and at Thrissur 1880. Drawn and photographed by Gopika Jayasaree	174
12.6	*Zhengyici* Beijing, photo over plan of typical classical theatre drawn by Jack Chen	175
12.7	Oil painting by an unknown mid-19th-century Chinese artist of a waterside open-air performance	177
13.1	Liverpool Everyman 2011. Architects Howarth Tompkins. Exterior over performance on thrust stage	180
13.2	Liverpool Everyman section over stalls level thrust without stage riser plan. Architects Haworth Tompkins	181
13.3	Theatre at Chateau d'Hardelot, Pas-de-Calais. Architect Andrew Todd	183
13.4	Stratford-on-Avon Plan 'B' Theatre Projects Consultants 14 December 2001	185
13.5	Royal Shakespeare Theatre 2010. New stage and auditorium over stage cutaway. Architects Rab Bennetts Associates advised by Charcoalblue	187
13.6	RST Swan Theatre 1986 within 1879/1932 shell. Architect Michael Reardon. Over open-air theatre of 2010 with Swan shell in background	189
13.7	Three Shakespearean theatres compared: Stratford Ontario 1957; Wanamaker's Globe 1997; RST revised 2010. Drawn by Gavin Green	190
13.8	The Yard, Chicago 2017 – concept drawing by Gavin Green over *Macbeth* curtain calls in opening season 2018	192

13.9	The Bridge 2017 Architect Haworth Tompkins, Three full tiers over long section over promenade performance of *A Midsummer Night's Dream*	194
13.10	Theatre Royal Drury Lane 2021. Renovation architect Haworth Tompkins. Photos of auditorium showing clumsy pre-2019 over the smoother 2021 revision	196
13.11	Theatre Royal Drury Lane: comparison of entrance level from 2021 over pre-2019	197
13.12	Same-scale comparisons: Theatre Royal Drury Lane holding 1,979, The Bridge holding 915, Olivier holding 1,150	198
13.13	Manchester Royal Exchange Theatre 1976. Architects Levitt Bernstein. Structure supported off pillars over curtain call for *Lord Arthur Savile's Crime* 1982	200
13.14	Orange Tree February 1991. Architects TPC. First preview of opening production of *All in the Wrong* by Arthur Murphy	202
13.15	Three productions at Regent's Park Open Air Theatre 2010–2015	204
14.1	King's Theatre Edinburgh 1906: male and female caryatids over three-quarter view of auditorium after renovation of 1985 and before that of 2024	216

FOREWORD

by Sir Richard Eyre

It should be a simple task to design an object for a unique purpose. The designers of bicycles collaborate with race-winning cyclists to produce a perfect racing machine; the designers of vacuum cleaners enlist a multitude of users to test their inventions in a myriad of domestic settings. The designers of theatres know better: they turn their backs on centuries of empirical wisdom and consult the practitioners only as a tiresome matter of courtesy.

How else to explain the existence of so many auditoriums that are wholly unsuitable for an art form which, uniquely, exploits the scale of the human figure, the sound of the unamplified human voice, and the disposition of mankind to tell each other stories? There is a reason for this: modernism, the sovereign credo of twentieth-century art, has deemed theatre, with its vulnerable dependence on living human performers occupying the same space as several hundred spectators and its reliance on the frail force of the human voice, to be outdated, irrelevant and redundant. But theatre cannot be abstract, cannot be conceptual, cannot depart from tradition: it is always determined by the relationship in the present tense between performer and public in an auditorium which enfolds them both.

It's astonishing that so many theatre architects in the last century could ignore these self-evident truths and could think that by defying their predecessors they could provide congenial spaces to perform and watch plays and musicals. But, as Iain Mackintosh points out in his indispensable and inspiring book, modernism will turn out to have been 'a blip on the architecture of the theatre space... engendered by an incomplete understanding of a functionalist philosophy which quite simply neglected the role of audience'.

Iain Mackintosh has put his knowledge and experience to practical use, not only as the maker of the one triumphantly successful space in the National Theatre building – the Dorfman (né Cottesloe) – but as an inspirational adviser to generations of directors, producers and civic bodies. In this book he charts with great clarity the history of theatre design from Wagner's Festspielhaus to the unyielding brutalist spaces of the late twentieth century, arguing conclusively what any actor instinctively knows: that a horseshoe-shaped auditorium clad with wood and plaster is the most favourable form for an auditorium, as good for sightlines as it is for vocal clarity.

I wish theatre architects of the last few generations had spent time listening to the irrepressible author of *Theatre Spaces*. Only recently – with the collaboration of Mackintosh and architect Michael Hopkins on the new Glyndebourne auditorium and the partnership of Steve Tompkins with director Nick Hytner and producer Nick Starr on the Bridge Theatre – has it been demonstrated conclusively that if architects want to make good theatre buildings, they must learn from those who know how to make good theatre.

As a postscript I should add that I've worked happily in several post-sixties theatre spaces – newly designed or architect adapted – such as the Phoenix in Leicester, the Minerva in Chichester, the Everyman in Liverpool, the Almeida in Islington, Hampstead Theatre, the Chocolate Factory and the Archevêché in Aix-en-Provence, and I've also slogged away in uncongenial and ill-designed theatres but, like all directors, writers and actors, if I've had a success in them my complaints have been muted. While this may show that the power of good theatre, like the cry of a baby for its mother, can survive any obstruction, it should not be taken by impresarios, local authorities and philanthropic visionaries as an invitation to allow architectural theory and aesthetics to overwhelm the power of pragmatism necessary for any act of making theatre.

In the design of theatres, as in acting in them, theory will be as useful as an ice-maker in the Antarctic. It's a wonderful paradox that the most frequently cited ideologue of theatre, Berthold Brecht, should also have produced the most profound refutation of all theatre theory: 'The proof of the pudding,' he said, 'is in the eating.'

January 2022

An introduction and a summary

The subject is theatre spaces new and old from 1920 to 2020, why each type was designed the way it was and how they have been used to create the theatre experience. It is not a review of complete theatre buildings but of the central theatre spaces where performer and audience come together. There is hardly a mention of foyers or of backstage planning but there is some consideration of exteriors that give audiences a first taste of what awaits within.

It is not a history but rather a memoir, which is personal and hence selective. Inevitably one needs a perspective which only time can provide; some say this is at least fifty years. It was around the middle of my century, in 1960, that I chose a career in theatre and in the same decade Britain's National Theatre moved centre stage. The latter was conceived in the mid-1960s but not opened until ten years later in 1976. By then both the modernist style and the fan shape were being questioned as to whether they were appropriate for theatre spaces. I played no part in the design of the Olivier and Lyttelton theatre spaces but I did play a central role in the design of the third, the Cottesloe, which opened in 1977. Within a year, at a conference held in Munich, I gave a paper entitled 'Old and New: The Rejection of the Fan-Shaped Auditorium and the Reinstatement of the Courtyard Form'. My hat was in the ring.

Modernism in the theatre limited the functional to the quantifiable and ignored the qualitative. The challenge of providing theatre spaces where the audience enjoys playing its part had been taken for granted for a couple of centuries but was then being put aside. Perfect sightlines for well-seated audiences in neutral spaces were given the priority while the complex question of atmosphere was largely being ignored. Architects and their clients hardly discussed design issues such as colour and density. The purpose of the touches of frivolity present in the design of older theatre spaces had been forgotten. But this was about to change. Hence a central theme of this memoir is *Finding the Fun in Functionalism*.

An added problem was that many modern architects had used reinforced concrete as their principal building material. It was the impregnability of concrete that prevented successive leaders of the major theatres from altering their inheritance. Theatre spaces built of brick and plaster on the other hand had long been adapted to match changes in the arts of theatre.

At the same time some theatre people were reassessing the few fine old theatres that had survived both war and the property developer. Previously they had been thought of as pleasant spaces that would always be there if you preferred that sort of thing. But careful study was needed to establish how many of these had survived (in Britain about 20 per cent was the answer) and to work out how they might be nurtured to benefit both present and future.

As a memoir this is a hands-on account by one who learnt theatre in two phases. The first was a dozen years of taking the homeless Prospect Theatre Company, which I had co-founded, around many theatres in many countries, as well as to six successive Edinburgh International

Festivals and to London for half a dozen seasons. The second started in late 1973 when I joined the team at Theatre Projects Consultants. Theatres into the design of which I was drawn included courtyard theatres, opera houses, theatre spaces fabricated of builders' scaffolding within found space, old theatres and in one case transporting a magnificent old theatre space from Scotland to Florida. Being invited to conferences on five continents gave me an international perspective as well as growing awareness of the threat posed by internationalism to indigenous theatrical traditions in those cities that aspired to be 'world class'.

The newest problem faced by live theatre over the last decade is the transmission of 'virtual theatre' either to local cinemas or to the high-res TV sets in the homes of subscribers. Many performers hate it, knowing it is almost impossible to perform simultaneously both to a large live audience and to cameras fitted with a close-up lens. Can so-called 'virtual theatre' ever be more than eavesdropping on the magic of live theatre?

Will the closures of 2020 and 2021 caused by the Covid-19 pandemic trigger radical changes in the design of new theatre space? Unforeseen changes to theatre space had occurred in England after seventeenth-century closures due to the plague and the puritans. The new talking pictures worldwide at the end of the 1920s destroyed much live theatre and led to more radical change in the design of theatre spaces than hitherto thought. An awareness of unforeseen consequences to extraneous events in the past plus a study of how theatre space evolved from 1920 to 2020 may help live theatre to recover its central role in society.

ACT ONE

Pre-1920: Setting the scene and some early pioneers

1

Theatre is ephemeral while buildings endure. Some necessary background

The arts of live theatre are ephemeral while those of architecture endure

Live theatre connects actor to audience, each member of which has their own viewpoint and can choose on what to focus. Your reaction as a member of an audience includes more than laughter and applause. A single audience is a distillation of individual reactions. Each and every audience is unique. No two performances are the same. These are just a few of the distinct qualities which define live theatre.

After the event each member of an audience has their own memories. We can jolt these. We can consult the critics, though they most likely saw a different performance from ours. A photograph, a painting or even a digital recording of a different performance of the same production can remind us of what we ourselves had experienced. But these are but aides-memoires, no more. In this respect live theatre differs from film, television or any other permanent mechanical reproduction which can be re-examined at the press of a button.

The ephemeral nature of live theatre is essential to its magic. Only two elements endure after the revels have ended: the printed text and the physical theatre space in which the performance took place. Scholars and critics study the text but rarely assess the contribution to the live experience made by a particular theatre space. (Some cynics say that to a theatre critic sitting in the front rows of the stalls all theatre spaces are the same.) There are theatres in which the architecture is active and encourages the audience to play its part. There are also those where the architecture is deliberately neutral so as to place no barrier between actor and audience. Yet it is often the latter that fail to connect the one to the other.

Compare two opposite perspectives of a drama critic and a scholar. Brooks Atkinson writing in *The New York Times* of 31 October 1974: 'The theatre is not the thing. Nothing is really important except the performance on the stage. The sole function of a theatre is to provide a place where people can assemble and enjoy the show.' Contrast this with Christopher Baugh, who in *Theatre, Performance and Technology* of 2013 suggests that 'the architecture of theatre building and that of the performance space, which are frequently considered to be inanimate and neutral, mute and inanimate things into which theatre artists project their ideas, are in fact things that need to be constantly brought back to life and into fresh perspective, just like the text of a play.' This memoir supports the latter and traces developments of the last century by suggesting that as long as the Atkinson view prevailed the sense of fun was lost in creating the theatre space and that only when the Baugh position gained ground designers of theatre space started to find the fun in functionalism.

The remainder of this chapter sets out the background to much of my argument and clarifies confusions that you may encounter in other books on this period. It will be easier to understand the arguments that are elaborated later if the reader recognises at the outset that this book is less a dispassionate academic treatise and more a memoir by someone who had a hands-on career in the creation both of ephemeral performances and of the enduring theatre spaces in which they occur.

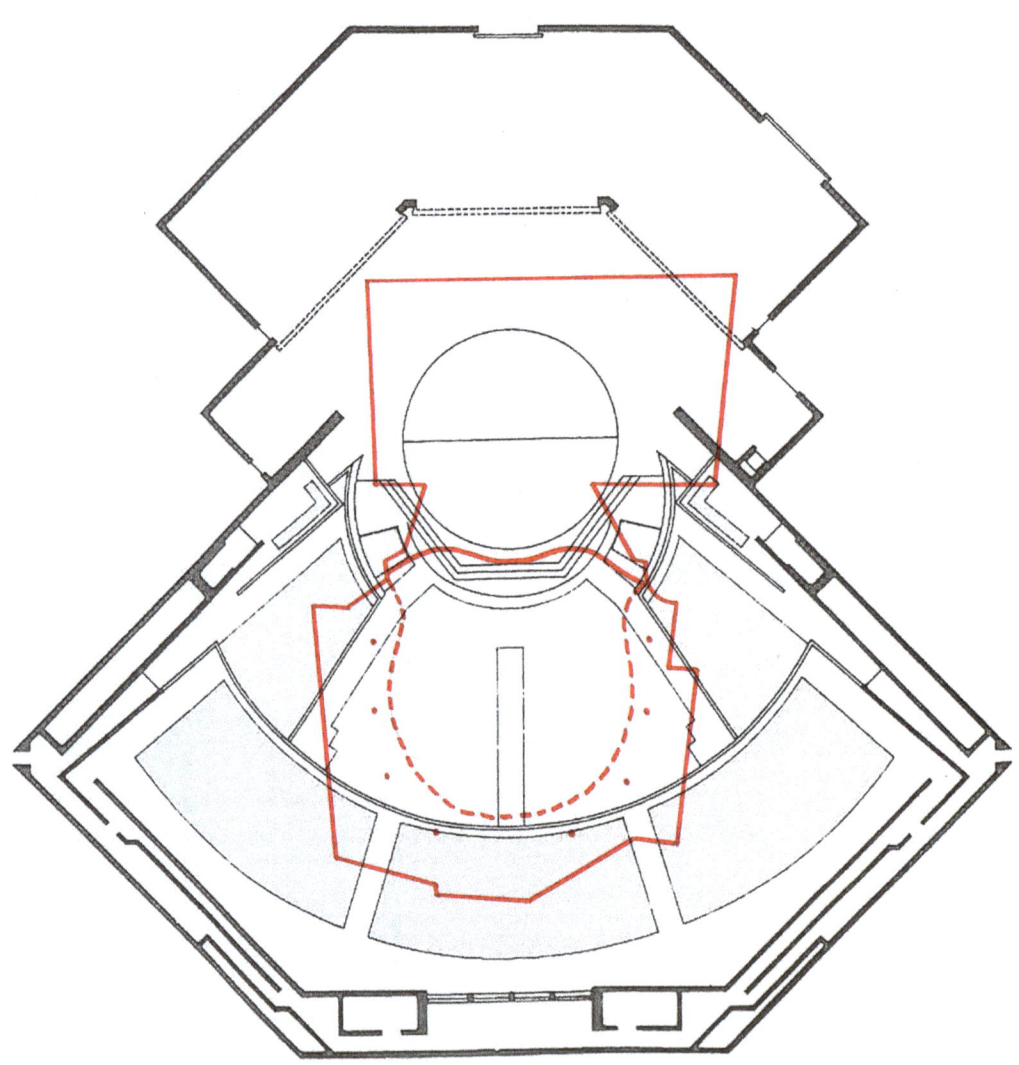

1.1 *Plan of the Old Vic overlaid on that of the Olivier Theatre.*

Some necessary backgrounds to my argument

First – do we start in 1920 or 1876?

In 1876 Richard Wagner's *Festspielhaus* opened at Bayreuth in Bavaria. From 1876 to 1920, a span of forty-four years, there were only twenty-two short summer festivals at this revolutionary fan-shaped theatre space. The older style of theatre architecture continued to flourish across Europe, pausing only for the First World War, while in North America the biggest theatre-building boom in history never paused. Everyone knew what a proper theatre looked like and felt like. At Bayreuth, although the baroque was retained for the decorative treatment of side and rear walls of the auditorium a totally new element was introduced. This was that the seating should be fan-shaped. The fan form did not filter down into mainstream theatre for a couple of generations, which is one good reason for the start date of 1920.

Second – the National Theatre as a reference point and as a cue for anecdote

When it comes to assessing the role of a particular architectural form in the theatre experience few generations have been lucky enough to build their own theatres but rather must accept what they have inherited. In 1987 Richard Eyre succeeded Peter Hall as director of Britain's National Theatre. Hall had served on the NT building committee and hence had been party to the big decisions on what sort of theatre space the main auditorium, the Olivier, was to be. In 1973 Hall had succeeded Laurence Olivier as director of the National Theatre Company. Hall's priority was to open the new NT as quickly as possible. He was in no position to question its design. Eyre, on the other hand, as the third director of the NT, took the job with foreknowledge of what was good and what was bad about the two main theatre spaces in the design of which he had played no part. His audition piece for the NT job had been a spectacularly successful production of *Guys and Dolls* at the Olivier in 1982 when it was discovered how well spectacular American musicals fitted the largest stage of Britain's National Theatre. In 1976 the intimate Old Vic, the NT's home since 1973, had been swapped for the enormous Olivier.

Towards the end of his own ten-year reign Eyre was trying to entice back to the NT the leading actor Albert Finney, who had not forgotten his unhappy experience in the leading role of *Tamburlaine*, the first production on the Olivier stage some twenty years earlier. Eyre was telling Finney that Peter Brook had recently declared that a theatre space was a musical instrument on which the actor plays. Retorted Finney: 'Yes, and who would make a violin out of fucking concrete?' Such was a leading actor's take on the brutalist fashions of the 1960s celebrated at Britain's National Theatre by architect Denys Lasdun. Concrete as a building material had been relatively cheap to pour but had resulted in an unyielding form almost impossible to alter without spending huge sums of money. How to adapt the new concrete theatres introduced problems much trickier than altering earlier ones built with steel, bricks and plaster. From the April 1997 edition of the *Newsletter* of the Theatres Trust, Britain's statutory body charged with the well-being of all theatres, here is Eyre's verdict on the Olivier as he stepped down after his *National Service* (the title of his memoir of those ten years): 'It's a hard stage on which to focus attention, hard to animate. Its monumental scale militates against intimacy and its enormous volume gives rise to lamentable acoustics.' The Finney anecdote and the forthright criticism of Eyre is a foretaste of what is to come.

Third – the different sorts of theatres contrasted: big and small, new and old

Playhouses and opera houses can be categorised in different ways such as those that seat between 200 and 400, which playwrights and actors often prefer, and those that hold many more either to make money for all concerned or to reach out to a wider cross section of the community. Both categories feature in this memoir. (The even smaller studios where often important experiments are undertaken are not debated here since, if successful, work there will filter down to larger theatre spaces.)

Another approach is to divide theatres into the new and old. The old is hardly homogeneous, especially those that have been rediscovered. In 1974 Peter Brook rediscovered the derelict *Bouffes du Nord* of 1876 in Paris and from the outset treated it as 'found space', with the tone and character of a fine but battered Stradivarius. He immediately realised that it should not be 'restored'. Contrast this with the Bavarian *Nationaltheater*, which is the German name of the great opera house of Munich designed by Karl von Fischer, which had opened in 1817. The second theatre of 1825 on the same site had been bombed to bits in the Second World War, providing an opportunity to recreate the first, which all agreed would be better than the second. This reopened in 1963 with a delicately reconsidered horseshoe auditorium and a new stage. Opulently finished and technically immaculate it is set in Munich's grand city centre. In contrast Brook and his team did as little as possible (though that subtly) to the *Bouffes du Nord*, which is to be found in a down-at-heel quarter of Paris, just round the corner from the Gare du Nord. The successful conjuring-up of their respective pasts was diametrically different and rightly so. Today each theatre is both old and new but in different ways.

Fourth – the audience listens, looks and reacts. The part played by 'spectacle'

In all theatres we both look and listen. Contrast live theatre with the heyday of radio drama in the 1960s and 70s when BBC radio producers such as John Tydeman introduced us to many new dramatists who later wrote for the stage as well as persuading leading actors of the day to play Shakespeare on radio. On radio you had to listen because there was nothing to look at.

If in that same era you might have seen the hit West End show *Blitz!* you may not remember the words or music of Lionel Bart, but you would probably recall the spectacle created by scenographer Sean Kenny. The word 'spectacle' requires analysing. It should not suggest only old-fashioned and exaggerated illusion. The *Oxford English Dictionary* offers a range of meaning for 'spectacle' from the straightforward early meaning – 'an impressive or interesting show for those viewing it' – to the mildly pejorative – 'a piece of stage-display or pageantry, as contrasted with real drama', which latter use arrived as early as 1752. Here, I use the first meaning but there are others quoted who assume the second. The reader must not think that I, in what some call an Oxbridge fashion, believe that listening is a more intellectual activity and therefore more significant than looking. Rather is it a question of balance.

That balance changes with the theatre space. On London's South Bank compare Shakespeare at the Olivier, which provides many visual opportunities for 'an impressive or interesting show' watched by an audience of 1,100 sitting in comfortable seats, with Shakespeare at the physically smaller Shakespeare's Globe half a mile downriver where audiences of 1,550 are offered little in the way of scenic spectacle beyond costumes and props. At the latter many at the sides have rotten sightlines and are tightly packed, both the 700 who stand in the yard and those sat in the tiers on backless wooden benches. No one is comfortable. At the Globe audiences first and foremost react to actors speaking verse rather than marvel at pictures set before them as at the Olivier. In different theatres the director must find the appropriate balance between looking and listening.

This introduces the third active participle nailed to my masthead, which is 'reacting'. An audience does not merely attend a performance. Tyrone Guthrie memorably reminded us that the French for to be present at a performance is *assister à*. Here is the most apposite prologue in English literature, from *Henry V*, when Chorus invites the audience to perform its role. I do not apologise for including this prologue in these opening pages. In *Architecture, Actor and Audience*, which I wrote in 1993, they were the last words in the book. Here they are up front. In almost every line 'your imaginary forces' are evoked:

> O for a Muse of fire, that would ascend
> The brightest heaven of invention,
> A kingdom for a stage, princes to act
> And monarchs to behold the swelling scene!
> Then should the warlike Harry, like himself,
> Assume the port of Mars; and at his heels,
> Leash'd in like hounds, should famine, sword and fire
> Crouch for employment. But pardon gentles all,
> The flat unraised spirit that hath dared
> On this unworthy scaffold to bring forth
> So great an object: can this cockpit hold
> The vasty fields of France? Or may we cram
> Within this wooden O the very casques
> That did affright the air at Agincourt?
> Oh, pardon since a crooked figure may
> Attest in little place attest a million;
> And let us, ciphers to this great accompt,
> On your imaginary forces work.
> Suppose within the girdle of these walls
> Are now confined two mighty monarchies,
> Whose high upreared and abutting fronts
> The perilous narrow ocean parts asunder:
> Piece out our imperfections with your thoughts;
> Into a thousand parts divide one man,
> And make imaginary puissance;
> Think, when we talk of horses, that you see them
> Printing their proud hoofs i' the receiving earth;
> For 'tis your thoughts that now must deck our kings,
> Carry them here and there; jumping o'er times,
> Turning the accomplishment of many years
> Into an hour-glass: for the which supply,
> Admit me Chorus to this history;
> Who prologue-like your humble patience pray,
> Gently to hear, kindly to judge, our play.

For Shakespeare's company there was no money for scenery and no mechanisms on stage other than a simple grave trap centre and an opening in the 'heavens' through which gods or fairies would occasionally fly. Actors on that stage were few in number. I believe that the 'crooked figure' which Chorus summons up for the battle of Agincourt signifies a number under ten.

One of the greatest swings of the pendulum to spectacle was recorded in 1806, when London was the richest city on earth. The two principal playhouses, Drury Lane and Covent Garden, had been rebuilt at a massively larger scale. Previously both had been of a scale suggested by the surviving Bristol Old Vic of 1766. Aghast that in 1794 the relatively narrow 28-feet (8.5m) wide stage opening of old Drury had been exchanged for the much wider 45 feet (13.8m) of new Drury the prolific playwright Richard Cumberland summed up the predicament thus:

> Since the stages of Drury Lane and Covent Garden have been so enlarged in their dimensions as to be henceforward theatre for spectators rather than playhouses for hearers, it is hardly to be wondered at if managers and directors encourage those representations, to which their structure is best adapted. The splendour of the scene, the ingenuity of the machinist and the rich display of dresses, aided by the captivating charms of the music, now in a great degree supersede the labours of the poet . . . When the animating march strikes up, and the stage lays open its recesses to a depth of a hundred feet for the procession to advance, even the most distant spectator can enjoy his shilling's worth of show.

Cumberland preferred irony to using the word spectacle in its pejorative sense. Earlier, in 1749 for the opening of his third season at the old Drury, actor-manager David Garrick introduced sardonic humour into his prologue for the season, when explaining the need for balance between looking and listening, between words and spectacle:

> Sacred to Shakespeare was this spot design'd
> To pierce the heart and humanize the mind.
> But if an empty House, the Actor's curse,
> Shews our Lears and Hamlets lose their force;
> Unwilling we must change the nobler scene,
> And in our turn present you Harlequin;
> Quit Poets, and set Carpenters to work,
> Shew gaudy scenes, or mount the vaulting Turk:
> For tho' we Actors, one and all, agree
> Boldly to struggle for our – vanity,
> If want comes on, importance must retreat;
> Our first great ruling passion is – to eat.

Fifth – this author's viewpoint: from Prospect to Theatre Projects Consultants

The reader is entitled to know where I come from. In autumn 1960, after the then statutory two years doing national service, which I spent mostly in Hong Kong as a Royal Artillery subaltern, and three years as an Oxford undergraduate reading politics, philosophy and economics at Worcester College, I joined the theatre profession. In summer 1960 I had been accepted by the BBC as a 'general trainee' but had been told first to get some experience of show business and come back in a year's time. In 1961 that promised invitation was repeated but I said no thank you. The reason was that in the intervening year, while resident stage manager of the Oxford Playhouse, I had designed an opera (the second production anywhere of Benjamin Britten's *The Turn of the Screw*, which librettist Myfanwy Piper and her husband the stage designer John Piper attended twice in the one week). In the same year and with Elizabeth Sweeting, then manager of the Playhouse, I had co-founded a theatre company. The distinguished show business lawyer Laurence Harbottle handed us the company Prospect Productions Ltd, which he himself had created for a single summer season on the end of a seaside pier to get his own hands-on experience of theatre management. (Prospect Productions later became known as the Prospect Theatre Company.) Over the next twelve years we took seventy-five productions to 125 theatres in twenty-one countries. In 1964 we invited Toby Robertson to become artistic director of our penniless company while he was earning real money in television. In 1965 Richard Cottrell, who had joined us earlier in 1962 when front-of-house manager at the Oxford Playhouse, became associate director and started to direct some of our productions while Robertson was away in the television studios. We were never distracted by having to run a building although we had associations first with the Oxford Playhouse and then with the Cambridge Arts Theatre. We were, literally, homeless with every Monday night a different theatre. I was able to book our productions into those theatres, big or small, where our shows played better than at the duller houses. In the provinces, outside of Oxford and Cambridge, this meant the Theatre Royal Brighton, the Grand Leeds, the Lyceum and King's theatres in Edinburgh, the Theatre Royal Newcastle and the newly restored 1788 playhouse in Richmond Yorkshire. Eileen Atkins, who in 1963 played Lady Brute for us in Vanbrugh's *The Provok'd Wife*, wrote in her autobiography *Will She Do?* of 2021: 'Restoration comedy is notoriously difficult, but once we were inside this beautiful little Georgian theatre we knew exactly how to play it.' Seeking out the right theatre spaces for the right shows and so pleasing both actors and audiences was one of the most rewarding parts of my job.

August 1969 marked the start of an *annus mirabilis* for Prospect. On our version of Guthrie's stage at the Assembly Hall Edinburgh Ian McKellen played the title roles in Shakespeare's *Richard II* directed by Richard Cottrell and in Marlowe's *Edward II* directed by Toby Robertson. Two sold-out seasons followed in London, at the Mermaid and the Piccadilly. For the British Council we played Bratislava and Vienna. Both productions were televised by the BBC. During my management of Prospect from 1961 to1973 we transferred eight shows to London, for which I made contracts with commercial managers such as Donald Albery, who owned many theatres, Binkie Beaumont of H.M. Tennent, Richard Pilbrow of Theatre Projects Associates and the Royal Shakespeare Company at the Aldwych. We also toured the world, always with the wise counsel of British Council drama and dance director Jane Edgeworth, who introduced us to *La Fenice* for the Venice Biennale and to Australia for the Adelaide Festival with Timothy West as *King Lear* leading the company. I was invited to join the British Council Drama and Dance Panel.

The choice of which theatres to play was at first a matter of instinct. In 1981 Declan Donnellan, who together with designer Nick Ormerod had founded the also homeless Cheek by Jowl company, was better able to articulate why the choice of theatre space was critical. When interviewed in 2003 for *The Open Circle, Peter Brook's Theatre Environments*, Donnellan explained:

> I think that a work of art cannot exist without a frame, and the frame is every bit as important as the work. A piece of theatre changes completely according to the space it's in – a fact to

which I have become increasingly sensitive, having spent most of the last twenty years on tour. This had often been a dispiriting experience; the increasingly prevalent cultural 'administrators' have tended to impose on us their latest 1,500-seat concrete bunkers, built to survive nuclear holocaust, replete with sleep-inducing armchairs ... In England at the National we have one vast space – the Olivier – which demands the energy of plutonium just to get things across to the front row, and is extremely constraining in spite of its size, and the Lyttelton with its audience cut in half on two shelves.

Donnellan went on to praise Brook's *Bouffes du Nord* in Paris because it was a space at once epic and intimate, which 'gives energy from the past life on its walls'. Since then, Donnellan has kept on touring, to 400 cities in thirty-eight years. Cheek by Jowl proved to be a stayer compared with Prospect which, after only twenty years, burnt its wings after succeeding the NT as principal tenant of the Old Vic. This led to Prospect placing less emphasis on touring. The Arts Council did not like that and withdrew its grant. Prospect went bankrupt.

Eight years before that, in 1973, the Arts Council touring department started to tell Prospect which theatres to play and often got it wrong – try playing drama in the Liverpool Empire or the Opera House Manchester that have the capacity and character more suited to the opera and dance which had become the Arts Council's priorities. This removed my most enjoyable role beyond balancing the budget and promoting the work of Robertson and Cottrell. Around the same time I had the opportunity to help in the creation of a new theatre space by assisting Edinburgh architects Law and Dunbar-Nasmith in their design of the 850-seat Eden Court Theatre in Inverness which was to open in 1976. My contribution was to suggest that we paper the walls with people. The key was the introduction of stepped side boxes, an idea lifted from a now vanished opera house of 1729 in Verona. Pilbrow, the founder of Theatre Projects Consultants (TPC), had been intrigued by this feature of the Eden Court design when the plans had been presented to the theatre planning committee of the Association of British Theatre Technicians (the ABTT) on which he and I both sat. Our task was to review proposals for new theatres presented by managements and their architects. In 1973 Pilbrow invited me to join him at TPC. I remained on the board of directors of Prospect until that foundered but changed my paid profession, from managing a theatre company to advising on the design of theatre spaces. For neither role was I qualified. For the record I never studied drama, English literature, history, architecture, acoustics, engineering nor even any physics. Lady Bracknell in *The Importance of Being Earnest* said it all: 'Ignorance is like a delicate exotic fruit; touch it and the bloom is gone.' I also curated exhibitions of theatre painting and architecture such as that of the Georgian Playhouse at the Hayward Gallery in 1975, and of 250 years of the Theatre Royal Covent Garden at the Royal Academy in 1982 having never studied the history of art. Always the enthusiastic amateur.

Almost immediately after joining TPC I conceived the design of the Cottesloe, which was the third, the smallest and the simplest of the three theatre spaces at the National (see Chapter 7). Design control for the third theatre space had been taken over from the architect by a committee of the NT led by director Hall and head of design John Bury.

Sixth – clarifying capacities of older theatres and the opening dates of the new ones

Until 1920 the priority for any new theatre was not form but capacity. To make profits it was necessary to sell seats to everybody and so the seat price ratio was about twelve to one from the best to the worst places. In London's West End this meant extreme luxury for those in the grand circle and front orchestra stalls and none at all for those in the gallery or on unreserved wooden benches in the pit situated behind the expensive orchestra stalls. What a member of the audience saw or heard depended largely on where he or she sat, which in turn was determined by the price he or she could afford. Take the Garrick Theatre of 1889 which now holds under 800 but crammed in 1,150 in 1912 (source *The Stage Guide* of that year).

In 1906 actor-manager Arthur Bourchier suspended the over-critical young critic Max Beerbohm from his press list at the Garrick Theatre. Beerbohm had to exchange his complimentary front stall seat (price ten shillings and six pence) for an unreserved place behind the stalls on a bench at the back of the tightly packed pit to which access cost one and six. In his *Around Theatres* of 1924 Beerbohm explained what then happened. On finding a place at the back of the pit he realised that 'the play had begun. Yes, there was a patch of yellowish light; and therein certain tiny figures were moving. They were twittering, too, these figures. I listened intently.' Beerbohm concluded: 'What seems like restraint to the man in the pit may seem like over-acting to the man in the stalls. And what seems like restraint to the man in the stalls may be a mere blank, a vacuum, to the man in the pit.' When sat in the front stalls Beerbohm had accused Bourchier of over-acting. Later Beerbohm wrote him an apology saying that he was the only actor who could reach the back of the pit.

This problem still exists in West End theatres, especially in those with three circles stacked over the rear stalls where seats are now priced at near top prices and extend far back to where once were the much cheaper and more densely packed pit benches. Some suggest that modern

1.2 *'Cheek by jowl', 1894 engraving of poorer pit patrons immediately behind expensive front stalls.*

democratically engineered theatres with a single circle are preferable in that they give near equal comfort and good sightlines to all. But do this and you get wider theatres with smaller capacities and fewer cheap seats. Such new 'democratic' theatres, with a much narrower range of seat prices, tend to become costly to visit and soon serve a rich elite rather than a wide cross section of society. Very low prices in the gallery and the in the unreserved pit immediately behind the highest-priced front stalls allowed nineteenth-century theatres to attract both young and old, penniless students as well as rich folk. The accompanying drawing by Charles Dana Gibson and captioned 'In a London Theatre' appeared in *Pictures of People* published first by Life Publishing Co. of New York in 1896 and four years later in London by John Lane.

There can be confusion if size is measured simply by seating capacity. Edinburgh's Royal Lyceum, which was designed in 1883 by C.J. Phipps, held 2,300 in 1912 (source *The Stage Guide* of 1912) and as recently as 1967 held over 1,300 when Prospect sold that number of seats for each capacity performance played during their weeks at the Edinburgh International Festivals of 1967 and 1968. At Edinburgh's Lyceum over the last fifty years 'improvements' have been made to audience comfort. Nobody now sits in the gallery or near a pillar lower down but the ceiling, three circles and side walls have not moved. The Lyceum now holds only 658, half the number Prospect played to and less than 30 per cent of the original capacity as built.

Now a warning about the dates quoted for new theatres. A theatre is generally dated by the year of its opening. This can mislead. The National Theatre on London's South Bank, which finally opened in 1976, had been conceived between 1962 and 1967. Design discussion had taken place in quite a different national mood than that of when it opened ten years later. In an email to me in 2017 Pilbrow summed up one important aspect of the euphoric mood of the mid-1960s: 'Only nutters were interested in the past; we were building the future.'

Supersonic Concorde first flew in 1969. The Beatles took the USA by storm. State education allowed a generation then thought of as 'working class' to reinvigorate the arts. But things changed in the 1970s while the future National rose oh-so-slowly on the South Bank. In the 1970s successive governments ran out of steam. Prime ministers had to cope with a failing economy and conflicting proposals on what to do about it. From 1973 Hall had the task not just of opening the oft-postponed National Theatre but of carrying the banner for an arts world suffering from shrinking subsidies. He had to take control of a National Theatre, conceived in an age of optimism and plenty, and open it in an age of austerity. The world was changing.

The new mood was eloquently expressed by director Michael Elliott in a BBC Radio Three broadcast in 1973 entitled *On Not Building for Posterity,* reprinted at my suggestion in *TABS* Vol. 31 No. 2. Elliot had been the last director of the Old Vic Company before the creation of the National Theatre Company and was the progenitor of the revolutionary Royal Exchange Theatre in Manchester which, ironically, was to open within weeks of the National. Said Elliott in 1973:

As one leans on the parapet of Waterloo Bridge pondering the huge mushrooming concrete of the new National Theatre all one's doubts centre round one question: was this the right theatre to build *now*? And if one cannot resist the answer 'no', it is good to remember the dilemma of those responsible. I served on the building committee of the National Theatre, and I remember those endless and agonising meetings as though they had taken place in the shadow of the ruins of some shattered tower of Babel. Every illustrious and experienced voice spoke in a different language, not only from his fellows, but different from his own the month before or the month after. We could all speak of vivid personal dreams of private theatres that held our fancy that week, but to analyse objectively the purpose of a National Theatre over the next century and design for it – that seemed for a long time almost impossible . . . Isn't it time we stopped lumbering our grandchildren with our mistakes – understandable mistakes, but mistakes nevertheless? Don't we need something different, something less expressive of civic or national pride, more reflective of changing taste – something perhaps less permanent? In future shouldn't we try to retain a certain lightness and sense of improvisation, and sometimes build in materials that do not require a bomb to move them? In short shouldn't we stop building for posterity?

Others went further: Stephen Joseph, philosopher of theatre-in-the-round, spelt that out with the suggestion that all new theatres should have a time bomb in the basement set at fifteen years.

Elliott went on to set out some alternatives. These included the thrust stages of Guthrie and the low-cost Young Vic of 1970. Such relatively simple theatre spaces and those created in 'found space', like the early Roundhouse, can arrive on the scene rapidly. National institutions on the other hand do not spring up overnight – the NT had taken a century to happen. Elliott had been on the panel which, in October 1963, had chosen the architect who was to design the National Theatre on the South Bank. Only ten years separated Elliott's endorsement of the modernist Lasdun as architect of the NT from his damascene moment quoted above which took place while watching all that concrete being poured for a national monument.

It was not only the National Theatre that took time. In 1982, five years after the National, the RSC finally opened the Barbican Theatre in the City of London. Much earlier, and soon after they had moved temporarily into the Aldwych in 1960, Hall and John Bury, then head of design at the RSC, had accepted the City of London's suggestion that one of the two centrepieces of their new Barbican Arts Centre be tailor-made for the Royal Shakespeare Company as its London home. Twenty years separate Hall and Bury working on its design and the opening, long after they had left the RSC. Thus 1982 as the date for the Barbican can mislead.

Seventh – unremarkable exteriors with memorable interiors and vice versa

Opportunities in Britain to trumpet a theatre's presence on a tight city centre site were rare. In mainland Europe the Royal, Princely or Civic theatres and opera houses proclaimed to both citizens and visitors the taste of those who had paid for the buildings. In Britain in 2021 only five surviving nineteenth-century theatres possess a colonnaded portico such as are familiar all over Europe. Three of the five are in London.

The facades of the over one hundred and fifty theatres designed by Frank Matcham, Britain's most prolific theatre architect, were comparable in style to that of an opulent Victorian public house. His rival, the older C.J. Phipps, had preceded Matcham into the *Dictionary of National Biography* by decades simply because his theatres looked like public buildings. Matcham did not make the *DNB* until 2004. His overdue inclusion was triggered by a fortuitous discussion at the high table of my old college as a guest of a retired Fellow who had recently become one of the editors for the Oxford University Press's addendum to the *DNB*, *Missing Persons*, which was to be published in 1993. Over the port I made the case for honouring Matcham, who was still being ignored by the establishment. I was invited to write his entry in just fourteen days. This finally made its way, verbatim, into the new *DNB* which was issued in many volumes from 2000 onwards. Around the same time, and quite independently of the OUP's change of heart, the first Matcham biography was published and the Matcham Society founded. He was at last being recognised as a giant of British theatre architecture.

Today no cultivated Frenchman, German or Italian would give a passing glance at Matcham's architecturally illiterate exteriors but they might wonder at the sheer theatricality of their interiors. With Lasdun's National Theatre some seventy years later the reverse is true. The exterior of the NT and the foyers have few enemies while the interiors of the Olivier and Lyttelton have few friends. In November 2016 *The London Review of Books* published a survey of eight books on brutalist architecture in which Lasdun's work featured prominently. One of these quoted the gasp of appreciation by John Betjeman in a letter to Lasdun soon after the opening of the NT: 'It is a lovely work and so good outside, which is what matters most.' The *LRB* printed my reply in the next issue stating that it is not the outside which 'matters most' but the theatre spaces inside.

Finally, the elephants in the room

Why cast the Olivier and the Lyttelton as the elephants in the room? Their bulk and lack of colour are certainly part of the problem. But at the centre was Lasdun's narrow definition of functionalism. Both the architects of theatre buildings and those who create performances therein need to check what is needed for live theatre to function well: how to achieve a balance between looking and listening, and above all how to create theatre spaces that delight an audience and prompt their participation in performance.

For many it is the role of shuttered concrete at the NT which comes first to mind. Enemies include not only Albert Finney but journalist and author Peter Lewis, who in 1990 chose a pertinent title for his pungent history of 1990: *The National, A Dream Made Concrete*. Lewis quoted Lasdun: 'It's modern. It's sculptural. It's not in any style except one's own'. Lewis concluded: 'The National opened with the handicap of being cast in the fashion of yesterday.' Friends of concrete include architect Patrick Dillon, who was a leading member of the Haworth Tompkins team for the most recent refurbishment of the NT building completed in 2016. Dillon was the author who, twenty-five years after Lewis, presented the alternative view in his lavishly illustrated love letter, *Concrete Reality: Denys Lasdun and the National Theatre*, published by the NT in 2015. Wrote Dillon: 'The NT reached the zenith in the mid-century's love affair with concrete.' He suggested that Lasdun's chosen material was the key to 'a classical purity of form and directness of expression, an architecture of mass and light that was timeless in its power and primal in its force'. In these pages I question whether the immutable qualities of shuttered concrete can ever support the ephemeral arts of performance.

2

Richard Wagner, Adolphe Appia and the spreading of the fan

Drawn to Bayreuth by the baroque, Wagner then chose to build a modern opera house

In 1870 Richard Wagner visited Bayreuth with the idea of creating a festival of his own work. His initial reason for choosing Bayreuth was the survival of the magnificent *Opernhaus* created in 1748 by the Margravine Wilhelmina, who was both a composer and the ruler of Bayreuth, an independent principality until 1779. This was and still is one of Europe's greatest surviving baroque opera houses. The acoustics are superb and the stage is very large, but the capacity is small – by 1870 scarcely 500. Understandably Wagner turned down the *Opernhaus* but not Bayreuth mainly because of the welcome he had received. He would shape his own opera house.

Wagner staged the first performance at his *Festspielhaus* on 13 August 1876. Garnier's Paris Opera had only just opened. The *Palais Garnier* cost 7.5 million gold French francs, which was ten times the cost of Bayreuth. In form Paris anticipates the end of an era while Bayreuth signals the start of a new one. But it was a slow start. Five years passed before there was a second season. The influence on theatre architecture worldwide of the then uniquely fan-shaped theatre space was hardly felt for half a century. Edwin O. Sachs in his monumental three-volume *Modern Opera Houses and Theatres* of 1898 remarked that 'its lines have not been imitated in any case but that of the People's Theatre at Worms'. (The latter was bombed in 1945 and has never been rebuilt.)

At Bayreuth Wagner had known exactly what he wanted. When the foundation stone was laid in 1872 he set out his aim:

> You will find in the proportions and arrangement of the auditorium and its seating the expression of an idea which, once you have grasped it, will immediately place you in a new and different relation to the stage spectacle that you are to see, a relation quite different from the one you had previously known when visiting other theatres. If this impression is pure and perfect, then the mysterious entry of the music will prepare you for the unveiling and clear presentation of onstage images that will seem to rise up before you from an ideal world of dreams and reveal to you the whole reality of a noble art's most meaningful illusion . . . you will be offered only the most perfect staging and acting.

No member of the audience would see the orchestra, sunk in what he christened 'the mystic abyss'. The arrangement of an almost unbroken fan of seating would focus the attention of an

2.1 *Bayreuth interior as built in 1896 before level inserted over boxes and below gallery.*

audience on 'a stage of the largest dimension for installing the most perfect scenery'. The acoustics worked superbly – for Wagner's music. Nobody would ever build such a theatre for Mozart, or indeed for anything comic. For Wagner 'the most perfect scenery' meant that the audience would be transported solemnly to the mythical Germanic world of the Nibelung and the Rhinemaidens. But Wagner's scenic style was as old-fashioned as both his music and the form of his theatre space was breathtakingly new. That anomaly persisted until after 1951, when Wagner's grandsons, Wieland and Wolfgang Wagner, reopened Bayreuth after the Second World War. As early as 1898 the visual style of Richard Wagner had been accurately described by playwright George Bernard Shaw as an 'intolerably old-fashioned tradition of half rhetorical, half historical-pictorial attitudes and gestures.'

There was one other pioneer who would have been able to supply the visual dimension lacked by Richard Wagner, and this was Swiss designer and architect Adolphe Appia. They never met – Appia was only twenty-one when Wagner died. In 1908 Appia had nailed the culprit: illusion. In the April issue of *La Vie Musicale*, published in Lausanne, he wrote: 'How should we define it? Is it the purpose of the setting? A tasteless joker might for his part reply that illusion is to dramatic art what Madame Tussaud's wax museum is to the sculpture of Rodin.'

Appia had trained as an architect though he hardly practised as such. In 1911 at Hellerau, on the outskirts of Dresden, Appia advised architect Heinrich Tessenow, who had never designed a theatre and did not ever work on another. Together they created one of the very first totally new theatre spaces of the twentieth century. It was a large unbroken single volume, 50 metres long by 16 metres wide and 12 metres high. It held more than 500 in a single well-raked block of straight rows. There was no proscenium. The side walls of the stage and of the auditorium were finished the same. For three years Appia did the settings and the lighting for choreographer and philosopher of eurythmic dance Émile Jaques-Dalcroze. Revolutionary Hellerau closed in 1914 and was not used again for performance until 1990 after the reunification of Germany, which is why Appia the pioneer must be mentioned here despite few of his achievements having taken place after 1920.

Appia was an even greater influence on theatre practice than on theatre architecture. His chief legacy must be the establishment of stage lighting as a major component in the art of the scenographer. In 'Art is an Attitude' (1927) he wrote: 'The actor rightfully occupies the first position. Next comes the spatial arrangement . . . Then follows the all-powerful lighting. The last place belongs to painted scenery, the role of which is definitely inferior to the other three elements.'

The fan as chronicled by the functionalist engineer George C. Izenour

To understand the ultimate victory for Wagner's fan shape one must turn to a much later champion of the fan, American engineer George Izenour, who published his monumental *Theater Design* in 1977. Here are 900 halftones and drawings, including his signature sections, which tell the story of theatre design from antiquity to the most recent of his own theatres. The history is good. The conclusion is wrong: it is that the fan shape is the only form of auditorium that is rational and works.

Izenour's language is tendentious in that what he does not agree with is labelled 'romantic' and hence wrong, while what he himself proposes is 'rational' and hence right. For him what is good is the unvarnished product of physics and engineering. Take seating: 'The fact of theatre seating derives from the obvious: the human body is more comfortable, the mind is more receptive, and the sensitivity to optical and aural stimuli is much improved for extended periods of time if the body remains more relaxed and quiescent in a position halfway between prone and standing.'

The fan shape of the seating that Izenour extolled was modelled on that of Bayreuth despite the fact the seats there offer no chance to relax, consisting mostly of thirty unbroken rows of seats with cane seats and hard backs. Each unbroken row then and now holds up to sixty-two operagoers. The seats are only 450 mm wide and have no arms. The rows are still generally set at around 700 mm back-to-back as they were in 1876. The steppings for each row remain today as built. Bayreuth held approximately 1,550 in 1876 and now holds 1,974. (The increase of 400 is largely due to the addition in 1930 of another level inserted above the rear boxes and below the original gallery.) Audience members the world over have increased considerably in height and girth over a century and a half but the space allowed per person in Bayreuth has not changed. Do not get taken short in *Das Rheingold*, which plays nearly two and a half hours without an interval. These tight dimensions may surprise but I took the measurements myself on a visit to Bayreuth in 1976 and recorded them in 'Newest and Oldest Theatres of Germany', printed in the Spring 1977 edition of *Sightline*. In 2019 I could scarcely believe these measurements were correct but they were checked by the press office at Bayreuth.

This contrasts with North America, where often capacities have reduced as legroom and seat widths have increased over the decades. The original Festival Theatre at Stratford Ontario, which is dealt with in Chapter 4, opened in 1953 with a tent roof. In 1957 a balcony was added, which raised the capacity to 2,262. A second major remodelling took place in 1997 providing more space for each theatregoer. It now holds only 1,800. Hence today at Stratford Ontario approximately sixty theatregoers relax in comfort in a similar-sized space into which Bayreuth packs ninety Wagnerites today, just as it did a century and a half ago.

In the late twentieth century Izenour's semi-reclining seats were pointed remorselessly towards the centre of the stage and were placed within a narrow fan strictly confined within 60 degrees. Izenour had used Bayreuth's archetypal fan shape to legitimise that form for his vast all-purpose auditoriums. In the 1960s Izenour's 'rational seating geometry' prescribed proscenium widths ranging from 11 metres for drama to 18.25 metres for symphony concerts. Using acoustic shells, flown ceilings and moving walls Izenour could transform these inevitably wide spaces into oddly proportioned smaller spaces, all of which were set out in what he described as 'rational fans'. For the Edwin J. Thomas Hall in Akron, Ohio, which was built in 1973, Izenour cites design as taking place in 'a continuous executive session for five days and nights attended by [his] team of designers and the client', the outcome of which was to change what had at first been intended to be three separate auditoriums into a single one providing many options, from a 3,000-seat concert hall to an 850-seat lecture hall/playhouse.

In any fan-shaped auditorium, all one sees of one's fellow theatregoers is the backs of their necks, which are hardly the most interesting part of the human anatomy. By contrast, in the half century 1870 to 1920 there took place the greatest ever building boom of more conventional proscenium theatres in which those present are always conscious of their fellows. Those that survive are well liked by both actors and audiences and are regarded as intimate.

It is hard to define intimacy. Tyrone Guthrie in his autobiography, *A Life in the Theatre* of 1960, put it poetically:

When human beings get together in large numbers for a great performer they will fuse their identity; each single person ceases to be himself and becomes a tiny bit of a single personality, that of an audience ... But let nobody fool himself that that collective monster is an intellectual thing! It is a great big mutton-headed baby, very easy to move to tears. The most unlikely people in the theatre will die laughing at vulgar jokes. I have seen an archdeacon kicking his gaiters in the air.

It is indubitably harder to get laughs in a large fan-shaped auditorium than in a tightly packed proscenium house. There are other factors, other than the fan, and these are colour and pattern.

At the Eighth World Congress of the International Federation for Theatre Research held in Munich in 1977 Rikard Küller, an environmental psychologist and author of *Architectural Psychology* published in 1975, presented his conclusions on how and why audiences react. He had measured the capacity of an audience to be aroused at the start of a show. He had connected electrodes to the brain of a group of people who had been placed in a room full of colour and pattern for, say, fifteen minutes before the show started and had taken measurements. He then compared their capacity to be aroused to a sample taken from a similar group who had been placed in a neutral grey room for the same length of time, before being exposed to the same stimuli as those experienced by the first group. Those who had been in the festive space laughed quicker and cried sooner than those who had been placed in the dull space. Most actors but few architects knew this already. For some of Küller's findings you must read his 'Psycho-Physiological Conditions in Theatre Construction' in the IFTR pre-conference introductions to some of the papers to be given by delegates at Munich, entitled *Theatre Space – Der Raum des Theaters*. At that conference, some young theatre makers and architects suggested to the modern functionalists that there were more things in heaven and earth than were dreamt of in their philosophy. Our numbers swelled over the following decades. We sought what it is in the architecture of the theatre space that encourages an audience not only to look and to listen but also to react. I was flattered to have my Munich riposte to Izenour's fan and in support of the courtyard form printed in 1978 in both *Theatre Design and Technology*, the Journal of the United States Institute of Theatre Technology, and *Theatre Research International* published by Oxford University Press.

Some playwrights had long known this. In 1955 Somerset Maugham wrote in the introduction to *The Artist and the Theatre*, the first catalogue of his collection of over forty eighteenth- and nineteenth-century theatre oil paintings researched and written by scholars Raymond Mander and Joe Mitchenson and published by Heinemann: 'The theatres they build now are severely functional; you can see from all parts of them what is happening on the stage; the seats are comfortable and there are abundant exits so that you run small chance of being burnt to death. But they are cold. They are apt to make you feel that you have come to the playhouse to undergo an ordeal rather than enjoy an entertainment.' In 1948 he had decided to leave his collection to the National Theatre, a notion which was then in limbo. A dozen years before Lasdun was appointed, Maugham gave the reason for his gift: 'It seemed to me that my pictures in the foyer and on the stairs of a new theatre would a trifle mitigate the austerity of the architect's design.'

In 1980 the board of the NT carried out Maugham's wishes. They hung most of the oils in the public areas and published a second catalogue in colour, also by Mander and Mitchenson, which I edited. Maugham was proved right about the austerity. The paintings of the players glittered. Unfortunately, after only a few years a couple of the smaller pictures were stolen. The NT took them all down, a move welcomed by Lasdun, and lent them to the Theatre Museum in Covent Garden, and when that closed in 2007 gave the collection to Bath. The larger ones now hang in the Holburne Museum and the smaller ones in a nineteenth-century theatre nearby.

Craig, Appia, Copeau and the *Vieux-Colombier*

The more famous proponent of the 'new theatre' was Edward Gordon Craig. Craig was first shown Appia's work in 1908 and declared him 'the foremost stage-decorator in Europe'. They finally met in 1914 at the International Theatre Exhibition in Zurich, but significantly Craig never visited Hellerau. Richard Beacham, in his article '"Brothers in Suffering and Joy": the Appia–Craig Correspondence' (1988), suggests the difference between the two: 'Appia was a contemplative, shy and reclusive person, who had an intense antipathy to publicity ... He greatly preferred to work in the background "behind the scenes". Craig was ... a man of large ... ego, who delighted both in self-advertisement and in aggressive advocacy of his ideas.' He had been bred on the stage, had himself been an actor and worshipped the actor-manager Henry Irving, who had been a lover of Craig's mother, Ellen Terry. Appia was a man of movement, inspired by music and the motion of the human body. Neither worked much in the theatre after 1920. Craig became a guru, not taking part but incessantly writing about what he had designed ages earlier. He did this in the pages of *The Mask* from 1908 to 1929, a total of eighty-seven issues, in which Craig wrote under both his own name and no less than sixty-four pseudonyms which implied that he had a large following of disciples. He could be generous: in his penultimate major work, a biography of Henry Irving written in 1930, he allowed himself to list the men and women who 'attempt to revitalize our European Theatre from within'. Craig had no doubts of who were pre-eminent: 'Two I place apart – Isadora Duncan and Appia.' The first of these two, Duncan, had died in 1927 at the age of fifty. She was Craig's lover and had borne him a son who perished soon after his mother. Appia had died in 1928 just two years before Craig placed him in his pantheon second only to Duncan.

One of the followers cited by Craig was Jacques Copeau, who does belong in the century because in 1920 he transformed his own recently acquired little theatre. He was no architect

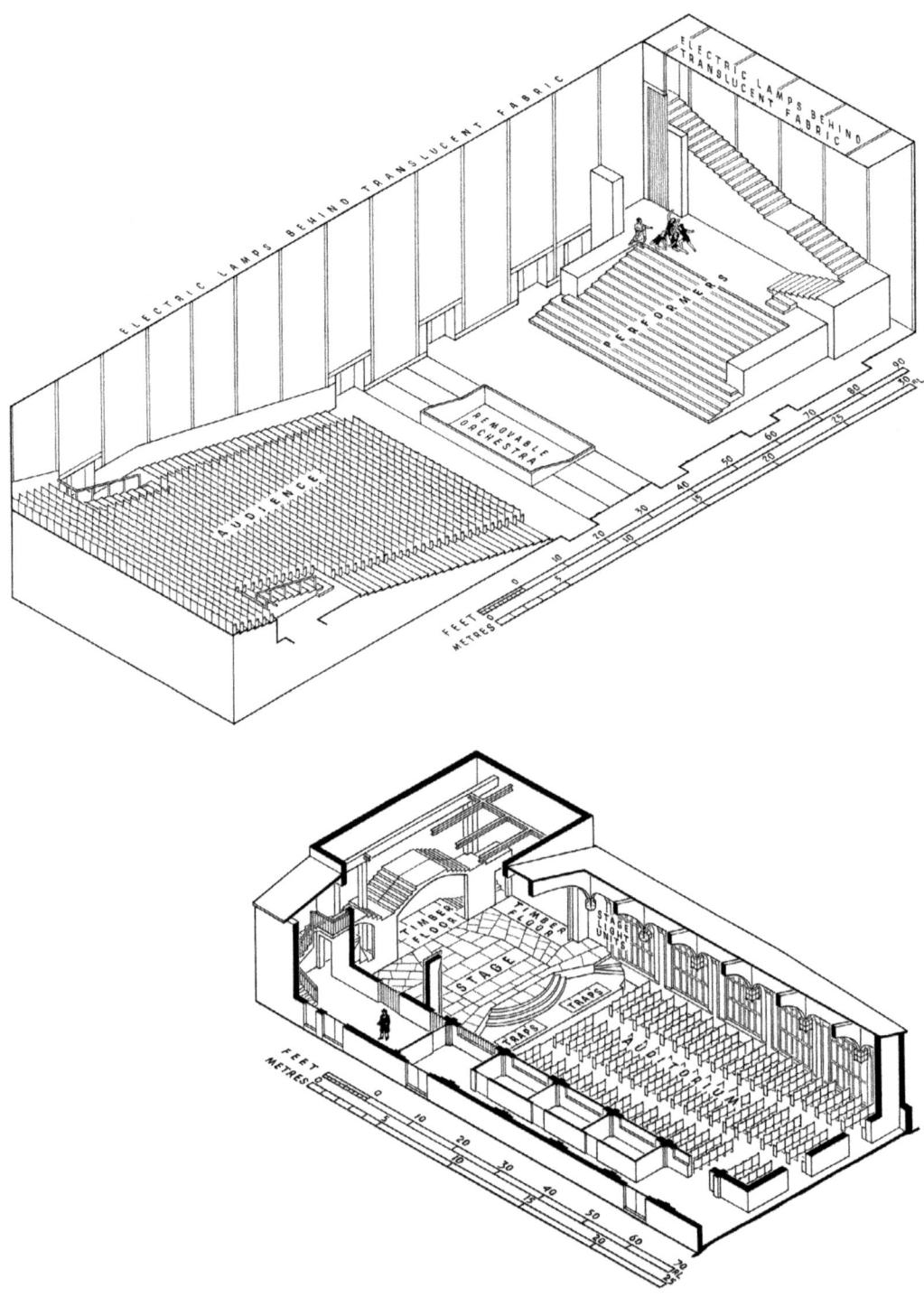

2.2 *Two isometrics by Richard Leacroft: Hellerau over Le Vieux-Colombier.*

and no stage designer but the leader of his own company at the dilapidated Paris vaudeville of *Athénée-Saint-Germain*. Central to his whole strategy was to create a new theatre space within the old. Copeau had money but not a lot. He had first met with both Appia and Craig in 1915. After only his second meeting with Appia Copeau reported to Craig that Appia's 'idea of stage settings emerging from the text, from the inner spirit of the dramatic work is a truism which he discovered before we did'. Copeau tackled his building when Paris had settled down after the First World War. He ripped out the proscenium and stage, replacing it with a permanent setting which is well documented in all theatre histories. This he called privately his Utopia and publicly *Le Vieux-Colombier*. It was a long rectangular space, only 15 metres wide and 37 metres long and is relatively low-ceilinged, the small scale of which was to make his theatre as appropriate for drama as the much larger Hellerau was for dance. *Le Vieux-Colombier* was a huge success. It worked for comedy because its vaudeville past helped shape its dramatic future. Today it is the third theatre of the *Comédie Francaise*.

In 1957 director Norman Marshall wrote in *The Producer and the Play*:

My own recollections of the productions I saw at the *Vieux-Colombier* during the early twenties are that they were simple, sincere, and very well acted. Admittedly the theatre itself was somewhat startling on first acquaintance because it was so unlike any other theatre one had ever seen. It was simply a long narrow hall at the end of which shallow, curving steps led to a platform with a door on either side, and at the back, a couple of pillars, and a stairway leading to a balcony.

Electricity throws a brighter light on theatres old and new

The replacement of gas lighting by electricity was to have a major influence on the art of theatre. For some this was a shock. In 1891 Henry Irving had introduced electricity into his Lyceum. On her return from the summer break his leading lady Ellen Terry wrote:

When I saw the effect on the faces of the electric footlights, I entreated Henry to have the gas restored, and he did. We used gas footlights there until we left the theatre for good in 1902. The thick softness of gaslight, with the lovely specks and motes in it, so like *natural* light, gave illusion to many a scene which is now revealed in all its naked trashiness by electricity.

In 1903 Matcham lit his new Buxton Opera House with electricity, although to please the actors he did retain the gas footlights. In 1979 I helped restore the Buxton theatre in a team led by engineer and acoustician Derek Sugden. We reconnected the gas main to the central 'sun-burner' in the auditorium ceiling. In 1903 the main function of a 'sun-burner' was not so much lighting but ventilating the auditorium by drawing out the foul air from the auditorium and without mechanical assistance through a 'chimney' above and replacing it with fresh air introduced naturally through grills in the side walls. There were no moving parts and it worked. Today in the climate emergency when there is much interest in efficient natural ventilation it is worth remembering that in the age of gas the theatre had the problems of natural ventilation partially solved.

While at first the electricity did not provide answers to lighting both the actor and the setting, technical developments would in time allow others to develop stage lighting to a pitch that Appia and Craig had only dreamt of. In 1882 Appia had seen Wagner's *Parsifal* at Bayreuth, which was lit wholly by gas until 1888. In *Parsifal* the Temple of the Holy Grail was a recreation of the Baptistry of the Duomo at Sienna. Appia wrote:

> When the curtain went up on the scene of the interior of the Grail Temple, the painted scenery had to be sacrificed to the darkness necessitated by the scene change – imparting a marvellous life to the setting. As the lights started to come up, the illusion was continuously dispelled until finally, in the full glare of the border lights and the footlights, the knights made their entrance into a pasteboard temple.

Norman Bel Geddes and Walter Gropius, neither of whom ever built a theatre

A less well-known early pioneer is American Norman Bel Geddes. He never built a theatre but designed many. His Theatre No. 6, published first in *Stage Lighting* by Harold Ridge in 1928, who features in the next chapter on the Festival Theatre Cambridge, and two years later in Geddes' own book *Horizons* of 1932, is for a stage facing a 90-degree fan covered by a single 60-feet-high domed ceiling over both stage and auditorium. Putting aside for a moment the disastrous acoustic consequence had it been built, one must wonder if Bel Geddes's cosmic imagination lodged in the mind of Lasdun, who was eighteen in 1932. It seems unlikely that Lasdun did not have a copy of *Horizon*s with 200 illustrations of Geddes's ultramodern designs, from theatres to motor cars, from liners to airships, from shop window displays to freeways. All these designs can be found at the Harry Ransom Center of The University of Texas at Austin. They look after them on behalf of the Norman Bel Geddes estate.

Lastly, no account of unbuilt modern theatres of the 1920s is complete without the better known *Totaltheater* of Walter Gropius, designed in 1927 when he was director of the Bauhaus. Plans of the unbuilt *Totaltheater* appear in all the studies of modern theatre architecture. At first sight it offers a clever solution to the newly perceived problem of flexibility. The stage revolve is within a larger revolve which is shared with part of the audience. This seems attractive when viewed in plan, but looked at in section one is aware that most of the audience is seated to the front in a shallow raked block which recedes into the distance, worse than at Chichester as built. The huge volume and the shape of the roof is like that of Theatre No. 6 and that would have meant similarly rotten speech acoustics. It too would have failed the actor.

Yet the pioneering twentieth-century modernist architects who did not build their designs for theatres did influence succeeding generations. Maybe this is because, while the drawings of the unbuilt fascinate, there never was an opportunity to discover their fundamental flaws.

# ACT TWO

1920–1976: The march of modernism

3

The Festival Cambridge, Stratford-upon-Avon and early days of the National

My interest in the Festival Theatre aroused

There has to be a good reason to include in a memoir a theatre which closed a couple of years after I was born. The reason is that from 1964 to 1967 I ran the Prospect Theatre Company from what had been the men's dressing room of the semi-derelict Festival Theatre Cambridge of Terence Gray. My curiosity in how the Festival had worked as a theatre was aroused. Research over the next forty years culminated in a visit in July 2016 by a hundred plus members of the Society for Theatre Research as part of their conference on Regency theatre held at Downing College. We covered both the Wilkins and Gray eras of the Barnwell/Festival Theatre. Many were surprised quite how good was Wilkins's 1814 auditorium, with which most were familiar only from the entry on Norwich in James Winston's *The Theatric Tourist* of 1805 and from Elizabeth Grice's scholarly *Rogues and Vagabonds* of 1977, which provides a definitive account of the circuit theatres of East Anglia up to the middle of the nineteenth century. Later, in 1984, it was Richard Leacroft who, in *Theatre and Playhouse: An Illustrated Survey of Theatre Building from Ancient Greece to the Present Day* formed the connection between the two distinct eras of Wilkins and of Gray in the same building and later with the Theatre Royal Bury St Edmunds of 1819, Wilkins's final addition to the Norwich circuit of which he was both the architect and, from 1815, the owner. Bury St Edmunds is dealt with in Chapter Nine.

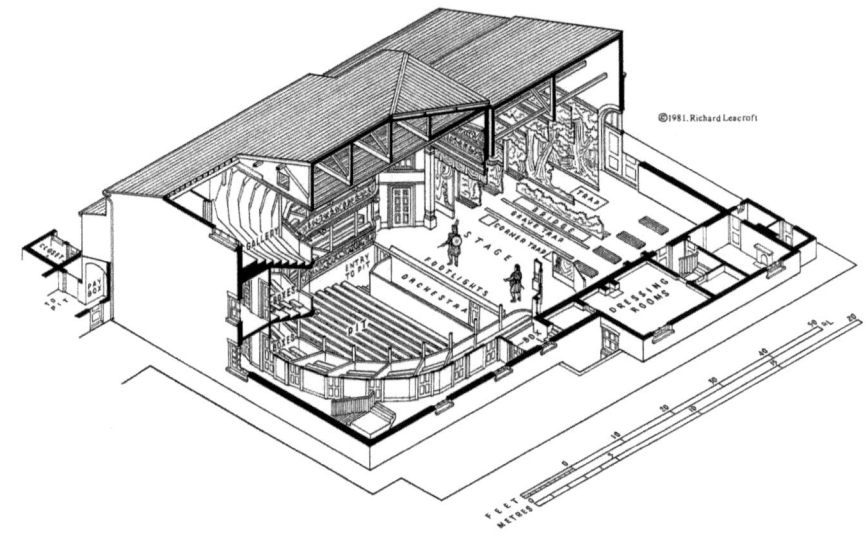

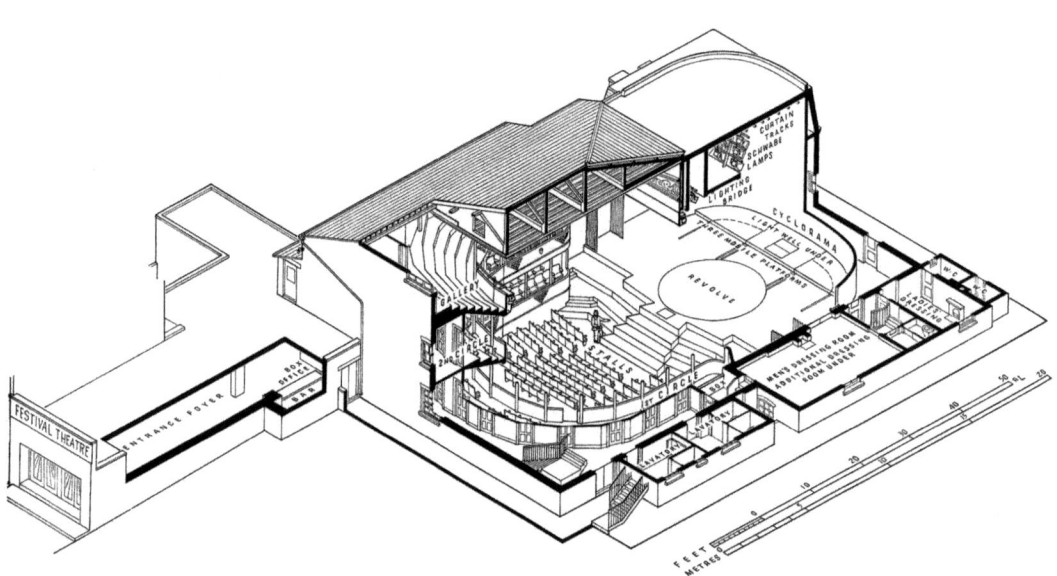

3.1 *Two isometrics by Richard Leacroft: Wilkins' Barnwell Theatre Cambridge of 1814 over Gray's Festival Theatre of 1926.*

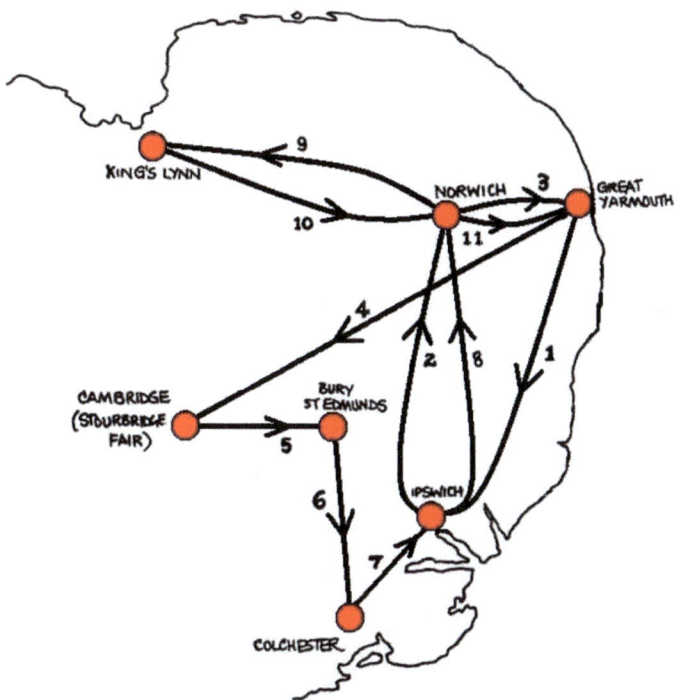

3.2 *Cambridge Festival Theatre auditorium 1926 over map of Norwich company circuit.*

In 1926 two major events had taken place in the development of British theatre architecture. The first was the opening by the 31-year-old Terence Gray of the Festival Theatre, much of which survives to this day though it has not been used as a theatre since 1940. The second was the partial burning of the original 1869 Shakespeare Memorial Theatre at Stratford-upon-Avon. The theatre space of 1869 was replaced in 1932 with a new one which in turn was completely remodelled in 2011. Meanwhile the flame for a National Theatre in London flickered into life and then went out.

Terence Gray acquires and remodels what had been the Barnwell Theatre

Gray came from a prosperous Anglo-Irish family and could afford his own theatre space. He had had no previous theatrical experience, not even at Cambridge University where he had lasted just one year at Magdalene College. In 1924 he acquired the old 1814 Barnwell Theatre, which by then was a semi-derelict Salvation Army Hall. The 1814 theatre was the second to bear this name, the first being a temporary structure which was hardly surprising seeing that the Norwich company visited Cambridge but once a year for the Stourbridge (or Stirbitch) Fair held in the area surrounding the present theatre which was then outside the city's boundaries.

Gray kept Wilkins's apsidal four-level auditorium, which he re-seated to hold 400 in a space that once held 700. He ripped out both the proscenium and the original raked stage and replaced it with one of the most modern open stages in Europe. He renamed it the Festival Theatre and it opened on 22 November 1926. Here prominent figures of the British theatre made their mark early in their careers, including Tyrone Guthrie. Gray realised some of Gordon Craig's visions. Guthrie was not yet thirty when he was a guest director there in 1929. One of the most remarkable followers of Gray was his Anglo-Irish cousin, choreographer Ninette de Valois, born Edris Stannus. When in 1976 she walked into the new Olivier Theatre she immediately linked it to her cousin who, fifty years earlier, had appointed her his resident choreographer at the Festival Theatre.

In 1933, after running Britain's finest *avant-garde* theatre for seven years, the disillusioned Gray left Cambridge, first for his vineyards in France and then, during the war, for his racehorses in Ireland. As a working theatre the Festival declined. It closed in 1940 and was bought by the Arts Theatre to become a scenic workshop and costume store. This was an adroit move by George Rylands, known as Dadie to generations of Cambridge men. He was mentor to many members of the Marlowe Society who would go on to have distinguished careers in the theatre, including Peter Hall, Toby Robertson, Trevor Nunn and Ian McKellen, all of whom grew ever more easeful with Shakespeare's verse thanks to Dadie, who was not only a Fellow of King's College but chairman, from 1946 to 1982, of the 650-seat Arts Theatre founded in 1936. Rylands could not abide Gray's approach to the classics. The latter emphasised the visual and cared less for the verse. By using the Festival as a workshop and wardrobe Rylands ensured that this monument to the tiresome Gray could never be reopened as long as he controlled the Arts, which soon had a monopoly of professional theatre in Cambridge following the demolition of the New Theatre in 1956. Rylands encouraged audiences first to listen. Gray invited his audience first to look. They could not have been more different.

To reach my office in the Festival I walked across the stage. Here and in what had been the stalls was all the clutter of a stage carpenter's scenic workshop. Behind the boarded-up fronts to the three encircling tiers were racks of costumes which the Arts hired out. Yet even then it was a pregnant theatre space.

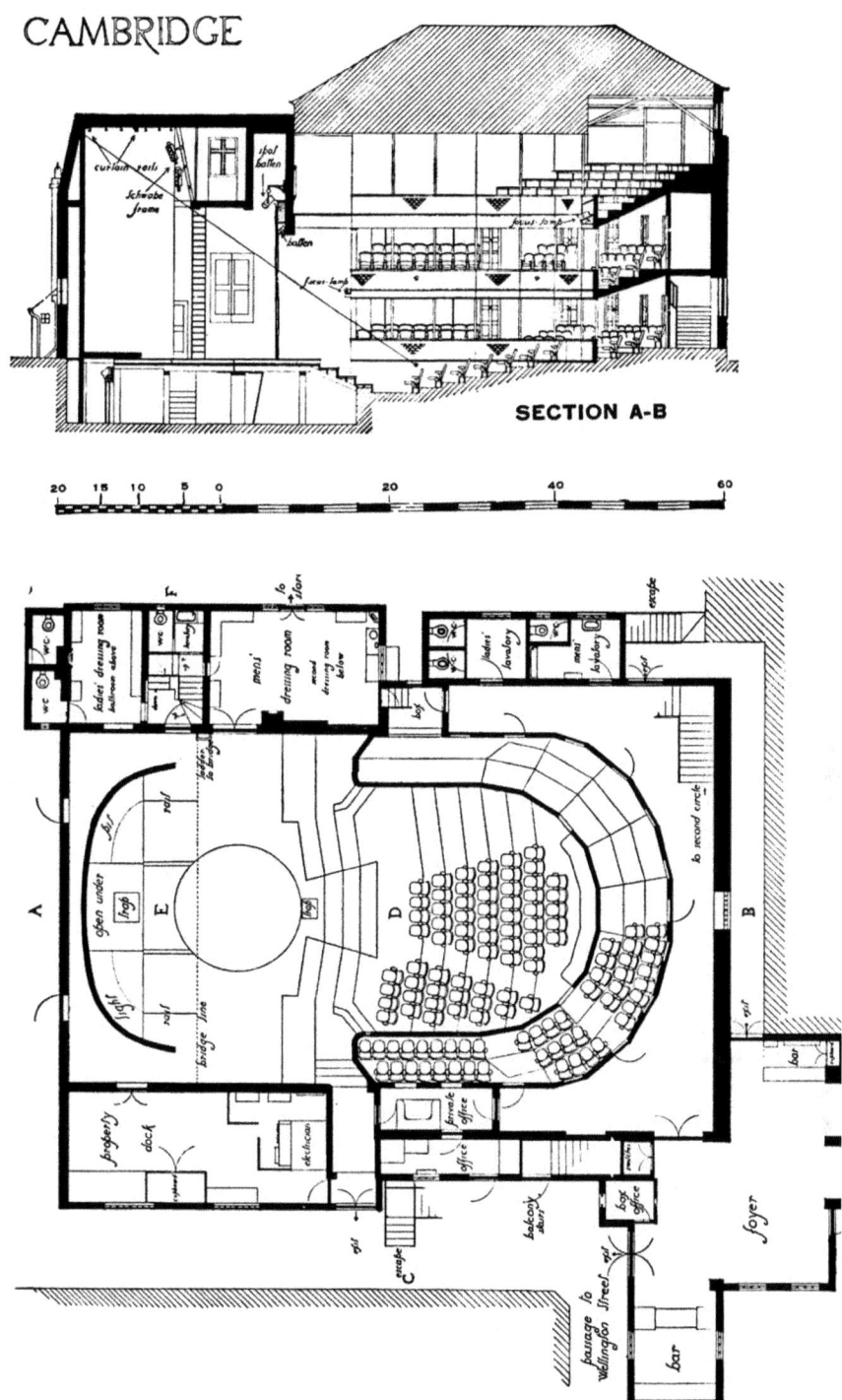

3.3 *Cambridge Festival Theatre section over plan 1926.*

The clutter of workshop and wardrobe having since been cleared away, the work of both Wilkins and of Gray lies open to view. The Festival has been well cared for since 1998 by the Triratna Buddhist Community. This would have pleased Gray, who embraced Zen Buddhism for the last thirty years of his life. Those who wrote of the Festival in the years before its rescue by the Buddhists could hardly judge the Festival as a theatre space. It is only in the present century that we have been able to comprehend the whole space with the superimposed tiers exposed to view and both pit/stalls and stage cleared for worship. What we now realise is that it was in the juxtaposition of the Georgian four-level auditorium of 1814 and the modern open stage of 1926 that much of the magic resided. Ironically Gray would have preferred a single-tier auditorium formed in a quadrant fan. Gray was lucky that he had not acquired a modern and essentially cold fan but rather Wilkins's intensely theatrical apsidal courtyard.

We know his preference for the fan from his written advice to the Governors of the Shakespeare Memorial Theatre at Stratford for the development of their winning design. In 1928 he recommended that the new Memorial Theatre should be a one-tier fan-shaped house. In contrast, at Cambridge Wilkins's three-tier auditorium embraces you. At the top is a gallery and below that the grand circle, originally arranged in boxes and latterly in two rows of seating. Below that is a similar stalls circle wrapping round conventional stalls seating with two diagonal aisles leading down from the stalls circle by which the actors could reach the stage. At the Festival there were no footlights, no orchestra pit and no formal edge to the stage, just a broad flight of steps.

Look to the right and the left and see that the original proscenium-arch doors and stage boxes flanking the former acting forestage have vanished along with the proscenium. Centre stage is the 4.5-metre-diameter revolve and beyond that the solid cyclorama 12.2 metres high with a surface not only perfect for lighting but also performing a vital acoustic function to contain the actor's voice. Above is a solid soffit at 12 metres with no suspended scenery to soak up the sound. On the line of the 1814 proscenium arch there is a massive steel and concrete bridge spanning the whole width of the stage, on which was a revolutionary seven-colour lighting system by the German lighting firm Schwabe to light both the permanent cyclorama and action taking place on and around the relatively small revolve.

The technical director and head of lighting was Harold Ridge, who was Gray's principal collaborator in the whole scheme. There was an architect, Edward Maufe, who contributed little and was better known for his churches such as Guildford Cathedral, though he did do one other theatre, the Oxford Playhouse in 1938. Ridge has left us one of the best-documented technical accounts of any new theatre. His *Stage Lighting* of 1928 (with a second edition in 1930) focuses on the Festival itself after a general discussion of the theory and practice of stage lighting. There is a preface by Norman Marshall, who was the first stage manager at the Festival and later was invited back to direct productions. Marshall comes back into this story as vice chairman of the building committee for the National Theatre.

Ridge got the whole building measured and drawn by F. Wynne Thomas. There are also both a fine photo of the auditorium and a series of production photos taken from the centre of the stalls circle. Elsewhere there survive 109 numbers of *The Festival Review*, the copiously illustrated programme produced by Gray for each show over the seven years of his regime. There exist only two other full accounts of this forgotten theatre: a biography of Gray by Paul Cornwell *Only by Failure: The Many Faces of the Impossible Life of Terence Gray* (2004) and *Terence Gray and the Cambridge Festival* by Richard Cave in the Chadwyck-Healey *Theatre in Focus* series. The latter consists of fifty individual slides and ninety-seven closely printed and well-researched pages of text. Guthrie wrote on his year at the Festival as director of productions in 1928/29, in his *A Life in the Theatre*, published in 1959. Marshall also wrote copiously about

3.4 *Cambridge Festival Theatre:* Oresteia *1926 over* The Provok'd Wife *1927.*

the Festival Theatre, in *The Other Theatre* of 1947 and in *The Producer and The Play* of 1957 and 1962. Nobody else was writing about how new theatre spaces were being used from the point of view of the one whom today we call 'the director' but whom Marshall still called 'the producer' as was the custom at that time.

Gray invites his hero, Gordon Craig, to the Festival in 1927

Marshall once wrote: 'It is extremely difficult to write about Gordon Craig without taking sides.' Marshall does just that. For him Craig was impossible. Foremost there is the business about the screens. Problems arose on their first outing, for Stanislavsky's *Hamlet* in Moscow in 1911 with designer Craig in attendance. The troubles there seem to have stemmed from how to move free-standing folding screens on the stage of the Moscow Art Theatre which was raked 1:20. In the Patent itself (No. 1771 dated 1 September 1910) Craig maintained 'this device is self- supporting and unlike scenery or curtains, does not require to be suspended from above. The screens may be mounted on castors and provided with struts if desired.' Sounds simple but the brief section on double hinging and castors is unconvincing and nowhere is it suggested how the screens could be moved on a raked stage and reset during the action without having to drop the front curtain, the avoidance of which had always been a main requirement.

The second set of screens, acquired by W.B. Yeats in 1911 for the old Abbey Theatre in Dublin, which also had a raked stage, seem to have worked satisfactorily. It is possible that their movement there was not as complex as what Craig had offered to Stanislavsky in Moscow. Maybe they did drop the front curtain. A third set was acquired by Gray in 1926 for the Festival, where he had flattened the original raked stage when installing his revolve and where the full-width front curtain was rarely used.

Screens were as important to Gray's vision of the 'new theatre' as they were to Craig. Ridge wrote: 'Realism is not practised in this theatre ... The permanent equipment consists of many dozens of screens made of three-plywood, which can be used separately or hinged together; they are all 4 feet wide and vary in height from 10 to18 feet ... The dimensions of the separate units of this scenery allow it to be built up in any way, as with a child's box of bricks.' There is no mention of whether they were moved other than in the interval. More likely they were securely fixed to the revolve, which did turn in full view.

Marshall tells of the entire *Hamlet* set in Moscow collapsing like a pack of cards: 'Craig had given little thought to the technical problem of how the screens were to be made to stand up safely and yet still be mobile.' In 1927 Gray invited Craig to the Festival to advise on their set of screens which, Marshall explains in *The Producer and The Play*,

> allowed finely effective settings, provided we made use of the theatre's exceptionally elaborate and flexible lighting equipment. But to rearrange them, even during the intervals, was a considerable task ... we tried in vain to discover how he (Craig) had envisaged them being moved in view of the audience. I remember him standing on the stage peering in puzzled silence through his pince-nez at these screens, as if pained by their obstinacy in remaining so immobile.

Craig did not, I think, ever mention Gray in his writings. Nor did Gray Craig after his editorial in the first *Festival Theatre Review* of November 1926, when he had written admiringly: 'great art is always ahead of its time, and its contemporaries cannot therefore be expected to appreciate it. That is why Gordon Craig and Appia are only now gaining a full measure of appreciation.'

I had often wondered why it was that Gray never again referred to Craig. I finally discovered why when a guest of Marshall for lunch at the Garrick Club in 1979. I asked him what else happened on Craig's only visit to the Festival in 1927 other than the revelation about the impracticality of Craig's screens. Marshall replied, most civilly, that Craig was still alive and in his nineties. He did not want to hurt him. He then told his lunch guests this story which he never set down in print. I risk quotation marks in this abbreviated version of what I recall and contributed to *Sightline* Vol. 15 No. 1 of Spring 1981, a few months after Marshall's death.

It was the end of the first season. I was there. Gray had managed to persuade Craig to come to Cambridge on one of his rare visits to Britain. After the evening's performance Craig thanked us all and accepted Gray's invitation to luncheon at the theatre restaurant the following day. It was an excellent meal, as it always was in Gray's own restaurant where he insisted on the highest standards, and Craig was most complimentary of both the food and wine. As with all theatre meals much time was spent in gossip and pleasantries. At the end of the meal Gray leant across the table to Craig and addressed him with the greatest courtesy:

'I would be greatly honoured if you would accept this, my invitation, for you to design and direct a play of your choice here at the Festival.' There was a long pause. Craig was visibly taken aback.

He recovered: 'But my dear Gray, I would demand total control.'

'Naturally. I will go further. You may have total direction of the whole theatre. The opening has been a great strain. I need a holiday and there is no one else in the world to whom I would rather entrust this theatre.'

Another pause.

'But I would demand eight weeks' rehearsal.' Here it was Gray that paused. The economics of the Festival and of the university calendar dictated that the vacations, sometimes as short as six weeks, were spent rehearsing the eight individual productions presented weekly in the three university terms of only eight weeks each.

'Agreed,' said Gray.

'But I would have to rebuild the theatre.'

Gray did not falter. Despite having just spent a small fortune of his own in creating the Festival, with the intent of achieving Craig's ideas, Gray replied: 'Certainly. I will arrange for my architect to attend us tomorrow and to receive your preliminary instructions.'

Craig demurred. The following day he had to leave early to go to Smallhythe in Kent to see his ailing mother, Ellen Terry, who died the following year. He said that he was most interested in the opportunity and would be in touch by letter as soon as he had returned to his home in Italy.

Some weeks later the letter arrived from Florence. Gray showed it to me. Craig thanked him for lunch and asked the name of the vineyard which produced that excellent and unusual wine they had drunk with the meal.

'Never,' Marshall concluded, his voice getting louder and his face redder as it always did when he felt passionately, and he certainly was passionate in his antipathy to Craig, 'Never let it be said that the whole British theatre turned its back on Craig. The theatre that was inspired by him and which realised all that was realisable of Craig's concepts was placed at his complete disposal. Craig turned Gray down and never referred to him or his theatre ever again. Craig was a dreamer, totally unrealistic, and never a man of the theatre. Nobody could work with the man and he knew it.'

Marshall's anecdote rings true. In the first edition of *The Festival Theatre Review* the previous year Gray had praised Craig, talking of his advanced theatre-craft that 'speaks through simple architectural forms piled together expressionistically and aided by the immense lighting facilities placed at our disposal by the advance of science'. But after that visit in 1927 neither Ridge nor Gray ever referred to Craig again.

The Memorial Theatre Stratford-upon-Avon of 1932

The story of the 1932 theatre starts from the moment of the discovery, on the evening of 6 March 1926, of the fire which seriously damaged but did not destroy the first Memorial Theatre of 1879. Immediately the chairman of the governors and three-time mayor of Stratford, Archibald Flower, took charge. By the end of April, Flower had formed an advisory panel of the good and the great – the director of the National Gallery, the president of the RIBA (the Royal Institute of British Architects) and the dramatists James Barrie and Harley Granville-Barker. There was to be an architectural competition run by the RIBA, who would select the winner. The director for the past seventeen years, William Bridges-Adams, was to be consulted about the design of auditorium and stage. But despite the assistance of Harley Granville-Barker his requests, having been considered by the governors, were mostly cut from the final brief handed to the contestants on the grounds that they did not want to tie the architects' hands. The governors preferred simply to state: 'The promoters desire a building, simple, beautiful, convenient, a monument worthy of its purpose.' This account is taken from chapter six of Sally Beauman's *The Royal Shakespeare Company: A History of Ten Decades* of 1982. What the promoters got was a seemingly intractable modernist auditorium seating 1,000 in fan-shaped stalls, circle and gallery. However, this theatre space was gradually made to work over the next three quarters of a century.

The winner of the competition was the twenty-nine-year-old Elisabeth Scott, a modernist whose understanding of functionalism was, in order that all should see the whole acting area, all must sit within a narrow fan. Of the result Bridges-Adams wrote in 1943, some dozen discreet years after his retirement in 1931: 'What we eventually got when the architects, pressure groups, quacks and empirics had finished with us, was the theatre, of all theatres in England, in which it is hardest to make the audience laugh or cry.' Actor Baliol Holloway, who had worked in both the old and the new Stratford theatres, commented: 'You can just about see the boiled shirts in the first row. It is like acting to Calais from the cliffs of Dover.'

What is not known about young Scott's winning entry is whether it was in fact her own work. She qualified in 1924, only three years before the competition was announced. She was then working in the practice of Maurice Chesterton. Richard Wilson, Sir Peter Hall Professor of Shakespearean Studies at Kingston University, wrote in his article 'Bonfire in Merrie England' in *The London Review of Books* of 4 May 2017: 'Maurice Chesterton's daughter, Dame Elizabeth Chesterton, herself an eminent architect who died in 2002, confided in a late interview that the competition entry had been falsely "submitted under Scott's name", and that her father never ceased to worry about the fraud: "Obviously, he had a conscience." Elisabeth Scott was never associated with another major building.' Wilson believes that Maurice Chesterton was the real designer of the 1932 Memorial Theatre.

There were three Chesterton cousins: as well as Maurice Chesterton, the architect, G.K. Chesterton, author, poet and dramatist, who in 1925 got the third cousin, A.K. Chesterton, the post of drama critic for the *Stratford-upon-Avon Herald*. A.K. soon became well known to

3.5 *Drawings by Richard Leacoft of* Künstler Theater *Munich 1908 over Stratford-on-Avon 1932.*

Archie Flower. A member of an already right-wing family, in 1929 A.K. Chesterton joined Oswald Mosley's British Union of Fascists.

In 1928 the Stratford establishment was susceptible to the romantic but slightly sinister notion that Shakespeare's 'Merrie England . . . that distant but shining country' was 'unlike the England of today' (Wilson quoting G.K.) and that Stratford on May Day, with its Morris dancers and maypoles, furnished 'an imaginative picture of the very soul of England' (Wilson quoting A.K.). Right-thinking citizens of Stratford-upon-Avon thought that their town might play a role in England analogous to that of Wagner's Bayreuth in Germany. In 1929, when the designs for the new theatre were being prepared, the Chesterton cousins advised Flower and his architect to visit Germany. Theatre buildings visited included, in addition to the Bayreuth *Festspielhaus*, the *Künstler* art theatre in Munich which opened in 1909 and was destroyed in the Second World War. In Richard and Helen Leacroft's *Theatre and Playhouse: An Illustrated Survey of Theatre Building from Ancient Greece to the Present Day* of 1984 we have Richard's sketches of both the *Künstler* and Stratford as built.

Incremental changes to the 1932 Memorial Theatre

Shepherd's auditorium of 1932 was constantly changed over seventy-four years until it was completely replaced by a new auditorium in 2010. By 2007 when it was demolished the capacity was 1,500, 50 per cent more than it had been when built. In 1935 150 places had been added in the gallery. In 1951 architect Brian O'Rorke tacked an extra row to the front of the circle and added three boxes each side, the better to connect audience with actor. In the stalls two more rows were squeezed in by reducing row-to-row distances. Most of the seats in the stalls were made two inches narrower. In the gallery comfort was actually increased when backs were added to the original benches. (This was the Stratford of the mid-1960s to which I toured Prospect during their winter seasons, which also included the Sadler's Wells Opera Company and the Royal Ballet.)

Under the new leadership of Trevor Nunn, another box each side was added at dress circle level, and above some gallery slips were brought right down to the proscenium. For the 1976 season those side galleries were brought through the proscenium to encircle a stage which now asserted itself by thrusting back through the proscenium and being flanked by angled wedges of seating. The sum effect was to make the theatre more intimate. Laughs came quicker, acoustics were better, audiences were younger by reason of the places in the admittedly distant gallery being sold for a fraction of that charged for the best seats in the stalls.

Incremental changes were possible at reasonable cost because of the inherently flexible nature of steel and brick. The cost was much less than it will ever be to change the reinforced concrete of the Olivier or Lyttelton. This is a different point from whether changes would ever have been permitted by Lasdun when alive or, after his death in 2001, by successive guardians of his flame. The NT had been listed Grade II * in 1994. Scott lacked the clout of Lasdun. She was never consulted on the generally beneficial alterations although she did not die until 1972 at the age of seventy-four. There is no record of what she thought about the changes to her theatre. If it was her theatre.

The next sea change in theatre architecture, the open thrust stage, bypassed Stratford-upon-Avon for half a century until the successful introduction of the smaller but more Elizabethan

Swan Theatre of 1986. Meanwhile a footnote is needed on the not very much that was happening with the project for a National Theatre, not in Warwickshire but in London.

Murmurings of a National Theatre from 1937 to 1950

In 1937 a site was found for the mooted National Theatre opposite the main entrance to the Victoria and Albert Museum. The architect was Sir Edwin Lutyens. There was to be one auditorium seating 1,040 with a single balcony like all those new cinemas built on both sides of the Atlantic. The detailed design of this dull auditorium was never worked up by either Lutyens or his collaborator Cecil Masey, who is best known for his extant Wimbledon Theatre of 1919 and the Phoenix on the Charing Cross Road of 1930.

Three things stopped this dream of a National Theatre in its tracks: the declaration of war in 1939, the proposal of a better site on the South Bank of the Thames and the death of Lutyens in 1944. After the war the long-standing National Theatre building committee was chaired by Sir Bronson Albery, who was both a theatre owner and the doyen of theatre producers of the day. The committee included his son Donald Albery, actors Sir Laurence Olivier and Sir Lewis Casson, theatre directors and scholars Hugh Hunt and Norman Marshall and designer historian Richard Southern. At its twenty-seventh meeting held in April 1950 O'Rorke, the newly appointed architect for the National Theatre, showed a model of his auditorium, which was fan-shaped with a single gallery. The minutes recorded:

> The matter was fully discussed, the Committee being of the opinion that, while it was desirable that perfect sight lines from every seat in the house should be arranged, this unfortunately was not possible except in a fan-shaped theatre, to which the Committee had always been strongly opposed involving, as it did, the sacrifice of that intimacy which the Committee felt was so desirable.

I am indebted to Richard Pilbrow for drawing my attention to this early and unequivocal statement that intimacy was a principal goal for a National Theatre. The paradox that fan-shaped auditoriums with perfect sightlines are not intimate theatres while all intimate theatres include some seats with bad sightlines had not yet been fully grasped. The first century of National Theatre murmurings had offered little discussion of the character of the theatre space save for this unequivocal statement made by distinguished men of the theatre whether intimacy could be achieved with a fan. Thereafter nobody questioned the relentlessly efficient seating of both the Olivier and the Lyttelton with perfect sightlines. Neither turned out to be intimate.

In the 1920s and 30s the design of theatre space had developed, interestingly at Cambridge and disappointingly at Stratford-upon-Avon. The highly decorated, tightly planned and hence intimate theatres of the half century 1860 to 1910 were dismissed as hierarchical, old-fashioned and irrelevant. The functionalist modern movements in both theatre and architecture had not and never would establish what were the design ingredients that would encourage a sense of community and a feeling for fun.

4

Guthrie's thrust stages

From Elsinore in 1936 to Edinburgh in 1948

There are many strands in Guthrie's early professional life which must be woven together if we are to understand how he came to conceive and then champion the thrust stage. Foremost is his own romantic account of the life-changing moment at Elsinore in 1936, when torrential rain fell just a few hours before a gala opening of his *Hamlet* for the Old Vic with Olivier as Hamlet and Anthony Quayle as Laertes. This forced Guthrie to move his production from the ramparts of the castle to the ballroom of the hotel where the company was staying. Guthrie set the chairs out on three sides of a playing area. Wrote Quayle in his autobiography of 1969, *A Time to Speak*:

> It was a brave move, for there was no time to rehearse; entrances, exits, positions, all would have to be improvised as we went along. Younger members of the audience were provided with cushions and instructed by Tony in his most governess-like manner to sit on the floor – and like it; members of the Diplomatic Corps, the elderly and distinguished guests were perched on slender ballroom chairs; everyone else had to stand, climb on benches and tables, or otherwise fend for themselves. Actors and audience alike rose to the occasion. Challenge drove the actors through. I do not know what pulled the audience along – they must have been damnably uncomfortable – but by the end they had caught fire . . . It was the performance that night that planted in Tony's mind the idea that Shakespeare could not be acted in a proscenium-arch theatre but demanded presentation almost in the round. The idea turned into resolve, and the theatres he built with Tanya Moiseiwitsch are the result.

The next significant moment in the development of the thrust was the decision to stage the 1554 play, *Ane Satyre of the Thrie Estaitis* by Sir David Lyndsay of the Mount, at the Assembly Hall Edinburgh in 1948 for the second three-week-long Edinburgh International Festival. Dramatist James Bridie had proposed to Guthrie that he direct this hardly known pre-Shakespearean play. The seven-hour playing time needed to be cut and the unfamiliar ancient Scottish dialect made more intelligible to a contemporary audience. For that Bridie suggested dramatist Robert Kemp, with whom Guthrie got on well. A particular sort of hall or place was needed, said Guthrie, and decidedly not a conventional theatre. Guthrie himself takes up the story in his autobiography *A Life in the Theatre* of 1960:

> We set out to find a suitable place to stage the play. Bridie, Kemp, William Graham of the festival office and me, in a noble old Daimler with a noble old chauffeur, lent by the

municipality. We visited big halls and wee halls. Halls ancient and modern, halls secular and halls holy, halls upstairs and halls in cellars, dance halls, skating rinks, lecture halls and beer halls.

The rain continued to pour . . . our Daimler careered wildly from a swimming bath, which we were assured could be emptied, in the extreme east of the city, to the recreation hall of a steam laundry in the city's extreme west. Darkness was falling; the streetlamps were reflected in the puddles . . . I was beginning to be acutely conscious that I had led them all a wild goose chase. Then spake Kemp in a tone of one who hates to admit something unpleasant: 'There *is* the Assembly Hall.' The minute I got inside I knew we were home. It is large and square in the Gothic style of about 1850. It has deep galleries and a raked floor sloping down to where, in the centre, the Moderator's throne is set within a railed enclosure . . .

The Scottish Kirk, with its austere reputation, might have been expected to take a dim view of mountebanks tumbling and painted women strutting before men in its Assembly Hall. On the contrary, no difficulties were raised; no one suggested censoring the bluer portions of the text or issued fussy interdicts about tobacco, alcohol or dressing rooms. There was a single stipulation: no nails must be knocked into the Moderator's throne.

The stage was a try-out on my part; a first sketch for the sort of Elizabethan stage I had long hoped, somehow and somewhere, to establish. The Moderator's chair and the table before it, in the centre of the hall, were enclosed under a platform reached from each of three sides by steps. Behind, and above the fourth side, a gallery was reached by two flights of stairs.

4.1 The Thrie Estaitis *at the Assembly Hall Edinburgh 1948 drawn by Richard Leacroft.*

Guthrie concluded:

> One of the most pleasing effects of the performance was the physical relation of the audience to the stage. The audience did not look at the actors against a background of pictorial and illusionary scenery. Seated round three sides of the stage, they focused upon the actors in the brightly lit acting area, but the background was the dimly lit rows of people similarly focused on the actors. All the time, but unemphatically and by inference, each member of the audience was being ceaselessly reminded that he was not lost in an illusion, was not at the Court of King Humanitie in sixteenth-century Scotland, but was in fact a member of a large audience, taking part, 'assisting' as the French very properly express it, at a performance, a participant in a ritual.

The Assembly Hall was and still is the solemn meeting place for the Annual Assembly of the Church of Scotland whose powers, as the established church in Scotland, are enshrined in the Act of Union of 1707 between the two sovereign nations of the United Kingdom of Great Britain. The hall had been built in 1859, not for the established Church of Scotland but for the sterner Free Church of Scotland, which was born in the Disruption of 1843 when more than half the congregations of Scotland marched out of their kirks and the ministers out of their manses in the belief that the Church of Scotland was in the pocket of the landowners. The two churches reunited in 1929 and from then on met in what we now know as the Assembly Hall.

Guthrie's great-grandfather, the Very Rev. Thomas Guthrie, had been Moderator of the Free Church of Scotland in 1862. My own grandfather, the Very Rev. Hugh Ross Mackintosh, was Moderator of the General Assembly of the Church of Scotland in 1932 and hence head of the Church of Scotland. The Moderator, who is elected, presides powerfully for just the one year and cannot be re-elected. The portraits of both of our ancestors hang in the building still. The fact that my grandfather was Moderator was one of many reasons why I sought an invitation for Prospect to play the Assembly Hall following our two earlier Festival appearances at the Lyceum theatre, which ambition was realised in 1968.

In 1948 the audience discovered that this sixteenth-century pageant of a play, presaging the Scottish Reformation, which was to enter its final phase in 1560, had found its true home. We cheered when Dame Sensualitie was banished to where she would be made welcome, Rome, and applauded when Duncan Macrae, as the Pardoner Flatterie, received his just deserts in the stocks. We understood why it was right and proper that King Humanitie should take counsel from Divine Correction, played by the magisterial Tom Fleming, and that all this should happen here, in the Assembly Hall of the Church of Scotland. I was there, an eleven-year-old schoolboy in awe at this evocation of a Scottish dramatic tradition of which few had been aware. Kemp had cut more than half the play and made most of the medieval Scots accessible. Having arrived to live in Edinburgh barely three years earlier I struggled to translate a little for my maternal grandfather, up from Bristol where I had been born.

Guthrie's stage was small: 4.5 metres wide and only 8 metres deep, surrounded by his steps on which the uninvited fourth estate, the common people, could crouch for involvement. The three estates (the Prelates, the Nobility and the representatives of Royal Burghs) had processed down the long aisles between the audience packed on to hard benches, 1,350 of them in total. On three sides of the lower area at the General Assembly there sit the ministers and the elders. Above are three galleries, with stepped seating and good sightlines, for the public. In the middle of the fourth side, behind the Moderator and Clerks, there is a shallow gallery which during the General Assembly is set aside for the High Commissioner who, for the duration of the Assembly,

4.2 *Festival Theatre Stratford Ontario 1957 over Guthrie Theatre Minneapolis*, The Three Sisters *1963.*

represents the Monarch. For *The Thrie Estaitis* there was placed here a vestigial curtained inner stage behind which the Moderator's chair was concealed. Above was a safe refuge for the corrupt Catholic Lords Spiritual. The cast of actors, musicians and extras was enormous and, with their banners but not much scenery, provided all the spectacle you could wish for. You looked and you listened. You reacted to the ritual. This was Guthrie involving us all.

From Edinburgh to Stratford Ontario and then on to Minneapolis

Guthrie's success was unique and not only for the fact that he had to revive the production twice in the Assembly Hall for the Festivals of 1949 and 1959. His achievement led directly to the invention of a totally new form of theatre, something that has never happened elsewhere as the result of a one-off special occasion. The Assembly Hall became the principal venue for guest drama companies at the Edinburgh Festival, starting with Richard Burton leading the Old Vic Company in *Romeo and Juliet* and more lastingly with the building of three new Guthrie thrust stage theatres: at Stratford Ontario, at Minneapolis USA and at Sheffield England.

On 24 March 1952 Guthrie had addressed the Shakespeare Stage Society in London: 'There will be no improvement in staging Shakespeare until there is a return to certain basic conditions of the Shakespeare stage. There is no need for an exact replica of the Globe Theatre, but it is essential to make contact between players and audience as intimate as possible.' Less than eight weeks later, in May 1952, Guthrie received the first overture from a small Canadian town in Ontario, fortuitously named Stratford and built on the banks of a River Avon and which had heard of *The Thrie Estaitis*. Guthrie was immediately invited over to discuss a festival season of Shakespeare. Just twelve months later, in July 1953, Alec Guinness opened in *Richard III* in a hastily erected tent over freshly poured concrete steppings. This first auditorium held 1,500 and had a 260-degree wrap-around. The roof was a temporary tent which was replaced in 1957 by the permanent structure with a second tier giving a capacity of 2,250. When much later I visited Stratford Ontario, Guthrie's successor, Michael Langham, and Moiseiwitsch had made further wise but minor modifications to the stage area.

At Stratford Ontario and at all succeeding Guthrie thrust stage theatres there were the two diagonal vomitories. These were ramped entrances pierced through the front rows of the auditorium for the actors to make quick entrances downstage. These are what Michael Boyd felt he could do without at the new Stratford-upon-Avon in 2010.

So far this account of the Guthrie thrust stage has not featured a major contribution from an architect. Minneapolis provided just this. From the start there was a tension between the chosen local architect Ralph Rapson and the 'old firm' of Guthrie and Moiseiwitsch. Guthrie disapproved of the appointment of an architect who had built only one indifferent university theatre. But being questioned all along the way by an intelligent younger man from a completely different background was just what Guthrie need. They quarrelled – 'creative tension' is the euphemism. Rapson's contribution of asymmetry and jaggedness in detailing was brilliant though somewhat grudgingly accepted by Guthrie and Moiseiwitsch. However, when in 2006 a later artistic director, Joe Dowling, and the Guthrie Theatre's governing body commissioned a new building on a new and better site from distinguished French architect Jean Nouvel, they insisted that the main auditorium and stage, which had been the joint creation of Guthrie, Rapson and Moiseiwitsch, be faithfully recreated within Nouvel's otherwise entirely new building.

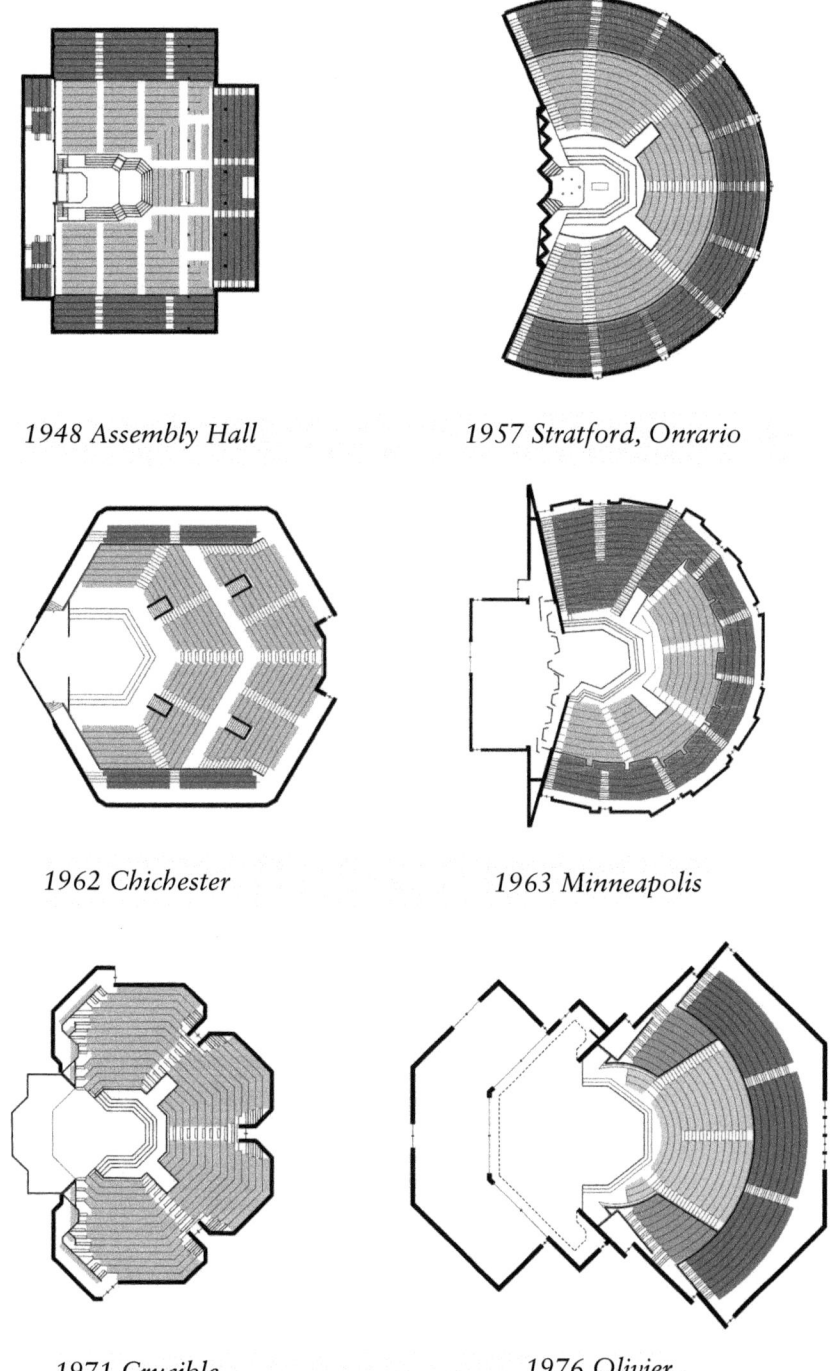

1948 Assembly Hall

1957 Stratford, Onrario

1962 Chichester

1963 Minneapolis

1971 Crucible

1976 Olivier

4.3 *Same-scale comparisons of six thrust stages. Capacities: Assembly Hall 1,350; Stratford Ontario 2,250; Chichester 1,350; Minneapolis 1,400; Crucible 1,000; Olivier 1,150.*

Chichester and the Vivian Beaumont without Guthrie

Two other new thrust stage theatres opened in the early 1960s, both of which strayed too far from Guthrie's path, one in Britain and the other in New York. In 1962 there came the Chichester Festival Theatre, founded by a former Mayor of Chichester, Leslie Evershed-Martin, who had been inspired by Stratford Ontario through watching a BBC television programme. He did not visit that theatre until his own was nearing completion. He appointed as architects the partnership of Philip Powell and Hidalgo Moya, who lived locally. Neither had built a theatre before. Evershed-Martin presented them with a pretty site but one with an abnormally high water table, which turned out to be significant. He gave them a small budget and decreed that neither he nor anyone else should interrupt them while they produced a design. At the time there was no artistic director and no staff. The architects therefore had no guidance other than what they had gained from a quick visit to Stratford Ontario. Much of what many would think essential was left out. Within Powell and Moya's office the young project architect, Christopher Stevens, explained the cause of some of obvious shortcomings at a Manchester University conference held in 1962, the year after the opening of Chichester: 'At the beginning, we certainly didn't expect scenery . . . If we had had to have all the space and equipment necessary to handle full-scale scenery we couldn't have done it without a lot more money.' (This admission is included in *Actor and Architect*, edited by Stephen Joseph in 1964, which contains papers given at that conference by Richard Southern, Tyrone Guthrie and Sean Kenny.)

Much of what was missing for the handling of scenery was added bit by bit over more than half a century in a series of extensions and modifications, the latest being in 2014. At the centre there remains the original theatre space which is difficult to alter due to its inflexible hexagonal structure. It still lacks the vomitories dedicated to the actors which Guthrie regarded as a *sine qua non*. The first architect whom Evershed-Martin had approached had been another local one who had to tell Guthrie, who was briefly involved at the very outset, that the site was waterlogged and that as result vomitories could not be excavated. The actors would have to share a flight of steps with the front rows of the audience, entering from the foyer. Guthrie gently disengaged himself from the project and did not see Chichester in action until the second season.

Comparatives of six successive thrust/open stages realised between 1948 and 1976 show the Guthrie flame both burning and flickering: the Assembly Hall, Stratford Ontario, Chichester, Minneapolis, Sheffield Crucible and the Olivier. The six drawings were selected from the twelve which originally appeared in *The Guthrie Thrust Stage: A Living Legacy* which I edited for the ABTT to accompany the British entry for the architectural section of the Prague Quadrennial of 2011. The six selected were for Tedd George to include in the book by his late father, Colin George, which he edited in 2021,*Stirring Up Sheffield: An Insider's Account of the Battle to Build the Crucible Theatre*.

In an email to me of 30 July 2013. Colin George explained how Guthrie wanted to dissociate himself from Chichester but in a supportive sort of way. Guthrie had become a close friend of George in 1967 when design had started on the Crucible:

> Aware of the contrast with Chichester, Guthrie advised me [George] in a letter of 16 October 1969 – 'you must be careful not to get us all into the position of running down the architecture of Chichester. It is no good; but it's not nice or politic to say so. I think it is relevant that the entire jing-bang at Chichester cost less than the heating-cooling system alone at Stratford Ontario or Minneapolis. Commend them for getting it up so splendidly reasonably, which we can truthfully do, and infer that it might have been better if there had been more dough to spend.'

4.4 *Opening production of* Amadeus, *Chichester Festival Theatre after 2014 renovation by Haworth Tompkins.*

That Chichester lacked the design involvement of Guthrie and Moiseiwitsch is clear from the hexagonal geometry and the fact that the tip of the thrust stage did not reach out as far as the centre of that hexagon. This forced too great a share of the audience to be positioned to the front of an overwide stage which at 9.39 metres was twice the width of the stages of the Assembly Hall, of Stratford Ontario and of Minneapolis. The mostly frontal Chichester audience suffered also from being seated on too shallow a rake, only 13 to 19 degrees as opposed to the 21 to 28 degrees of the true Guthrie theatres. This was caused by the roof over the stage and auditorium being unusually low, under tension cables which hold up the hexagonal roof and are anchored to the six corners of the building. The result was an unusually inexpensive theatre space which cannot easily be altered. In 2014 Haworth Tompkins did what they could to the auditorium while transforming much elsewhere.

Four years after Chichester, in 1965, there opened the Vivian Beaumont Theater at the Lincoln Center New York. This was an expensively engineered compromise between thrust and proscenium stages and was finally judged unsatisfactory as either. Designer Jo Mielziner wrote that architect Eero Saarinen and he had hoped to design two theatres. Neither 'believed in anything but single-form stages. We were both completely opposed to a multiform Stage . . . if our original proposition had been accepted one of them would have been pure Thrust Stage and the other pure Proscenium. We were overruled . . . However, the Lincoln Center gave us months of exploratory time and supported the cost of experimental designs and models.' The committee then decided that the Vivian Beaumont should have a dual-form design so that 'it could be used either as a Proscenium Theatre or as an Open-Thrust Stage . . . We pointed out that to meet the production schedule of a company in repertory it would be imperative to install expensive automatic mechanical equipment.'

The theatre opened in 1965 and soon abandoned repertoire. In the end what the Beaumont got was neither a proscenium theatre nor a true thrust but an open stage which like the Olivier was too wide. Much of the expensive machinery was removed having been scarcely used. Three years earlier, at that conference at Manchester, Guthrie had spoken presciently about the plans for the Vivian Beaumont then under construction.

> You press an electronic this and you pull a something else that, and lo and behold! a whole lot of seats shuffle out of sight and disappear into thin air. An apron stage thrusts itself forward. And there you are in another form. On paper it is extremely ingenious. I could be very wrong but my belief is that it is neither as good as it could be as a proscenium theatre, nor as good as it could be as a thrust stage.

Guthrie was spot on.

Success of the Sheffield Crucible of 1971 with Guthrie very much involved

The decade ended with a resounding success with the Sheffield Crucible. Guthrie and Moiseiwitsch had been involved from the outset, advising director Colin George and architect Nick Thompson of Renton Howard Wood Levin. The Crucible opened in November 1971. In an interview on Radio Brighton, recorded just after he had stood on the stage of the almost complete Crucible, Guthrie had said: 'It's going to be an eye-opener when they open the new theatre in Sheffield – this I think will be the best example of a thrust stage yet.'

George liked to compare the Crucible to what had gone before. In an email to me of 2013 he wrote:

> Chichester's thrust stage was too wide, the rake of the seats not steep enough, and the centre of the roof too far back from the stage. It is over the centre of the stage itself at Sheffield. Chichester cost £100,000 to build, Sheffield spent a million pounds on its theatre – ten times that of Chichester. This is not to denigrate in any way the effort of Evershed-Martin and his supporters. The city council of Sheffield, one of the largest cities in England, was able to give £330,000, the Arts Council another £330,000, and the remainder was raised privately. Sheffield at that time was a world centre for the steel industry.

Christopher Baugh, who was on a planning group for the Crucible, recalls George and Moiseiwitsch identifying the centre of the roof to the Crucible theatre space as being directly over the natural focus of the acting stage. George had identified that focus on any stage as being of nine feet (2.75 metre) diameter and named it 'the magic spot'. Baugh remembers the gleam in George's eyes when he recalled that to build the Crucible the contractors placed the huge crane precisely on the magic spot.

In *Stirring up Sheffield*, a memoir co-authored with his son Tedd, George records the controversy stirred up in 1969 by opponents of a deep thrust stage When the Crucible had started construction a Mr Cotton, who had enthusiastically supported the creation of a civic theatre in Sheffield but was bitterly opposed to the choice of a thrust stage, elicited support for his cause from Olivier. The latter found himself batting for the wrong side:

> I don't know whether or not you have seen the designs for the new National Theatre, but therein I believe the audience/actor relationship to have achieved its most perfect design in a thrust stage theatre. The audience seem to take hold of the stage like a pair of pincers and yet do not seem to be blowing a draught from the port or the starboard quarters. I find as an actor that more than a quarter circle is a wee bit disconcerting.

A quarter circle is that subtended by the precise 90-degree angle that drove the wide fan of the Olivier Theatre.

Olivier later apologised to George for this misjudged letter. The controversy over the Sheffield thrust had a happy ending when the Crucible turned out a great success. Unfortunately, at the National Lasdun had taken on board Olivier's misgivings about the thrust stage after the latter's experiences at Chichester but overcorrected what Olivier had perceived as a fault. This was audience seeing other audience over his shoulder when he was standing centre stage. Olivier disliked Chichester because the wrap-around went too far, while Guthrie disliked Chichester because the wrap-around did not go far enough. How Guthrie would have hated the Olivier Theatre. Sadly, he died a few months before the Crucible opened and five years before the opening of the Olivier.

In the *Sheffield Telegraph* of August 1969, when George was asked why a thrust stage he replied:

> Theatre has reacted to television and the cinema ... A thrust stage possesses a quality those forms of entertainment lack – personal contact between actor and audience. It is three-dimensional in a way the others can never be. The audience sitting on three sides are aware both of the performance and of the other spectators enjoying and being moved by it. A shared experience like being in a football crowd or at a revivalist church meeting.

For an account of how the new Crucible impressed when it opened in 1971 you must turn to *The Architectural Review* of February 1972 for an article by Michael Elliott, who wrote of Guthrie: 'At Elsinore and Edinburgh he invented, and the word is invented not rediscovered, a new way of approaching production.' But while Elliott pinpointed some practical advantages of the thrust stage – more people closer to the stage plus less scenic possibilities leading to less costly settings and more use of the imagination – he also emphasised the downside of Guthrie's austere, non-scenic approach. Elliott explained that 'Guthrie may have rescued the actor from behind the proscenium but ... he failed to rescue what design at its best can create for the actor and the audience. Immense flexibility and pace of stage action he achieved, but by chucking everything else out of the window ... These theatres have a certain visual aridity.'

The Young Vic of 1970

Frank Dunlop founded the itinerant Pop Theatre Company in 1966 having played the Assembly Hall Edinburgh twice. He gained a home when the Pop Theatre Company was translated into the Young Vic Theatre Company under the wing of the National Theatre. He briefed young architect Bill Howell to build him 'a cross between the Elizabethan Fortune Theatre, Guthrie's Assembly Hall and a circus.' This is exactly what Howell achieved. It was the simplest and cheapest 400-seat theatre ever built. On opening in 1970 it was intended to last but five years. The improvements wrought by Haworth Tompkins in 2006 were not to the original square plan but consisted of necessary technical matters like stage lighting and ventilation. The original performance lighting over the entire space had been crudely clamped to two-inch pipes and accessed from below. Now there is a grid of standard lighting bridges. The consequent raising of the ceiling allowed the addition of a second balcony with a single row of seating. Everywhere the seating is more comfortable than were the original tough wooden benches. They still lack arms but the back cushions now identify your place. This in a theatre at which for the first thirty years your ticket let you into your chosen level but left it to you to sit where you liked (a practice followed at first at both the Cottesloe and the Tricycle).

The square form of the main auditorium allows the celebration of centrality, most vividly in the 2017 production of *The Life of Galileo*. Yet the Young Vic remains essentially a Guthrie thrust stage theatre. What few now recognise is that the 'magic spot' of the 980-seat Crucible's thrust stage and at the Young Vic in thrust format, which is now just one of the possible

4.5 Life of Galileo *at Young Vic 2017.*

arrangements at this much smaller theatre, are both precisely under the centre of their roofs. These two theatre spaces opened within fourteen months of each other in 1970/71.

The end of thrust stage drama at the Assembly Hall for the Edinburgh Festival

The Assembly Hall's use as the main venue for drama at the official Edinburgh Festival came to an end a few years short of the fiftieth anniversary of *The Thrie Estaitis*. Each year there had been three weeks of eight performances a week. That is twenty-four performances per Festival, each with a capacity of 1,350. The shows generally sold out. Thus, attendances at each Festival totalled over 30,000. That is about 1.5 million attendances over the lifetime of the Assembly Hall as a thrust stage theatre for the festival.

Why did it stop? In 1999 the Assembly Hall became the temporary home of the newly created Scottish Parliament until their new building was completed down at Holyrood. The new government paid for the temporary removal of most of the old uncomfortable benches on three straight sides of the main floor. The layout for the parliament had at its centre easy concentric semicircular curved rows, in contrast to the stern rectilinear geometry of the Hall. All was supposed to be reversible in the Grade A listed Assembly Hall, but after the parliament left for its new building at Holyrood the Church of Scotland decided to keep the semicircular seating. Such is the arrangement now used by the Edinburgh Fringe, who each year rent the Assembly Hall for the Festival.

A thrust that did not happen until sixty years later

All could have turned out differently had a thrust stage theatre been built in Britain soon after *The Thrie Estaitis*. In his autobiography *A Time.to Speak* Anthony Quayle tells a tantalising story of when, in 1950, he offered Guthrie co-directorship of the Memorial Theatre in Stratford-upon-Avon. Quayle, who had taken over in 1948, was overworked but on the crest of a wave. He had introduced to what had been a provincial backwater the likes of John Gielgud, Laurence Olivier, Ralph Richardson, Peggy Ashcroft and Michael Redgrave. Guthrie had contributed a fine production of *Henry VIII*. Quayle fleshes out an anecdote, starting with his delight at Guthrie's immediate acceptance of his offer of a co-directorship. But there was a condition:

> I have one great ambition. And that is to build what I call my Tin Globe. It all sprang from that first night in Denmark which you will remember very well. I want to build a theatre with a permanent set surrounded by audience on three sides in order to bring the people nearer to the actors and so communicate far more in the way Shakespeare himself did. All this proscenium-arch acting is merely a version of opera. Rubbish.

Quayle knew Guthrie was right. To reach the back of the gallery at Stratford his company had to give operatic performances. Asked to state exactly what was his condition Guthrie replied: 'That you build my Tin Globe right here beside the Avon in this garden behind the old theatre. It'll be an eye-opener for the people. They'll see how far, far better it is than that dreadful shoe box in which you are acting now.' But what was to be done with the existing theatre? 'Bulldoze it and push it into the river,' smiled Guthrie. To Quayle's protestations that the governors would never allow that he answered with a shrug: 'All right then. I'll build it somewhere else and you must go on looking for a co-director. But this I assure you, build it I shall. It may not be in this country at all. So much the worse for this country.' Quayle concludes: 'And that was the end of that. He went and built it in Canada.' Stratford-upon-Avon took sixty years from that moment in 1950 to the opening in 2010 of the thrust main stage that Guthrie would have recognised.

5

Germany's building boom and Anglo-American Shakespeare

West Germany sets the pace for the building of new theatres

Of all European countries in the post-war years 1948 to 1970 it was West Germany which built most major new theatres, more than forty in fact. Six were pure opera houses seating between 1,400 and 1,850. Some comprised an opera house of various sizes alongside a playhouse plus a third studio. Three were pure playhouses. A further score, holding between 750 and 1,100, lacked their own companies and received productions from those that had. All were built and paid for by generous city or state governments. This German theatre-building boom, excluding East Germany, is dealt with in detail in *The Modern Theatre* by Hannelore Schubert of 1971. This became the authoritative guide for the many theatre architects and technicians from other countries who took themselves off to Germany on study trips.

Most German city centres had been flattened in the war. The reinstatement of the civilising arts of opera and the drama had a much higher priority than in the victorious countries. The quickest way was to recreate the theatrical experiences of the past but dress these in smart new modernist clothes equipped with the latest technology. However, a few great theatres from the eighteenth and nineteenth centuries did survive and were soon lovingly restored.

In 1975 I was a guest of the West German government, on a visit arranged by Brigitte Lohmeyer, their cultural attaché, who had become a friend at many an Edinburgh Festival. I chose the theatres I wanted to visit and the government arranged every detail, from the welcome in Berlin (on the plane itself, not at the barrier) to seeing that it was either the architect or the director of the theatres on my list who showed me round. I chose their finest old and their best new theatres: in Bayreuth both Wagner's 1876 *Festspielhaus* and Wilhelmina's 1748 *Markgräfliches Opernhaus*, and in Munich the reconstituted rococo 1753 *Cuvilliés Opernhaus* and the 1901 secession *Kammerspiele* as well as the already mentioned Bavarian *Nationaltheater*. The new theatres and opera houses were strangely similar: cool, efficient and well equipped. They were all picture-frame proscenium houses, as were the few old ones that were being meticulously restored. But two new ones stood out for very different reasons.

In West Berlin I was taken to the 1963 *Freie Volksbühne* by architect Fritz Bornemann, who showed me an effective playhouse holding 1,047 with a single wrap-around balcony. The intimacy achieved had surprised Laurence Olivier and his National Theatre Company when they visited in 1965. The experience resulted in Olivier allowing an increase of 100 seats in the brief for the Lyttelton. It was a pity that he did not advise Lasdun to wrap round the single balcony at the Lyttelton as at the *Freie Volksbühne* rather than allowing him to run his balcony in an almost straight line, side wall to side wall.

The second surprise was the magnificently asymmetric *Badisches Staatstheater* of 1975 in Karlsruhe. The asymmetry makes it uncompromisingly different from the other new opera houses in Germany from the 1960s and 1970s. My guide was the principal architect, Helmut Bätzner, who spoke perfect English. I asked about the design of the magnificent decorative doors set into the asymmetric shuttered concrete auditorium. From the naturally lit foyers each door was distinctively enamelled in strong colours and each was a different height and width. Large, elegant handles had been engineered to exert pressure and seal the soundproofing. There were no sound or light lobbies. I did not question the safety mechanism for exiting the auditorium as I knew that would have been solved in an efficient German way, but did wonder about the arrival of latecomers which would obviously let light into the auditorium. Bätzner smiled and said slowly: 'I do not understand. What is this English word "latecomer"?'

Both asymmetry and side 'ski slope' or 'toboggan' balcony boxes shared one drawback in that the resulting perfect sightlines meant wider stages. The universal snag with this is that more intimate presentations are framed not by the architecture of the auditorium at that crucial point where performer and audience should meet, but by severe black technical mounts which dampen the mood and apparently distance the acting area. This is alienating for Mozart, for operetta and for the comedy which continued to flourish in the few surviving narrower and more flamboyant nineteenth-century houses.

In 1989, before the Berlin Wall came down, I gave my paper, 'The Impact of Eighteenth- and Nineteenth-century Theatre Architecture on the Theatre of the Twentieth Century', from the stage of just such an interior, that of the Hungarian State Opera House in Budapest which acoustically and architecturally is a match for the Paris *Palais Garnier*. It had just been beautifully restored to celebrate its centenary in September 1984 and offered a warm embrace to a nervous visiting speaker.

American influences on English playhouses for Shakespeare 1948–1997

In the summer of 1969 American actor Sam Wanamaker was canvassing support for his project to rebuild Shakespeare's Globe close to where the original had stood. He sought out Toby Robertson and myself at our London office. Prospect was enjoying its *annus mirabilis*, which had started with the ten-week season at the Piccadilly Theatre of our 1969 Edinburgh productions of *Edward II* and *Richard II* which played for every performance to 102 per cent (a figure certified by the Albery management of the Piccadilly who counted standing in the take but not in the capacity). Wanamaker's pitch started with a panoramic sketch of a rebuilt Globe sitting snugly on Bankside beneath lightly sketched-in skyscrapers which would finance its construction. When it came to thoughts for the theatre space itself he had just the two images: the familiar drawing by de Witt of the Swan Theatre ca. 1596 and a photo of the Elizabethan Theatre in Ashland Oregon of 1959, where an audience of more than 1,000 is seated across a wide fan recognisable from so many modern auditoriums. All but those in a very few token side seats have a frontal view of a permanent half-timbered wall-to-wall 'Elizabethan' facade modelled, it is said, on that of the Fortune.

Wanamaker was uncertain whether a modern London audience would want to stand in an Elizabethan yard, and suggested that there might be stalls seating to the front like at Oregon but

5.1 Antony & Cleopatra *at Shakespeare's Globe 1999.*

removable. (He carried a photo to prove it). The scholars rightly dissuaded him from doing this but he persuaded them to allow him to hedge his bets by insisting on many more *ingressi* than are shown by de Witt, the better to connect the yard with the first encircling tier. Weary standees in the yard, thought Wanamaker, could retreat up only a few steps and sit in the lowest tier. While the de Witt drawing shows only the two *ingressi* Wanamaker insisted that there might have been more and so a further eight were introduced. Since the authorities also required four exits directly to the outside world this made fourteen breaks in the lowest tier in the Globe as reimagined in 1997.

Had the floor of the front row of that first encircling tier been pitched at stage level then things would have been much better. Coincidentally the two great scholars who could draw, Richard Southern and C. Walter Hodges, had each imagined alternative Globe reconstructions, one with the floor of the front row of the lowest tier at stage level and the other with the floor much lower and the top of the lower tier front lining through with the stage level. Wanamaker and his architect, Theo Crosby, therefore had a choice. In 1997, encouraged by Wanamaker, they chose the latter and thereby made their only mistake in what was otherwise a most successful project. Over the thirty years it took to happen the rebuilding of Shakespeare's Globe was at first dismissed by the English theatre establishment as Disneyland for the tourists. But the establishment was wrong. From the outset this unsubsidised Globe drew the town as well as the tourists and a younger audience all paying less than upriver at the Olivier with its perfect sightlines and government support.

Neither Wanamaker nor Crosby lived to see their take on Shakespeare's Globe finished. The keeper of the flame on matters architectural since then has been Jon Greenfield, who had joined Crosby at Pentagram in 1986. There were many committees. In the first decade of the twentieth

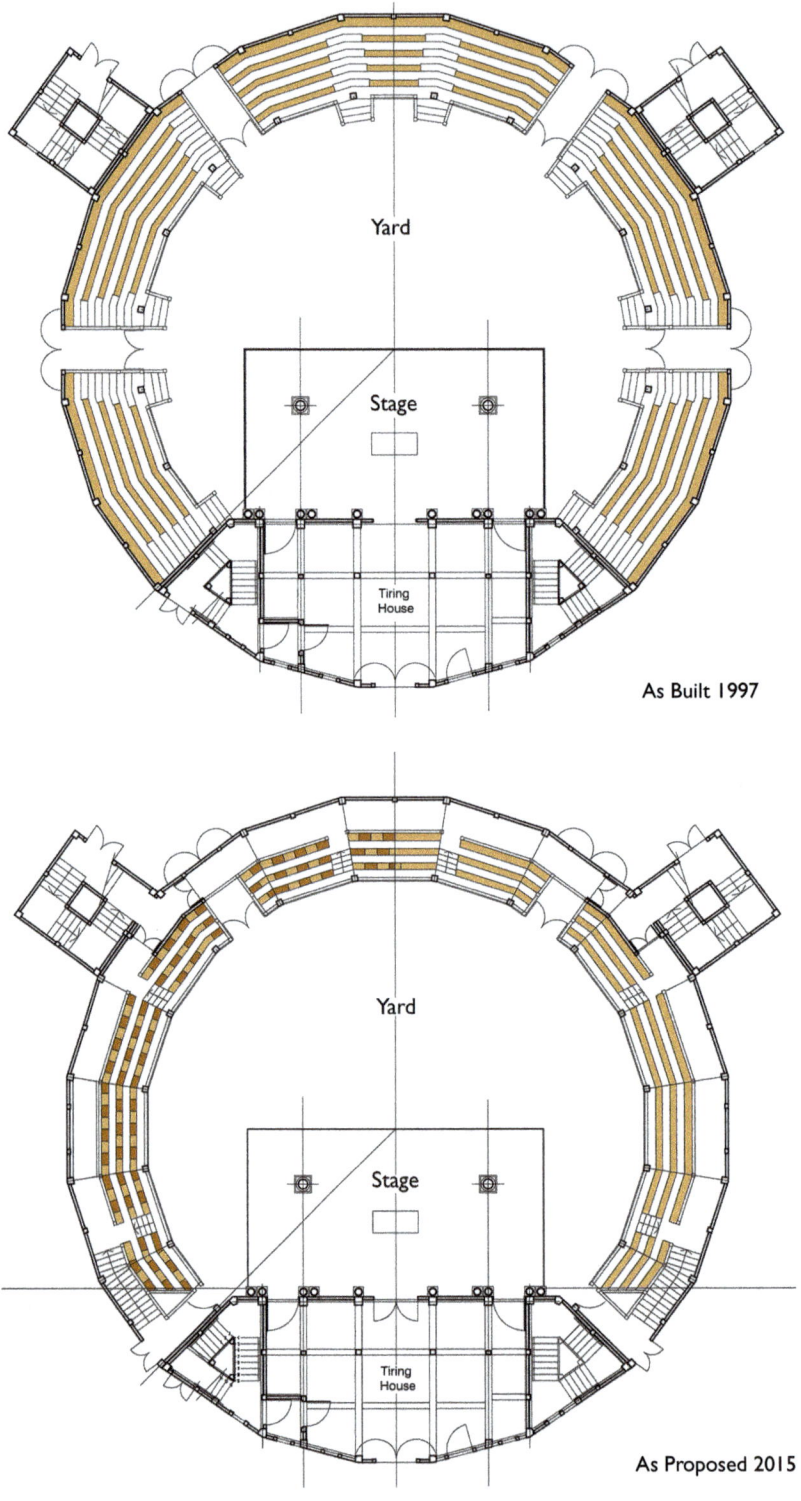

5.2 *Two plans of Shakespeare's Globe yard level: as built in 1997 over proposal of 2015.*

century colleagues were finally persuaded to raise to stage level the almost unsellable bays in the lowest tier on each side of the stage, and this did make a difference. But to date there have not been the resources to raise the main centre section, reroute the access and lose almost all the *ingressi*. How to achieve this has been worked out by Greenfield. When this does happen, as is indicated in the accompanying drawings, no one will be more pleased than Mark Rylance, who was actor-manager of the Globe from 1995 to 2005. Rylance had experienced the downside of the first tier being pitched so low. As completed, the eye line of the standing actor on stage hit not the eyes of audience seated in what should be the best places but the blank plaster of the wall above their heads. When the Covid-19 plague struck in 2020 Greenwood had already drawn the plans to show how matters can still be put right when there is the money.

The fan shape is adopted by many new British theatres from 1969 to 1979

By the 1960s fan-shaped blocks of seating for all had become the way for anyone designing new theatres. Perfect sightlines and comfort for all, and good acoustics, were important to the designers of not just the National's Olivier and Lyttelton theatres of 1976 and of the Barbican of 1982. Up till then most new playhouses in Britain had found no problem in fulfilling these two functional requirements of legroom and sightlines simply because they were much smaller. Five near identical and mostly satisfactory new theatres, each with a fan-shaped and well-raked unbroken block of seats for about 550 facing a proscenium approximately 10 metres wide, had opened within seven years: at Leatherhead in 1969; at Stirling in 1971; at Cardiff in 1973; at Derby in 1975; and at Clwyd in North Wales in 1976. Both Leatherhead and Derby were designed by Roderick Ham, whose later New Wolsey Theatre at Ipswich of 1979 holding but 400 signalled a small but significant change in the design of smaller theatre spaces by way of a single continuous horizontal balcony wrapping round both auditorium and stage.

Similar in form to these theatres, but dangerously bigger, was the New Repertory Theatre at Birmingham of 1971, with 920 seats in a single fan facing a 15-metre opening. That is wider than that of the London Coliseum. This replaced the 'old' Rep of 1913 that still survives holding half as many with the stage precisely half the width of the 'new' Rep. This was one of the first misfortunes that resulted from a theatre client asking an architect for 'the same only bigger'.

The Old Vic and Stratford theatres changed but the Olivier and Lyttelton never

The original Globe of 1599 was destroyed by fire in 1613 and rebuilt the following year. That second Globe closed in 1642 and perished some years later. The present National had its 45th birthday in 2021 and its two main theatre spaces have not been altered. This immutability contrasts with that of the two other British 'national theatres', the Shakespeare Memorial Theatre and the Old Vic.

The National Theatre Company occupied the Old Vic from 1963 until 1976. This 1818 theatre had been completely remodelled in 1880 and after that its proscenium zone was reshaped six times between 1927 and 1963. In 1914 it became the home of the Old Vic Company with a largely Shakespearean repertoire. This was the company that was replaced by the National Theatre Company in 1963. What links Stratford-upon-Avon and the Old Vic is not just Shakespeare but the fact that these two national playhouses were often altered in the crucial area where actor and audience meet. Successive directors had differing ideas. They were able to carry alterations out at modest cost because both were built of steel, brick and stucco, which can be adjusted. A full account of the development of both can be found in my article with nineteen images: 'Scene Individable or Poem Unlimited' in *The National Theatre: The Architectural Review Guide* edited by Colin Amery and published by The Architectural Press in 1977.

In contrast no significant alterations have been made to the Olivier or Lyttelton other than wrapping some of the originally exposed shuttered concrete 'temporarily' in soft black material to ameliorate the doubtful acoustic and to tone down its overassertive pale colour. In the next chapter all three major British brutalist theatre spaces – Olivier, Lyttelton and Barbican – are considered, both how they were designed and the question of whether it is because they were cocooned in hard-to-shift concrete that they have never been improved as theatre spaces.

6

The Olivier, the Lyttelton and the Barbican theatres

The National Theatre of 1976 approached through the rebootings of 1998 and 2016

As the millennium approached the National Theatre building needed attention. The NT was then thought of as both a new building, being unlike almost all other theatres, and as an old one because it had been in use for more than a generation. Much has now been done at the National building and yet both the Olivier and Lyttelton theatre spaces have survived as built. The reason for the Olivier and Lyttelton themselves not having been altered as taste and society had evolved was not wholly due to a lack of money. In 1998 architects Stanton Williams spent £43 million retuning the NT building for the twenty-first century. In 2016 Haworth Tompkins spent even more doing more of the same. The cost of the two renovations, added together and updated to 2016 prices, was approximately £190 million. Indexed to 2016 prices the 1976 original cost of Lasdun's National (£16 million) translates approximately to £85 million. Thus the sum of the two rebootings of a 1976 theatre cost, in real terms, twice what it cost to build it in the first place. The original costs and the 2016 costs come from the NT. The updating of 1976 and 1998 costs to 2016 prices was calculated for me by John Clarke, the best British quantity surveyor of his generation to specialise in performing arts buildings. The 1976 National Theatre was originally built to a tight budget. It was a bargain. Only Chichester of the larger British theatres built since 1945 cost less in real terms calculated either per seat or per square metre.

Where did the money go in the improvements? First there were changes to the front of house. People wanted to eat. The requirement for a restaurant had arrived at a late moment in the design process, the GLC having thought that playgoers would walk over to the Festival Hall restaurant to eat. At a late stage Lasdun cleverly managed to insert a small restaurant, but that was all. At the opening little more than a sandwich was available elsewhere.

Early on the management inserted a bookshop, the need for which had not been foreseen in the brief. Lasdun disliked clutter and at first opposed anything more than a small booth in the Lyttelton foyer. The original emphasis on arrival at his theatre was preparation for an occasion. Every evening the pilgrims, glass in hand, could enjoy an hour's worth of free music before the show. Since then the world and theatre has changed and the foyers now buzz all day, not necessarily with theatregoers. Some are meeting friends and others are hunched over laptops. The foyers now are less of a preparation for a formal occasion and more of an informal meeting place for the like-minded.

Bigger expenditure was incurred because the building had been planned in the age of the motor car. The NT as built was a traffic island with anti-clockwise car circulation and a *porte cochère* as a drop-off at the main entrance at the riverside apex of the 45-degree axis. Off this perimeter road there were originally four ramps up or down to an underground car park with capacity now reduced to space for 400 cars – say 1,000 theatregoers – with access by two ramps only. Today most people arrive on foot.

In 1998 the NT gained a prominent and purpose-designed bookshop, which Stanton Williams established in the by then superfluous *porte cochère*. Lasdun did not approve. He also dug his heels in on the proposed removal of the now largely redundant pedestrian level linking the upper Olivier entrance to the platforms of Waterloo Station. When these walkways had been cut short on the Festival Hall side both Stanton Williams and the NT board wanted to lose the upper walkway on the NT side of Waterloo Bridge but Lasdun did not. The Lyttelton foyer remains in the shadow cast by this vestigial walkway which has for decades taken you on the level only as far as the Hayward Gallery.

Vehicular access on the river side was originally required not only for theatregoers arriving at the *porte cochère* but also for refuse lorries picking up kitchen and other waste from a collection point placed on that side. This accounted for the impression that the NT when built had turned its back on the Thames. In 2016 the NT was finally opened up to the river walk, which had itself been elegantly redesigned. The main entrance has been re-established at the riverside apex of the 45-degree diagonal axis. The bookshop is now bigger but has been pushed back into a building also possessing many revenue-earning coffee shops. Meanwhile, at the rear of the building, views of the backstage workshops have been imaginatively created for the public. A necessary expenditure was incurred on the mechanical services – heating, ventilation, etc. – which in almost all theatres need revisiting every thirty or so years.

Changes to the theatre spaces unwelcome to Lasdun, a believer in the *Gesamtkunstwerk*

This has been a brief explanation of why big money had to be spent other than within the Olivier or Lyttelton. Leaving aside until the next chapter the one theatre space that was revisited, the Cottesloe, which became the Dorfman, one must ask why in either 1998 or 2016 improvements to the two main theatre spaces were not made. There are probably three answers.

The first was an article of faith of the modern movement. Lasdun had trained at the Architectural Association in the late 1930s. This was when a galaxy of modern architects emigrated from Germany to London, including Walter Gropius, Mies van der Rohe and Berthold Lubetkin. The almost untranslatable German word *Gesamtkunstwerk* proposes that a building is a total work of art. The whole building and its contents should be conceived as a single entity. This unwavering article of faith meant that the whole – the exterior, the foyers and the theatre spaces – had to be consistent in style, in texture, in geometry and in character.

After completion Lasdun saw the NT management as being the custodian of his creation. The NT's job, as he saw it, was to put on stage shows, which were their works of art, and not tinker with the building which was his. As artists they should respect each other's roles. The NT directors, designers and actors on the other hand were members of a profession which for centuries had a more proprietorial attitude to the buildings in which they worked. They are grateful to the architect when his theatre spaces set off their work to advantage, but what if the theatre spaces fail them? The drama, which is by nature an ephemeral art, can be ruthless when, after a shift in purpose, taste or fashion, the architecture of a theatre space intrudes rather than liberates.

After only twenty years the NT gave up trying to change what they had inherited within the Olivier and Lyttelton. As early as October 1995, in a fax to Christopher Hogg, chairman of the NT, Richard Eyre, director of the NT, had explained that he could not change the Olivier because 'it would require the entire reconstruction of the building... and there was no guarantee that the acoustics would be improved'. On the Lyttelton: 'It is structurally impossible to change the relationship of the circle to the stalls without dismantling the whole auditorium... The auditoriums are WHAT THEY ARE. I have long come to terms with this.' Coping with the theatre space you've got is what every director does for every production and every actor does in every performance. But it is different when you are the director not just of a show but of the whole place. You are responsible for the remaining years of your contract. You have learnt what's wrong with the space but know also that a cure is neither permissible nor affordable. You realise grimly that your successor will just have to cope. Eyre recognised his predicament when, in a platform lecture on the stage of the Olivier in 1989, a pleased Lasdun quoted the poet Arthur Clough to support his resolution not to allow any change to his rooms: 'Pure form nakedly displayed / And all things absolutely made.'

Later, Eyre asked himself why 'absolutely' to Lasdun meant that the concrete had to be 'impregnated in the pattern of a million pine planks'. In an email to me in June 2020 he wondered whether this shuttering was the brutalist equivalent of flock wallpaper. Eyre was not alone. In 1977 Colin Amery, in his *Architectural Review* guide, spoke of 'the rigorous purity of one architectural ethic'. In the penultimate sentence of his conclusion he wrote: 'Our successors may well be mystified by our enthronement of concrete as a thing of beauty and puzzled by the unrefined nature of so many of the surfaces and the almost total banishment of colour.'

Unique scenic opportunities of the Olivier stage

The second reason for not changing the Olivier is more positive. In the 1980s a new generation of stage designers discovered the potential of the Olivier for contemporary spectacle. In summer 1979 a distinguished team of British scenographers, led by John Bury who was by then head of design at the NT, won the Golden Triga which is the premier award at the Prague Quadrennial of Stage Design and Theatre Architecture.

The Prague Quadrennial had been founded in 1967 and was supported by both Czech and Soviet governments in the belief that what theatre performance looks like, as opposed to what is heard, is not political. From the outset the PQ was a genuinely international event which brought together theatre people from both sides of the Iron Curtain. However, much of theatre performance in Prague turned out to be subtly subversive, as I discovered when visiting the PQ in 1976 and 1979. This was the country where it was no surprise when a playwright, Václav Havel, became the first president of free Czechoslovakia after the Iron Curtain was dismantled in 1989.

Great Britain is the only country to have won the top prize of the Triga three times in the fourteen PQ competitions held from 1967 to 2019. One of the greatest challenges for Britain's scenographers from 1975 onwards had been how to realise the scenic potential of the Olivier. This took time. The first musical to cause a sensation on the Olivier stage was the already mentioned production by Eyre of *Guys and Dolls* in 1982. The design by John Gunter had been deceptively simple. New York City was evoked by hanging, in the vast void over the Olivier stage, every neon light you had ever imagined on Broadway. The eye was led down to the performers at stage level.

It was a second designer, Bill Dudley, who in 1988 for Dion Boucicault's *The Shaughraun* made magic mountains and much else rise up from below the Olivier stage by being the first to exploit the drum revolve. This had not been used at all for the first five years and then from 1982 to 1988 only either as a standard revolve at stage level or as a goods lift to bring up scenery from the workshops and rehearsal rooms three floors below. However, this unique device had been designed to do much more. The drum revolve contains three semicircular platforms that can separately rise or fall. It is literally the centrepiece of the Olivier stage which itself is at the centre of the whole building. It was Dudley who first used the D-shaped elevators to marvellous effect. Now the revolve and its unique elevators scarcely stop. Stage designers are constantly discovering new scenic opportunities presented by this unique invention of Pilbrow and his engineer partner Richard Brett. In 1966 they had been instructed by the building committee that the stage facilities of the Olivier Theatre were to be 'dictated by scenic possibilities'. The drum revolve was the result and this was central to the achievement of their goal.

Scenic possibilities lead to excessive width which leads to bad acoustics

Scenic spectacle at the Oliver was successful firstly because of the uniqueness of the stage design, complete with drum revolve and three-dimensional flying, and secondly because of the width of the Olivier stage. The acting area in 2020 was a circle with a diameter of 16.7 metres. This circle is centred on the drum revolve, which has a diameter of 11.5 metres. This acting area projects in a near complete semicircle into the auditorium. The width is almost the same as that of the proscenium of Radio City Music Hall New York of 1932, which seats 6,000 and where you need a line of thirty-six high-kicking Rockettes to fill that opening. Or to make comparisons nearer to home, the scenic opening of the Olivier stage is wider than that of either the Royal Opera House Covent Garden or the London Coliseum, which are England's largest opera houses. Fabulous scenic effects can be staged at the Olivier under a fly tower that can handle scenery of any shape and at any angle. The lighting positions in the auditorium are optimal. The drawbacks are first that it is difficult to transfer productions from the Olivier to other stages and second that it can be expensive to fill such a large stage. There are only 1,100 paying customers. Compare this with the Theatre Royal Drury Lane as renovated in 2021, which has a narrower 12.8-metre proscenium/scenic opening/acting area but nearly twice the capacity (see Chapter 13).

Was all that space necessary? The acting stage is much wider than that of any thrust stage theatre anywhere. The actors must either address each other across this considerable width or, if director and designer have delineated a smaller acting area, be bounded by a lot of empty space on each side. Such a *cordon sanitaire* can separate actor from audience as much as any architectural proscenium arch.

All that space contributes to the main problem, which is that the Olivier has a dreadful acoustic for the spoken voice. Lasdun had no acoustician on his team when working up his design. His first scheme, Scheme A, dated March 1964, had 1,000 people in a single-tier

115-degree fan facing a wide pictorial stage without a proscenium. Then came undated Scheme B after the phrase 'a stage in the corner of a room' had been coined. This room was to be delineated by a solid concrete balcony which squared off the space. The geometry of a 90-degree auditorium fan extended to a right-angle point immediately upstage of the acting area. As first envisaged a single ceiling united stage and auditorium. Only minimal flying would have been possible and then only through gaps in the ceiling. This ceiling disappeared when it was decided that the acting area was to be supported by full scenic possibilities. Acoustic consequences of placing the 'stage in the corner of a room' do not seem to have been addressed.

Henry Humphreys was the acoustician in Lasdun's team but was not appointed until December 1966 when he was referred to as the noise control consultant, for which it is thought that he was paid an annual fee of £100. Lasdun had in fact already settled the fundamental fan shape without any specialist acoustical advice. Hence it was too late for Humphreys to offer strategic advice on the inherent acoustic problems for wide, fan-shaped rooms. In 1975, the year after Humphreys died, Sound Research Laboratories took over the sound commissioning of the Olivier and Lyttelton theatres. Richard Cowell started on a damage limitation exercise that was to last thirty years, working first for SRL and then for Arup Acoustics when that was formed in 1980.

In 1975, before the Olivier opened, Cowell found it 'too reverberant'. There were long confusing reflections and strong echoes. In October 2016, when Pilbrow organised a seminar in the Olivier in celebration of the fortieth anniversary of the NT on the South Bank, Cowell asked the rhetorical question: 'Why was Olivier standing so far upstage on opening night Royal Gala (25 October 1976) when to bring the theatrical space to life he wanted to play downstage? It was to avoid a strong echo from the balcony front!' The solutions to this and to the unwanted side reflections, were to install 'extensive sound absorbent material added in the ceiling void, in corners, on the side walls closest to the stage, front ceiling panels and on the balcony front'.

A useful introduction to how to equip large modern theatres with as good an acoustic as the narrower old ones can be found in Michael Barron's *Auditorium Acoustics and Architectural Design* of 1993 (with a second edition in 2009 where there were additions made to the chapter on new opera houses such as Glyndebourne but not to the pages on playhouses). To a layman on matters acoustical two essential elements emerge from Barron. The first is that the angle of the side walls should provide good and rapid side reflections for acceptable intelligibility, and the second is that there should not be too much volume. The side walls at the Olivier provide bad side reflections because the fan is too wide. Secondly the volume of the Olivier (excluding the stage and fly tower) is 13,500 cubic metres, which is 11.6 cubic metres per person. Compare this with the Barbican, which has the same capacity but a volume of only 4,160 cubic metres, which is 3.6 cubic metres per person. The volume of the Barbican auditorium per person is thus one third of that of the Olivier. At the Barbican the actors in straight plays generally do not wear microphones.

Over forty years many solutions to the Olivier acoustic problem have been attempted. After transferring his *Racing Demon* and *Arcadia* in 1995 to the open stage of the Vivian Beaumont New York, which had and still has its own acoustic problems, Eyre persuaded the NT to spend £350,000 on a Dutch sound enhancement system for the Olivier involving many hung microphones and over 100 loudspeakers. Initially this was pronounced a success, but Nunn, who followed Eyre in 1997, had it all removed two years later. So much for 'state of the art' technology. Nunn then raised the entire playing area of the stage by a further amount so as to bring the by now curved stage edge out over the front three rows of stalls. Soon after succeeding Nunn in 2003, Hytner reversed all that. So much for intuitive thinking.

Much later the head of sound at the NT, Paul Arditti, who in 2015 became an associate director, persuaded Hytner that every actor should be individually miked for every show in both the Olivier and Lyttelton theatres and that their voices should mixed by a skilled technician, who also played the sound plot, from a position at the back of the stalls. At the 2016 symposium, Arditti confessed that he was no acoustician but riffed that every time a way was found to dampen unwanted sound reflections in an auditorium the sum of the energy coming from the actor is diminished. Two questions. First is to ask what the response from actors has been to being miked all the time. Regulars at the NT are cautious to criticise lest they are not asked back. Senior friends are more forthcoming. Actor Timothy West has suggested to me that microphones take away from the actor the ability to control space in all three dimensions. Critic Michael Billington told me that microphones 'flatten things'. Same point.

Lastly, was the removal of surfaces providing bad reflections compensated for by the introduction of surfaces providing good ones? The answer is 'no'. It is impossible to work out where in the Olivier such surfaces could be placed because the room is basically the wrong shape as well as having the wrong volume. How did this happen?

The building committee, its composition and its relationship with the architect

The minutes of the building committee of the National Theatre Company have been discussed in depth for the first time in Richard Pilbrow's *A Sense of Theatre: The Untold Story of the National Theatre* (forthcoming). The committee was chaired by Lord Olivier with Norman Marshall as co-chairman. This tried valiantly to do its job but spoke with many voices, met irregularly and was answerable to two separate entities: the South Bank Theatre and Opera House board (known simply as the SBB after a new opera house for Sadler's Wells had been dropped from the project), whose job it was to build it, and the National Theatre board, whose job it was to run it. The existence of two distinct boards controlling a single project could lead to confusion. How did the National Theatre building committee and the architect cope with each being in an important sense the servant of two masters?

At the very first meeting of that committee, held on 3 June 1963 before architect Lasdun was appointed, Olivier opened by informing the members of his committee that 'we are to study the practical aesthetics'. Marshall added that the 'SBB will also need technical experts on such matters as Box Office, acoustics etc. over which it should be unnecessary to trouble this panel'. The second mention of acoustics took place at meeting number twenty-one on 6 November 1964, when the question was asked whether the balcony 'could be raised' in the 'one room' Scheme B which had been first submitted but two meetings earlier. Mr Minjoudt, a staff member of the office of Lasdun, who was himself not present, replied: 'In that case the volume goes up and you run the risk of trouble with the acoustics.' And that is all there in the minutes on acoustics.

Lasdun saw his relationship with the building committee rather differently from how the NT did. He had said to the chairman of the SBB (Lord Cottesloe) – his client – that he wanted to listen to the building committee's thoughts but that after that he should be left in peace to design the building. As the appointed architect he reckoned that he was being wholly reasonable. He did not want interference on aesthetics, which he regarded as his sole responsibility. The NT felt excluded. But they were not the client – only the user who had no contractual relationship with the architect.

If there had been someone on the committee who had actually built a theatre he or she might have been listened to by an architect who himself had never built one either. At the critical moments in the early development of the design there were just the two committee members with anything like that sort of experience: chairman Olivier and co-chairman Marshall. Olivier had opened Chichester but had had no part in its design. Early in his career Marshall had been the first stage manager at the innovative Festival Theatre Cambridge (see Chapter 3) but he had had no part in its design. The only person of stature in Britain who was involved in the design of new theatres which he subsequently ran was Guthrie, but he was never a member of the committee. This was probably because in 1963, when the new building committee was first convened, Guthrie was deeply committed to the imminent opening of his second theatre, the one in Minneapolis which bears his name.

On the scenic side there were three fine stage designers: Roger Furse, Sean Kenny, who was a qualified architect having graduated from the Dublin School of Architecture, and later Tanya Moiseiwitsch, who had closely collaborated with Guthrie. In April 1966 at the twenty-fourth meeting shortly after the death of George Devine, it was decided to invite three further people on to the building committee: Devine's widow, Jocelyn Herbert, who was a distinguished stage designer, Pilbrow and Guthrie. The first two accepted but Guthrie declined. In 1966 he was about to step down from being director of Minneapolis, though he was active there for a further three years and was also working with Colin George's team at the Crucible Theatre Sheffield which opened in 1971 (see Chapter 4). Directors on the building committee independent of the NT Company included Peter Hall, Peter Brook and Michael Elliott. From the NT itself there were Bill Gaskill, Frank Dunlop and John Dexter. Stephen Arlen was a member who not only had many years earlier worked at the Old Vic but had also been on the architect selection group in his capacity as administrator of the Sadler's Wells Opera during the days of the short-lived project for both the National Theatre and a new Sadler's Wells to be linked side by side on the South Bank. (This was Lasdun's original wider brief.) Kenneth Tynan, literary editor of the NT, was 'in attendance'. Of all those mentioned above Pilbrow is one of only three left alive in 2022, which is another reason why his *A Sense of Theatre* is important.

Every individual on the committee was worth listening to. But they often changed their minds and as busy professionals missed meetings while directing or designing shows. Brook irritated Lasdun when he advocated 'an empty space'. The minutes record a spat when Lasdun rejoined: 'From what Brook is saying all he seems to want is a bombed site in Bethnal Green. It's dead easy. And we could do it on the South Bank site but is this the National Theatre?' This was the meeting at which those present nodded agreement when the architect stated: 'We cannot get to the poetic till we have bled dry the functional.' They also applauded Lasdun who, after visiting the expensively adaptable Vivian Beaumont in New York of 1965, as well as Guthrie's theatres in Stratford Ontario and Minneapolis, correctly asserted that adaptability could not be made to work in a theatre holding as many as 1,000. (This is precisely what Guthrie had predicted three years before the Vivian Beaumont opened.)

Squaring the circle: fitting a scenic stage into a single room

Early meetings of the building committee had been bound up with the architect selection process. The second sequence, with Lasdun present as the chosen architect, took place from January to

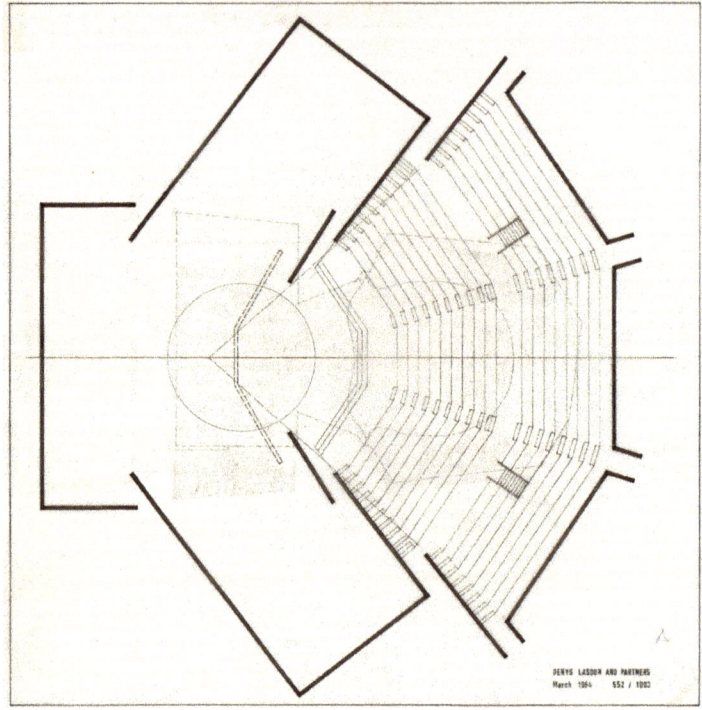
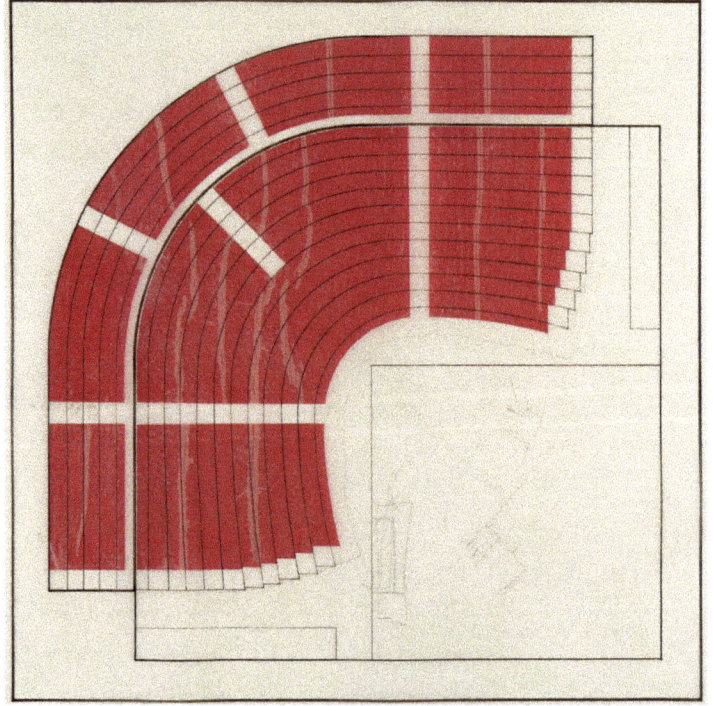

6.1 *Two Lasdun sketches for the Olivier: Scheme A over Scheme B.*

6.2 *Lasdun's model for the Olivier with setting envisaged by Jocelyn Herbert over photo of Olivier set up for* Small Island *2020.*

October 1964 during which Scheme B emerged – for 'a stage in the corner of a room'. Soon after that the Treasury confirmed that there was to be a second large theatre, though the capacity of what was to be the Lyttelton was not yet finalised. Scheme B superseded Scheme A, which was for an unbroken 115-degree fan.

There was then a hiatus because Lasdun had angrily decided he would work up his designs without meeting the building committee. This was prompted by a misleading leak of his intentions as printed in an unsigned article in *The Sunday Times* of 21 February 1965, illustrated with a crude diagram of 'a stage in the corner of a room'. Such was what the article suggested that Lasdun was designing for the NT, plus odd and often inaccurate diagrams of other theatres existing or proposed. There was some surprise at the amount of umbrage taken. The source of the leak was rumoured as being Peter Hall. It took fourteen months for matters to be patched up, during which Lasdun worked without meeting the building committee.

Meetings restarted in April 1966 with one at which Lasdun was not present. This was when the decision was taken to ask Pilbrow to meet with Lasdun and suggest to him what would be the spatial requirements for 'full scenic capability', the need for which the building committee had now agreed. They had concluded that 'the one-room auditorium is, in Scheme B, interpreted too literally. There must be the atmosphere of one room but the pattern of all stage facilities both behind and above the actor must be dictated only by scenic possibilities.' With hindsight one can say that for a committee to require in the one theatre space the atmosphere of a single room and at the same time extensive scenic possibilities was to ask for the impossible, and typical of a committee request.

The Chichester theatre was one room in that a single ceiling spans both stage and auditorium and had been important background for design discussions on Scheme B between 1964 and 1966. In May 1966 Lasdun had said of Scheme B: 'It is sharp, no compromising, anti-illusion theatre.' That sounded exciting. But it all turned out rather differently. When the Olivier Theatre finally opened nobody thought of it as having a stage at the corner of a square room. Few would grasp that the two side walls, if continued, would meet at a 90-degree angle at a point immediately upstage of the acting area. Rather do the endings of the side walls at the Olivier read as a very wide scenic opening waiting to be filled with wonders. Lasdun's design model, complete with a set dreamt up by stage designer Jocelyn Herbert, and a photograph from 2020 illustrate just this.

In January 1967 Pilbrow stepped down from the NT building committee on the appointment of his company, Theatre Projects, as technical theatre consultants to the SBB and Lasdun's design team. He continued to attend in his new capacity as a member of Lasdun's team. The committee met only twice more, in January 1968 and January 1969, to review developments in the design of both main theatres. Building started on site in 1970 and the first performances at the NT to paying audiences, for a few productions which had already been seen at the Old Vic, took place in the Lyttelton in March 1976. The first of these was the four-hour *Hamlet* of Albert Finney who later in the year had the distinction of opening the Olivier with *Tamburlaine the Great*. Hall directed both but then, somewhat surprisingly, chose Goldoni's *Il Campiello* to be directed by Bill Bryden for the Royal Opening of the National Theatre on 25 October 1976. This is a light farce which was going to be difficult to make work anywhere, let alone on the wide Olivier stage.

When the Olivier was being conceived in the mid-1960s there was little experience in Britain of open-stage theatres other than Chichester. As has been referred to in the fracas over the Crucible, Olivier disliked Chichester because he was aware that some of the audience saw past him to other members of the audience seated opposite. This objection ignored the fact that audience on three sides was not only a prerequisite of all the best modern thrust stages but had also been a central feature of the open-air theatres of Shakespeare's day, where the platform projected into the centre of the yard.

The brutalist character of the concrete National

While the above explains to some extent the form of the Olivier we need to look elsewhere for its character. This was ultra-modernist due chiefly to the use throughout of shuttered concrete in a style that became known as 'brutalist'. Not all modernist buildings of the period were brutalist. Modernism is a philosophy. Call a mid-twentieth-century architect a modernist and he or she would have been pleased. Call a mid-twentieth-century architect a brutalist and he or she might have been uncertain whether it was meant as a compliment or insult. The term derives from the French expression *béton brut*, which means rough cast concrete and was first used to describe the *Unité d'habitation* of the *Cité Radieu*se at sunny Marseille in the south of France which had been completed in 1952 by Le Corbusier.

The National Theatre was one of the final flowerings of the short brutalist era in British architecture which, insofar as arts spaces were concerned, had started with the nearby Queen Elizabeth Hall of 1967. The brutalist exterior of the NT continues to please many people. The foyers provide a sense of occasion in which the brutalism of shuttered concrete does play a part. The problem is that within the Olivier and Lyttelton the brutalist concrete is often antithetical to all but the biggest styles of theatre making. Emphasise the concrete with light and the large angular forms distract in a way that more articulated and inherently festive schemes do not. Fail to honour it and it sulks.

Hall visited Epidaurus for the first time in 1975 when interviewing Lasdun for the London Weekend Television arts programme *Aquarius*, season nine episode one. As is customary, coins were dropped by the guide in the centre of the circular *orchestra* to be heard by those at the back. Hall: 'I didn't hear, you didn't hear, they didn't hear but they believed they heard.' Lasdun: 'Well they want to hear.' And so on in a strange twenty-minute exchange when Lasdun tries to explain the 'calculated modifications' to the apparently simple geometry made by the original architect working within that still ravishing landscape. The NT archives hold a copy of the *Aquarius* programme which is worth puzzling over. Seven years later in 1982 Hall took to Epidaurus, after a successful run at the Olivier, the NT's production of *The Oresteia* in a version by poet Tony Harrison. It is now held that there were no acoustical problems for this production at either theatre. But there are also conflicting opinions which would be worth disentangling.

The influence of Ancient Greece on the design of the Olivier

Why after so much discussion shared by the architect and the building committee did the English National Theatre settle on a form inspired by Ancient Greece? The monumental theatre of Epidaurus was built of stone and has endured for more than two millennia. It is said that Epidaurus was first built by Polykleitos around 340 BC, which was after the death of the four greatest Greek playwrights – Aeschylus, Sophocles, Euripides and Aristophanes. There is no evidence that any of their plays were ever performed at Epidaurus. The theatres those great

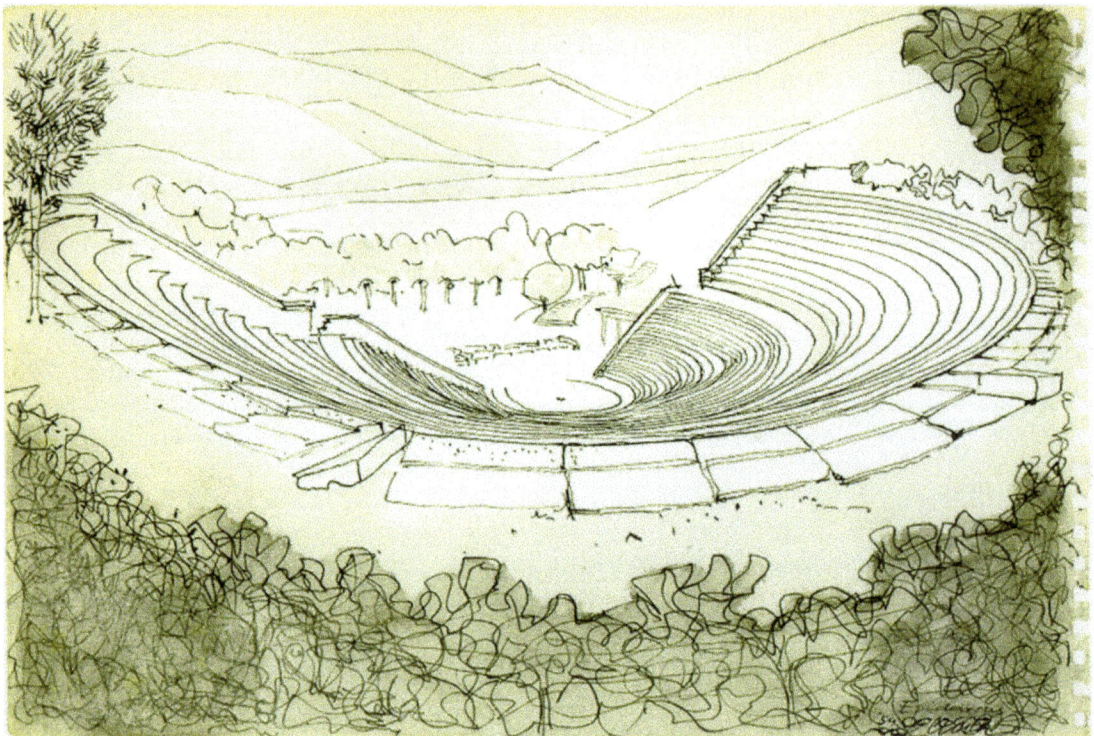

6.3 *Epidaurus sketch by Onno Greiner 1959.*

Greek playwrights knew were almost certainly smaller than even the first Epidaurus, which almost certainly ended at the present cross gangway and probably held but 6,000. Behind that, further rows were added nearly two centuries later in Roman times that more than doubled the capacity up to the oft-quoted 15,000, which is what Epidaurus holds today.

Lasdun must have believed that a 90-degree wedge of this ancient form would work dramatically and acoustically in the twentieth century partly by reason of the original 220-degree fan having worked for what was then supposed as being much larger audiences 2,000 years ago. But the acoustic part of this reasoning neglects the fact that at Epidaurus there were no unwanted late reflections from side walls to muddy intelligibility because there were no side walls. There was also no ambient sound – no aeroplanes or road traffic in the fourth century BC. Place a roof over and confine the audience within the side walls of the 90-degree fan as at the Olivier and unwanted reflections are introduced. Acoustics for open-air theatre are fundamentally different than for indoor spaces. The style of performance in ancient times was also quite different from that needed for the repertoire envisaged for Britain's national theatre.

In his autobiography, *Making an Exhibition of Myself*, published in 1993 Hall asked himself how Epidaurus had influenced Denys Lasdun in designing the Olivier: 'It seems to me now that while the Olivier is a great theatre, it bears as much relation to Epidaurus as St Pancras Station does to Venice. But inspiration has to have a beginning. Lasdun had a vision of a fine modern theatre after he saw those great stone benches at Epidaurus, sweeping round in a half circle.'

Lasdun explained when interviewed by Colin Amery for *The Architectural Review* in 1977: 'We searched for a single room embodying stage and auditorium . . . an open relationship that looked back to the Greeks and Elizabethans and, at the same time, looked forward to a contemporary society in which all could have fair chance to see, hear and share the collective experience of exploring human truths.'

However, we still need to ask how Hall's production of *The Oresteia* succeeded in the actors being heard both at the Olivier and at Epidaurus in 1982 without mechanical reinforcement. There seem to have been a number of reasons. All Hall's actors faced downstage when speaking. The principals wore full masks in character and did not turn to look at any other actor. The masks had been carefully researched and designed by Jocelyn Herbert. The chorus, wearing identical masks, took turns to speak solo and sequentially which also made for clarity. The actors spoke to the measured rhythms determined by playwright Tony Harrison and composer Harrison Birtwistle. *The Oresteia* played to near capacity at the Olivier for sixty-five performances. At Epidaurus the NT's company manager, Michael Hallifax, recalls that the show opened to an audience of only 3,000, which is but 20 per cent of that much-touted 15,000 capacity. Hall preferred to remember it differently in his autobiography: 'Every word of the difficult texts was heard by some 15,000 people at each performance. There is no amplification, yet no need to shout. Provided the ends of the lines were sustained and the consonants kept distinct. The sound was crystal clear.'

A larger audience of 7,000 did attend the second performance. The stage manager reported that the audience roared their applause at the end when the actors took off their masks. Hall and his creative team were vindicated. Lasdun was not present. The focused bowl of the Olivier worked well for highly stylised Greek drama, as did Epidaurus. But it did not follow from the unamplified success of *The Oresteia* at the Olivier that the English classics or new writing would work as well as had been hoped at Britain's National Theatre.

It is sometimes forgotten that Hall did return to Epidaurus in 1996, as a guest director for the NT with *Oedipus*. For the two performances at Epidaurus radio microphones were cunningly installed in the masks of the actors and loudspeakers placed in the auditorium at Hall's request and to the consternation of the Greek management.

Lasdun later offered his own explanation of what went wrong in 'Olivier Theatre Acoustics', which was a section in his report to the board of the NT: *A Strategy for the Future – Denys Lasdun and Partners 1989*.

> There has been a tendency for a long time to bring the acting area further forward into the auditorium than had been the intention when the Olivier Theatre was designed, with the result that performers are taken further away from helpful reflecting surfaces. Despite advice that, acoustically, it would be better to keep the acting area further back this situation was perpetuated when the new raised stage was installed which brought the acting area even further forward to its present position. As a result, a series of echoes and late sound reflections which did not exist previously are now being generated with a consequent deterioration in intelligibility in certain positions.

It is worth remembering that Peter Hall and John Bury raised the entire stage area by about 28 centimetres soon after the Olivier opened, to the level where it has remained to this day. It seems that Lasdun did not mention this in his report of 1989. Both sightlines and acoustics were part of the problem.

When an architect suggests that actors should move upstage to make better contact with the audience you wonder if they are on the same planet. Needless to say Eyre, who was in the fourth year of his tenure, makes no reference to this study in his diary of the decade in which he served as director of the NT, *National Service* published in 2003.

Not much discussion on the Lyttelton

With the 894-seat Lyttelton proscenium theatre things were much simpler. At the building committee it was known as the 'any other business' theatre and discussed at only three meetings. Apologist Barnabas Calder reported that Lasdun shared 'the prevailing view that the proscenium theatre was simply a matter of people facing a stage, where they could both see the action and hear clearly'. Prevailing where? Forty years earlier, in 1922, in *The Exemplary Theatre* Granville-Barker had deplored frontal theatre, by which he meant those with long straight rows facing the stage in which 'people sat blinkered like horses. However excellent the performance which would be as flat as if – however excellent the dinner – the diners sat at a long table all facing one way.'

This strategy was typical of Lasdun's narrow perception of functionalism. At the Lyttelton the seats are all in near straight rows of audience and point perfectly at a wide stage. No matter that those in the balcony can be unaware that there is an audience below, and vice versa, the sightlines for the upper audience having been engineered precisely to cut off at the edge of the stage. When in 1968 the building committee was shown what was proposed they suggested that placing seats at the side might increase intimacy. Lasdun retorted that he would need a written instruction from the board to include seats with bad sightlines. The minutes also recorded: 'The majority opinion was that this [Lasdun's proposal for the Lyttelton] had not yet reached the degree of dynamic excellence required for a proscenium theatre solution.' Were the committee concerned about form or about atmosphere? Calder, in 'A Concrete Violin', which was the ironic title he gave to his chapter on the National in *Raw Concrete: The Beauty of Brutalism* published in 2016, reports this exchange. Olivier: 'How can we get the atmosphere of an old theatre in a new one? Plaster and wood is better for the voice. Acoustically the theatre at Antwerp, which has plaster and wood, is best for me.' (Olivier was referring to the horseshoe *Bourla Schouwburg* of 1834 not the nearby modern *Stadsschouwburg*.) Lasdun: 'Engaged intensity is the central thing. We cannot duplicate the furnishings of an old theatre except by pastiche.'

Pastiche and the proscenium theatre

'Pastiche' was one of the rudest words in the modernist's language. But what most of the members of the committee were interested in was form not furnishings. That it was possible to create modern proscenium auditoriums that reinterpret successful old forms is illustrated by both the Forum Billingham, which opened in 1968 with Elder and Lester as architects and Michael Warre as theatre consultant, and Eden Court Inverness of 1976, architects Graham Law and James Dunbar-Nasmith with John Wyckham as theatre consultant assisted by myself in the planning of the stage and auditorium. Both Billingham and Inverness were conceived at around the same time as the Lyttelton. There was no pastiche to be seen in either. But neither would have pleased Lasdun or Izenour because some seats in the side boxes have less than perfect sightlines, the side walls having been papered with people. The principal function of side

6.4 *Eden Court Theatre Inverness 1976 taken in 2009.*

seats and the boxes was to wrap audience and actors in what was to feel like a single room, though in a proscenium theatre stage and auditorium are separate. At the Lyttelton Lasdun ensured that there were neither bad sightlines nor pastiche. NT associate Bill Bryden christened it 'the best cinema in London'.

Perhaps the outcome at the Lyttelton would have been different had there been more agreement on the simple matter of the width of the proscenium which the straight rows of seating for 894 faced. There is a fixed proscenium of 13.6 metres which can be narrowed down with adjustable black masking to 9 metres (29 feet 6 inches). Once again, if you mask in 6 feet each side with 'neutral' panels then this not only ruins the sightlines from the ends of the near straight front rows, but also frames the smaller-scaled productions with funereal black. Black masking alongside grey concrete does not encourage laughs.

Here are some of the misgivings quoted from the minutes of the NT building sub-committee meeting on 26 June 1966, at which members were shown a model of the proscenium theatre, yet to be christened the Lyttelton. Hall: 'Conventional and boring... like a shoe box', 'Mistakenly puritan'; Elliott: 'Uninspiring'; Marshall: 'Dead at sides'; and Olivier: 'Germanic'. As chairman the latter diplomatically concluded that 'the design fulfilled the brief of enabling every member of the audience to see the stage properly and that this was the most important requisite for the proscenium theatre'. Lasdun took the chairman's words as approval for his proposals and that was that. There was evidently no shared language to discuss anything more elusive than the functionality of sightlines. Aesthetic support had come from just the one committee member, designer Jocelyn Herbert: 'Good that it is adamant and strong.'

What to do now?

What next for the two main theatre spaces at the National? It is hard to see a way of changing the Olivier both to accentuate the positive and to eliminate the negative. The only approaches must be either to play spectacular musicals or to breed epic horses for this particular course, such as *War Horse* of 2007, the second production of Peter Shaffer's *Amadeus* of 2016 or the Empire Windrush saga *Small Island* of 2019. The Lyttelton on the other hand can be fixed. Keep the concrete box and do not change what you see from the foyers. Gut the box and insert an egg, by which I mean an auditorium that takes as a starting point some variation of timeless sacred geometry. The resulting narrower-shaped space might mean raising, slightly, the roof over the auditorium and making modifications to service areas beneath the stalls. The present capacity would be maintained. Side seats for people papering the walls would be sold at much lower prices than are the cheapest at present. The loss would be compensated for by higher prices for the best seats. A wider range of prices for a more diverse audience and a warmer atmosphere for all. Architecturally it would be a surprise gift from one generation to another: an egg decorated with people packed within a plain concrete box without so as not to disturb the *Gesamtkunstwerk* – until you got inside.

The genesis of the third theatre at the National, the Cottesloe, conceived in October 1973 and opened in March 1977, comes in the next chapter. Before that here is a short account of the origins of Britain's third major modern concrete theatre, the Barbican, which opened as the London home of the RSC in March 1982.

The design of the Barbican from 1958 to its opening in 1982

The Barbican Theatre, holding 1,150, is the second major component of the Barbican Centre and shares foyers with the larger Barbican Concert Hall. Other elements include an exhibition gallery, a library, cinemas, trade halls and restaurants etc. plus, nearby, the Guildhall School of Music and Drama which has its own theatre spaces. On completion the whole was claimed to be the largest arts centre in Europe. It is threaded so tightly into the 35 acres of the Barbican Estate that they had to paint luminous lines on the high-level pedestrian walkways from the underground stations on the perimeter to guide patrons to the arts centre hidden in the middle. Soon after the opening there appeared in *The Times* a thumbnail cartoon by Marc, pen name of Mark Boxer, showing a police sergeant at a desk over which is the sign 'Missing Persons'. The sergeant is asking a tearful woman: 'Madam, have you tried the Barbican?'

The whole Barbican Estate is finished in the brutalist style. The subtle difference with the National is that while at the former the concrete was carefully shuttered, at the Barbican it was painstakingly hammered. As for the theatre spaces in the Barbican auditorium there is also a lot more warm-toned timber in evidence. Importantly for the better speech acoustics at the Barbican theatre is that auditorium volume per seat is a third of that of the Olivier.

The design of the Barbican Theatre had proceeded in two phases. The first in 1959 had been the development of a design for the theatre space by architects Chamberlin, Powell and Bon in conjunction with theatre consultant Richard Southern. The latter's own sketches dated 1958 are now in the Bristol University Theatre Collection. The second step was a recommendation, made in 1964 by opera director and arts consultant Anthony Besch, that the main elements in the arts

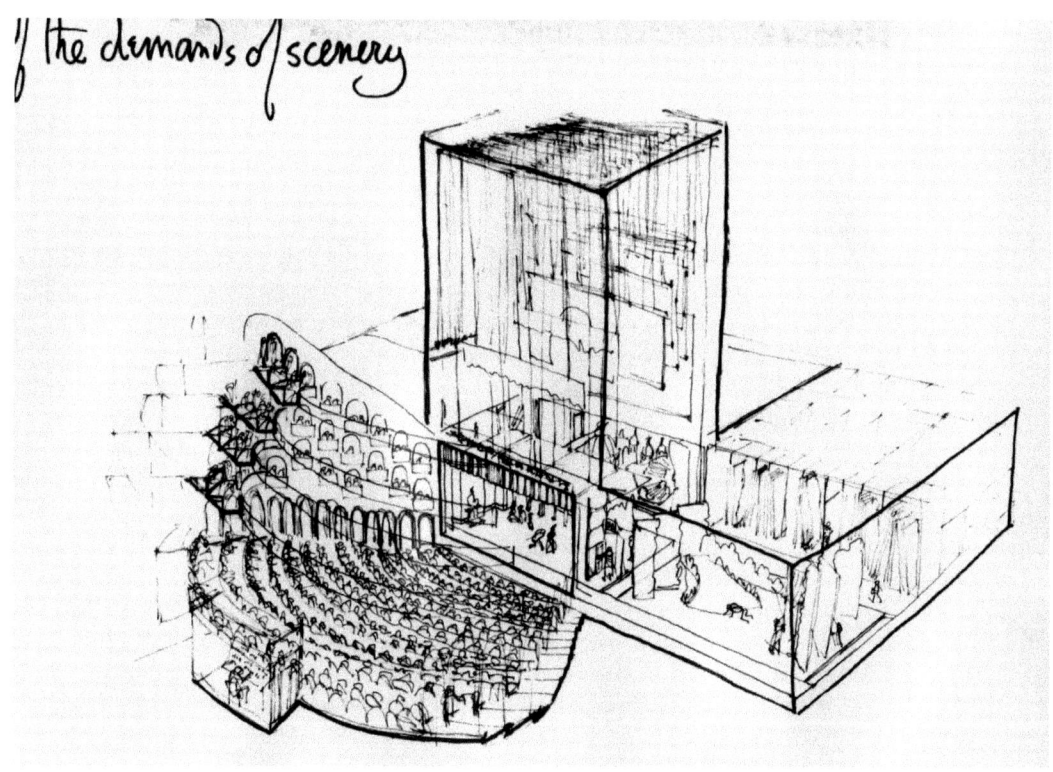

6.5 *Two Barbican sketches – Richard Southern 1959 and Elizabeth Bury 1968.*

centre should be bespoke spaces designated for particular professional groups. The London Symphony Orchestra, known as the LSO, were to be principal tenants of the Concert Hall. A comparable theatre company was needed for the theatre. Who could that be?

Peter Hall had become director at the Stratford-upon-Avon theatre and company in 1960 at the age of thirty. The name had been changed to the Royal Shakespeare Company. He soon arranged for a lease for three years of the Aldwych Theatre as the RSC's London base while looking for a permanent building. (They stayed at the Aldwych for over twenty years until moving into 'their' Barbican theatre in 1982.) In 1961 Hall was in full expansionist mode. After asking Sean Kenny to sketch a remodelling of the Memorial Theatre with a full thrust and inviting the Arts Council to pay two thirds of the cost, he was not downhearted when they turned him down. He then directed his phenomenal energy towards finding a permanent home in London for the RSC.

Hall was introduced to Marie Rambert, who had been assistant to Nijinsky for the premiere of *The Rite of Spring* in 1913 and had studied with Émile Jaques-Dalcroze of Hellerau fame. In 1926 Rambert had founded her own company, the Ballet Rambert. In 1933 she created the Mercury Theatre, which was a simple small building on a valuable site at Notting Hill which might be extended. In 1962 a potential planning deal for a major theatre on the site emerged after a developer had declared that he could enlarge the site, make money and include a theatre holding 1,000. The Rambert needed a theatre partner who would take up half the fifty-two weeks while they were on tour in the winter. The RSC would be a perfect match as Hall wanted to split the year: Stratford in the summer and London in the winter. It was not to be. Almost immediately the City issued an invitation to the RSC to become the main tenant of the Barbican Theatre. The RSC told Rambert that they had decided to go elsewhere and so the tantalising combination of these two highly creative companies collapsed.

Enter John Bury

To advance the Barbican Theatre project Hall brought off a double coup which amazed both the Governors of the RSC and the Arts Council: that the RSC would not have to raise any capital while the rent at the Barbican would be modest – less than at the Aldwych – and that there were plans already on the architects' drawing board which would need some but not too much development by the RSC head of design, John Bury.

Compare the Southern concept design of 1958/59, already endorsed by the architects, with what opened in 1982 and you will find that Bury retained many features introduced by Southern such as the triple galleries that step forward as they get closer to the stage, the shallow fan of the main seating, the absence of aisles and the notion of individual doors for each row which Southern had envisaged would close automatically as the house lights dim. The first main element which Bury introduced was a half-hexagon raked thrust modelled on that which had been introduced at Stratford in 1961. Second was the double-cranked safety curtain which could be engineered by Theatre Projects. This was a useful development on the single-cranked safety curtain, falling on the orchestra rail/edge of the forestage, that had been installed in the mid-1970s in theatres as diverse as the *Badisches Staatstheater* Karlsruhe, Eden Court Inverness and the University Theatre at Warwick University in the design of which Bury had collaborated. The third important element he introduced was the stepped 'toboggan' side boxes pointing at the stage which were familiar from many of the new German theatres. These ideas were governed by Bury's intuitive attitude to what makes a good theatre.

6.6 *Full auditorium at the Barbican Theatre.*

In the mid-1940s, after active service in the Fleet Air Arm, Bury had decided against studying chemistry at university and instead joined the touring Theatre Workshop of Joan Littlewood before they moved into the near-derelict Theatre Royal Stratford East in 1953. Ten years later he joined Peter Hall's RSC at Stratford-upon-Avon. Bury, like Hall, had not trained for the theatre in any formal way. They collaborated first at Stratford and then Glyndebourne and later at the NT, in the design of which Bury was not involved but Hall had been. They worked together on the design of only this one theatre space, the Barbican, but ironically neither ever worked there. Its innate style gives it the theatricality absent from the more prosaic Olivier. This is largely the influence of Bury, to whom wise architects listened. The detail design was done in 1968, as the accompanying image of that date by his wife and design partner Elizabeth Bury shows. However, it did not open until 1982.

In the Glyndebourne programme for the 2001 season, the first after Bury's death, Hall opened his appreciation thus:

> John Bury – stage designer extraordinary, costume creator, lighting genius, advisor to architects on how to build theatres and to theatre directors on how to run them – changed the face of stage design . . . He had the daring originality of a great abstract artist, combined with the care and precision of an old-fashioned craftsman. He had no formal training. Yet his progress as a young man was so inevitable, so driven by his passion to create, that it should be lesson to all those who seek today to make systems and qualifications (all of the bureaucracy of art) more important than originality itself.

My own vote is for the Barbican as a theatre space rather than the Olivier or Lyttelton

The resulting Barbican theatre has a form and finish which is warmer than either the Olivier or Lyttelton. A perfectionist might reduce the width of the Barbican auditorium by slicing out two or three seats a row on the centre line. As it is, this must be one of the best British theatres seating more than 1,000 of the last fifty years. Yet the Barbican stage is wide. When we, as audience, are asked by Chorus in *Henry V*, 'Can this cockpit hold the vasty fields of France?' one is tempted to shout back 'Yes' – though with less emphasis than at the Olivier.

Some people hated the whole place: in 2002 the then director of the RSC, Adrian Noble, persuaded the governors to leave the Barbican in the mistaken belief that when the RSC wanted to come to London they could simply book a West End theatre. This was never going to work because commercial theatre owners prefer to keep their options open in the hope of a profitable long run while a repertoire company like the RSC must plan well ahead. But others, including Greg Doran, the next director of the RSC but one after Noble, liked the Barbican theatre and as a result the RSC returned as a regular visitor.

Not every feature attracts at the Barbican. The extensive subterranean public areas at the theatre are shared with those for the Concert Hall and echo with emptiness unless the intervals coincide. The dressing rooms are underground and depressing. As to which of Britain's two major modernist theatres succeeds as a whole building, Barbican or National, there can be no doubt: Lasdun's whole building, now carefully renovated, succeeds almost everywhere except where it matters most – in the Olivier and Lyttelton theatre spaces. Hence my vote would be for the National Theatre as a building and the Barbican as a theatre space. But neither the form nor the character of these three modernist theatres have been emulated elsewhere. The theatre profession found them too wide. Meanwhile brutalist concrete, whether shuttered or hammered, has indubitably gone out of fashion.

ACT THREE

1976–2020: The past informs the present

7

The Cottesloe and other courtyards

Where the Cottesloe happened approached as 'found space'

The Cottesloe, the third theatre space at the National, happened in a very different way than either the Olivier or the Lyttelton. Construction was already under way when Lasdun was instructed to defer the third theatre, then referred to as the studio. He adroitly left a bricked-up void under the Olivier, upstage right, and beyond that the shell of a two-level foyer for an audience of 200. This was to have its own entrance off the perimeter road on the east side.

Within a year of being appointed director, Hall turned his mind to what he preferred to think of as the third theatre. In his 'Policy Thoughts for the New South Bank to the National Board', dated 28 February 1973, he discussed 'The Studio. Third Auditorium of the National Theatre'. This was to have three roles: first as 'a Laboratory for advanced work and this work should be done by the leaders of the profession'; second as the headquarters for the National's own Mobile Touring'; and third as 'a facility for all the young creative groups up and down the country. We should invite them to use our facilities. It is important that new talent can use the National Theatre and attract their audiences to our building.' Hall then finessed the compliance of both National Theatre and South Bank boards.

I did not see this paper until after initiating my design for the Cottesloe between 22 October and 10 November of that same year. A small informal meeting had taken place in the TPC office at 10 Long Acre attended by Pilbrow, Bury and senior TPC technical consultant Alan Russell. We sat around a cardboard model of the empty bricked-up void, 66 feet (20m) long, 56 feet (17m) wide and 41 feet (12.5m) high. Next day I was shown this void. It would have made a serviceable hangar for a medium-sized Zeppelin.

The 1973 genesis of the Cottesloe design

Bury's steer was given verbally on behalf of the NT directors. It was threefold: first, a licensed capacity of 400, which was twice the capacity that had been envisaged for Lasdun's studio theatre; second, one of the functions of this third theatre was to be for the recording of productions brought down from the stages of the big theatres upstairs (hence the need for a flat floor option), and third that it was to cost as little as possible. I asked Pilbrow if I could borrow the cardboard model and come back with thoughts after a long weekend.

The task was to come up with a solution for a 'found space' in a new building. Knowing nothing of what had gone before and realising that any design solution had to cost little

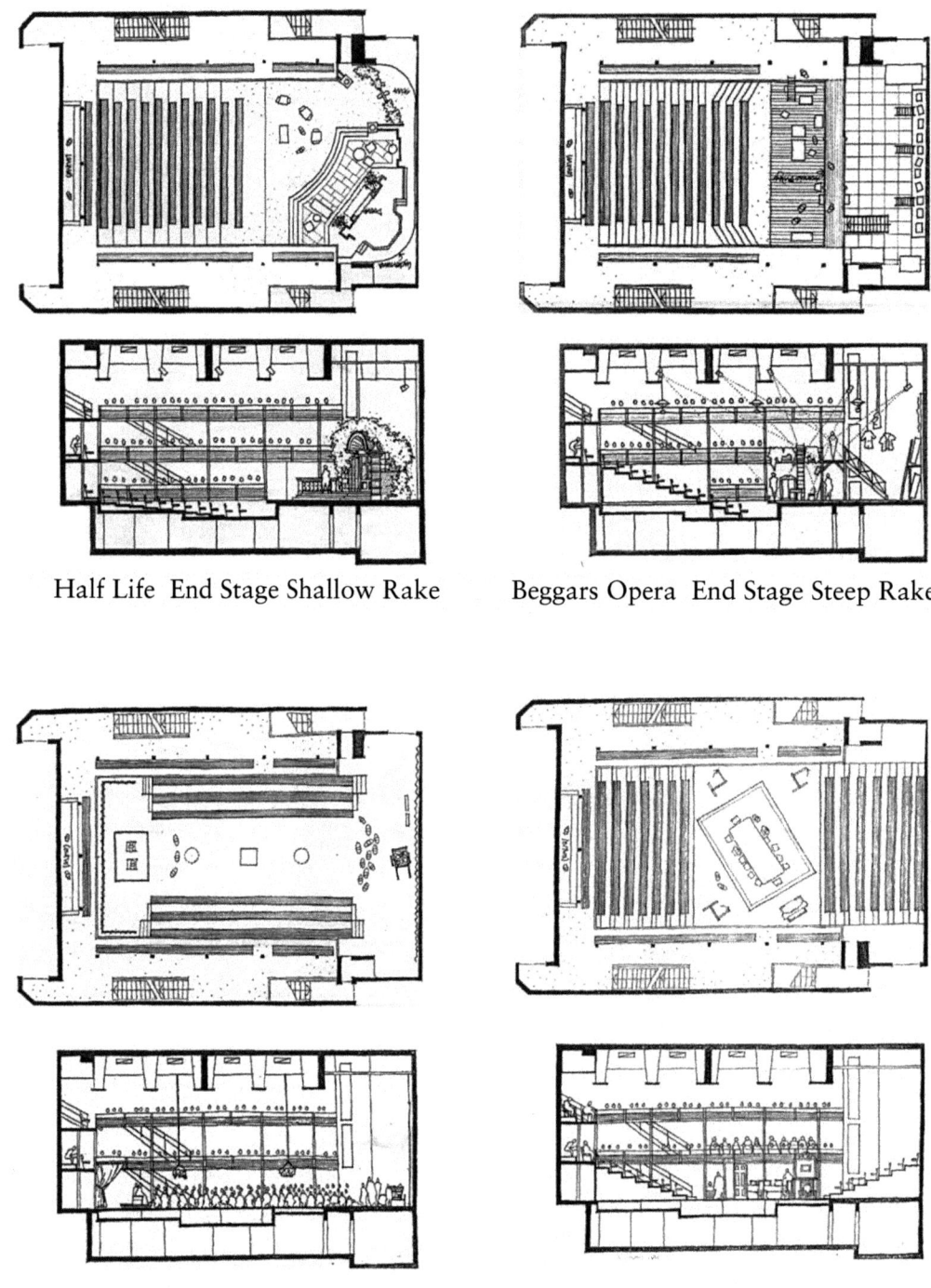

7.1 *Four sketches of Cottesloe layouts:* Half Life *1977,* The Beggar's Opera *1982,* Fuente Ovejuna *1992 and* The Voysey Inheritance *1989.*

7.2 *In The Mysteries at the Cottesloe, God on top of a fork-lift creates a world lit only by candles.*

concentrated the mind. The eventual cost of the Cottesloe when it opened in 1977, excluding minimal fees, was £350,000, which was 2 per cent of the total building cost of the entire National of £16,000,000 – the latter figure taken from the NT's website.

The approach I adopted was to create a 'framework for freedom'. The framework was inspired by the small rectangular galleried playhouses of the late eighteenth century of which I had had direct experience of the only surviving one, the freshly restored 1788 Georgian Theatre Richmond, Yorkshire. This was where, in 1963, Prospect had presented the first play staged there for over a hundred years: Vanbrugh's *The Provok'd Wife*. My enthusiasm for such spaces was illustrated in the exhibition which I devised for the Arts Council of Great Britain in 1975 at the Hayward Gallery next door to the NT: *The Georgian Playhouse: Actors, Artists, Audiences and Architecture, 1730–1830*. The freedom consisted of the central void, which could contain a 'pit' with padded bench seating facing a conventional end-stage, or which could be a place where the dream of French stage designer Pierre Chaix might be realised: 'The spectacle should no longer be confined to the stage but should invade the entire space.'

I proposed fixed steel balconies on three sides, with the existing foyer level providing the middle level for the auditorium. At stage level was the most flexible of all conceivable arrangements, an empty hole. Over this was a removable flat floor at stage level, which was about three metres above an already built basement floor. In this hole production manager Jason Barnes and his team could realise levels, entrances, traps, or whatever proceeded from the imaginations of directors and designers. Action and audience could happen wherever. The only limit on their freedom was the framework, which was scaled in the manner of many a courtyard of an inn or country house. The only predetermined arrangement for the centre was the flat floor option requested by Hall. For me the flat floor option had been triggered by the promenade production by Luca Ronconi of *Orlando Furioso* by Ludovico Ariosto, which had been staged so breathtakingly on a floored-over ice-hockey rink at the Edinburgh International Festival of 1970.

It was this flat floor capability that director Bill Bryden, who had also seen *Orlando Furioso*, and designer Bill Dudley put to such brilliant use for their *Lark Rise* and *Mysteries* promenade productions in years two and three of the new Cottesloe. When someone called me to say, 'You will never guess what they have done to your theatre: they have taken out all the seats!' I murmured to myself 'Hooray! And so soon!'

The task at the outset was to reconcile the format of an end-stage, which would give the required capacity of 400 (including some standing at the sides), with the opportunity to experiment with other actor/audience relationships. This studio theatre was to be different in feel from the as-yet-unfinished main theatres. Workmanlike finishes and simple seating, as found in the better fringe theatres of the day, were reflected in much lower admission prices than those charged upstairs. There were no assigned seats, just assigned areas where firstcomers got the best places on continuous tip-up padded bench seating with no arms. The audience at the Cottesloe travelled at the back of the plane, not in club class as in the Olivier and Lyttelton.

An unforeseen effect of there never being enough money was the loss, after the first few years, of the shallow rake option for end-stage when going quickly and frequently from the steep rake, which reached the middle level, to a playing area other than end-stage. The steep rake end-stage format was favoured by many directors. Meanwhile the removable flat floor in the centre, covering the hole, was the starting point for many other arrangements. To achieve this the NT soon acquired an off-the-peg retractable seating unit on wheels. This system provided the steep rake and the flat floor option but not the shallow rake. It was too large to be taken out of the theatre and had to be parked when not needed under the lower balcony at the entrance end, which inhibited some of the other staging options. The best thing to come out of the refurbishment in 2015 of the Cottesloe as the Dorfman was a single if expensive mechanical solution that can be set for either steep or shallow raked seating or as a flat floor at stage level or even lower.

The Cottesloe design evolves rapidly

Back to 1973. Bury, having liked my weekend's work, found a model maker to create a first at 1:96 then another at 1:24. Bury showed these to Hall and then to his colleagues on 6 December. The following day Hall wrote:

Dear Iain,

Yesterday John Bury showed the Policy Committee, which is principally my associate directors, the revised model of the Cottesloe Theatre. They were, to put it no stronger, delighted and enchanted. Please accept my congratulations and thanks for all you have contributed to its evolution. We are now more than ever determined to see it built. And the quality of its conception is sure to make our task easier.

Kind regards, Peter.

On 12 December I replied: 'Thank you very much for your generous letter. It is exciting when an idea gets a life of its own so quickly. This is due entirely to the encouragement and assistance of John and of my new colleagues at Theatre Projects.'

Somebody now had to tell Lasdun, who had not been involved in any of these discussions, that he was being asked by the NT to detail for construction an already approved proposal 'by others'. He was informed that the design concept had come from someone he had never heard of at Theatre Projects Consultants, who in any case Lasdun had thought of as technical consultants not as theatre designers.

One day in January 1974 Pilbrow, Bury and I attended Lasdun's office in Queen Anne Street. We entered his inner office where the model already approved by the NT stood on the table. I turned to Bury and Pilbrow to check who was going to open the batting. They said nothing and made me a sign. Lasdun, whom I had never met, seemed angry. He prowled. He then pointed at the columns on the top level, three feet back from the leading edge of the balconies. I had intended these to pass through the top balcony to meet up with the already existing ceiling over the whole space. Lasdun: 'What are those?' Me: 'Er, those are part of the web which weave audience and actor together in, er, a shared experience.' Lasdun: 'I don't understand metaphysics. Columns are to hold up the roof. I have already built the roof. Take them out.'

And that was that. I only met Lasdun once more, in 1976 shortly before the opening of the National, at a large meeting of the whole design team. (It was said that this was the first and only meeting of the whole design team as Lasdun preferred one-to-one meetings with his specialists.) We were all instructed that any questions of design were to be referred to him personally. Some years later Pilbrow showed me his unequivocal reply to Lasdun's letter 'instructing' him that Theatre Projects was not to be credited with the concept design of the Cottesloe. Pilbrow ignored this and always credited me. And it is to Bury I owe a subsequent introduction to George Christie which set up the design process for the new Glyndebourne, of which more later. Both were generous friends to whom I am ever grateful.

During detailed design, my only contact with the architects was with Peter Softley, Lasdun's professional partner, who cheerfully agreed to everything I suggested. In the void there was in what was to be upstage right a single square free-standing concrete column which held up one corner of the Olivier fly tower above. This stood well clear of the internal walls of the Cottesloe space. I asked for an identical concrete column to be built stage left which would serve no purpose beyond symmetry. Softley arranged that. Both columns (the functional one and the matching pair) were made to look more functional by adding a vertical slot for side lighting. Softley's collusion did not stop there. The contractors had already started work in the Zeppelin hangar when it occurred to me that the floor-to-floor heights between galleries were going to be too great. The audience here should be compressed and feel they might have to duck to avoid beams overhead while the actors in the centre walked tall. Softley agreed to reduce each of the floor-to-ceiling heights within the galleries by 150 mm.

The technical matter of theatre equipment was not in the control of TPC because not only was there no money for the customary process of design, specification and tendering but also because Pilbrow, Brett and the TPC team were heavily engaged upstairs dealing with tardy contractors. The equipping of the Cottesloe over and above the creation of the steel galleries was tackled as if it was for a future production that everyone liked but for which there was no realistic budget. The technical director of the NT at the time was Simon Relph, who presided over a series of problem-solving ad hoc meetings. The absence of stage lights was solved by the realisation that some of the older lights that the NT were able to bring over from the Old Vic, which they were leaving, would be sufficient for the Cottesloe and that there was just enough petty cash somewhere to buy standard lighting and sound control desks off the shelf. The rostra needed for fresh audience layouts for individual productions as they occurred would be paid for out of the show budgets.

A modular courtyard for an unknown future

An unknown future had to be thought of alongside the immediate exercise of making bricks without much straw. Courtyard theatres must be modular so that arrangements not yet dreamt of can be accommodated in the years to come. At the Cottesloe the search for a module started early on with the positioning, immediately within the side walls, of internal staircases up or down which theatregoers would find their way from the mid-level foyer to their seats on the level above or below, a journey which contributed to their total experience. Within these side staircases were gangways for audience or actors to circulate at all levels. Between these gangways and the single continuous front row of seating there was a narrow space of statutory width where a second row of standing audience could lean on rails linked to the steel columns that held up the galleries. Their heads would be directly over those of the single seated row in front, which meant that the second row would have acceptable sightlines. Total up these spatial needs at the two sides and the remaining clear width in the central void was 9.9 metres or 32 feet 6 inches.

A width of 9.9 metres is roughly the size of the proscenium arch in most medium-size London theatres and hence a scale familiar to directors, designers and actors. Divide by six and you get 1.65 metres, which is the perfect distance between the balcony supporting columns which a standing person could touch with outstretched hands. Divide by twelve and you get 825 mm, which at that time was judged an acceptable row-to-row depth for a fringe or experimental theatre. Divide by eighteen and you get 550 mm, which is a generous space width per person in continuous bench seating. Double 550 mm for the statutory width for a gangway.

To touch base with ancient English measures: the width between Cottesloe galleries of 32 feet six inches is as near as damn it 33 feet, which is two medieval rods of 16 feet six inches. The rod was the unit of measurement for centuries for the setting out of almost all buildings from domestic property to cathedrals. The width of the proscenium opening at the 1788 Georgian Theatre Royal Richmond is one rod. The width of my mid-nineteenth-century house in Clapham in which this book was written is one rod. The length of a cricket pitch is precisely four rods, 66 feet or 22 yards, information which one Friday evening many years later in Bangalore woke up my audience of young Indian architects.

It was tightness of planning which differentiated the Cottesloe from the two generously spaced large theatres upstairs, which even then seemed to me windy and thus not good for comedy. The flexibility of the Cottesloe differed from those 'adaptable' studios in that it did not come with a set of diagrams showing how motors and levers could produce this or that predetermined actor/audience relationship. There being no money for such devices the balconies on three sides provided the framework while the central void provided the freedom. In presenting 'The Cottesloe Cockpit' to the NT directors in November 1973 I quoted from Christopher Marlowe's *The Jew of Malta* lines which spoke of 'men of judgement' who would 'enclose infinite riches in a little room'.

My use of the word 'courtyard' as a description of the Cottesloe stuck. This new tag did not signify any one format of theatre – such as thrust, in-the-round, proscenium, traverse, etc. – but did suggest adaptability. Courtyard through association also indicated the character of the space to be shared by actor and audience in whatever way director, designer or playwright might choose. Better than using the adjective 'flexible', which suggests the shunting around of predetermined seating blocks into variations on a single theme. Often such shunting takes place on an impermeable flat floor which means that for all the pre-arranged variations the feet of the actor and of the front row of the audience are at the same level. The absence of a stage riser can be difficult for the actor. Ask any comedian who likes to have half his or her audience below eye level and half above. With no stage riser and the consequent steep rake, you get but two rows below eye level and the rest above. Actors call this acting at the bottom of a well.

Soon after the Cottesloe opened in March 1977 I visited the Christ's Hospital School theatre at Horsham in West Sussex designed by Bill Howell, who had died tragically in a car crash only months before its opening. His first achievement as a theatre architect had been creating the Young Vic in 1970 for director Frank Dunlop. The success of the Young Vic had led visionary school master Duncan Noel-Paton to seek out Howell for Christ's Hospital. I discovered that the Cottesloe courtyard was in no way unique. The chorus of courtyards that follow spans the forty years from Christ's Hospital in 1975 to the opening of the Bridge in 2015.

Priorities change for the Cottesloe/Dorfman and for the Polonsky Theatre, NYC

Any good theatre needs revisiting by future generations, especially if they have different priorities. In September 2015 the Cottesloe of 1977, which sat 350 plus fifty standing, reopened as the Dorfman with a design team led by Steve Tompkins. In the club class Dorfman standing was abolished and comfort increased for all. This was reflected by increases in the prices of admission as the NT needed the money, subsidy levels having fallen. The loss of standing still seems slightly odd. The young cheerfully stand in the Royal Opera House and at Shakespeare's Globe, not to mention at Glastonbury – 100,000 of them stood in 2022 for Paul McCartney at the Pyramid stage. Why not a few standees at the third theatre of the National?

In 2008 I had been commissioned by the NT to suggest what improvements might usefully be made to the Cottesloe should money be available. Barnes and ex-TPC head engineer Brett were co-authors. A by-product was statistics carefully researched by Barnes. In the first twenty-one years, from 1977 to 1998, when first Hall and then Eyre were directors of the NT, fewer than half of the productions were in end-stage and the rest in one of the other forms – long traverse, short traverse, promenade, cruciform, in-the-round, three-sided thrust, diagonal staging, etc., etc. Compare this with the first five years after its reopening as the Dorfman in September 2014 when the proportion of end-stage productions increased from 46 per cent to 60 per cent. Had later generations of NT directors and designers become less interested in formats other than end-stage, or had priorities shifted to maximising box office by encouraging end-stage because that form had the highest capacity? Unless about half the productions in a courtyard theatre are staged in the centre as opposed to end-stage the public are entitled to ask why a theatre has so many side seats with indifferent sightlines. In the eighteenth and nineteenth centuries the managements of both horseshoe and rectangular auditoriums would cover over the stalls at stage level and organise balls and banquets. In winter in eighteenth-century Dublin the Theatre Royal regularly presented actual horse races along the length of that central space.

In 2013 there had opened the Polonsky Theatre, home of Theatre for a New Audience in Brooklyn NYC which had been closely modelled on the Cottesloe. As built the clear distance between the side galleries at both had been similar, at 9.9 metres at the Cottesloe and two feet wider for the Polonsky at 34 feet 6 inches. This plus an extra two feet in height from stage level to lighting bridges made the Polonsky windier for its seating capacity of only 299 compared with 450 at the smaller Dorfman, the total cubic volume of which is less than that of the Polonsky. But if the latter had held 399 rather than 299 this would have involved more stringent NYC building regulations, increasing capital costs, while the theatre unions would have required larger minimum salaries, which would have increased running costs. The design team at the Polonsky, led by architect Hugh Hardy and advised by TPC America, in the persons of Pilbrow and John Runia, were working to different parameters than those controlling architect Tompkins and his team in London who, when revising the Cottesloe, had been instructed by the client to pack them in.

The Polonsky is the only new theatre space reviewed here that has stuck to the neutrality of the 'black box'. During the gestation of the Cottesloe in the early 1970s the insistence of black throughout was the only aesthetic difference between Bury and me. When the steel for the Cottesloe galleries arrived on site it was primed red. At Bill Howell's courtyard theatre at Christ's Hospital his steel galleries are clad in timber which has been stained red. But at the NT in 1976 there had been no discussion: black it had to be because that was how such studio theatres were then dressed.

More courtyards: Bracknell, Calgary and Salford

In the 1980s and 1990s there came more courtyards in which I was involved. After the Cottesloe there was the Wilde Theatre Bracknell where director Gavin Henderson brought together two people involved in a couple of galleried theatres that he liked, Axel Burrough of Levitt Bernstein architects, who had worked on the Royal Exchange Manchester of 1976, and me by reason of the Cottesloe. The result at Bracknell was a courtyard on three levels holding up to 400, this time not rectangular but square in form with entrances set diagonally at the four corners with boxes over. It is a flexible space: fixed galleries on three sides with freedom in the centre. Wrote Francis Reid in the *Architects' Journal* of June 1984: 'The overriding strength of the Wilde Theatre is that, whatever form is in use, the shallow balconies link with the main seating to ensure that the audience is always more than just the sum of the parts. An individual will always be aware of the rest of the audience.'

Next in 1986 for me came the Martha Cohen Theatre Calgary designed in conjunction with Alberta architect Joel Barrett. This was an apsidal-shaped three-level courtyard, framed in wood and set off from the encircling walls which were also wood clad. As at the Cottesloe internal staircases connected the audience levels. These were also reached by dramatic bridges from the foyers spanning the narrow surrounding voids which, with their vertical banners, played different acoustic roles depending on whether the banners were up or down.

The Calgary theatre was cloned in 2000 as the Quays Theatre at the Lowry, Salford. When detailing my sketch design for the Quays with architect Michael Wilford I suggested that we might find useful a visit to Calgary, reachable by direct flight from Heathrow, where the Martha Cohen had been in use for more than ten years. No, they were too busy to do that and anyway they liked my design. When I asked whether we might now talk colours for the steel and wood

7.3 *Opening performance at the Wilde Theatre Bracknell 1984.*

structure within the outer brick apsidal form Wilford said, 'Yes. Red.' And that was that. Everything red. A touch oversimplified but certainly preferable to the black everywhere at the Cottesloe. Some of us had smiled when John Gielgud, having experienced all three theatres at the NT (including, in 1977/78, *Half Life* at the Cottesloe, which transferred easily to the Duke of York's and then to Broadway), was reported as saying of the new National: 'The theatres are perfectly terrible. The only one that is any good is the Cottesloe and that is painted black like a coffin.'

In 1989 a second similar but slightly smaller apsidal theatre was conceived by me for Westminster School Connecticut, which was elegantly detailed by an alumnus architect, Graham Gund based in Boston. The accompanying image shows the headmaster addressing the house before a piano recital.

Tim Foster, theatre architect, who specialised in school theatres

In 1979 Tim Foster and I were both working for TPC and were asked to suggest a design for a new theatre for Dulwich College, which had been founded by Elizabethan actor Edward Alleyn. The College was so pleased with Foster's design that they agreed that if he could set up his own architectural practice they would employ him as architect with the safety net of the well-

7.4 *The flexible Martha Cohen Theatre Calgary 1985:* Angels in America *over* Candide.

7.5 *Westminster School Connecticut Theatre 1988.*

established TPC as theatre consultants. Foster was soon successful with his own practice, Foster Wilson Architects, which quickly gained a wide range of clients with an emphasis on drama teaching at both schools and universities. In 2014 Foster's distinction in this field was recognised when he became chair of the Architecture Commission of OISTAT, the International Organisation of Scenographers, Theatre Architects and Technicians, a prestigious position which he held until 2020.

The Inigo Jones pedigree of the Vanbrugh at RADA and of the Wanamaker Playhouse

Two further courtyards which wear their pedigrees on their sleeves are the Vanbrugh Theatre at the Royal Academy of Dramatic Art in Gower Street London, which opened in 2001, and Hall Two at the Sage Gateshead of 2004. My involvement with Bryan Avery at RADA came about after a regular meeting of the theatre planning committee of the ABTT to which architects and their clients brought their proposals for informal discussion. The meeting with the RADA group in April 1995 was not easy. Avery had successfully coped with an exceptionally narrow site in Gower Street. The only matter that needed further debate was what sort of a new theatre to build

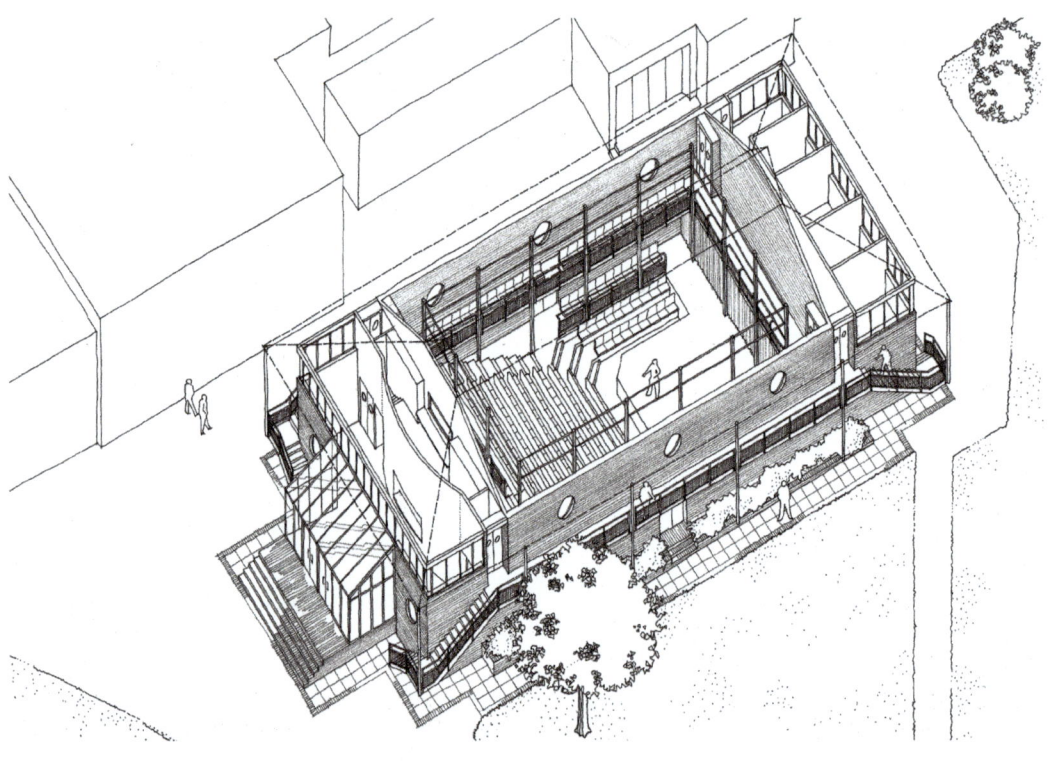

7.6 *Edward Alleyn Hall Dulwich College 1983: Tim Foster's axonometric over-audience photo.*

as centrepiece. At the ABTT planning meeting he had showed us a fixed single-rake auditorium not unlike the Mermaid. This would have allowed little variety in staging, which is important for teaching students. At a subsequent smaller meeting Avery and I hit it off, both of us being smitten by the rigorous *ad quadratum* geometry of architect and stage designer Inigo Jones.

Avery confirmed this by handing me a photocopy of an article he had co-authored with an optometrist headed 'Beauty is in the Eye of the Beholder', which suggested that the ratio of the vertical to the horizontal in the human field of vision is one to the square root of two, which is the key to the sacred geometry to which the likes of Jones and Avery subscribed. For the tercentenary of Jones's birth in 1973 a major exhibition of his work had been held at the Banqueting House of 1622 in Whitehall where he had staged masques for the court of King Charles I. *TABS* of September 1973 published my article on his drawings of theatre spaces which included those then catalogued as '7b and 7c' and which are held by my old Oxford college, Worcester.

In this article I suggested that they were for the Cockpit in Drury Lane of 1617. Shakespearean and Inigo Jones scholar John Orrell had come to the same conclusion. Together we convinced the indefatigable Sam Wanamaker that these drawings were the oldest extant designs for an English-speaking indoor playhouse. Globe architect Theo Crosby, Orrell and I were instructed to prepare sketch proposals for the reconstruction, next to their Globe, of what all then referred to as 'the Inigo Jones Theatre'. My contribution to further research included the

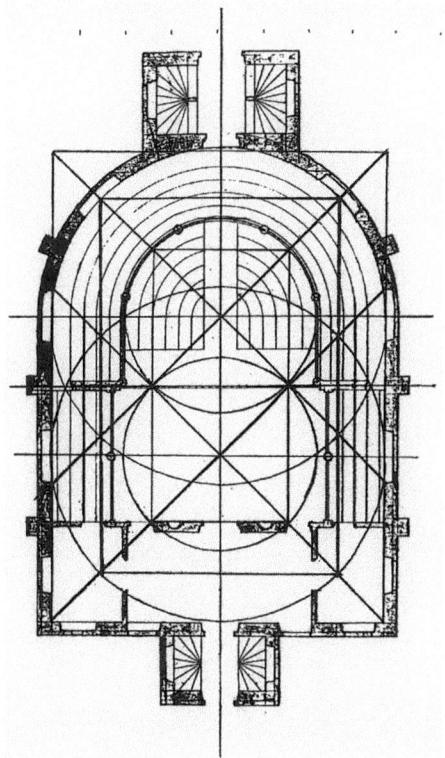

7.7 *Iain Mackintosh sacred geometry overlay on plan originally supposed by Inigo Jones himself.*

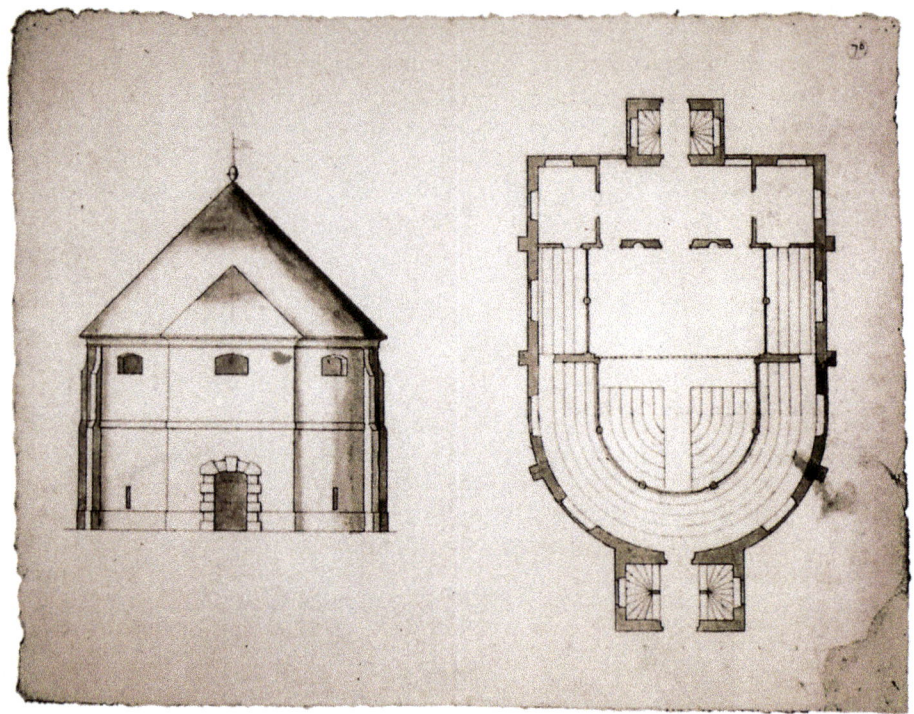

7.8 *Pair of supposed Inigo Jones drawings once known as 7b and 7c and now as H&T 10 and H&T 11. Worcester College, Oxford.*

7.9 *Sam Wanamaker Playhouse 2014 adjacent to Shakespeare's Globe 1997.*

relevance of *ad quadratum* geometry so favoured by Jones. Sadly when Wanamaker was alive there was money only for the shell, which was used as a rehearsal space for nearly twenty years. Much later, in 2005, when at last there was hope of raising the cash for the interior, the architectural scholar Gordon Higgott convinced most people that these drawings were not by Inigo Jones but by his assistant John Webb, that they were not realised and dated not from 1617 but from 1660, the year of the Restoration and thus forty-four years after the death of Shakespeare. The Globe management cunningly decided that 'The Inigo Jones Theatre' was to become 'The Indoor Jacobean Theatre' before it became, appropriately, the Sam Wanamaker Playhouse on its opening in 2014. The drawings were slightly modified with straight facets at the apsidal end which, on the seventeenth-century drawings, was shown as semicircular in plan. It was agreed, somewhat fancifully, that this was what the indoor Blackfriars playhouse of 1596 might have looked like. I suggested that the same drawings might have been Webb's proposals for the remodelling of a Jacobean theatre originally built by Jones. That debate will continue.

Meanwhile, Avery and I were working up the new Vanbrugh theatre at RADA, which opened in 2001 at a time when those drawings were still being attributed to Jones rather than to Webb. The *Architects' Journal* of 3 May 2001 wrote: 'Avery, with Iain Mackintosh of Theatre Projects Consultants, has shown a deft touch in responding to RADA's brief. Essentially the new theatre had to be an exemplary training ground for students who had to truly understand the nature of theatrical projection to prepare them for work in much larger theatres of different forms and scales.' Usually the designers of theatre space are asked to make a large space feel more intimate than the capacity suggests. This was the only time we had been asked to aim for the reverse.

Hall Two at The Sage Gateshead

The architects for The Sage Gateshead were chosen by limited competition between seven selected practices. The brief called for three principal components: a 1,600-seat concert hall, primarily to be the home of the Northern Sinfonia, England's oldest chamber orchestra, and Hall Two which is a 450-seat smaller hall for which Folkworks, a unique organisation devoted to traditional music of the north-east, was the prime mover. The winning architects were Foster and Partners. The partner in charge was Spencer de Grey and the project architect Jason Flanagan, who later created his own practice, Flanagan Lawrence.

Theatre Projects were appointed as consultants at The Sage because we had worked on many concert halls as well as theatres across the world. Hall Two was a unique challenge: it had to work for string quartets, for jazz or folk and for theatre of the sort that defies definition. It had occurred to me that here might be an opportunity to experiment with a five-sided geometry which allows the blurring of there being a centre line. For one of the other shortlisted architects, Keith Williams, I had sketched a galleried pentagon. Foster and Partners were happy to run with this idea, which was helped by our drawing which placed Vitruvian man, as drawn by German polymath Heinrich Cornelius Agrippa, over the 5/10 side form. Flanagan and I with our teams then set about detailing the space with the active involvement of acoustician Bob Essert, who was then working for Arup Acoustics.

An audience of 450 was accommodated on two ten-sided galleries while below, at the lowest five-sided level, there are five retractable wedges of seating. If all these were extended at the same time this would provide for music or theatre-in-the-round. If but three of the five retractables were extended and more seats added in the centre this would allow the performers to occupy one end of the room. On 27 October 2005 Charlotte Higgins wrote in the *Guardian* of her evening with the Lindsay String Quartet in the recently inaugurated Hall Two which she reported was 'an intimate, beautiful space that can be re-configured so the performers are in the centre or at the side. Tonight, they were in the centre. There's visceral intensity to being so close to performers that you can almost feel their breath. You start to feel bound up in the drama.'

Tim Foster wrote in the Winter 2005 edition of *Sightline* (the ABTT Journal of Theatre Technology and Design) of having attended at Hall Two to hear a high energy ten-piece band from Mexico:

I was struck by how much more fun it was than a lot of dreary theatres I have seen and this set me thinking about the differences between the design of spaces and for drama and for this type of music . . . there are very few purpose-designed spaces for popular music which is not generally considered worthy of serious architectural consideration. I don't suppose that Iain Mackintosh has been to many gigs in his time, but nevertheless his principles of 'sacred geometry' work just as well here as they do in a theatre. The fact is a successful performance space with a proper sense of intimacy and focus will work for any kind of live performance from hip hop to *Hamlet*.

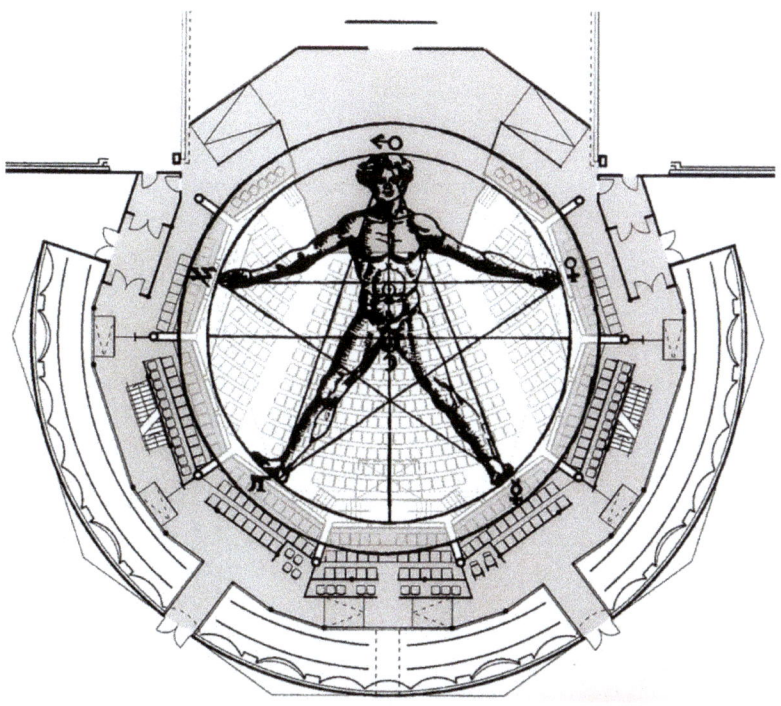

7.10 *Hall Two Sage Gateshead: 2004: TPC proposal over in-the-round performance.*

One of the best of all courtyards: The Swan

The pick of the courtyards from the end of the twentieth century is one with which I had no connection: the Swan at Stratford-upon-Avon of 1986. It occupies the apsidal shell of the auditorium for the first Memorial Theatre which burnt in 1926 and was replaced in 1932 by the brick building (see Chapter 3) which included a new theatre sited next to the shell of the 1879 auditorium that was retained as a rehearsal room. It was Trevor Nunn, artistic director of the RSC from 1968 until 1986, who persuaded the Governors of the RSC to consider the conversion of this into a truly Shakespearean but at the same time contemporary theatre space. The collegiate RSC team which joined Nunn to nurse the project from dream to completion over ten long years included the scholarly couple of John and Anne Barton.

The architect they chose was Michael Reardon who, before the Swan commission, had tried to interest Nunn 'in doing some of his work not in theatres but in galleried churches, because it seemed to me that the architecture of such buildings had the power to draw the audience together in a way that modern theatres do not'. Warwickshire-based Reardon was Surveyor of the Fabric to two cathedrals: Birmingham and Hereford. An article of his faith was that 'the best theatre, like the best religious worship, can still create a sense of community'. In *Making Space for Theatre*, edited by Ronnie Mulryne and Margaret Shewring in 1995, Reardon summed up the approach: 'We set out to create a very strong architectonic form – a framework within which the actor and the audience would exist on equal terms and interact. This was of course what Trevor wanted and, I suppose, is the exact opposite of the "black box" approach that had prevailed at Stratford.' He was alluding to those designers including John Bury, Abd'Elkader Farrah and Christopher Morley who often created sparse, dark-toned settings that set off brilliant costumes and properties.

There were two principal reference points. In 1978 an RSC small-scale tour of *Twelfth Night* with Ian McKellen as Sir Toby Belch and co-directed by Nunn started its tour at Howell's Christ's Hospital Theatre of 1974. 'And *there*,' wrote Nunn, 'pretty much in every detail, was the kind of space I was dreaming of. Michael already knew of it . . .' This is taken from Mulryne and Shewring's *This Golden Round* of 1989, which celebrated the design and the first three seasons at the Swan. Second was a later charcoal sketch by designer Tim Furby who was Reardon's right hand in matters theatrical. This sketch swayed any doubters at Stratford-upon-Avon.

The naturally stained woodwork introduced by Reardon at the Swan was wrapped in the newly exposed nineteenth-century Warwickshire brick of the shell of the first theatre. Ever since, both profession and public have enjoyed what Adrian Noble, RSC director from 1990 to 2003, called 'this easy relationship. The space humanises the epic; makes public the private; and enables a secret grief or joy to be shared honestly.' Included in *The Golden Round* are magnificent architectural photographs by Martin Charles who bequeathed his images to the RIBA archive. That book's cover image is reproduced on page 189 in Chapter 13.

Courtyards holding less than 400 lead to the request for 'the same only bigger'

Small courtyard theatres make little economic sense. Those who run new small theatre spaces holding, say, 300, and have forgotten the mark-up for greater capital costs or of paying for casts who can cope with a larger scale, have said to me, 'It's a nice theatre, Iain, but if you had understood theatre economics you would have put in 450 seats.' When building them one with 600 seats they would say, 'It's a nice theatre, Iain, but if you had understood theatre economics you would have put in 850.' And so on. Others just ask the architect on day one: 'I want the same only bigger.' Is there a limit to the size of a courtyard theatre and is that perhaps that of the successful Bridge Theatre discussed in Chapter 13?

8

Worthy scaffolds: Brook's empty space and spaces found by others

An early scaffolding theatre

The first scaffolding courtyard theatre I knew of was in Pittsburgh, Pennsylvania where such a theatre had been erected in found space for a trial twelve-week season in 1975. Its founder, artistic director Ben Shaktman, visited the Cottesloe in the summer of 1977 and sought me out as a fellow spirit. Neither of us drew breath for a couple of hours. In Pittsburgh Shaktman had collaborated with stage designer Peter Wexler. There was no money and the city lacked any theatre company of its own. With a load of Safeway scaffolding they built a courtyard theatre, tall and elegant, on three levels holding 300 in a found space. More places were added over the years until the capacity reached 470. It was taken down in 1998 having lasted more than twenty years. That site was not the best and the Pittsburgh Public Theatre moved to a better one downtown and into a newly built 'proper' theatre holding 650. The director was Eddie Gilbert.

Eddie Gilbert and the remodelling of the St Lawrence Centre, Toronto

This introduces one of those curious theatrical connections. In 1980 Gilbert, an old university friend with whom I had collaborated at the Oxford Playhouse, moved from Winnipeg to the major producing theatre in Toronto, the St Lawrence Centre, which had opened as recently as 1970. It had been modelled, badly, on the already discussed and fundamentally flawed Vivian Beaumont in New York. Gilbert decided to close it and completely remodel its auditorium. Hearing that Theatre Projects Consultants of London was opening an office in New York he got in touch with me. In March 1983 the remodelled St Lawrence Centre reopened and was the first completed project in North America of Theatre Projects Inc.

Gilbert realised that the St Lawrence Centre as built would never work as a thrust stage. Canadians knew what a real thrust was like: Guthrie's Stratford Ontario had been built just over two hours away down the road. But could the St Lawrence be transformed into an intimate proscenium playhouse and maintain a capacity of 860? We got to work on a new auditorium together with architect Ron Thom, who in 1973 had designed the similar-sized and most successful Shaw Festival Theatre at Niagara, Ontario. The rest of the St Lawrence could not be changed for political reasons, it being not easy to find money to remodel a civic centrepiece completed only ten years previously. The low-cost transformation worked and Gilbert's company was renamed 'the Canadian Stage Company'.

Arguments for using inexpensive scaffolding in found space: The Tricycle

In an Elizabethan playhouse and at the Swan there is a rhythm between the vertical and the horizontal, which is achieved by both being woven of wood. These days if you want to create a free-standing modern courtyard theatre within found space and have little money timber columns will be too expensive. But you can afford builders' scaffolding. This means you can't cantilever the balconies. You have to lose the supporting columns which balance the horizontal with the vertical as they did in a Shakespearean courtyard. Fine, you will say, except for those sitting behind a column. Yet steel scaffolding has always been only two inches (50 mm) diameter and interferes less with the field of vision than does a timber column which must be at least twice as thick to take the weight of the tier above.

The most successful steel scaffolding theatre in the UK has been the Tricycle in Kilburn, London of 1980. It caught fire in 1987, the fire having spread from an adjacent timber yard. The roof collapsed but underneath the scaffolding stood unscathed and was reused when ceiling and roof were rebuilt within two years. Wrote drama critic Irving Wardle in *The Times* of 23 September 1989: 'Good places for performances are easily destroyed by attempts to improve them, and the best news is not its handsomely redesigned foyers or its community activities but the fact that the stage and auditorium look exactly as they did before the 1987 fire.' There were small changes such as capacity being increased from 200 to 235. The *Daily Telegraph* theatre critic Eric Shorter noted that 'the audience congregates close together. It is this sense of cluster which increases our capacity to pay attention.' Nicolas Kent, director of the Tricycle from 1994 to 2012, claimed that strangers struck up conversations on those armless benches resulting, he claimed, in three marriages and countless adulteries.

This most friendly atmosphere was enhanced by architect Tim Foster's idea to construct the tier fronts of stout blue canvas that yielded to the knee. The authorities accepted this as safe on the grounds that if it was safe for the cockpit of an ocean-racing yacht in a force nine gale it would be safe for a theatre in Kilburn. The canvas was laced to an American scaffolding system which Foster had chosen from many. This came in 4-feet, 6-feet or 8-feet elements which allowed the easy application of a geometric rationale to the plan. In *The Empty Space*, which is an edited transcript of his four Granada Lectures of 1965, Brook sought 'the mystery of theatre, and in the understanding of this mystery lies the only science . . . It is not a matter of saying analytically what are the requirements, how best they could be organised – this will usually bring into existence a tame, conventional, often cold hall.' For many including myself the mystery of sacred geometry is now an integral part of that science.

The Tricycle's antecedents also include the Theatre Royal at Richmond Yorkshire of 1788 as the accompanying pair of photos show. Here the show can spill over into an auditorium which at the time was lit almost as brightly as the stage, which helped make auditorium and stage a single room. The Tricycle was similar except that there was no solid proscenium arch and the main structural material for the stage, like that for the auditorium, was the same scaffolding, which was available only in orange. After the fire the old scaffolding was painted red. In the proscenium zone, curtains or scenery could be attached to the scaffolding if for a particular

8.1 *Audiences in the Tricycle Theatre Kilburn 1980 and Georgian Theatre Royal Richmond Yorkshire 1766 restored 1963.*

production. Stage and auditorium could be either a single space or two rooms. The scenic opening, for the latter, between the parallel arms of the audience balconies was but 20 feet (6.09 metres), only slightly wider than Richmond.

The single-room option of the scaffolding Tricycle is not easy to achieve in a 'proper theatre' where stage and auditorium are distinct spaces, as in the more conventional Kiln that followed the old Tricycle. That had lasted thirty-six years and closed in 2016. The free-standing scaffolding structure was then dismantled and retained for use elsewhere. Director Indhu Rubasingham had succeeded Kent in 2012. She decided that what was needed was a proper theatre with more seats in place of the small and underequipped Tricycle. A large sum of money was raised. The new theatre space opened in 2018. The flexibility inherent in low-cost free-standing builders' scaffolding was replaced by a more sophisticated structure using every inch of space of the old dance hall. The difference between the old Tricycle and the new Kiln was summed up in a conversation with drama critic Michael Billington: 'The Kiln is sleeker.'

For the theatre worker there are important advantages. There are now safe lighting bridges where previously brave technicians propped up a ladder against one of the four steel trusses which were the only purpose-built elements in the old structure otherwise made of builders' scaffolding. At the new Kiln the scenic opening is now 8.8 metres, which is wider than that of either the old Tricycle or the Royal Court where the proscenium is but 6.4 metres wide. Why is width important? Narrowness makes for intimacy. It is hard to raise a laugh on the wide stages of the Olivier and Lyttelton. The narrow Royal Court stage makes for greater focus on both actor and on new writing.

There are two other links between the Cottesloe of 1977 and the Tricycle of 1980. Both were inexpensive. The Cottesloe cost a fraction of the two big theatres at the NT. The total all-in cost of the entire Tricycle theatre when it opened in 1980, much of it erected by the theatre company's own staff, was £150,000. This is around £1 million at 2018 prices. Compare this with the £7.5 million spent on the 2018 remodelling of the Kiln, which lifted the capacity to 292. There are now individual and comfortable seats with arms which award each member of the audience his or her own personal space. The second link was that both were 'found spaces' where the starting point for the design was a rigid rectangle.

Two worthy scaffolds in found spaces: São Paulo and Hackney

The next three worthy scaffolds were created in very different found spaces. The first of these was not so much a found building but a narrow urban lot behind a dull street facade in São Paulo, Brazil. Inspired by artistic director Zé Celso two architects, Lina Bo Bardi, born in 1914 and who had emigrated from Italy in 1946, and Edson Elito, born in Brazil in 1948, created the unique *Teatro Oficina*. The long narrow site is hemmed in on one side by existing buildings and threatened on the other by an unscrupulous developer. On each side are the scaffolding galleries which were detailed by Elito in 1994 after the death of Bo Bardi in 1992. I visited it in 2000 when invited to the second Espaço da Cena Latino in São Paulo, organised by stage designer José Carlos Serroni, with whom I had shared platforms at the Prague Quadrennials of 1995 and 1999.

I did not see a show but did walk along the sloping internal street which leads nowhere. On one side there are no openings but there is a waterfall. On the other there is a vast glass window, with a tall tree, roots outside and branches within. A few of the audience are at 'stage' level

8.2 The Bacchae *at the* Teatro Oficina *São Paulo Brazil in 1996.*

while most cling to three levels of scaffolding. Above, halfway up the street, the roof slides open. The space can hold a little over 400 in great discomfort. Sometimes fires are lit. All the elements are conjured. The performance mood is captured by the exceptional photo of *The Bacchae* by Euripides which in Brazil is referred to as the *Bacantes*. This was the show which I would have liked to have caught. Zé Celso's take on Euripides, like the space itself, had evolved over the years. It was in 1966 that the near naked cast was first presented in this, the final version of the space. An unusual Samba School is setting off for the Carnival. In what he described as a 'tragicomediaorgy' founder Zé Celso played the wise Dionysus, wise because he had been both Man and Woman. In *The Theatre Times* of 25 February 2017 critic Felipe Vidal, who had seen the original production in 1966, explained that the ruler Pentheus is 'a politician of a new generation ... and represents the resumption of retrograde, racist, sexist and xenophobic thinking against the libertarian and libidinal Dionysus and his followers'. In 2019 reality caught up with the drama when ultra-right-wing Jair Bolsonaro became President.

The scaffolding galleries contribute much to the mood of the wildly illogical T*eatro Oficina*. Of this child of three talented people, one actor-manager and two architects, Rowan Moore wrote, in *The Guardian* of 11 December 2015, of

> this wall of galleries built out of scaffolding which serve the orgiastic performances of the theatre's creator Zé Celso, who has claimed that the idea came to him when, on an acid trip

and running from the police, he found himself trapped against a solid wall. Teatro Oficina has challenging sightlines, hard seats and is very much not the shape theatres are meant to be but is all the more intense for that.

No wonder architectural critic Moore placed it first in his list of the ten best theatres in the world.

The second of the three scaffolding theatres set in an unusual place was a more conventional end-stage temporary theatre holding 750 that was ingeniously fitted into an about-to-be-demolished film studio in North London, the Gainsborough Studios. The season lasted only twelve weeks in summer 1999. Here Ralph Fiennes gave his *Coriolanus* and *Richard II* for director Jonathan Kent, who had invited Steve Tompkins to work his magic on a small budget. Tompkins was the man of the moment. The buzz was good for his Royal Court, which was to open the following year. This prompts a digression on the Royal Court.

A diversion on the first theatre project by Haworth Tompkins

Haworth Tompkins were the youngest of the five practices I had suggested to the English Stage Company that they interview – these were the days before the lengthy 'procurement rules' of the European Union, adopted soon after by the Arts Council. Late in 1994, the technical staff of the Royal Court had called in a fellow director at TPC, Jerry Godden, because they thought that some corrections were needed both to the sound system and to a structurally dangerous fly tower. They were thinking of applying to the National Lottery for a grant of £3 million. On my first visit I suggested to general manager Graham Crowley that they might go for more money with a more ambitious approach and could benefit from employing an architect. 'Oh my God,' groaned Crowley. 'Do we really need one of those?' Nevertheless, selection wheels were set in motion. The brief was deliberately vague. We – that is, some members of the board, some senior staff, plus Godden and I – spent a day interviewing five architects. We tactfully withdrew when the five firms were reduced to two. One was the theatrically inexperienced Haworth Tompkins, which I had a hunch about and whom I had met only recently on a romantic but unfulfilled project for the conversion of a small factory in the East End of London into a theatre space. The other was Levitt Bernstein, represented by Axel Burrough, who had already done such a great job on what had been their first theatre, the Royal Exchange Manchester (see Chapter 13).

The director of the Royal Court, Stephen Daldry, met the shortlist of two. He chose Haworth Tompkins for two good reasons. First, the Court had a long tradition of supporting young talent and in 1995 Daldry was thirty-five and Steve Tompkins thirty-six. Second, if Levitt Bernstein could make such a good job of their first theatre why not Haworth Tompkins if, like them, they were supported by a theatrically experienced design team?

Tompkins soon made a totally original contribution to the project which was that nobody owned the earth under the road in front of the theatre and that the council had no plans for the redundant subterranean ladies' lavatory in the middle of Sloane Square. Tompkins suggested digging out under the road, reaching out to that stair in the square and in between constructing a subterranean warren of theatre bar, lavatories and a bookshop. The complexities of acquiring a long lease on *terra incognita* caused a five-month hiatus which nearly did for the whole project. It was five years from appointment of the design team to opening night, during which time the

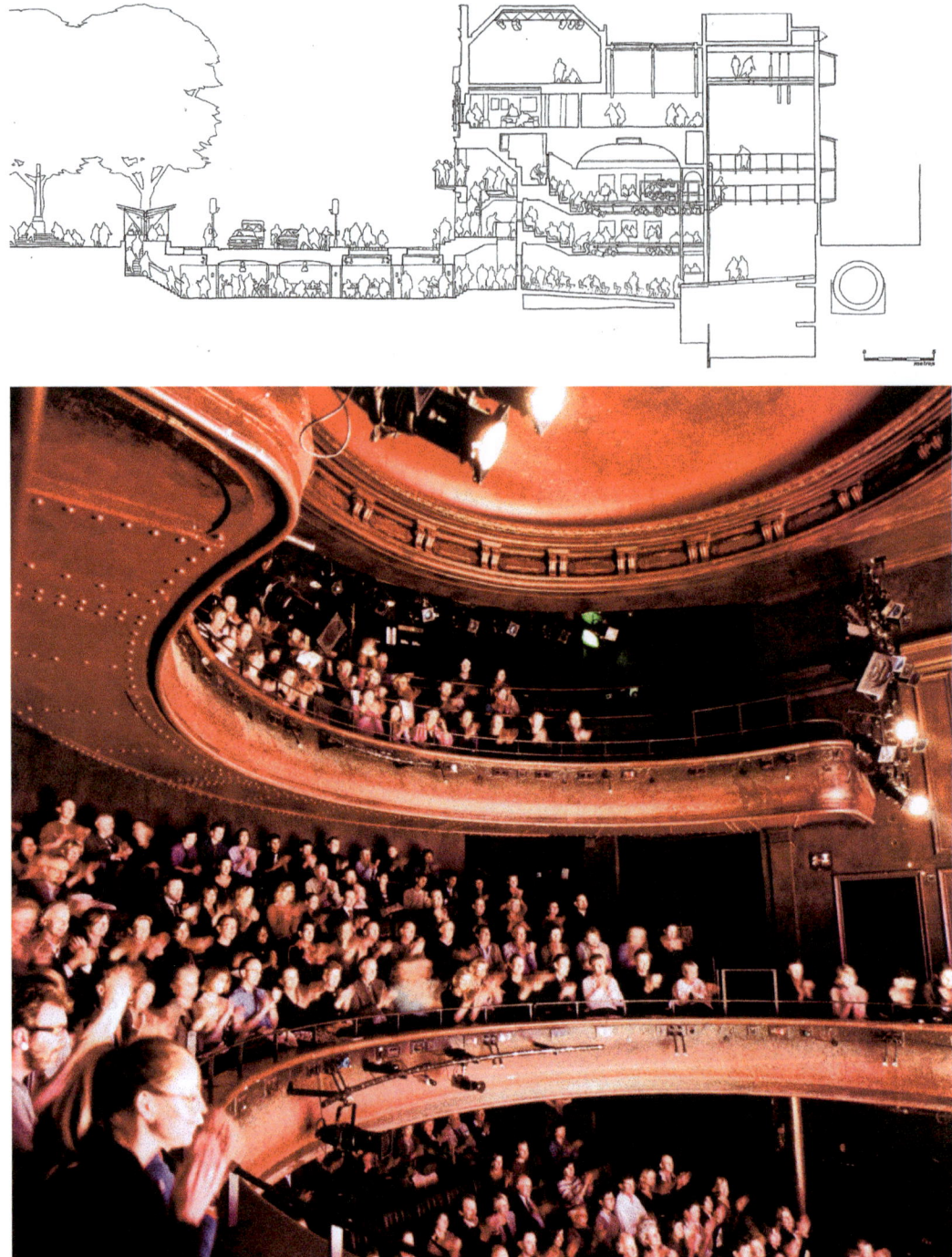

8.3 *Royal Court Theatre 1888 renovated 2000: long section of extension to Sloane Square over auditorium.*

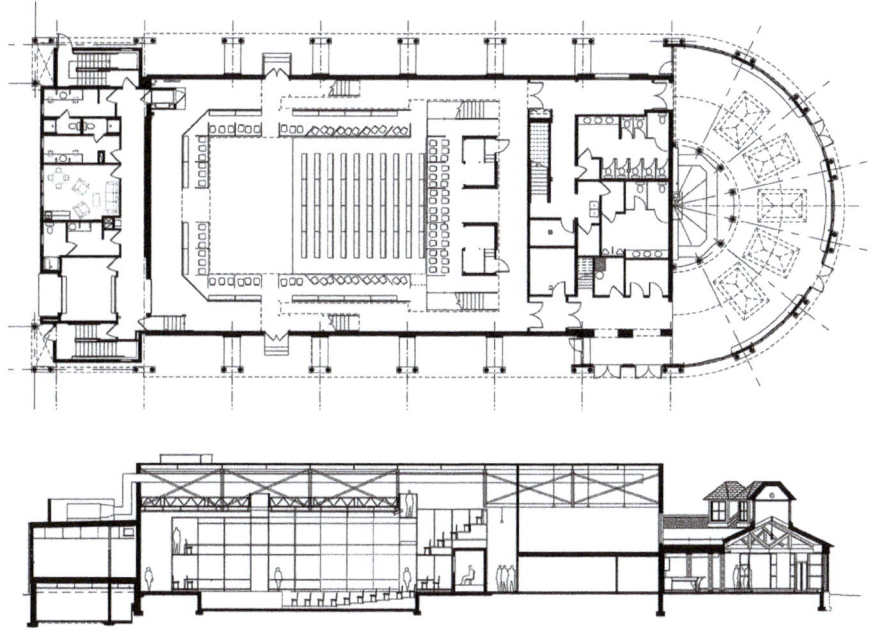

8.4 *Tina Packer Playhouse Lenox Massachusetts 2001. Architects' drawings over auditorium.*

Court decamped to the similarly small-scaled Duke of York's. Time allowed Tompkins to make a second original contribution which was to find a fresh aesthetic for the renovation of old theatres, especially those that had a convoluted history. At the beginning of the twentieth century Harley Granville-Barker and later George Bernard Shaw had done some of their best work at the Court. It was a cinema from 1932 until it was hit by a bomb in the Second World War. It reopened in 1952 and in 1956 the English Stage Company, under the direction of George Devine and managed by producer Oscar Lewenstein, chose the Court as their home for new playwriting.

Tompkins's approach to decoration of such a time-honoured relic was radical. He rejected the usual approach with dilapidated old theatres, which was to research the original colours and then gild away. Instead, Tompkins could be found, after the builders had left of an evening, up a ladder, chipping away at the plaster to reveal either 'an interesting surface' or the structural steelwork beneath. He would attach a puzzling note to the contractors instructing them not to clean up as this was the finish he wanted. Tompkins intuitively understood that the very fabric which has enclosed the ephemeral retains memories. It has to be said that such a deceptively simple approach can cost a lot of money; £25 million was resourcefully raised by Daldry and the Royal Court chairman, dramatist John Mortimer QC. Such an approach can best be summed up in the enigmatic words of playwright Eugene O'Neill in his play of 1928, *Strange Interlude*: 'The only living life is in the past and future . . . the present is an interlude . . . a strange interlude in which we call on past and future to bear witness we are living.'

A scaffolding theatre for Shakespeare and Co. in Massachusetts

In 1978 a Briton, Tina Packer, founded Shakespeare and Co. at Lenox in the Berkshires of western Massachusetts. There the wealthy and cultured of near equidistant Boston and New York had, for over a century, emigrated for the summer to build their own three-storey mansions, politely known as 'cottages'. Packer's company performed in the open air in the gardens of Edith Wharton's cottage before acquiring a nearby property which had most recently been a boarding school. Here were many outbuildings, one of which had been built by the US Army during the war, a Quonset hut, one of over 150,000 which were manufactured in America during the Second World War.

The Quonset hut at Lenox had later become a school gymnasium that doubled as a dreadful flat-floor theatre with a raised stage added at the far end. A semi-sprung timber floor had been laid over a concrete slab. The roof was sound and had wooden transverse trusses tied front to back with steel members. All this supported a quadrant-shaped tin roof which would clearly need insulating against the drumming of the occasional downpour during the summer season, which lasted from mid-June to mid-October. Into this empty found space we might just fit a 450-seat courtyard. The snag was that the clear height measured barely 18 feet (5.5 metres) from existing flat floor to the underneath of the transverse trusses. We wanted to create a new Shakespearean playhouse with an audience on three levels: pit and two encircling tiers. How to achieve this with only 18 feet clear height?

We ignored the banal existing raised stage and dug a one-metre-deep hole in the middle of the main floor slab, 32 feet across and 50 feet from front to back (9.7 metres by 12.25 metres) and far enough away from the walls so as not to disturb the foundations. The original slab level, with fresh timber floor, was to be the new stage level backed by a 'house' which completed the

8.5 Théâtre des Bouffes du Nord *Paris 1878 acquired by Peter Brook 1974. Photo by Jean-Guy Lecat, a key member of Brook's team.*

rectangular courtyard theatre fabricated of scaffolding. Such is the third and very permanent scaffolding theatre in an usual setting,

On three sides of the hole we stacked audience on two levels with canvas fronts laced on to the scaffolding, an idea lifted from Foster's Tricycle. The tiers were four feet deep front to back with space for a single row and some standing behind. The centre area was dug out to three feet below slab level and equipped with padded pit benches easily arranged either for end-stage or for an Elizabethan-style Guthrie thrust. Beyond the main hall was a semicircular new-build foyer and bar opening out onto a terrace with fine views of the whole property. The architect was George Marsh of the Boston firm Payette with whom I had collaborated earlier on a modest school theatre elsewhere in Massachusetts. The Founders' Theatre Lenox, now renamed the Tina Packer Playhouse, cost only $2.5 million (£1.9 million) and opened in summer 2001.

Peter Brook's *Bouffes du Nord* in Paris and the Majestic in Brooklyn

It is now the moment to examine two 'proper' but derelict theatres found by Brook and his team: the *Bouffes du Nord* of 1876 which became his home and the younger Majestic Theatre Brooklyn of 1904 which was to become Brook's temporary New York base. The latter is now called the BAM Harvey Theater after Harvey Lichtenstein, who was the president of the Brooklyn Academy of Music from 1967 to 1999 and had a fine record of presenting experimental dance and drama. Lichtenstein and Brook were a good match.

The finding of a worthwhile derelict theatre is a rare romantic adventure. What Brook was seeking was 'a glowing space'. What appealed to him about both was their warmth. He analysed what makes a space at once intimate and epic. It was 'the rigorously mathematic rightness of the proportions. Proportion is harmony.' Jean-Guy Lecat, who had joined Brook as technical director in 1975, identified some of the qualities that made the *Bouffes* intimate:

> I think it has something that has to do with the height: paradoxically the higher the ceiling in a theatre, the more intimate it feels, whereas a low ceiling makes a space feel big. Something one doesn't find in other theatres is the vertical accent of the columns: the eye is always stopped at the balconies and never seeks further so we see half the volume.

It was the unusual plan of the *Bouffes* that had contributed to its failure in its original arrangement as much to its success in its reincarnation. The plan scheme of the *Bouffes* is elliptical, as are many fine multi-tiered horseshoe opera and playhouses, but uniquely elliptical in that this ellipse was not set on the centre line but at right angles to it. The result had been both rotten sightlines from the sides to a proscenium stage and an uneasy junction between the worlds of actor and of audience. The original oval ceiling was supported by sixteen identical arches, eleven for the audience, three for a narrow proscenium, which was eight metres wide, plus one blank arched panel each side of the proscenium. In 1876 there had been twelve rows of stalls in a shallow curve following a conventionally bowed orchestra rail. Brook's team did not restore this curve and instead chose the geometry of the balconies to introduce just five more steeply radiused rows to embrace the front half of an acting area, the centre of which was moved forward through the proscenium arch. The warmth of the old plaster walls allowed intimacy for

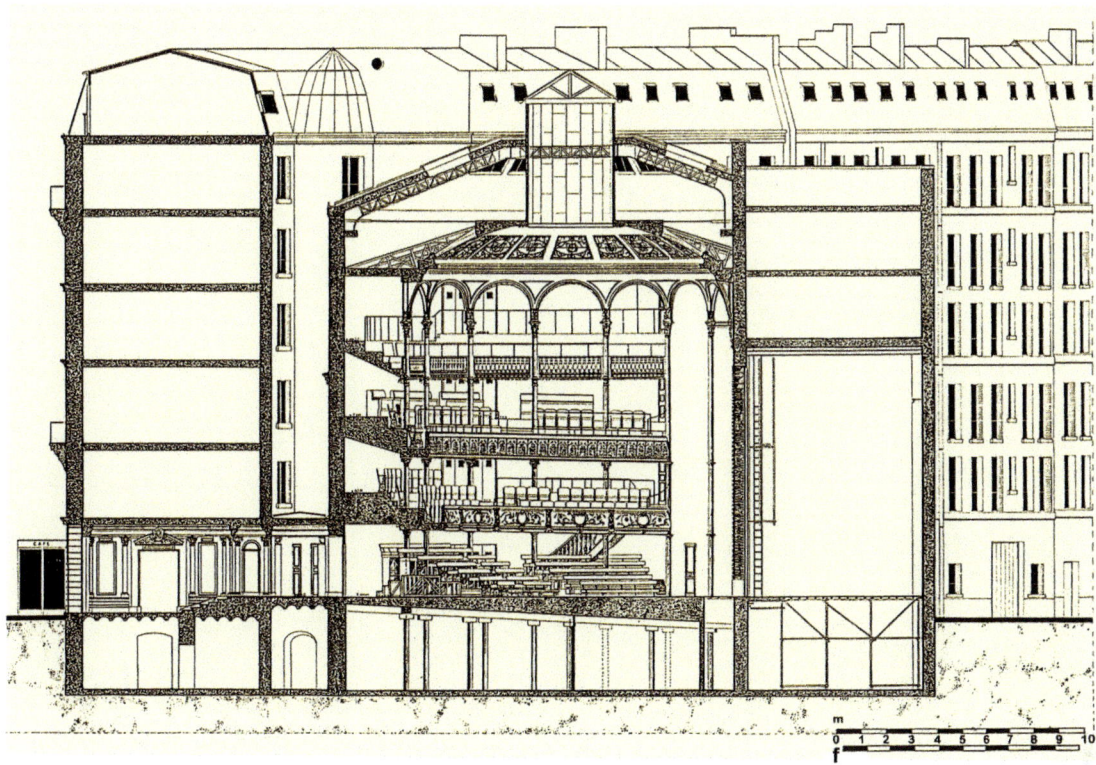

8.6 Théâtre des Bouffes du Nord, *long section, as adapted for Peter Brook and drawn by Jean-Guy Lecat.*

The Cherry Orchard and grandeur for *The Mahabharata*, the plaster having been lovingly distressed by designer Chloé Obolensky, who had joined Brook in 1982.

Brook met the derelict *Bouffes* at just the right moment in 1974. A reduction in volume of the empty fly tower by the recent conversion of the top half into offices had made good acoustics even better. Although I had earlier visited the *Bouffes* I did not see a show there until *Impressions de Pelléas* in 1992. However, I did see Brook's *Mahabharata* and *Cherry Orchard* at the Majestic in Brooklyn New York City in 1987 and 1988.

In 1987 a New York season for *The Mahabharata* had been dependent on finding the right venue. The rediscovery of the Majestic by Brook, Lecat and Lichtenstein was triggered by the latter remembering the existence of the boarded-up wreck in dark and dangerous Fulton Street Brooklyn where, in happier days, Noël Coward and Ethel Barrymore had played. It had become, briefly, a cinema and had finally closed in 1968. The trio had already inspected and rejected every other alternative.

The Majestic held 1,800 when built in 1904 by J.B. McElfatrick and his son W.M. McElfatrick, who jointly built over two hundred theatres throughout the USA. In 1986 on the day that the derelict Majestic had to be assessed this had to be done in the dark. The safety curtain could not be raised, and all they had were hand torches. Yet they all felt that the Majestic was the answer – there was just the practical question of how intimacy could be achieved. Over lunch

8.7 *Majestic Theatre New York 1904 as adapted for Peter Brook 1987 by Jean-Guy Lecat and Hardy Holzman Pfeiffer Associates architects.*

Lecat sketched out a possible solution, Brook accepted it and Lichtenstein said that he would raise the money.

In 1904 those at the back of each level at the Majestic saw the stage as through a letter box, their sightlines curtailed by the level above. Lecat's solution had five key components. First raise stage level by 1.5 metres and carry that acting level out into the auditorium. Second take off the front rows of the middle level and carry the remaining seating there at a constant radius down to the new thrusting acting area. Third chop off the front five rows of the top tier to remove said letter-box effect for the back rows of the seating in the level below and rake what was left more steeply. Fourth seat the whole remaining auditorium with armless padded benches as at the *Bouffes*. Fifth remove box fronts but keep the boxes, now four a side rather than six, for actors and musicians not for audience – and certainly not for stage lights. A well-known firm of New York theatre architects, Hardy Holzman Pfeiffer Associates, were employed by Lichtenstein to carry out the wishes of the *Bouffes* team in such a way that the theatre could be used by others after they had left. For the cost of only $8 million New York had acquired a 'new' 860-seat theatre. Subsequently it was smartened up with 'proper' seats and used as an occasional cinema, which some regard as a pity.

The regeneration of the Majestic in 1987 benefited not only from experiences gained at the *Bouffes* but also from the fact that this was a well-proportioned theatre which could withstand radical and rapid remodelling. For *The Mahabharata* the apparently bare stage was alternately huge and intimate as that epic demanded. At the end of *The Cherry Orchard*, Madame

Ranyevskaya and family depart their empty home, inadvertently leaving their elderly servant locked inside the once-friendly house now full of emptiness. On the night I was there much of the audience must have been unfamiliar with Chekhov's play and so applauded Firs' final entrance having mistaken it for the first of the curtain calls.

Finally in New York, one more of Lecat's temporary transformations: of the Vivian Beaumont theatre at Lincoln Center. The 1965 Vivian Beaumont had failed as either a thrust stage or a scenic theatre, as Guthrie had forecast (Chapter 4). I had first visited the Beaumont in early 1977 to see Joseph Papp's New York Shakespeare Festival company in *The Threepenny Opera*, which used microphones, one of the last shows before Papp gave up. It had been dark for three years when Brook's team was searching for somewhere in New York with a natural acoustic for *La tragédie de Carmen* that had opened at the *Bouffes* two years earlier. Lecat said he could fix the Vivian Beaumont for *Carmen* and keep the capacity of 1,140. He succeeded. I saw that production: ninety minutes, four principals, no chorus and a chamber orchestra. The limited season ran for a full six months in 1984.

The theatre seemed much smaller than I had remembered from the earlier visit. Lecat had brought the scenic opening down to nine metres and the back wall of the vast scenic stage appeared so much closer than before. All done with apparently solid concrete/timber walls which I thought then to be part of the mooted reconstruction, which it turned out never happened. The 'walls' around the stage plus an apparent ceiling were theatrical artifice. This resulted in unassisted acoustics at the Beaumont finally working. Empiricist Lecat had been up in the roof tearing out the original absorption with his bare hands. New York producer of *Carmen* Roy Somlyo wrote in *The Open Circle*, published in 2003: 'Jean-Guy Lecat has never been given the credit he deserved for turning the Vivian Beaumont from what Joseph Papp termed "unusable" into a viable performance space.' After Brook and team had gone the theatre soon went back to business as usual: mostly amplified musicals with the performers individually miked and for which the Vivian Beaumont, like the Olivier, is well suited.

A ballroom and a shipyard adapted for single shows presented by Bryden and Dudley

Playwright Tony Harrison's three-part reworking of medieval Mysteries had been seven years in the making. The trilogy was titled *The Mysteries: Part I The Creation; Part II The Nativity; Part III Doomsday*. The creative team was led by director Bill Bryden, designer Bill Dudley, musician John Tams and production manager Jason Barnes, who had also transferred Cottesloe productions to many different places.

The Lyceum had closed after Gielgud's *Hamlet* in 1939, the theatre having been acquired by the London County Council for a road-widening scheme in the Strand that fortunately never happened. After the war, the LCC sold a lease to Mecca, who needed a ballroom having been asked to vacate the Royal Opera House which had become theirs for the duration. The result was the Lyceum Ballroom, which opened in 1951 and was run by Mecca until 1984. The stage level had been extended to the back of the stalls, leaving the two circles above complete with their original seats. Hence most of Bertie Crewe's florid auditorium of 1904 was still there.

It occurred to me that a superfluous flat-floor dance hall within a dusty Edwardian theatre, unused as such for nearly half a century and situated at the other end of Waterloo Bridge from the NT, might be a good place in which to present *The Mysteries* to more people than could ever be fitted into the Cottesloe. The opportunity had been occasioned by NT director Hall's announcement that, at the close of the final season of *The Mysteries*, he would close the Cottesloe, the government subsidy being insufficient to run three theatre spaces. I persuaded Pilbrow that his producing arm, Theatre Projects Associates, might bring the Cottesloe company across Waterloo Bridge if private backing could be found. Anthony Field, who had been finance director of the Arts Council of Great Britain before becoming vice chairman of Theatre Projects, said he could do just that and the project went ahead.

I negotiated a twelve-week season with the Mecca manager. I was unaware that there was a developer's plan afoot to turn the Lyceum into a casino at the end of our season. Fortunately for the arts of theatre the developer, Brent Walker, got into lengthy trouble and was wound up after a serious fraud trial.

Reanimating the Lyceum as a live theatre after a gap of forty-four years was not easy. But the season became a well-publicised success which contributed to the changes of heart which led to the casino proposal being stopped in its tracks. In 1996 the Lyceum was converted back into a successful live theatre. From 1999 to 2022 a single musical, *The Lion King*, has held that stage.

Another instance of unusual promenading took place in Govan in 1990 when Glasgow was European City of Culture. Special funds were made available and the same team of Bryden and Dudley took over an abandoned shipbuilders' yard. Bryden described the evening thus: 'We build *The Ship* – the liner in fact – and at the end of the evening it is launched.' In the engine shed of shipbuilders Harland and Wolff Dudley created, in steel, a liner that was launched into an infinity of smoke at the end of a slipway once that half of the audience seated in three galleries which formed the steel ribs of the hull had left their places and been given the task of removing the timber supports prior to the launch. This ship/theatre, long and narrow, held 550 seated and 350 promenading.

Dudley pulled these threads together in his programme note for *The Ship*:

> During the last 1,000 years the most successful European theatres have all pretty well followed the same lines and the same size. The Shakespearean theatre, the small Victorian music halls, the Spanish courtyard theatres, all have the same dimensions, with a horseshoe of galleries above a pit-like space in the middle. All the best theatres – the theatres that actors love to act in and audiences to be in – have the same approximate size and basic ground plan. If you take away the nautical aspect, that is what I've done here in *The Ship* . . . It's certainly the most ambitious thing that I've ever designed . . . well if you take it off the slipway, it would make a very good theatre.

One summer evening I was lucky enough to witness a launching of Dudley's ship.

9

Regenerating the old offers an antidote to modernism: English theatres of the eighteenth and nineteenth centuries

The Almeida Islington and the Lawrence Batley, Huddersfield

Reflections on what the nineteenth century can offer theatricality as an antidote to modernism start, perhaps surprisingly, with two buildings that had been places of worship before becoming theatres. The Almeida in North London had been built in 1837 for the Islington Literary and Scientific Society. In 1890 it was acquired by the Salvation Army, who added a wrap-around balcony and stayed there until 1955. In 1980 it became a theatre, having evolved gradually under the watchful eye of architect Mark Foley, who worked for Pierre Audi, a young opera and theatre director. He had bought it to run as a simply appointed performance space. The Almeida opened with an eclectic policy of presenting major innovative musicians and companies such as Cheek by Jowl, Joint Stock and Théâtre de Complicité. When Audi became artistic director of the Dutch National Opera in 1988 he had less time for the Almeida. In 1990 Ian McDiarmid and Jonathan Kent began a twelve-year reign as joint artistic directors. Many of their productions transferred to the West End.

Seating only 325, the Almeida is now a theatre space at once epic and intimate. It has seventy-five more seats than the physically less interesting Donmar, the only other London fringe theatre that has been comparable in achievement. Both the atmosphere and the geometry of the Almeida are special. When in 2014 Rupert Goold's award-winning production of *King Charles III* was transferred to Wyndham's, they took the apsidal back wall of the Almeida with them, replicated in painted fibreglass. And then on to Broadway.

In 1994 what had been a large Wesleyan chapel in Huddersfield before being gutted to fit in four full-size squash courts was converted into a theatre. These were removed by the Kirklees local authority's own architects, for whom I conceived a newly constructed courtyard on three levels which opened in 1994. The connection between preaching and play-acting was here harder to sense because the original interior had long since vanished. But both the Almeida and Huddersfield raise the tantalising thought of how church and stage connect, something some of

9.1 *First night Lawrence Batley Theatre Huddersfield 1994 within already gutted chapel.*

us had realised when forty years earlier the drama had arrived at the Assembly Hall of the Church of Scotland for the Edinburgh Festival.

Wrote music critic Andrew Porter in the *Guardian* of 19 November 1994:

> The star of this year of the Huddersfield Contemporary Music Festival was a place: the Lawrence Batley Theatre, a 477-seater created within a great Wesleyan chapel that Joseph Kaye, in 1819, built to sacred harmonic proportions – harmonious proportions based on the, rod, pole or perch and on 4, 3 and 2 – that were respected by Iain Mackintosh, a member of Theatre Projects Consultants and author of *Architecture, Actor and Audience*, who was prominent in the planning of the Edinburgh Festival Theatre and the new Glyndebourne; the Batley crowns a year of triple triumph. It is a three-tier courtyard theatre at once neo-Georgian and modern, flexible, as old stages were, to advance through the proscenium and command 'the position of power'; ridotto-ready to throw stage and auditorium into a one-level ballroom.

1976 and the start of a movement to save historic theatres

The move to awaken the best old theatres was gathering support among both theatre folk and conservationists in the mid-1970s just when efficient new modern playhouses were being proudly unveiled. The theatre profession had hitherto assumed that Britain's romantic provincial theatres would always be there. In the Second World War fewer British theatres had been lost than in continental Europe. But in Britain the problem was that commercial developers were substituting slick supermarkets for empty Empires. Bingo offered a reprieve only for some. It was not just the distant provinces that suffered. Actor Robert Eddison told me that immediately before the Second World War he could tour the inner and outer London suburban theatres for half a year and still sleep each night in his own bed in Chelsea. By the 1970s most of these and many more in the provinces had gone. In America and Britain both the theatre profession and the wider public began to realise that much of what was left of our theatrical heritage might not survive if nothing was done.

In 1976 the League of Historic American Theatres was founded, America having lost in peacetime an even higher proportion of their fine old theatres than had wartime Europe. In the same year, the UK Parliament passed a private member's bill which set up the Theatres Trust 'to promote the better protection of theatres for the benefit of the nation'. The procedure for a private member's bill is arcane. Few become law. They are usually one of many parliamentary procedures for airing a topic which, if it strikes a chord with both members of parliament and the public, may result in government action. The Theatres Trust Bill was unusual in that it immediately received cross-party support and speedily became law. Supporters included Hugh Jenkins, the left-wing Labour MP for Putney who had been a Minister for the Arts in the government of Harold Wilson.

Jenkins became the first part-time director but lacked both a salary and a desk. The Trust's first chairman, the ubiquitous Lord Goodman, found funds from a well-advised Greater London Council committee set up to ensure that the right groups received 'death bed grants' on the winding up of the GLC in 1986. The Theatres Trust received the freeholds of the Garrick and Lyric theatres. The assignment of the long lease of a third, the Lyceum where *The Mysteries* had been staged in 1985, was bungled and in lieu the Trust now receives in cash from the current owner of the Lyceum a sum equivalent to the price for four best seats for every performance. The total receipts, from the two leases and these tickets, provide the Trust with an annual income independent of government. In 2019 this was worth over £550,000 and covered two thirds of the Trust's then current annual expenditure. The balance is raised from private sources.

In September 1976, the Arts Council of Great Britain announced a cut in its annual Housing the Arts budget from £1.15 million to £0.5 million. This seed money had brought in the capital funding principle of one third from central funds (ACGB), one third from the local authority and one third from the private sector, which had led to the creation of new theatres in Leatherhead, Sheffield, Cardiff, Derby and Clwyd. Nevertheless, in 1976, disturbed perhaps by cost overruns and building delays on the NT, the Arts Council shied away from the creation of new theatre buildings.

In October of that year I gathered signatures for the customary letter of protest to *The Times* and a project was born. The creation of the Theatres Trust had made people realise that nobody knew what old theatres in Britain had survived the bombers and the developers. In 1957 actress Vivien Leigh had led a procession down Whitehall to protest at the GLC granting permission for yet another office block in place of the magnificent 1835 St James's Theatre which had been managed by her then husband, Laurence Olivier. They failed to stop the developer. In 1971 London suddenly lost the Granville Theatre of Varieties in Fulham of 1898 with its unique ceramic-tiled auditorium by Matcham. This led to the GLC starting a register of all the surviving theatres in London. The Trust did not know where to start in the rest of England because nobody knew how many theatres had already been lost and which of the dark ones were sleeping beauties worth reawakening.

A self-appointed task force then happened with the aim of publishing a guide to remaining historic theatres and lists of the lost ones. The group included Christopher Brereton, John Earl, Victor Glasstone and Michael Sell. We met irregularly in my office at Theatre Projects in Covent Garden on Saturday mornings. Along the way we were helped by too many to mention. We took five years to find out what Britain had left of its theatre heritage. None of us were paid. Our slender resources to meet minimal expenses were made up of private and public money. The latter included £5,000 from the ACGB, who had sent our good friend Peter Longman, who ran their Housing the Arts department from 1969 to 1978, to check up on us. In 1982 there came the first gazetteer of Britain's theatre heritage, at that time defined as theatres built before 1914, *Curtains!!! or A New Life for Old Theatres*, edited by Michael Sell and myself. To write the foreword we invited Ken Dodd, who had reopened the Theatre Royal Nottingham five years previously. In *Curtains!!!* Dodd celebrated '**theatres** – temples of arts, emporiums of fun, forums of debate and argument which still provide audiences and performers alike with that most magical experience of our lives – a live show!'

An exhibition opened at the Museum of London before touring to towns with theatres under threat. The tour was in the hands of historian David Wilmore, who was and still is the only man in Europe to be awarded a PhD for a thesis on nineteenth-century stage machinery.

At *Curtains!!!* we had found that of the 1,000-plus theatres in use between 1900 and 1914, 85 per cent had been demolished or irretrievably altered. Of the 15 per cent of theatres that remained 9 per cent were in use and 6 per cent, which was almost seventy theatres, were dark but possibly rescuable. One must always remember there were and still are grey areas of music halls, cinemas and flat-floor halls which have some but not all the accepted attributes of a theatre. Qualitative judgements are easy for an unofficial organisation. I proposed the principles of the *Guide Michelin*: *** (exceptional, worth a special journey), ** (*vaut le detour*) and * (excellent). As a group we made decisions and rarely argued. We were not interrupted because if you are a self-appointed homeless group nobody knows who you are, where you are or to whom you are beholden. Of the ninety-eight pre-1914 theatres then in use we designated fifty-four either *** or ** and a further sixteen *.

The Theatres Trust now knew where most of the sleeping beauties slept. Take just two, both ***, which in 2021 were still awaiting the arrival of Prince Charming: the Opera House Tunbridge Wells of 1902, which has been a pub since 1996, and the uniquely *chinoiserie* Grand Clapham Junction of 1900, a live music venue since 1991.

In 1986 Earl, previously of the GLC's Theatre Department, became the first director able to devote all his energies to the Trust. He held the post until 1995. As distinguished a scholar was Glasstone, who contributed essays about the pantheon of hitherto hardly known theatre architects. Many of the images in *Curtains!!!* came from his own incomparable collection, much of which is in his *Victorian and Edwardian Theatres* published by Thames and Hudson in 1975. I served as a trustee of the Theatres Trust for the then maximum three terms, from 1984 to 1991. Michal Sell together with Earl edited the follow-up guide: *The Theatres Trust Guide to British Theatres 1750–1950: A Gazetteer*, published in 2000 during the reign of Earl's successor as director, Peter Longman.

The rejuvenating of five great theatres

Such is the back story to the restoring of many British theatres of the eighteenth and nineteenth centuries. What follows, in date order as originally built, is a selection of five successful projects.

Interspersed are reflections on wider issues of how to handle our theatre heritage. But first a note on the official classification of historic buildings administered by a government agency now named Historic England, which is slightly different from the *Curtains!!!* star rating system lists and rates the best buildings and places which are to be protected by law. (Scotland, Wales and Northern Ireland have comparable systems.) In 2010 there were in England 374,000 listing entries for all types of buildings excluding churches. Of the relatively few theatres so listed in England 92 per cent were Grade II, 5.5 per cent Grade II * and 2.5 per cent Grade I. It is this top 8 per cent which matter most and where the movers and shakers of both live theatre and conservation interact. The first four theatres below are listed Grade I. The fifth, the Nottingham Theatre Royal, is Grade II*. All five were rated *** in *Curtains!!!*

Bristol, Theatre Royal, also known as the Bristol Old Vic. 1766 Thomas Patey. Many minor alterations to stage and auditorium between 1800 and 1881. Modern interventions to the whole building by Peter Moro 1973, Andrzej Blonski 2012 and Haworth Tompkins 2018.

Bury St Edmunds, Theatre Royal 1819 William Wilkins. Alterations 1906 by Bertie Crewe. Closed 1925. Partially restored by Ernest Scott 1965. Further modern interventions by Purcell, Miller and Tritton 1992 and Levitt Bernstein 2007.

Richmond Yorkshire, Theatre Royal 1788 architect unknown. Restoration 1963 by Richard Southern and Richard Leacroft. Further restoration in 1996 by Nick Allen.

Newcastle upon Tyne, Theatre Royal 1837 John and Benjamin Green. New auditorium 1895 Walter Emden. Another new auditorium 1901 Frank Matcham. Modern interventions by Renton Howard Wood Levin 1988 and Sansome Hall 2012.

Nottingham, Theatre Royal 1865 C.J. Phipps. Alterations to auditorium 1890 by C.J. Phipps and 1897 by Frank Matcham. Modern intervention by RHWL 1978.

Theatres are heavily used public buildings and need to evolve as society changes, not least in matters of safety and in the provision of facilities both backstage and front of house. However, any irreversible changes to the theatre spaces occasioned by the fashion of the day need dispassionate scrutiny. Of major mistakes the worst has been the flattening of the raked stage of the Bristol Old Vic in 1973 together with the loss of all the early-nineteenth-century under-stage machinery.

Three Georgian playhouses: Bristol, Richmond Yorkshire and Bury St Edmunds

Val May had been artistic director of the Nottingham Playhouse from 1957 to 1961 when he moved to Bristol. The magnificent 770-seat new Nottingham Playhouse opened in December 1963 having been designed by the foremost theatre architect of the day, Peter Moro. May had been closely involved. At Bristol, May quickly got Moro appointed as architect when, in March of 1966, the bicentenary year for the Theatre Royal, also known as the Bristol Old Vic, a possibility arose of acquiring the adjacent Coopers' Hall of 1744 and converting that into a grand new entrance. Much else was done to the 200-year-old theatre, which reopened in 1973. It was the product of the closest of collaborations between May and Moro who, however, had no experience of historic theatres. Neither understood why their stages had been raked for two centuries. Did they not realise that the rake was there for practical reasons which are still relevant today and not merely to set off historic perspective scenery as many had imagined?

I first saw pantomime at Bristol. (I must admit a bias to Bristol where I was born in 1937 and where, after the war, I made my first visits to any theatre when down from Edinburgh to visit my maternal grandparents in Clifton.) This was before May and Moro stripped out the entire raked stage, including the traps which made much of the magic. The Demon King would disappear down a 'fast-rise trap' stage left only to pop up, in the twinkle of an eye, through its pair stage right. But by 1973 May and Moro removed the magic machines and substituted a flat modern stage under a twentieth-century fly tower. This almost turned a unique Georgian playhouse into a picture-frame proscenium theatre, which had not been the original intention.

In 2002 a thorough conservation plan was undertaken by Donald Insall Associates advised by scholars Wilmore and Jane Root. Together they cited more than two dozen significant alterations in 236 years. However, they were unable to pinpoint the exact date when the Bristol Old Vic lost its proscenium-arch doors or the years when the forestage was cut back bit by bit. My guess is that it lost the doors and most of its forestage during major works in either 1831 or 1835 and had the little of what then remained of the forestage removed in 1881 by theatre architect C.J. Phipps.

In *The Theatres Trust Guide to British Theatres 1750–1950* Earl and Sell used their strongest language for this 'incredibly destructive act' and deplored the substitution of 'an inappropriately flat stage for the raked stage that the form and sightlines of the auditorium demand'. This was no mere antiquarian quibble. At the time the raked stage at Bristol was removed Stratford-upon-Avon was already ten years into a thirty-year period when the RSC played on a semi-permanent 1:18 rake installed over the 1932 flat stage. At the Old Vic in London in 1963 a 1:18 raked stage was inserted by Sean Kenny and laid, complete with revolve, over the original 1:24 rake. This stayed there until the NT left fourteen years later. At the Bristol Old Vic itself artistic director Richard Cottrell, an old friend and colleague from Prospect days who had succeeded May in 1975, introduced a 'temporary' rake laid over the flat Moro stage which remained there for most of Cottrell's five-year term. May and Moro had been out of step with the leaders of the theatre profession. But for the stage crew a flat stage does make life easier. The substitution of technically easy flat stages for actor-friendly rakes keeps on happening and has even been instigated by otherwise intelligent theatre consultants. Only recently one such took out the raked stage of 1902 in the listed Grade II * Theatre Royal York and substituted a flat stage, an inevitable consequence of which was the old shallow stalls were replaced by a steep rake. The last row of these now barges into the front of the dress circle.

The worst of unintended consequences at Bristol is that the precise positioning of the downstage supporting structure for the Moro/May fly tower will make it expensive to reintroduce the proscenium-arch doors that were a *sine qua non* for all Georgian playhouses – assuming the scholars can agree exactly where exactly these doors were. The downstage supports for the massive 1973 fly tower almost certainly occupy the space in plan where once were those all-important doors.

There are two aspects to this disaster which need spelling out. First, the Bristol Old Vic is the oldest playhouse in the English-speaking world which has been in continuous use. (Put aside the claims of Drury Lane and Covent Garden where successive buildings have occupied different parts of ever bigger sites.) At Bristol the theatre space did not change in either scale or position. Well before Moro, this Georgian playhouse already had a strong decorative flavour of the nineteenth century, starting as early as 1800 when architect James Saunders angled the flat auditorium ceiling when inserting a gallery. As late as 1881 Phipps introduced much of the decorative detail we see today. And yet despite all this the Bristol Old Vic remains in essence a Georgian playhouse.

9.2 Bristol Old Vic auditorium renovated 2012 by Andrzej Blonski architect over studio by Haworth Tompkins Architects 2018.

Second is that for many years nobody was quite sure how the acting area of forestage and proscenium doors in the less well-documented Georgian playhouses were arranged. Neither Southern, who was the first to publish with *The Georgian Playhouse* in 1948, nor Richard Leacroft, whose *The Development of the English Playhouse* was published in 1973, understood quite how the Georgian forestage shrunk in depth in the first decade of the nineteenth century. The forestage and proscenium-arch doors did not just vanish overnight when changes in taste and technical advances in lighting allowed the performer to retreat upstage into a picture-frame proscenium. Southern, who was involved with the theatre department of Bristol University from 1947 to 1969, never offered a conjectural layout of the original Bristol forestage of 1766. Leacroft's 1973 book did not explore the gradual shrinking of the Georgian forestage, nor did his second major book on the subject, *Theatre and Playhouse: An Illustrated Survey of Theatre Building from Ancient Greece to the Present Day* of 1984.

In 2018 Tompkins completed a comprehensive reorganisation of the remainder of the Bristol Old Vic. The entrance, now dressed in its own twenty-first-century style, was shifted to roughly where it had been in 1766. Inside is a friendly foyer on more than one level and of great height, the end wall of which reveals the entire outside of the back wall of the auditorium, exposed by Tompkins as if just discovered. The theatre now seats 540 and the milling space in the foyer is carefully limited in area to encourage the hustle and bustle of theatregoing. The contrast with the grand entrance through two floors of the grandiloquent Coopers' Hall of 1744, which May and Moro had introduced as a new foyer and which lasted until 2016, could not be greater. Tom Morris, formerly of the Battersea Arts Centre, where he had worked with Tompkins, and an associate director of the National Theatre, was appointed director of the BOV in 2009. Morris and Tompkins quickly agreed to put back the clock at the *piano nobile* of the Coopers' Hall and restore it as a well-proportioned assembly room for which appropriate uses would be found. Underneath the Coopers' Hall is an old cellar in which Tompkins created a galleried studio theatre full of character and possibilities for audiences of up to 180. Before Tompkins was appointed the restoration of the main house had been supervised by architect Andrzej Blonski, who had had the advantage of having worked for Moro on the 1973 renovation.

The only other two extant Georgian playhouses awoken in quick succession from long slumbers are the Theatre Royal of Richmond Yorkshire of 1788, reborn in 1963, and the Theatre Royal Bury St Edmunds of 1819, brought back to life in 1965. The Richmond theatre had closed in 1841 and had been completely altered below stage level where stone arched wine cellars were introduced occupying the whole basement. This meant that both the stage machinery and the seating in the pit had to be surmised. The evidence for how far the Richmond forestage had originally extended out into the auditorium had vanished and what was recreated in 1963 was a shallow forestage typical of the early nineteenth century rather than the 1788 original which probably came out a further four or five feet. It was a mercurial young Bristol scholar, Mark Howell, who first proposed the precise extent of Richmond's original forestage by creating a temporary platform, the forward edge of which rested on the 1963 orchestra rail. Howell brought fellow drama students from Bristol University up to Richmond and performed excerpts from plays of the period staged on his evocation of the original acting forestage. His conclusion was that in the first decades of the nineteenth century the original deep Richmond forestage had been cut back as others had been elsewhere. Howell's more accurate arrangement is available to users today, though when this is reinstated there is no orchestra pit, which in 1788 must have been where the front rows of seating are today.

In 1963 Prospect had presented the first play for 100 years at the Georgian Theatre in Richmond in the shape of Toby Robertson's production of Vanbrugh's *The Provok'd Wife* with

9.3 *Theatre Royal Bury St Edmunds: a 1906 full house over auditorium renovated in 2007.*

a young Eileen Atkins in the title role. She wrote in her 2021 autobiography *Will She Do?*: 'Restoration comedy is notoriously difficult, but once we were inside this beautiful little Georgian theatre we knew exactly how to play it.' The show then transferred to the West End and played the Vaudeville where it flopped in that flat-on-frontal auditorium of 1926.

The earliest argument for the actors' retreat upstage into a pictorial stage was the aesthetic one advanced by George Saunders who, in his *Treatise on Theatres* of 1790, argued:

> The great advance of some stages into the body of the theatre is too absurd, I imagine, as ever again to be practised. The actor, instead of being so brought forwards, ought to be thrown back at certain distance from the spectator's eye, and stand within the scenery of the stage, in order to make a part of that pleasing picture for which all dramatic exhibitions are calculated.

Some of the theatre managements of the day were supportive of Saunders, welcoming the opportunity to install additional money-making front rows in much of the space once taken up by the original deep forestages and orchestra pits.

In Georgian theatres the audience surrounded the actors on three sides of the stage just as they had in Shakespearean open-air playhouses and on the forestages of Jacobean and Restoration indoor playhouses. See the recreation of both Shakespeare's Globe on London's Bankside and, a few yards away, the candlelit indoor Sam Wanamaker Playhouse, based on seventeenth-century drawings which are discussed in Chapter 7.

The restoration of the Theatre Royal Bury St Edmunds of 1819 presented slightly different problems. Southern at first thought it a Regency theatre built without proscenium-arch doors, which certainly had been lacking in Wyatt's Drury Lane of 1812 though they were re-installed by Samuel Beazley in 1822. All were surprised in 1961 when workmen clearing the clutter of its later life as a barrel store, after both stage and stalls areas had been stripped down to the bare earth, discovered door frames in the curved coves each side of the proscenium arch. They also found one of the two magnificent original doors which was copied to make a pair. A hasty restoration got under way.

In 1963 brewers Greene King, whose head office and brewery were next door, had moved their barrels out and had granted a twenty-one-year lease for a peppercorn to a quickly formed trust. The theatre which was to reopen in 1965 had closed in 1925, less than twenty years after the fashionable London theatre architect Bertie Crewe (d.1937) had partially remodelled it. Crewe had those proscenium-arch doors plastered over and the forestage cut back. The electricity was installed and the overflowing auditorium redecorated with Edwardian exuberance. *The Stage Guide of 1912* tells us that it then held 'about 800'. Now the capacity is 360. The new manager in 1906, the flamboyant Eade Montefiore, had aimed high when he reopened with a week of grand opera presented by Britain's only touring opera company, the Moody-Manners. Their repertoire consisted of *Faust* (Monday), *Carmen* (Tuesday), *Lohengrin* (Wednesday), *Maritana* (Thursday), *Cavalleria Rusticana* and *I Pagliacci* (Friday), *Tannhauser* (Saturday matinee) and *The Bohemian Girl* (Saturday evening). Montefiore did not last long. Variety twice nightly was tried and in 1910 the motion pictures. Neither succeeded. Bury lost its only live theatre.

After 1965 and for the first ten years Bury enjoyed a roller coaster of precarious finance and glorious success. An actor-manager in the old mould, George Baker, moved his own company, Candida Plays to Bury St Edmunds. Baker invited Noël Coward over from Switzerland for *Private Lives*, with which Baker had chosen to open his first season. The next year he presented the seventy-fifth anniversary production of *Charley's Aunt* which had had its world premiere in 1892 at this very theatre. In 1968 Prospect visited for the first time, with Richard Briers as

Richard in *Richard III*, and again in 1973 with Derek Jacobi in the title role of *Pericles*, another Robertson production on its way to international festivals at Edinburgh, Baalbek, Cairo and Athens. In 1975 success was crowned by a 999-year lease being granted to the National Trust and the theatre being listed Grade I, then one of only ten such in the whole of England and Wales.

My own involvement at Bury had started in 1963, having been introduced to the theatre by friend and Prospect colleague at Oxford Elizabeth Sweeting, whose involvement with Suffolk dated back to when she had been general manager of the Aldeburgh Festival. I was involved at Bury up to 1979, when I was commissioned by the National Trust to write *Pit, Boxes and Gallery: The Story of the Theatre Royal, Bury St Edmunds 1819 to 1976*. For this Leacroft, accompanied by wife and co-author Helen, researched an isometric of Bury as it was in 1819 which appeared first in that National Trust guide and later his own work where comparisons were made with the Barnwell Theatre Cambridge

I joined the building committee chaired by Lord Euston. His was the courtesy title of the eldest son of the Duke of Grafton, who was a direct descendant of that duke who, in the first years of the eighteenth century, was both Lord Chamberlain and the patron of the Norwich theatre company. Their circuit stretched from King's Lynn in the north to Colchester in the south and to Cambridge in the west (see page 29). Author and playwright Angus Wilson, who lived locally and was enthusiastically involved from the outset, could not have dreamt up a better cast for Euston's committee. There were the brothers Blackburne, who ran a first-class

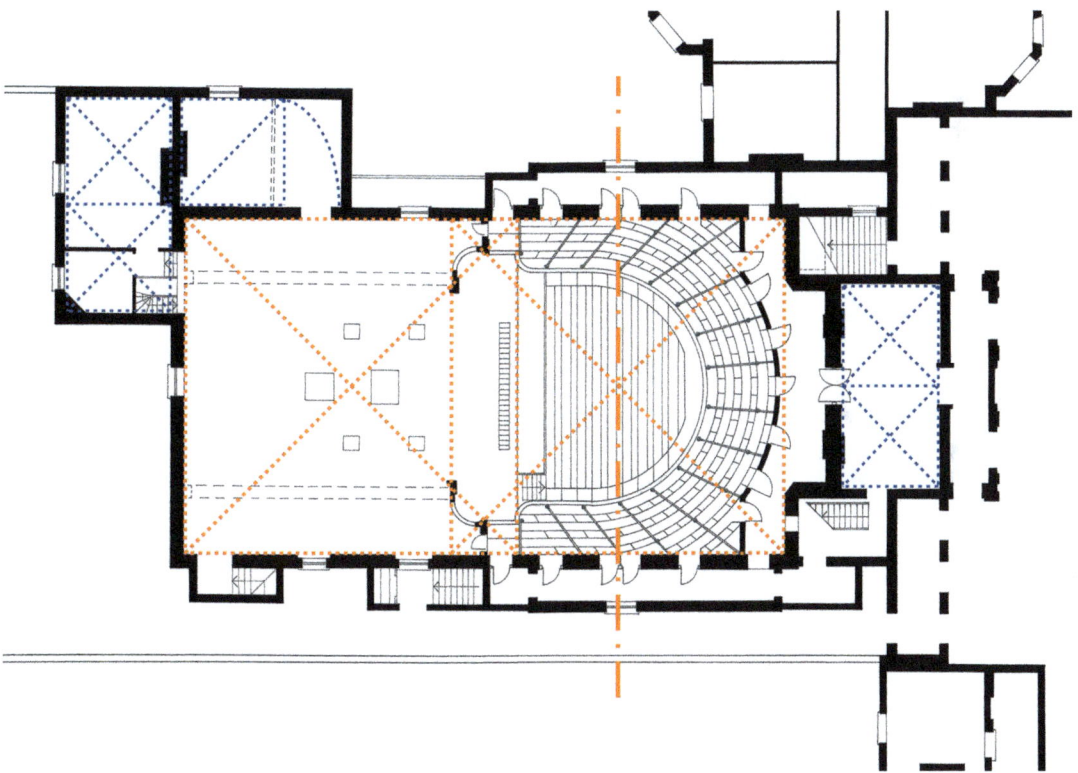

9.4 *Theatre Royal Bury St Edmunds 1819, William Wilkins' geometry explained by Axel Burrough of Levitt Bernstein.*

preparatory school up the road, the distinguished Air Vice Marshal Stanley Vincent, who had flown and fought in both world wars, plus Doris Pleydell-Bouverie and Olga Ironside-Wood, either of whom could have inspired the character of Lady Billows in Benjamin Britten's comic opera *Albert Herring*, set in Suffolk. All contributed huge amounts of energy. The only thing lacking was expertise in what were the essential elements of a late Georgian playhouse which ought to be recreated if they had already been removed.

We all made mistakes. I did not oppose the installation of a new flat stage. I failed to champion the original raked one as was evident from the holes for the supporting beams in the side walls. Today the upstage actor on the flat stage loses those of his audience sat at the back of the shallow stalls. The well-meaning local architect, Ernest Scott, inserted a centre gangway in those stalls because he liked the look and this was what you then found in an Italian horseshoe-shaped opera house, and anyway that is what they had at Bristol at the time. Now we know that this was an error and that no Georgian playhouse ever had a centre gangway. In 2007 the architect Axel Burrough for Levitt Bernstein established the precise *ad quadratum* of Wilkins's original geometry and got a lot right which we had got wrong.

Half a century later the stage at Bury is still not raked. Neither has the original forestage been reintroduced. What is now offered is the alternative of forestage or orchestra pit when originally the latter had been permanently placed on the audience side of a permanent forestage. Later I discovered that not only had the stages of Bristol and Bury St Edmunds been flattened but that the *Markgräflisches Opernhaus* Bayreuth of 1748, the *Cuvilliés* Munich of 1753 and *La Scala* Milan of 1778 are also three of the great European theatres of the eighteenth century both to have lost their forestages and to have had their stages flattened. At Bayreuth this happened in 1961 and, as at Bristol, the original stage machinery was removed. The forestage was cut back and staircases at the side were introduced to provide entrances to the orchestra area for the musicians, who originally would have entered on the level of the parterre where many of the audience stood. The Bayreuth theatre was meticulously photographed for *Baroque Theatre* by Margarete Baur-Heinhold in 1967. Then, in 2018, when most of the fabric and all the paintwork was being restored, further 'improvements' were made. The little that was left of the original forestage was made removable to allow the musicians to play immediately in front of the proscenium arch on the spot where the performers sang standing on the long-gone 1748 forestage. Why? The technicians who bring the Bavarian State Opera from Munich to the *Markgräflisches Opernhaus* for an annual season have found it more convenient to treat this gem of an eighteenth-century theatre as a nineteenth-century picture-frame stage so that their existing picture-frame productions of eighteenth-century operas from the similarly emasculated *Cuvilliés* could fit more easily. Throughout Europe directors, stage designers and all-powerful technicians have decided that revivals of eighteenth-century operas should now take place on flat stages and the singers perform behind the proscenium arch five metres upstage from where the acting forestage once was. The decoration may be authentic, but how they are used is not.

Two ninteenth-century provincial theatres with porticos: the Theatres Royal of Newcastle and Nottingham

The exteriors of both Richmond and Bury were always modest. In contrast the larger Theatres Royal of both Newcastle upon Tyne and Nottingham have porticos with the customary six

9.5 *Newcastle Theatre Royal 1837 over interior by Frank Matcham 1897.*

columns just like those of three of the grandest London theatres: John Nash's Theatre Royal of 1821 in the Haymarket, Samuel Beasley's Lyceum of 1834 and Charles Barry's 1858 Royal Opera House in Covent Garden. (These are the only five remaining nineteenth-century British theatres which announce themselves so grandly.) Both Newcastle and Nottingham occupy central and spectacular city centre sites. Newcastle opened in 1837 at the top of the curved and rising Georgian Grey Street and Nottingham in 1865, dominating Theatre Square in the city centre. Nothing beats the sense of occasion of arriving for a show through a Corinthian colonnade.

Inside both Newcastle and Nottingham there have been major alterations to the auditoriums due to fires and changes in fashion. Newcastle's first interior was by the original local architects John and Benjamin Green, who must have admired Samuel Beazley's 1822 remodelling of the auditorium of Benjamin Wyatt's Drury Lane. Later at Newcastle there came entirely different auditoriums by C.J. Phipps, Walter Emden and finally the present one by Frank Matcham which is one of his finest and dates from 1901. This has been twice tweaked, in 1988 by theatre architects Renton Howard Wood Levin and again in 2012 by Sansome Hall guided by historic theatre consultant David Wilmore.

For the last fifty years Newcastle has been thought one of the best touring dates for drama. Some touring theatres are great for drama, musical theatre and pantomime and yet have stages just big enough to accommodate opera, ballet or musicals. Others are perfect for the latter but on the large side for drama. The Theatre Royal Newcastle has long been pre-eminent in both groups. It is also good for intimate comedy, which cannot be said of many overlarge touring houses new or old. What is that quality? It has much to do with character and little to do with capacity: Newcastle held 1,850 when Matcham built the present auditorium which now holds 1,250. Compare this with the more soberly decorated Grand Theatre and Opera House Leeds of 1878 which now holds 1,550. The latter is a theatre in which it is harder to raise laughs but is perfect for opera and has since 1977 been home to Opera North. Or take the 1906 King's Theatre Edinburgh which in 2019/20 held 1,315 and works for both pantomime and grand opera, perhaps due in part to the decadent style of those four fruity caryatids from the Viennese baroque on each side of the proscenium. The capacity may be reduced to nearer 1,100 when the renovations are realised in 2025. *The Stage Guide* capacities for the King's are as follows: 1912 – 2,500; 1948 – 1,950; 1971 – 1,602.

Newcastle maintained a unique status in English provincial theatre for nearly forty years from 1977 to 2014 as the third home of the Royal Shakespeare Company. The RSC presented four- or five-week-long annual visits between their summer seasons in Stratford-upon-Avon and winter ones in London. When the Royal was being renovated in 1988 the RSC maintained their annual visits to Newcastle by moving to the superb 1867 Tyne Theatre and Opera House which is listed Grade I. This had been 'rediscovered' in the mid-1970s after sixty years as a cinema during which time both auditorium and stage had been hardly touched, the latter with the most complete nineteenth-century wooden stage in Britain. Wilmore fully restored this stage and the original timber machinery twice – the second time three years after the first following a disastrous backstage fire on Christmas Day.

The indefatigable chairman of the Tyne Theatre and Opera House, Jack Dixon, staged many successful amateur seasons. In May 1963 he decided to celebrate the return to theatrical life of the Tyne in style with a professional gala. For a single performance he hired an entire production of Puccini's *Tosca* from Welsh Opera, put Newcastle's Northern Sinfonia in the pit and engaged a star cast led by Placido Domingo. We felt the building shake when, at the surprisingly bouquet-free curtain calls, a woman advanced down the centre aisle and handed something to the conductor who handed it to the first violins who handed it to the woodwind who passed it up to the streetwise Domingo. He held it up for all to see: a single red rose in an empty bottle of Newcastle Brown Ale.

Why did Newcastle become a third home for the RSC? The innate quality of the Theatre Royal? Was it because the Tyne local authorities offered funding from the outset? Was it because Britain's leading actors relished playing the Theatre Royal? More likely it was because the long-serving and powerful financial controller of the RSC, Bill Wilkinson, was himself a Geordie.

Nottingham may have a portico like Newcastle but here the resemblance ends. In the late 1960s the Theatre Royal was the most battered relic of the once prosperous Moss Empires chain of touring theatres. Half a mile away there was Britain's finest new repertory theatre, the Playhouse, which had opened in 1963 with *Coriolanus* directed by Tyrone Guthrie and starring John Neville in the title role. Neville, Peter Ustinov and Frank Dunlop were the three joint artistic directors. Against such competition there seemed little hope that the run-down Royal could attract the funds for a renovation. But the city council did buy it and paid for a thorough makeover completed in 1978. A concert hall for 2,500 was soon added alongside by the same architects who did the Theatre Royal, Renton Howard Wood Levin.

The main asset of the Theatre Royal was its prominent site and that portico. There was little else to commend it. Phipps had altered his own interior twice, in 1884 and 1890. In 1897 along came Matcham, who added on the east side a second theatre, a variety house named the Empire,

9.6 *Nottingham Theatre Royal: 1837 auditorium renovated 1978 by architects RHWL.*

which was demolished in 1969 to ease road traffic and provide better pedestrian access to the Theatre Royal.

The Phipps/Matcham auditorium was refashioned in 1978. The colour scheme was one of the first by Clare Ferraby, wife of architect Nick Thompson, who was to become the leading decorator of theatre interiors of her generation. The predominant tones of green are just right. There is enough but not too much gilding. It having been impossible to disentangle late Phipps from early Matcham, we the design team concocted some eclectic takes on the style of both. At the back of the dress circle we introduced an arc of boxes with good sightlines derived from a similarly placed glazed screen at Phipps's 1883 Royal Lyceum Edinburgh. At the back of the unchanged shallowly raked stalls, where once were the pit benches, we placed a colonnade which was sheer pastiche but allowed the circulation from foyer to stalls to work for the first time. It is easy to forget that when all these theatres were built, both in the West End and in the provinces, the grand front door was used only by those patrons who had paid high prices to sit in the first circle or the front stalls, behind which were the denizens of the pit benches who, along with the gallerygoers, had their own mean entrances. Hence when trying to democratise these Victorian and Edwardian theatres it has always been difficult to revise the circulation to allow all the audience to enter through the front door and percolate either into the now unbroken stalls or on higher levels by the new main stairs linking levels which were originally strictly separated.

That the public areas worked well was made clear on the night of 7 February 1978. It is the custom with new or renovated theatres that the first performance is 'Builders' Night', sometimes called 'The Hard Hat'. Everybody who has been involved in any way dresses to the nines and makes an occasion of the evening. All are entertained for free in both auditorium and bars. This is generally the dress rehearsal for Official Opening on the next night attended by the Lord Mayor, the Lord Lieutenant, etc. The management decided to stage both on the same evening. They asked Ken Dodd to do the honours: at six o'clock the Builders' Night and at 8.30 pm the Official Opening by the Lord Mayor. Come 8.25 pm, Ken Dodd was considering whether to finish his first show. At last, the well-tickled first house of 1,140 left to be replaced by another 1,140 who had been cheerfully drinking in the bars and foyers. Then it happened all over again at a greater length. We reached City Hall for the Mayor's reception after midnight. Nobody complained and we had the best of opening-night parties. Only the tattyfilarious Ken Dodd from Knotty Ash could have reopened the Theatre Royal 'Twice Nightly'.

Back to the recurrent subject of raked stages. At Nottingham the old fly tower and whole stage had to be replaced. In the rebuild Theatre Projects Consultants created a completely new stage house in which there was one surprise: the original raked stage was replaced with a new raked stage. It had been my job to poll the managements likely to visit pre- or post- West End tours of plays, musicals, touring opera and dance, both classical and modern. The answers surprisingly favoured a traditional raked stage, that is 1:24 or a half-inch to the foot. Most other touring theatres of that scale were still raked, as were those of London's similar-sized theatres. Another reason was that there was the need to maintain good sightlines from the back of the shallowly raked stalls to the prone figure of a dancer anywhere on stage. The floor of the last row in the stalls at the Nottingham Royal was and still is lower than the front edge of the stage. Hence there is a very shallow rake for those twenty rows of stalls. This is a plus in that it allows for the three circles above to be packed tightly down, one level above the other, giving a wonderful intimacy to the whole auditorium. However, a shallow rake in the stalls facing a flat stage would make it difficult for most of the stalls audience to see a prone figure and this was the deciding factor at Nottingham.

Many years later I was to discover another significant reason why for centuries playhouses and opera houses had permanent raked stages, in Britain at half an inch to the foot (which is 1:24) and in Europe anywhere between 1:15 and 1:30. This is because a singer or actor standing on a raked stage naturally leans slightly backward to retain verticality and such a posture opens the chest, enabling him or her better to project the voice. This was suggested to me in late 2020 by scenographer and scholar Christopher Baugh, who recalled working as a stagehand at Bristol before the rake was removed. I checked with Timothy West, brought up in Bristol, who had played the BOV both when raked and flat during half a century of touring. He recalled that the theatres he enjoyed most had rakes. Next I talked to Elizabeth Bury, widow of John Bury and his design partner, who confirmed that the semi-permanent rake at 1:18 at Stratford-upon-Avon was John's gift to the RSC. Hall, then but three years into the job as director of the RSC, had immediately realised its worth during the epic season of *The Wars of the Roses* of 1963 and 1964. In short, actors like raked stages while technicians hate them.

In a live theatre it is the sightline to the human figure that matters most, not the sightline to the whole proscenium picture frame as it does in a cinema. Moro once told me that the only mistake he thought he had made with the Nottingham Playhouse auditorium was to pitch the circle too high as he had been told that the back row of the well-raked stalls had to see the top of the proscenium opening. This latter requirement, which had arrived in live theatre buildings from the cinema in the 1930s, will be explored later.

10

Regenerating the old offers an antidote to modernism: A couple of twentieth-century Scottish theatres reborn – one in Edinburgh and the other in Florida

Few cities have considered renovating theatres from the 1920s. The two chosen here were created in 1921 and 1928. Their surprising resurrection happened in different ways and for different reasons.

Dunfermline, Opera House 1921 J.D. Swanston. Totally new auditorium and stage within an older theatre building of 1903. Closed 1955. Auditorium dismantled rather than demolished 1982. Shipped to Sarasota, Florida, and re-erected inside a new building for Asolo Theatre Company by Stuart Barger 1990, advised by Theatre Projects Consultants.

Edinburgh, The Festival Theatre, formerly Empire Theatre 1928 W. and T.R. Milburn. Until 1963 used as the home for ballet (despite a raked stage) for the International Festival. It then became a bingo hall. Reopened as a theatre for one Festival in 1991. Completely rebuilt save for the auditorium by Law and Dunbar-Nasmith in 1994, advised by Theatre Projects Consultants.

From Dunfermline to Florida

Scotland has ten good pre-1920 theatres. Most are by well-known British theatre architects, but one, the King's Edinburgh of 1906, is by two architects whose work is unknown outside Scotland. Or rather was. They were James Davidson, who did the exterior, and J.D. Swanston, who did the interior. The only surviving theatre interior designed by Swanston other than the King's Edinburgh was that of the Opera House Dunfermline. This now stands within a new theatre complex in Sarasota, Florida. From 1921 to 1982 this fine auditorium had been in Dunfermline, unloved from 1955 when it had closed and then became an electrical store. Actor Denise Coffey had attended Dunfermline High School in 1948 and played the Opera House early in her career. In the 1980s she spread the word that it was under threat from a developer then in league with the borough council. She persuaded the authorities to think again. Finally,

10.1 *Opening in 1990 of Dunfermline Opera House,* now the Mertz Theatre, now with stretched proscenium, in Sarasota Florida, *over same when derelict in Dunfermline, Scotland.*

when nobody was prepared to save the Opera House as a whole, it was decided to save the interior. The auditorium was surveyed by students at the Edinburgh College of Art's department of architecture taught by Dunbar-Nasmith, who among so many other things was a member of the *Curtains!!!* team. George Younger, the then Secretary of State for Scotland in Her Majesty's Government, was advised by the Scottish Arts Council and they in turn by *Curtains!!!* Younger ruled that the building itself, which had little architectural merit, could only be demolished if the developer not only paid for the survey but also arranged to cut out the fibrous plasterwork so that the theatre interior could be re-erected one day somewhere else in Dunfermline. By the end of 1982 the plasterwork had been packed away in a container parked nearby. The council lost interest. The shopping mall was never built.

Four years later, in the summer of 1986, my colleague at TPC, David Staples, rang me from Florida to ask if I still had that 'theatre in a suitcase'. Soon the chairman of the board of the Asolo Theatre Company of Sarasota, Elizabeth Lindsay, who was of Scottish descent and had trained as an architect, was over in Edinburgh with her family for the International Festival. Dunbar-Nasmith showed her the container full of plasterwork. Wearing a smart white boiler suit and wielding a powerful torch she emerged saying Sarasota would be honoured to have it. The Scottish Arts Council, technically now the owner of the plasterwork, agreed a deal and design commenced. One of the conditions was the Asolo company would employ three new

10.2 *Lyric Theatre Hammersmith 1895 as translated to new site 1979.*

consultants to their design team led by Sarasota architect Stuart Barger. The three were architect Dunbar-Nasmith, plaster worker John Grandison, son of Leonard Grandison of Peebles whose firm had cut out the plasterwork for storage, and myself. We were beholden to the Scottish Arts Council for whom we had to ensure that every detail of Swanston's interior was faithfully reproduced in Sarasota. That city had been founded by John Hamilton Gillespie, born in Edinburgh in 1852. In 1886 Gillespie had been sent by his father to Sarasota, where he became its first mayor in 1902.

Moving a theatre 4,000 miles sounds mad. But it had been done before – sort of. The 1895 Lyric Theatre in Hammersmith (a borough on the west side of London) was ill placed on a tight little site next to a noisy rail track. Before the old Lyric was demolished in 1966 Matcham's plasterwork was cut out and stored. Thirteen years later fresh plasterwork moulded from casts of the old was inserted by the Borough of Hammersmith into an undistinguished concrete shell. This was pitched over a supermarket on a more central site further from the railway. Architectural critic Clive Aslet in *Country Life* of 15 November 1979 waxed enthusiastic: 'Re-creating Matcham's auditorium has been *a tour de force*. It is also an object-lesson scoring easy points off the modern architecture downstairs which – as the National Theatre shows just as clearly – has no vocabulary with which to be frivolous. All the more reason that we should guard the masterpieces of gaiety we have left.'

Four hundred yards or 4,000 miles, the problems are the same. A demanding detail the two managements had in common was that both wanted their original 24-feet (7.3 metres) prosceniums widened to 28 feet (8.5 metres). This sounds simple until one realises that the delicate webs of arched prosceniums had to be spun afresh so that they looked as though the stage had always been that wide. At the Lyric George Jackson Ltd (founded 1780), advised by Eric Jordan of TPC, and at Dunfermline in Sarasota Grandison of Peebles (founded 1886) both seamlessly stretched the originals. At the latter I suggested we employ as plaster workers and decorators the leading firm in this field, Conrad Schmitt of New Berlin, Wisconsin. I had seen their work on tours with the League of Historic American Theatres from Boston to Milwaukee, all of which had auditoriums dating from between 1898 and 1926.

We nearly made a bad mistake at Sarasota. Drawings and moulds were supplied for all the pieces of the jigsaw puzzle save one: the precise *bombé* curve of the lower circle front to which the original plaster cartouches would be attached. On site I attempted a sketch and handed it to a vast cigar-chomping plasterer and returned an hour later. Flat-chested. It happened again. 'Wadyawant? Jus' you tell me.' 'A bit more Dolly Parton?' 'Now you're talkin'.' Dunbar-Nasmith and I were told to come back after lunch. We were shown a perfect *bombé* curve, which a French–English dictionary translates as 'rounded' or 'bulging'. The adjective is as appropriate to a circle front as to a French chest of drawers.

A 28-foot-wide proscenium fronting a fully equipped stage and a capacity of 500 was precisely what the well-established Asolo Theatre Company needed. Swanston's architecture would support an audience that relished the idea of attending live theatre in an historic Scottish theatre space. The new Provost of Dunfermline had become an ardent supporter. He, Dunbar-Nasmith and I wore the kilt for the opening night on 27 January 1990. Tears were shed when Sarasota's own pipes and drums paraded to greet the audience in front of this much-travelled theatre. A dozen years later Sarasota Florida was twinned with Dunfermline Scotland, two communities far apart which had been brought together by a treasured theatre space.

The former Empire becomes The Festival and 'one of the best theatres in the world'

This Swanston auditorium had opened in Dunfermline in 1921. The Empire Theatre Edinburgh, which was to reopen as the Festival Theatre, had been built slightly later in 1928 by T.R. and William Millburn of Sunderland on the site of an earlier and smaller Empire by Matcham of which no trace remains. The second Edinburgh Empire was a variety theatre playing twice nightly and so one the most important spaces in the old front of house was the hall for the audience attending the second house to queue indoors out of the rain until the first house left. Backstage there were minimal dressing rooms. The 1928 stage at the Empire was shallow and, surprisingly, raked – probably the last one in Britain to be so built. The inadequate Empire, as it was then, was surprisingly home to the ballet at the Edinburgh Festival from 1947 to 1963. In 1954 Robert Helpmann appeared as Oberon and Moira Shearer as Titania for the Old Vic in Shakespeare's *A Midsummer Night's Dream* with an orchestra in the pit playing the whole of Mendelssohn's score. At the close Oberon and Titania flew away stage left, '. . . Make no stay/ Meet me all at break of day', courtesy of Kirby's Flying Ballet. Only four months previous Laurel and Hardy had played the Empire on their penultimate week of a farewell tour of the theatres of the British Isles.

In 1963 owners Moss Empires gave up live theatre and turned the Empire into a bingo hall and was no longer thought of as having any place in the long-term future of the performing arts in Edinburgh. One reason was that over a period of fifteen years Edinburgh was gripped by the saga of the Castle Terrace Opera House which never happened. This turned out, surprisingly, to be a good thing for the arts in Edinburgh, though few saw it that way at the time.

The confusion started in 1964 when a developer planned to demolish the 1883 Royal Lyceum and, with the cooperation of the city, substitute a theatre which would function as a playhouse for most of the year and as an opera house during the International Festival. In the same year I had started booking Prospect tours into the Royal Lyceum, always with my sights set on getting Prospect invited to the official Edinburgh Festival, which dream was realised in 1967. At the Lyceum I was wheeled before the convenor of the arts and libraries committee who explained that the Lyceum would be replaced by a modern auditorium with a curtain which could be drawn across the circle to reduce the capacity from 1,500 at Festival time for opera to 700 during the rest of the year for drama. I nervously suggested to the elderly convenor that such devices had been tried elsewhere and had failed. 'Laddie, if it doesnae work onywhere else is nae reason why it shouldnae work here in Edinburgh.' There was no answer to that.

Over the next decade plans for the Edinburgh Castle Terrace Opera House grew ever more ambitious. There were four successive schemes for ever larger buildings. By 1974 the brief was for a 1,400-seat theatre suitable for opera, musicals or epic drama, with a studio in the basement and connections to a retained Lyceum. A press release announced that the design team had visited twenty-one theatres in West Germany.

Meanwhile Scottish Opera had sussed out that this Edinburgh project was going nowhere just as parallel proposals for a fashionably modernist cultural quarter were going nowhere in Glasgow. The latter would have set, side by side, a concert hall, an opera house for Scottish Opera and a new home for the Glasgow Citizens Theatre – a sort of Lincoln Center transposed from warmer New York to damper Scotland. This was finally abandoned to the relief of both Scottish Opera and the Glasgow Citizens, who preferred their nineteenth-century homes to anything modernist. Either in Glasgow or Edinburgh a ghetto for the performing arts would have been a disaster. In 1974 Scottish Opera, homeless since being formed in 1962, had been offered Phipps's 1895 Theatre Royal for a song by Scottish Television who had been using it as a television studio. The design team was led by the multi-disciplinary practice Arup Associates, the chair of which was acoustician Derek Sugden who was to play a significant role in the yet-to-happen new Glyndebourne. He got Phipps's masterpiece back into operatic use in under a year.

The Castle Terrace Opera House project had many snags. First, it was unlikely that a 1,400-seat auditorium could work acoustically for both opera and drama. Second, a capacity of only 1,400 seats (less with the introduction of a large orchestra pit for opera) would be too small to make economic sense for opera at Festival time. Third, it was a tricky site, tucked away in a largely residential terrace behind the Usher Hall and a block away from Lothian Road and city life. The early schemes on this dour site faced typical nineteenth-century Edinburgh tenements with a sideways and upwards glance up the backside of the Castle Rock, hardly the prettiest part of this gigantic landmark. The final design did swivel the building through 45 degrees to face north-east. This would have given a better view of Princes Street below. The fourth reason was that the introduction of monumental concrete, which was to work for the imminent National Theatre on the sunnier banks of the Thames, would have been glum under a northern sky. In September 1975 the plug was finally pulled on the Castle Terrace project. The sole redeeming feature of the resulting office block that filled the 'hole in the ground' was a new home for the Traverse Theatre company which had outgrown its earlier site in the Grassmarket.

Such was the background when in 1975 Sandy Dunbar, director of the Scottish Arts Council, made the initial move that led to the recasting of the Empire Theatre as the Festival Theatre some twenty years later. I had known Dunbar from when he had been the first director of North-Eastern (later Northern) Arts in Newcastle when we reopened the Georgian Theatre Richmond in 1963. He had followed the fortunes of Prospect which, between 1967 and 1973, presented nine productions at successive Edinburgh International Festivals, three of them at the Lyceum and six at the Assembly Hall. We had also toured our productions to the Lyceum and King's theatres in winter. Dunbar knew that I had recently become a theatre design consultant with TPC and had had a small role as a consultant to Law and Dunbar-Nasmith in the design of the soon-to-open Eden Court Theatre in Inverness. Dunbar asked me if, in the wake of the demise of the Castle Terrace Opera House, I would undertake a study for the Scottish Arts Council on using what already existed elsewhere in the city to fill the gap, in both the short and long term. The study was to include the potential of the three Edinburgh theatres larger than the Lyceum: the King's (1906), the Empire (1928) and the Playhouse (1929). When I asked Dunbar if I might involve Law and Dunbar-Nasmith he said that would be my decision. I gave them a call and we set to work. We had only a few months and immediately found difficulties, such as there appeared at that time to be no extant set of drawings of the King's.

There had just been a local government reorganisation. The new Lothian Region Council, which lasted less than twenty years from 1975 to 1994, included Edinburgh. (Later the City was to recover its responsibilities for strategic planning.) In 1975 we looked at the Playhouse briefly. Though it had a fly tower it had never been used as a live theatre, only as a super cinema. Backstage it had been built over a geological fault, and this plus the fact that the street level behind the slanting back wall of a shallow stage was three storeys lower down meant that it would be very expensive to extend the stage. The only advantage seemed to be its seating capacity of 3,000, which made it one of the biggest auditoriums in Britain. We concluded that the stage would be too small for Edinburgh's major lyric theatre and the auditorium too large for most touring shows. The Lothian Region promptly bought it. There were to be many changes of ownership. It reopened finally in 1993 and soon found its true role as a money-making venue for long runs of touring hit musicals modified to fit the odd-shaped stage.

With the Empire a bingo hall and no likelihood of a new Opera House, there remained only the King's and the Lyceum as principal venues for an International Festival city. In our report delivered to the Scottish Arts Council in 1976 we recommended that the Empire be bought and rehabilitated. Then everything went quiet, not least because Dunbar retired in 1980. After a few years enter two other movers and shakers: Frank Dunlop, director of the Edinburgh Festival from 1984 to 1991, and Sandy Orr, chairman of Scottish Opera. Together they championed the Empire. Dunlop booked it for the 1991 Festival, using the old stage plus temporary seating in the stalls that had been converted for bingo.

'Why temporary?' was the reaction. Soon a design team was appointed which reunited Law and Dunbar-Nasmith with TPC. We had liked the Empire for three reasons. First, the auditorium could hold 1,900 in the two circles complete with their original seats and the stalls where we would install new seats to match the old which had been ripped out for the bingo. There also appeared to be space between the auditorium and the street at the front to extend the dingy entrance squeezed between two three-storey shops with something bigger and brighter. At the back of an enlarged site there was room for a completely new stage and facilities to take the biggest opera productions likely to be invited to any international festival.

Of course, there was no money. But there was an enthusiastic source of some seed money in Lothian and Edinburgh Enterprise Limited, a quasi-governmental organisation created in 1990 in the heyday of the Lothian Region. Its role was both to encourage enterprise and to control costs. By the time we opened in June 1994 barely £20 million had been spent in actual building costs. (For total costs one must add professional fees and the modest purchase price.) Compare the total cost of the 1994 Helsinki Opera – £110 million – or of the 1990 Bastille Opera in Paris – £300 million. In retrospect the Empire/Festival theatre in Edinburgh cost a tiny sum, which nevertheless had to be finessed. Frank Dunlop had suggested that it could all be done for an even lower figure than that spent initially on the Theatre Royal Glasgow. Had he not the project would never have started. One day in Edinburgh I asked the vastly experienced Dunbar-Nasmith whether the client meeting we were about to attend was the one at which we would tell the client that the building would inevitably cost £2 million more than the figure previously placed in front of them. 'No,' said James. 'If you do we will all be fired and the project will stop. To tell them the truth would be irresponsible.' Dunbar-Nasmith was to receive a knighthood in 1996 for services to architecture and conservation. The citation did not mention that from 1981 to 1985 Sir James had also been deputy chairman of the Edinburgh Festival Society, the Lord Provost being *ex officio* chairman. Nobody knew better than Dunbar-Nasmith which levers were to be pulled and which left untouched in the Byzantine arts world of Edinburgh.

The Empire project was nearly cancelled more than once. To save it on one occasion a private donor gave £1 million on the condition that it be renamed the Festival Theatre, knowing that no city councillor could face the headline in the newspapers: 'CITY CANCELS FESTIVAL'. None of us on the design side were responsible for the clincher, which was a two-inch-thick management study which stated that no running subsidy would be needed from the city given the 'commercial' 1,900-seat capacity. There was just enough truth in this unlikely assertion to convince politicians: after all, there were many more seats at the Festival Theatre than at the aborted and vastly more expensive Castle Terrace Opera House. This optimistic study had been written before it was realised that the renovated 3,000-seat Edinburgh Playhouse would cream off the profitable blockbuster musicals.

10.3 *Festival Theatre Edinburgh built as Empire Theatre 1928 renovated 1994.*

It is surprising that the question of capacity was not discussed at the time. Had the Castle Terrace Opera House not been abandoned in 1975 opera would then have had to be presented in a house which would have seated only about 1,250 when the largest orchestra pit was in use. Today the Festival holds 500 more than that even with the option of the largest pit.

One of the reasons why the Festival Theatre's auditorium with a maximum of 1,900 seats is so compact with such good sightlines is that in both upper levels the narrow seats from 1928 survive with the original tight back-to-back measurements – as they do at the older Bayreuth *Festspielhaus*. This lack of legroom is acceptable to the Edinburgh public today only because these are the historic original seats. Wider seats and more legroom in the circles would have not only reduced capacity by 15 per cent but would have made the whole project unaffordable due to the high cost of reshaping the tiering of the two steel cantilevered circles. At stalls level, where we had to buy the matching new seats, we were able to increase the back-to-back measurements of each row and, in order to perfect the sightlines, to 'dish' the rows of seating. The latter means that the ends of the rows rise gradually from the centre, and incrementally towards the back, starting from the front rows near the orchestra rail where the rows are horizontal end to end. This was a device I had learnt from visits to American theatres of the same period.

I had quickly organised a short North American tour of some of the period auditoriums which had decorations which might be relevant from Cleveland, Ohio to Toronto, Ontario. Included in the group were the Edinburgh City architect Stuart Henderson, Jim McFarlane of Lothian and Edinburgh Enterprise Limited, which had provided the seed money, Colin Ross, partner in charge for Law and Dunbar-Nasmith, and Ross's colleague, project architect

Michael Hamilton. The outcome was to invite two of the best North American interior decorators to come over separately and each paint a full box front and entablature adjacent to the proscenium. They were to do this in a manner which they thought would best present the Milburns' auditorium of 1928 to an audience of 1994. We had deliberately not taken the antiquarian approach of establishing the original colour scheme. We all knew what we had was a battered bingo hall, arrayed in the stock Moss Empires colours of the day, which Ross memorably described as 'an old Edinburgh floozy dressed in flock wallpaper'. The two firms were Conrad Schmitt, who had served TPC so well at Dunfermline in Sarasota, and David Hannivan, whose decoration of the Elgin and Winter Garden Theatres in Toronto had impressed us all on our quick tour. These two specialists would show us how they might give the kiss of life to an old floozy.

When the Empire auditorium was clear of scaffolding the two firms came in turn to decorate a box and related plasterwork next to the proscenium: Schmitt was first, audience left, and a fortnight later Hannivan, audience right. Four of us gathered to make a recommendation to be forwarded to the client. The four were Ross, Dunbar-Nasmith, Graham Law and me. Law broke the silence: 'I know which one my wife's hairdresser would prefer.' We chose the other, by Hannivan.

Hannivan floated glazes over a darkish base redolent of the period and the gilding was muted. The effect was as if theatregoers had been smoking cheroots for decades. Schmitt on the other hand had celebrated every opportunity to gild the plaster detail which was, after all,

10.4 *New facade of Festival Theatre Edinburgh 1994.*

second rate. The Milburns' Empire had never been grand, having been finished in the simplest of styles in the gathering depression of 1928. Ross's scheme compensated by fitting out the auditorium with the sort of light fittings that the Milburns' client could not afford at Edinburgh but had a year later at their grander Dominion Theatre in London.

Ross's *coup de théâtre* was on the gently curved glazed space between street and auditorium. At street level there is now both a friendly all-day bar and an open box office. These flank the foot of the grandest axial stair ever built for any theatre in Britain. This takes you up effortlessly to all three levels of the auditorium and on the way offers two lofty fully glazed foyers. At their south end they offer a hitherto undiscovered axial view straight down The Bridges to Robert Adam's General Register House, completed in 1788. The arc of Ross's sensational fully glazed front facade to the Festival Theatre of 1994 stands a few yards from Adam's Old College buildings for the University of Edinburgh, started in 1788 and finished by William Playfair in 1831. Both are beautifully proportioned. No wonder that the Cockburn Society, the statutory but independent guardian of Edinburgh's architectural heritage, took just fifteen minutes to approve and applaud Colin Ross's proposal for an utterly modern glass-fronted facade, the only one to grace a public building in the Athens of the North. to the same theatre space as it was for Laurel and Hardy in 1954 and as it became forty years later.

The Festival Theatre bids audiences welcome as they enter off Nicholson Street. It also bids them farewell. On 15 June 2019, a gala performance of Scottish Opera's *Magic Flute* was staged to celebrate the twenty-fifth anniversary of the Festival Theatre. At the curtain's fall the entire audience chose, as they always do, to cascade down the grand stair and leave by the main front doors. They could have chosen other exits for quicker routes to their cars or to public transport. They instinctively prefer Ross's unique grand stair, big enough for a large audience to leave *en masse*.

Raymond Monelle, respected music scholar, conductor and jazz pianist, had written music criticism for the monthly *Opera* magazine since 1969 on joining the Faculty of Music at the University of Edinburgh. None of the design team ever met him. In *Opera* of September 1994, he summed up the fairy tale of how the Festival Theatre was reborn as Edinburgh's opera house:

> All this time the old Empire stood in Nicholson Street ... But the scanty backstage and the dowdy front of house made the theatre unsuitable, everyone thought, as a regular opera house. Then – one of the miracles of opera history – someone suggested that the old auditorium be renovated, with a brand-new backstage area and audience concourse, effectively creating a sumptuous new theatre for a mere £21 million ... The result is an auditorium of just the right size, holding 1,900 people, combining spaciousness with intimacy, with the largest stage area in Britain (9,300 square feet) and dressing rooms for 180 artistes, coupled to an extraordinary front of house with an all-glass frontage that makes the bars and cafes blend with the street outside ... The world's operatic community must be told of its glories and magical acoustics ... So we had better proclaim it loud and clear: whether we consider matters practical or acoustical, we have suddenly woken up to one of the best theatres in the world.

These last two chapters have dealt mainly with old theatres which were given a new life. They have been tested in use and one does not have to rely on promoters' puffs as happens with the latest wonders. There are more recent re-generations of fine old theatres holding 1,000 plus which await the test of time. A few are reviewed in Chapter 13.

11

New opera houses from Glyndebourne to Dallas. Elsewhere some starchitects upstage the performers

Glyndebourne 'likely to remain a landmark for many years to come' – Michael Barron

Glyndebourne has been the archetypal English summer opera festival since it started in 1934. The eccentric enthusiast John Christie had inherited from his grandfather a country house that was not itself architecturally interesting but was beautifully sited in the Sussex landscape. Here Christie built his own small opera house at the east end of the family home, having first acquired some experience of theatre management by taking a short lease of the Opera House Tunbridge Wells in 1925. When opened, Christie's own theatre had a seating capacity of only 300 but a pit large enough for a small symphony orchestra. He constantly made improvements by adding a fly tower, magnificent dressing rooms and more seats. The narrow auditorium was extended: to 433 in 1936, to 600 in 1952 and by 1977 to 850.

Christie and his wife, soprano Audrey Mildmay, had been frequent visitors to German opera houses. The Christies at first focused on Bayreuth and Wagner and it was only later that this shifted to Mozart, which was more suitable for Mildmay's voice. In November 1933 Christie was introduced to conductor Fritz Busch, who had just left Germany in disgust at the new Nazi regime and was soon joined by fellow countryman Carl Ebert, who remained as director of productions until 1959. The triumvirate was completed in 1934 by Austrian-born Rudolf Bing, who became general manager. For the first six seasons before the war this trio had total artistic control of what was produced on the stage while Christie looked after the building, ensuring that his opera house had the intimacy and the acoustic appropriate for Mozart. There was no regular architect though one was called in to advise on the design of the original fly tower.

After the war things did not start well. An association with Benjamin Britten fizzled out after two of his operas, *The Rape of Lucretia* and *Albert Herring*, had their world premieres at Glyndebourne. Bing busied himself as co-founder and director of the Edinburgh International Festival where from 1947 to 1955 (with the exception of 1952) Glyndebourne took over the King's Theatre for the full three weeks of the International Festival to present opera of the highest standard.

Following the death of his father in 1962 George Christie inherited Glyndebourne. In 1977 he oversaw the final extension of the old narrow auditorium. As a 600-seater the form had been fine but with 250 more seats it was like one of those seventies airliners which has been 'stretched' too often by inserting additional sections halfway down the fuselage. In 1990 Christie wrote a letter to members of the Festival Society: 'We are going to pull down the opera house, before it falls down, because we feel an acute need for more ticket income and in order to accommodate as many more of you as possible.' But how many more? This was one of the many questions, along with how much it was going to cost, which occupied minds at Glyndebourne before a design team was appointed.

To get to this point Christie involved stage designer John Bury. Bury had joined the RSC in 1963, where he forged a close relationship with Peter Hall. They worked together at Stratford until Hall left there in 1968. Their partnership was resumed at the National Theatre in 1973, where once again Bury was head of design. Meanwhile they first collaborated at Glyndebourne in 1972 on Monteverdi's *Il ritorno d'Ulisse*. Over ten years in the old theatre Bury designed ten shows, mostly for Hall, culminating in Britten's *A Midsummer Night's Dream* in 1981. At the time of writing, this is still being regularly revived, since 2000 under the supervision of Bury's widow Elizabeth Bury who was, professionally speaking, 40 per cent of the designer known as John Bury. Said Christie of the Burys' opera designs: 'There was not a dud amongst them.' He also knew that Bury's expertise extended to the design of theatres, which was where he really did need advice. Elsewhere in the team Anthony Whitworth-Jones had recently succeeded Brian Dickie as general director, who had been at Glyndebourne for twenty-seven years. Bernard Haitink, the musical director, was about to leave Glyndebourne for Covent Garden. In 1989 Hall had resigned as artistic director in protest over Peter Sellars's production *of Die Zauberflöte*, set in a hippy Los Angeles with all its spoken dialogue cut. (Christie was surprised that his artistic director had not twigged this until a few days before the opening. It took a decade for them to make it up but finally they did.)

A longlist of nine British architects was assembled. In August 1988 he sent to each his deceptively diffident 'idle thoughts' which triggered the building finally created by Christie's chosen architect Michael Hopkins who, as Marcus Binney suggested in the aptly titled *Glyndebourne: Building a Vision* of 1994, had 'taken functionalism down a new contextual road'. Hopkins's brick building is celebratory rather than solemn, as had been so many of the functional modernist opera houses of post war Germany. It sits so well in the landscape'.

But what of the new Glyndebourne auditorium? Here Bury played a key role. Commissioned by Christie to prepare a feasibility study he had sketched a Germanic form of a fan within a box. He then had second thoughts and wrote to Dickie in June 1987:

> I must admit I am still very worried about 1,050 people on a continuous rake with no overhangs. If that is built to GLC specifications one ends up with the Olivier. My thinking at this stage is that if we are building an opera house it should be one. Not in stucco and cherub, but in wood if they will let us and on the German *Hoftheater* format . . . everybody squeezed into as small a volume as possible. Tradition without the pastiche! A Mozart house for Mozart operas.

It was this that led Christie to include in those 'idle thoughts' 'the feel of the auditorium. What it's going to be dressed in. It has to be hugely welcoming. Timber-clad, not plush, gilt or velvet. It has to be both functional and friendly.'

Hopkins was appointed in February 1989. Next came Derek Sugden of Arup Acoustics. Then in December of the same year Theatre Projects Consultants joined the team, having been interviewed by Christie, Hopkins and Bury. For TPC there were just the two of us, fellow

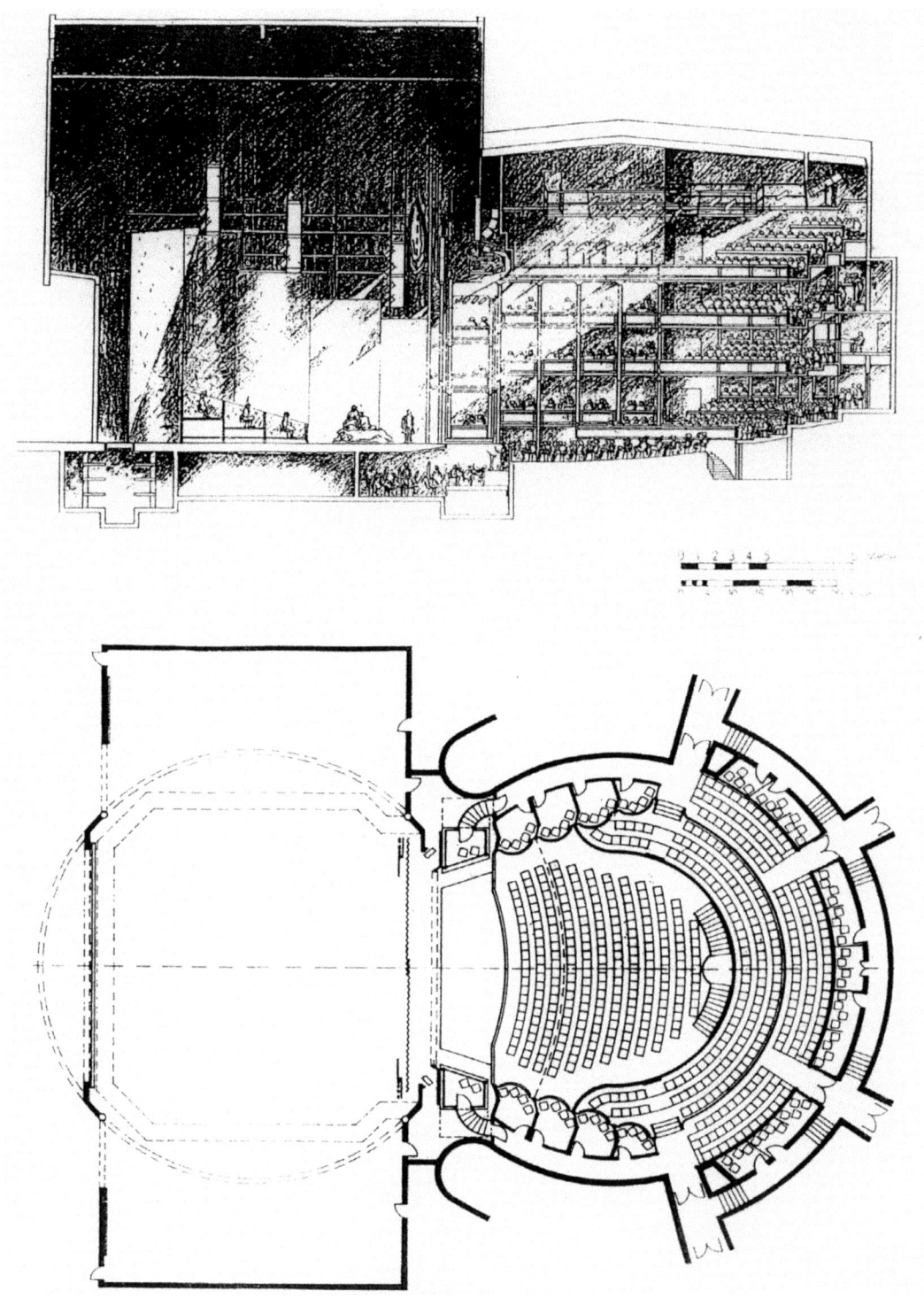

11.1 *Glyndebourne: TPC's concept design July 1990.*

director Alan Russell to advise on stage engineering and stage lighting and myself on theatre planning. At the outset we were sent a design by Hopkins with an auditorium rectangular in form which he had derived from Bury's first proposal: fan-shaped stalls and a single balcony plonked in a rectangular box. I thought there could be a different approach.

Bury having been a supporter of my idea for the Cottesloe, I wondered whether there was now an opportunity for him to do the same at Glyndebourne. Would Christie and Hopkins accept as a starting point a concept design from me? I discussed my sketches with Bury, who said go for it. My notion was worked up into a plan and a peopled section drawn by a young architect, Anne Minors, who had been a much-valued newcomer to the Theatre Projects team in 1984. Her eloquent drawing was first reproduced in my *Architecture, Actor and Audience*, published in 1993, the year before the new Glyndebourne opened in celebration of the sixtieth anniversary of the old one. A decade later Minors left TPC to form her own theatre consultancy which she ran for 20 years before forming a practice with her acoustician husband, Bob Essert.

The galleried horseshoe space with people papering the walls was, with Bury's active support, shown first to Sugden, to check that it would work acoustically, then to Christie and soon after to Hopkins in March 1990. Binney quoted Christie in *Glyndebourne: Building a Vision*: 'It was Mackintosh who convinced everybody that the horseshoe was the best shape. It happened remarkably quickly. We all felt that intimacy would be most easily achieved with the people in the audience wrapped round like wallpaper. That's something that neither the fan shape nor the shoebox does.' Hopkins preferred this inherently circular geometry to the rectangular box

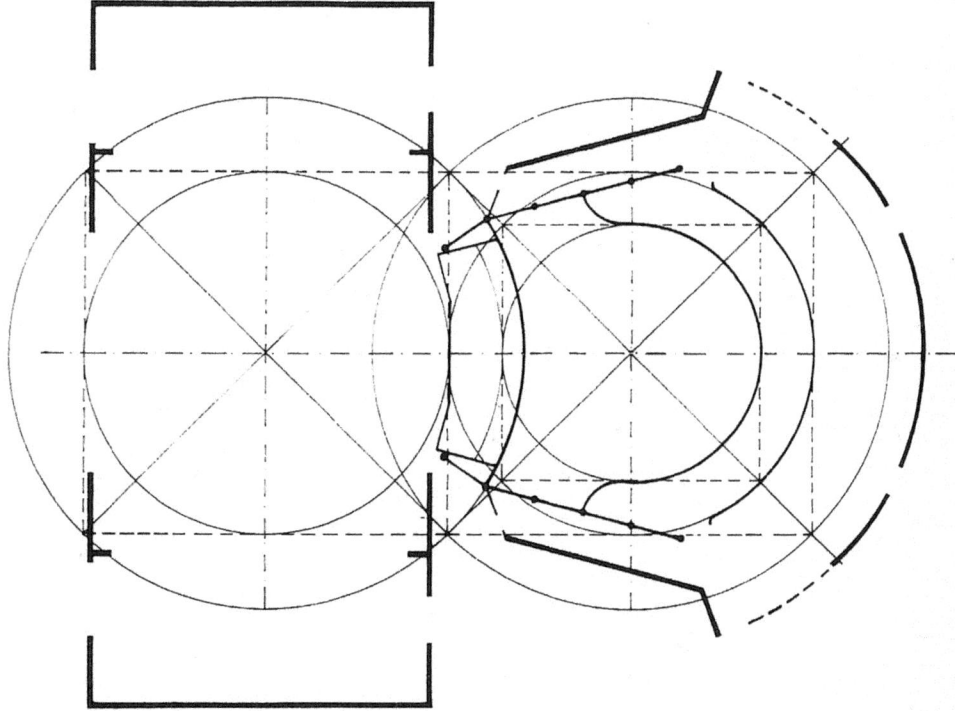

11.2 'Iain's mumbo jumbo' received by architect Michael Hopkins from TPC April 1990. The area of power, the vesica piscis, is occupied by the downstage singer, the conductor and the orchestra.

previously offered and we were off. I had long subscribed to Bury's mantra that 'the poetry lies in the geometry'. I put my geometry, reproduced in Binney's book, to Hopkins, who said with a twinkle, 'I think I can turn Iain's mumbo jumbo into architecture.' To which I replied, 'Michael, I choose to take that as a compliment.' We got on as well as any specialist design consultant should with a fine architect, disagreeing only about a few matters on which our wonderful client Christie would arbitrate.

Details of that horseshoe sketch which contributed to its intimacy include the stalls rear entrance which sets up the curved side aisles to the stalls. This was borrowed from Edward Barry's Royal Opera House Covent Garden of 1858 (although not reinstated in that form until 1999) and the lyre-shaped upstand for the rear three rows of the stalls stolen from the *Nationaltheater* Munich. Things lost in design development include the number of tiers, three instead of four. Capacity was maintained by the deepening of the top tier, where the acoustics are best, into a front gallery of three rows and an upper gallery of four. One fewer tier in the horseshoe made the all-important connections with the surrounding open terraces easier to realise and gave a better acoustic balance of side reflections from both the tier fronts and the side walls of the drum. My only regret at the time was that we lost the flexible proscenium zone. Christie and Hopkins preferred a cleaner junction between auditorium and stage. With hindsight I believe they were right.

There were a couple of critical moments during design. At the outset quantity surveyors Gardiner and Theobald had told George that a new theatre could be built for as little as £14 million. During design development our plans were costed at £22 million and the project was nearly cancelled. This was not the fault of the design team but due to errors by the cost consultants, who had done their costing before any of us had been appointed. Sugden, who led the multi-disciplinary practice of Arup Associates and knew a lot about quantity surveying, dissected G&T's earlier estimates of £14 million. They had omitted this and omitted that. The roof of the old theatre was not soundproof and had bats in its rafters. Yet this had been taken as the costing yardstick for the new larger roof. George decided that the revised construction budget should be £22 million and would never change.

Soon there was another costing by the now overcautious G&T. I was dug out of the management box at a dress rehearsal in the old theatre to see Christie in his library. Straight off he asked me whether he should sack the architects as he had just been informed that building costs had risen from £22 to £24 million. Pause for some quick thinking. I replied that the architects were first rate and should not be sacked. Nor should they be asked to design a cheaper building. But he, Christie, could reduce costs by modifying the brief. 'How?' he asked. Knowing it carried a £2 million price tag I suggested omitting the insertion of a totally new restaurant into the old dressing room buildings which open out on the main lawn. When he replied that a new restaurant was important to many of his patrons I suggested that this was precisely why it could become Phase Two. The following morning he made just such a decision and we were back to £22 million. Phase Two has never happened: the rich still like the old restaurant, which retains a certain charm, and the performers love the green room and their own bar in the old dressing room quadrangle connected to the backstage new dressing rooms and stage by invisible routes, of which the public are unaware, that pass under the main foyer.

As delicate a matter as cost control is the timetable. The ground plan of the new theatre overlapped with that of the old. Would two of the annual summer festival seasons have to be lost? It seemed likely. This could have jeopardised the entire project. Then the young project architect in the Hopkins office, Robin Snell – of whom more anon – came up with a meticulous

11.3 *Glyndebourne auditoriums: new opened in 1994 over old theatre demolished in 1992.*

plan which showed in detail that by using off-site pre-casting of concrete elements only the 1993 season would be lost and the new opera house could open on the exact sixtieth anniversary of the first opera house in 1934. Snell's plan convinced and so it was. That it was he who originated this solution I learnt only in 2021.

Christie always listened, made decisions and encouraged creative relationships within the design team. This was at the opposite end of the spectrum from the National Theatre where there were too many committee meetings, which were held irregularly, and too many conflicting opinions. At Glyndebourne it was quite different. During critical design development in 1990 the same eight people met fortnightly at the architects' office. Present at every meeting were Christie supported by Bury and Whitworth-Jones, the two Hopkinses – Michael and his wife Patty, who was also his professional partner – Sugden, Russell and myself. We were joined occasionally by structural and mechanical engineers from Arup, both called John, whose silence signified approval.

Two further anecdotes. The first suggests that the scale of new Glyndebourne is roughly right. A year or two after the opening and within months of each other I took around two groups considering their own new opera houses. The first, from Pilsen in the Czech Republic, where 75 per cent of the costs of a large repertoire were then being met by city taxes, said, 'Iain, this is a wonderful opera house, but we could never build one so big.' The second group, from a North American city, said, 'Iain, this is a wonderful opera house, but we could never build one so small.' In the USA there were no public subsidies as there were in Europe, just private donations and a greater dependence on the box office. Hence the capacities of their new opera houses were then around 2,200 to 2,500. Some of the earlier American ones were even bigger, such as the New York Metropolitan Opera and the San Francisco War Memorial Theater.

The second concerns auditorium lighting. Quite far into detail design I heard that Hopkins intended there should be no decorative light fittings on the front of the circles. I showed Christie a pair of diagrams which suggested that if there were no such fittings the emphasis would be on the outer walls of the auditorium, which as a consequence would feel large, while if there was some glitter on the timber tier fronts the auditorium would feel smaller. Christie instructed Hopkins to introduce tier-front fittings. I was told that the young members of his architectural team, who had been bidden to come up with a design solution, christened them 'George's Blackpool twinklies'. The result was the fittings, both elegant and modern, you see today. Years later Glyndebourne project architect Robin Snell, who actually designed the said fittings, suggested to me that the saga of the 'twinklies' was a good example of what is meant by 'creative tension'.

Meanwhile, colleague Russell negotiated necessary auditorium stage lighting positions without either compromising the architects' floating steel and concrete lighting bridge that crowns the circular auditorium chamber or cluttering the circle fronts with too much stage lighting. Encouraged by Bury he negotiated the best forward-of-the-proscenium lighting bridge ever installed anywhere. It was so much better than those massive, suspended, steel lattice beams which disfigure many theatres, old or new, looking as if they have been borrowed from a shipyard. Rob Harris of Arup Acoustic suggested that this curved bridge be so shaped in section as to provide additional reflections from the players in the orchestra pit. The architects detailed the whole to assist in leading the eye down to the performers. A team achievement.

Christie had cunning ways of controlling costs. He knew that a smaller building would always cost less. Accordingly he stated the new theatre had to fit between the organ room to the west and an existing tennis court to the east and that this was non-negotiable. Much effort was put into compressing the width of the stage, the extent of the wings and circulation both backstage and front of house so as to preserve that tennis court. Once construction had started Christie quietly moved the tennis court to elsewhere in the grounds.

Lastly on Glyndebourne why, you may ask, are there 1,294 places (1,250 seated and forty-four standing) in the new theatre when we had been originally asked for only 1,100, only 250 more than in the old? (In addition to the 1,294 there are thirty-six seats that have doubtful sightlines and are never sold but are kept for latecomers or staff.) In design development I offered Whitworth-Jones a priced seating plan, which he welcomed. It indicated a wide range from the most expensive seats to the cheapest, which ratios have been adhered to ever since. For the opening season of 1994, the prices ranged from £100 in the stalls and foyer circle to £30 in the top circle and £15 for seats in the side slips plus standing at £10.

Some operagoers at the sides may have less good sightlines but all can hear well. Crucially they raise the emotional temperature for us all. This was why we had advised that some of those occupying additional places at the sides should get in for a fraction of what is paid by the well-heeled. Christie saw the social benefit immediately. He had always been worried that the young and some of the locals could not afford Glyndebourne.

Soon after the opening there was a letter in a national newspaper from an indignant operagoer who, while not admitting that he had sat in the cheapest seats, said he could not see the whole stage and protested that he would have thought that by 1994 architects had learnt how to provide perfect sightlines. I seethed. Christie advised not rising to the bait. A week later, a happier patron wrote that she and her husband had already seen two operas, one standing and one sitting in those side places, and had booked there for the remaining three. Attending all five operas in the season she said would have cost them less than a single pair of best stalls for just the one. Point made.

The notices, all written in 1994, were good. Wrote Bernard Levin in *The Times* of 23 August: 'Basically, there are two kinds of beautiful opera house interior: the ornate, however lavish or delicate, and the geometrical, however severe or magical. And I swear by Pythagoras or Archimedes, nay by the very square on their hypotenuses, that the new Glyndebourne is so stupendously magical that it hypnotises the visitor into the belief that it could win prizes for lavishness.' Jonathan Glancey in *The Guardian* of 1 February added: 'Inside the auditorium, the project makes near perfect sense. Mackintosh and Hopkins have produced a big but intimate space. It has as near as one can get to a timeless quality.' Colin Davies in the July issue of *Architectural Review* wrote: 'The aim was to preserve the intimacy that was such an important characteristic of the original 800-seat auditorium. That aim has been achieved, apparently effortlessly. The new auditorium seats 1,300 but looks much smaller.' *Time Magazine* of 13 July reported: 'Says soprano Alison Hagley who plays Susanna in *Figaro*: "It's really more a circle than a horseshoe, and on stage I feel part of that circle. The audience is my friend and I am theirs."' On a more technical note, Michael Barron wrote in the second edition (2009) of his *Auditorium Acoustics and Architectural Design*: 'Overall the house offers as intimate an acoustic experience as one can expect. In visual terms the design cleverly reconciles the traditional horseshoe plan with modern architectural sensibilities. As a medium-size opera house design the new Glyndebourne Opera House is likely to remain a landmark for many years to come.'

At the Prague Quadrennial of 1999 the project won a unique gold medal in the architecture section, not just for the building but to honour the creative synergy achieved by the client team led by George Christie and the design team led by Michael Hopkins. This medal, which I had the honour to receive in Prague, hangs discreetly in the foyer at Glyndebourne along with a lot of other awards.

11.4 *Longborough Festival Opera 1998.*

Four smaller festivals: Longborough, New Garsington, West Horsley and Nevill Holt

Other country house opera festivals in England have shorter seasons than that of Glyndebourne where the main season lasts from mid-May to mid-August. Uniquely eccentric, Longborough is the brainchild of Martin and Lizzie Graham. In 1998 at Banks Fee Farm in a tranquil corner of Gloucestershire they created an opera house for 500 by extending an undistinguished modern farm barn, at the rear with a simple but good-sized stage and at the front with a brave classical facade on the pediment of which stand life-size figures of Mozart, Verdi and, at the centre, Wagner. The emphasis on Wagner contrasts with Glyndebourne, where Christie was glad that his father had been redirected towards Mozart. The Grahams, however, stuck with Wagner while at the same time creating an ambience which also works well for comedy. Conductor Anthony Negus convinced the Grahams that their Wagnerian ambitions could be realised with musical advantage at what might seem to be an unrealistically small scale.

For the Grahams' first Ring Cycle, completed in 2013, Negus had assembled sixty players in an orchestra pit that can take seventy-two. Delightful eccentricities persist: visiting once in a heatwave my wife and I enjoyed a pre-show speech from the stage by chairman Martin dressed in dinner jacket, black tie, white shorts and plimsoles. Their audience is fiercely loyal. We sit comfortably in stalls seats collected from Royal Opera House Covent Garden who, in 1995, had replaced their old seats with new ones.

11.5 *New Garsington Opera 2011. Architects Robin Snell and Partners advised by Iain Mackintosh. Interior over exterior.*

New Garsington at Wormsley, which opened in 2011, is that rarity among English summer operas: a 600-seat purpose-built opera pavilion with no side walls set on a green field site – literally. It has a largeish stage and an auditorium with perfect sightlines. At its precursor, Garsington Manor at Garsington village, nearer to Oxford, Leonard Ingrams had from 1989 presented short summer seasons of opera out of doors on a south-facing terrace. A stark demountable auditorium of scaffolding holding around 500 on a steep rake was tucked between terrace and high trees. At the rear of the acting area was a hinged canopy, somewhat like a pram hood, which rose over the performers at the hint of rain. In front of the picturesque terrace most of the pit musicians were sat not under the stage but under the first rows of the audience, the feet of whom were two or three feet above stage level. An unusual arrangement with a conductor who was invisible to the audience, different in detail from Bayreuth but similar in purpose.

In 2005, disasters struck. Ingrams died tragically of a heart attack at the age of only sixty-three. At the time he was locked in a dispute with the inhabitants of the small, sleepy village of Garsington, who mounted campaigns against both the sounds of opera in the open air and of the operagoers' cars arriving up narrow country lanes. Injunctions were served. It seemed at first that Ingrams had won. The neighbours then resorted to noisy tractors and low-flying aircraft. However, in the same year that Ingrams had his heart attack the board appointed Whitworth-Jones as general director. (After having spent seventeen years as general director at Glyndebourne he had gone to Dallas, where he opened that city's new 2,200-seat opera house and then quickly decided to move back to Britain.) Whitworth-Jones realised that the Ingrams family's decision to cease opera on their own property was a blessing in disguise. They would find a new site, quieter and closer to London, and there fit in more seats.

They researched a score of possibilities. Once a site had been chosen, they would engage a scaffolding firm to provide a larger, more easily demountable auditorium and ask TPC to look after stage lighting and technical stage design. Whitworth-Jones asked me to accompany him to some shortlisted sites. Looking at the problems which would be encountered anywhere I suggested that employing an architect might help and TPC would be happy to join a team led by the right man. He sighed and said too many of his board were against having an architect as they believed that would increase costs. I reminded Whitworth-Jones of our Glyndebourne experiences, where costs had been controlled. We looked at each other and both thought of Robin Snell, the project architect on Glyndebourne who six years previous had set up on his own. Whitworth-Jones rang him the next morning.

Snell is a calm person as well as a talented architect. There was no detail in the brief he was given. His instructions were simply to design a demountable new home for the proven Garsington summer opera festival which would seat 600, 20 per cent more than the old. A secluded site was finally chosen at Wormsley Park in Buckinghamshire, home to Mark Getty. This was a scheduled Area of Outstanding Natural Beauty which would therefore require a pavilion of distinction. There were nearby farm buildings, some of which could become dressing rooms and other back-up spaces, a celebrated cricket ground, a pretty lake, a good shoot, no noisy neighbours and a deer ha-ha dividing lawns from the aforesaid green field. There was no budget. Just an instruction from a small board of directors to keep costs down. With help from friends from Glyndebourne days Snell got on with a design and so impressed his client that a more than modest amount of money was quickly found.

His opera pavilion appears to hover a few feet above the ground. It was designed as a deceptively simple kit of parts because the first ten-year tenancy agreement stated that it would have to be erected and then dismantled each year. Bob Essert was the acoustician and Dick Brett advised on aspects of the structure needed for lighting and scenic suspension. Once erected,

Getty liked Snell's opera pavilion so much that he told Garsington Opera that in the winter they need not remove it. The pavilion had been designed with straight lines and no curves to make it more easily demountable. Ironically it was this very limitation which led to the success of what was a carefully proportioned concept. No wonder this 'temporary structure' won eight architectural awards.

Early on, Snell and I had pegged out the site. Here is where the deer ha-ha comes in. Your standard ha-ha, as at Glyndebourne, is a shallow trench four or five feet deep which prevents cows or sheep straying from field to lawn. Such a device, which has a brick face on the lawn side only and a small slope on the other, is practically invisible and gives the illusion that the animals could wander over to meet the picnickers and vice versa. A deer ha-ha on the other hand is ten feet deep with a much higher brick wall on the lawn side and a longer slope on the field side. Deer, unlike cows and sheep, can jump. At Wormsley Park this protection gave us the line of the stage edge – some two metres on the green field side of the said vertical wall. This would allow the orchestra, sat at the lower ha-ha level in the field, to extend the customary distance under the stage which we set at the higher lawn level. Not to have made use of this ancient feature in this way would have meant either a bigger pit opening measured front to back, with dire effects

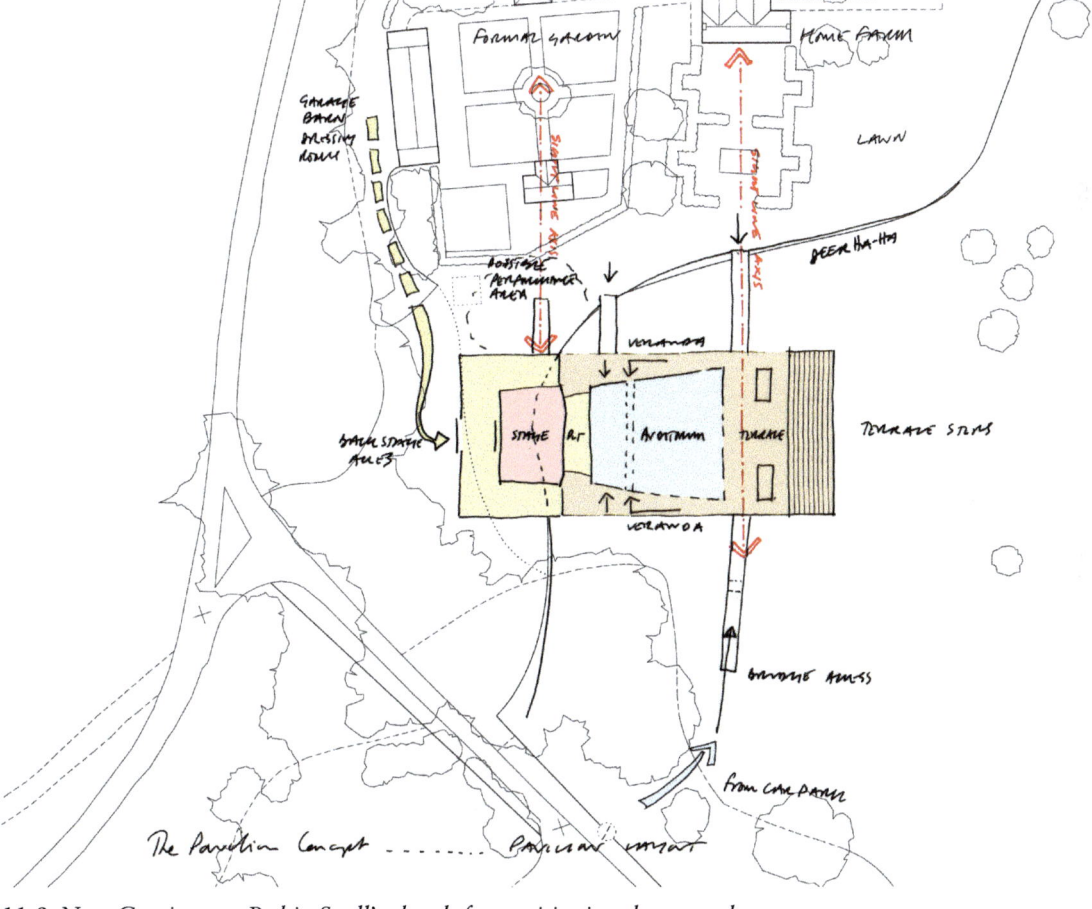

11.6 *New Garsington. Robin Snell's sketch for positioning the opera house.*

11.7 *Grange Park Opera: design and illustration by Tim Ronalds over photo as built by others.*

on intimacy, or much greater expenditure on building up the stage level, forcing the whole structure to rear up and appear too tall in the landscape.

Designed to be easily dismantled by successful contractors Unusual Rigging, new Garsington was relatively quick to build. It opened in May 2011, old Garsington, which was forty miles away, having closed in August the preceding year. Soon Getty paid Snell a second compliment by commissioning him to design a private dining pavilion on an island in the middle of the little lake at the foot of the hill where the theatre stood.

While the name Garsington was cheerfully passed from the old in Oxfordshire to the new in Buckinghamshire in 2011, the transfer of Grange Park Opera from the Grange in Hampshire to West Horsley Place in Surrey was not so happy. At the Grange in 2002 dynamic opera impresario Wasfi Kani had encouraged the conversion into an opera house of a derelict orangery, with cellar below, which had been built in 1823 beside William Wilkins's Greek revival country house of 1804. All was well for a dozen summer seasons. But in 2015 the two parties, owner and operator, fell out and spoons were counted. Kani left with much of the stage equipment plus her host's name. Now the opera at the Grange in Hampshire is called Grange Festival Opera while Grange Park Opera (*sic*) happens at Kani's new venture at West Horsley Place in Surrey. Got it?

The form of the auditorium of the first Grange had been determined by the height of the orangery plus excavated cellar below. The stalls there were steeply raked to meet not the first circle, which is normally at or near stage level in horseshoe opera houses, but at second circle because at the original Grange Park that was the entrance level for all the audience. In contrast West Horsley is new build on a flat site and all 700 audience enter at ground level. Nevertheless, Kani insisted on importing the steep rake from the smaller Grange Park. Above the steeply raked stalls are three complete tiers. The eye is led upwards. Performers in a theatre of this scale generally prefer that half the audience seems to be below their eye level and half above. They will liken singing in front of a steep rake, such as that of the 1967 Queen Elizabeth Hall on the South Bank, to pushing a boulder up a hill.

West Horsley Place is the 384-acre estate which author and broadcaster Bamber Gascoigne inherited in 2014 from his ninety-nine-year-old great aunt, the Duchess of Roxburgh. Kani shrewdly reckoned that this site, which is relatively close to London, would be a good alternative to the Grange in distant Hampshire where divorce proceedings had already started. Soon Gascoigne declared in an interview in *The Times*: 'They are planning to build the theatre tucked away romantically in a wood . . . Roll on the first night.' It did, but too quickly, in only eighteen months.

Her appointed architect, Tim Ronalds, designed a magical 'theatre in a wood' surrounded by abandoned parterres, ancient crinkum-crankum brick walls and secret gardens. Then, within a year, Kani sacked Ronalds and took over the design herself. Nothing wrong with the owner designing their own opera house without an architect, as this is what John Christie did at Glyndebourne in 1934. But to employ a fine architect and then sack him makes for complications. With an impossibly tight timetable and not much ready cash, there were siren voices whispering that this or that simplification would save both time and money.

But the problem was that Kani wanted to add as well as to subtract. This included an encircling colonnade because, as she explained to architectural critic Robert Bevan of the *London Evening Standard* (6 June 2019), she 'wanted a skirt around the building'. He wrote of Kani that 'whatever her admirable determination and opera programming nous, she does not possess astute design hands' and called it 'La Scala, by way of eBay and Ikea . . . It has some charm but is essentially daft.' To him Kani had described herself as 'a very driven person, a very annoying client'. Yet she gets things done and has cultivated a loyal audience not least by keeping them informed by sending them exotic *bonnes bouches* when closed during the dark days of the pandemic. However, the building, which will endure when the fine productions have been forgotten, is not as good as it might have been. On this wonderful site at West Horsley Park she could have offered not only first-class opera, which she does, but also a first-class building.

The design of a new opera house at Nevill Holt Hall, a Grade I listed building in Leicestershire, was a happier affair. A few performances of guest opera had been staged there by the ubiquitous Wasfi Kani from 2004 to 2012 in a tent set up in the square courtyard of a listed old stable block. In 2013, the owner of Nevill Court, David Ross, created his own opera company and decided to exchange the temporary tent for a small purpose-built opera house. He could afford to pay the cost and so fundraising was not a distraction. Services for both audience and performers are accommodated in the existing stables ranged on all four sides. The audience of 400 sit in gently curved stalls and a single circle which reaches round to grasp the stage.

Ross entrusted the work to young architects Witherford Watson Mann, supported by theatre consultant Anne Minors and acoustician Bob Essert. It opened in June 2018. Rare among theatre spaces discussed here, Nevill Holt is one I have not had the chance of visiting. Rowan Moore concluded in *The Observer* (13 January 2019): 'Its virtues are an intense level of thoughtfulness and discreet wit . . . It is a place that can make opera feel fresh and alive.'

In summer 2019 the new Nevill Holt Opera was one of six projects shortlisted for the annual Stirling Prize which is awarded to the best building completed in the preceding year. The Stirling had been founded in 1996, the year after Glyndebourne would have been eligible for the first such prize if it had opened in 1995 rather than 1994. To date, only one theatre has won this award, the 400-seat Everyman Theatre Liverpool of 2014 (see Chapter 13).

Almost all opera houses are of a comparatively fixed form in contrast to playhouses, consisting of stage, orchestra pit and auditorium. Discussions for a new drama space are more complex, starting with talk of form: end-stage with or without proscenium arch, thrust stage, in-the-round, traverse, promenade, etc. Hence architects generally prefer the more straightforward brief for an opera house. The smaller country garden opera buildings in Britain have been successful, driven not by committees but by imaginative and comparatively wealthy individuals such as Ingrams, Graham and Ross who are the successors to the European princes who built those delightful miniature court opera houses.

New opera houses in Amsterdam, Oslo and Dallas

Now for three larger, very different and most successful opera houses of recent decades. The Amsterdam Opera House, *Het Muziektheater*, which opened in 1986, is the link between the earlier German theatre-building boom and the achievements of a later generation. It holds 1,650 and announces itself on a wonderful site, the Waterlooplein, where five waters meet. The lead architect was Wilhelm Holzbauer, who had won a competition twenty years earlier. He is described in his Wikipedia entry as a 'pragmatic modernist'. While it was Holzbauer who suggested the linking of the opera house to a new City Hall it was the city government who insisted that after he, an Austrian, had won the Amsterdam competition, he should incorporate a design for an opera auditorium of 1956 by Dutch architects Bijvoet and Holt. A third distinguished architect, Cees Dam, who had married Holt's daughter, became a partner within the Holzbauer consortium, and it was Dam who had to reinterpret the design of a 1956 theatre space to fit within a 1986 opera house.

The *Architects' Journal* (19 November 1986) aptly titled my review of the result 'Double Dutch' and added in the header that I had found it 'a resoundingly cheerful building'. The form of the theatre space dates from that time when theatre architects thought that Ancient Greece was where you started. In Amsterdam the audience of 1,650 is arranged on three levels in a near semicircle of almost concentric arcs. A consequence is that they face the widest opera stage in Europe. This can be narrowed down, with panels, to a mere 16.5 metres, which is the width of the scenic opening of the London Coliseum or the Metropolitan Opera in New York, both of which have many more seats. At *Het Muziektheater* directors, designers and performers must cope with a stage which is too wide.

The cheerfulness starts in how the architects have handled the arrival of the public to the foyers arranged on this curve of the Amstel River. An inviting facade, articulated in seven well-proportioned urban facets, glows and glistens over the water and provides almost as much pleasure to the citizens on the opposite bank as to the arriving operagoer. He or she, after entering a small entrance foyer, mounts the gently curved stair which rises up to the first floor and the friendly pink-carpeted foyer where the audience assembles. The whole is well illustrated in images to be found easily on the internet.

At the start of the twenty-first century major cities in both North America and Europe were once again building new opera houses. Their auditoriums, post-Glyndebourne, are now generally

11.8 *Dallas Opera House 2010. Architects Foster + Partners advised by TPC.*

horseshoe in plan and have two, three or even four tiers wrapping around the shallowly raked orchestra stalls. The capacities of the two reviewed here are 1,400 and 2,300.

In one vital matter other than capacity new opera houses fall into two very different categories. One comprises those that are the homes of major subsidised opera and ballet companies, in which the works are created as well as performed. Within a single building performers and musicians rehearse, scenery is built and stored, costumes are made and the administration is housed. The Oslo Opera House of 2008 is the most successful of recent opera houses of this sort. One way of registering the difference between the two sorts is the size of their footprints. At Oslo the footprint is 18,460 square metres to serve a theatre with 1,400 seats, while the new one in Dallas has a footprint one third the size of Oslo, of only 6,160 square metres, yet has 60 per cent more seats – 2,300. The operas and ballets presented on the two stages are comparable in calibre. The difference is that all the preparations of the operas which happen on site at Oslo happen elsewhere at Dallas.

Hence in Dallas there are two distinct managements: that of the opera company and that of the building, which also books in and promotes all the other attractions: musicals, pop concerts, etc. The number of performances at the Margot and Bill Winspear Opera House in 2019 consisted of Dallas Opera thirty-four, Texas Ballet Theater twenty-two, visiting dance five, Broadway musicals twenty-two, and 'other', including symphony concerts, comedy and speakers, 118, making a total of 262 performances in the calendar year 2019. In that year performances of the Dallas Opera Company in the Dallas Opera House amounted to no more than 13 per cent of that total. The Winspear Opera House opened in 2010. It was the work of a largely British design team led by Foster + Partners as architects, partner in charge Spencer de Grey, with TPC as theatre consultants and Bob Essert as acoustician.

Oslo's new opera house is the home of *Den Norske Opera & Ballett* and opened in 2008 on a breathtaking site in Oslo harbour. A comprehensive brief was set out for an international competition which concluded in 1999. The winners were a team led by the Norwegian architectural firm Snøhetta. In 1988 the founders of Snøhetta, Kjetil Trædal Thorsen from Oslo and Craig Edward Dyke from Los Angeles, won a major international competition for the Alexandrina Bibliotheca in Egypt. Before Oslo Snøhetta had never built a theatre. An open competition too often leads to an eye-catching exterior which does not really work for the performers inside. In Oslo Snøhetta got the balance between exterior and interior just right. The brief had been written by Theatre Projects Consultants, as a result of which a TPC team led by Mark Stroomer and an Arup Acoustics one led by Rob Harris were appointed theatre and acoustical consultants. The Oslo auditorium echoes the horseshoe plan and the scale of Glyndebourne of fourteen years previous.

The principal reason why the Oslo Opera House will be ranked alongside Sydney as one of the best opera houses in the world is because the whole building sits so well on the chosen harbour site. It is unmistakeably Norwegian. The image of the exterior gives the idea. There is little to add to describe the brilliant idea of the architects of completing the entire building with sloping roofs, over which the public is invited to ascend and descend on foot, safely at all times of the year and at all times of day. This could happen only in Norway. This is a country of deep fjords and near-vertical mountainsides which citizens bravely enjoy at some time in their lives. Building regulations in Norway are different from those of the rest of Europe or of North America. There appear to be no conventional handrails but you are not going to fall off because the parapets and the changes of level are ingeniously detailed. In another situation such an exterior might be thought the conceit of a 'starchitect' but at Oslo it completes a whole building that functions well both inside and out and in every sense of that word.

11.9 *Oslo Opera House 2008. Architects Snøhetta advised by TPC.*

Enter the starchitects: their successes and failures

The first starchitect to succeed in transforming the reputation of an entire city had been Canadian American architect Frank Gehry who, in 1997, designed the Guggenheim Museum at Bilbao, then a run-down port in northern Spain. Thereafter cities sought out the starchitects for their flair and the prestige they brought with them. Meanwhile cost consultants immediately added a minimum of 15 per cent to their preliminary estimates before the selected starchitect even started work.

Museums and galleries were the first building types to attract the starchitect. It is relatively easy to provide a thrilling architectural context for the visual artist. But there are much more complex design parameters which must be observed for a new playhouse, opera house or concert hall where it is the ephemeral performances by living performers for whom the architect must provide a supportive frame, no more no less. The Sage Gateshead is a third starchitect success alongside Oslo and Dallas. Here Foster + Partners designed an exterior form which draws the eye of train passengers looking east when crossing the rail bridge over the Tyne. On a narrow site facing north an elegant triple-humped glazed shell makes an architectural unity of the three independently conceived spaces: Hall One (the main concert hall), Hall Two (discussed in Chapter 7) and between the two a rehearsal hall. The three are connected by swirling public spaces pitched above the final element consisting of a basement floor of congenial teaching spaces which, with the foyer above, are blessed with fine views overlooking the Tyne.

In contrast, consider another musical achievement which, like the opera house at Sydney of 1973, commands a harbour. The opera house/concert hall of Santa Cruz Tenerife in the Canary Islands was designed by starchitect Santiago Calatrava, a Spanish-Swiss artist and engineer turned charismatic architect. It was his first auditorium and seats 1,600 in a single dished rake of seating cut down the middle by a dead straight gangway. Above is a symphony of concrete curves which pulls the eye up to an apparent oculus over the front of the seating. It is hard to conceive a more effective way of cutting the performer down to size. Consult the internet and you will find plenty of eye-boggling exteriors and interiors.

The soubriquet *starchitect* often has a pejorative ring and suggests that famous architects can put eye-catching external form before the provision of a functional space for performers to share an experience with a live audience. However, we must also realise that there is no fixed formula for this and that architects who are true geniuses can surprise the overcautious. The asymmetric and truly original *Berlin Philharmonie* of 1963, which architect Hans Scharoun conceived and surrounded with the 'vineyard terraces' planned by acoustician Lothar Cremer, has long delighted players and audiences of 2,500. In 1975 I heard a concert given by the Berlin Philharmonic and the following morning was shown round by Scharoun's surviving architectural partner Edgar Wisniewski, who had studied music as well as architecture.

In Oslo the cloaking of auditorium and stage within Snøhetta's breathtaking glacier did not compromise what happens inside. All is well at Gateshead. In contrast one could say that what Calatrava achieved in the Canary Islands gave Tenerife a terrific landmark but at the expense of the performer.

12

Learning from the Netherlands, Berlin, Brazil, Australia and from Indian and Chinese cultures

The Netherlands

Working overseas or speaking at international conferences gives one the chance to see how other countries tackle universal issues differently. In the late 1970s I got to know Onno Greiner, architect of Amsterdam who built many theatres and cultural centres. My contributions to his later designs were small but the experience was deeply enjoyable. We shared views on how, in a well-designed theatre space, new or old, the audience assists the performer in the making of magic.

12.1 *Onno Greiner's* De Tamboer *at Hoogeveen 1990.*

At our first meeting, in 1974, Greiner introduced himself at Schiphol airport, sat me in his Porsche and set off at 160kph across endless flat polders to show me his work. These included the cultural centres of Hoogeveen (1960), away up in the north-east, and Amersfoort (1970), an hour from Amsterdam, where Greiner had his bureau. In 1990/91 I was to help him to replace both their original auditoriums. At Hoogeveen in 1990 this was to add to his earlier small auditorium, which had one tier and lots of 45-degree angles, a larger and more tightly planned 800-seat theatre which has two tiers and lots of curves. At Amersfoort it was to substitute for his first auditorium holding 450 a new 800-seater with three circles.

From the start I was struck by how economically his buildings had been conceived and second how performance was just one sort of thing which happened in a 'cultural centre' – a term which in the English language daunts while the Dutch *cultureel centrum* does not. They generally consist of an internal street leading to a theatre space off which cluster many spaces available for different uses. The mix was something which did not appear elsewhere until much later. The modest building costs of these Dutch cultural centres were paid for by the town, who also met the running costs. They are used for everything. In Sliedrecht I watched a matinee audience of schoolchildren leave, the seats in the centre quickly stacked and eight gleaming cars driven in for an evening's motor show. In Amersfoort I listened to the Chris Barber Jazz Band in the flat-floor galleried central space holding 1,000 for concerts and termed the town square. The next day it was to serve as the weekly food and flower market.

Most of Greiner's cultural centres were new build and were set out on a strict six-metre grid with an internal height generally of three metres. Each square was supported at the corners by concrete pillars. Each module was topped with a peaked roof carrying its own air extract and intake plus primary and secondary lighting. Occasionally there were double spans and, in the case of the town square, triple. This systematic flexibility kept down building costs. Much of the square stone paving was bedded directly on to the earth mixed with the right sort of sand.

In 1970 Biberach an der Riss, a small town not far from Munich, held a competition for a cultural centre or *Stadthalle*. This was open to any West German architect plus four foreign invitees. Greiner won. In 1977 I boarded a bus in Amsterdam along with many of Greiner's staff and some Dutch architectural journalists to head south. All were proud of the success in Germany of a Dutch architect. But there was a difference which shocked many of his staff: the finishes were not low cost as they were in the Netherlands. The roofs were of grand bituminous shingles, not simple zinc, and the circular light fittings hand-blown glass not paper. Movable walls, made of fireproof panels, were manhandled in the Netherlands but glided on silent motors at Biberach. Yet the philosophy was the same.

Meanwhile Greiner had revitalised the 1865 *Schouwburg* at Leiden, which seemed to me like a smaller version of London's 1871 Old Vic. Inside he avoided slavish restoration but rather sang a sympathetic descant when it came to colour and decorative light fittings. His central new/old chandelier was made of timber and the brackets on the tier fronts held hand-blown glass globes with a gold sparkle while those in the foyers shone with a subtler silver. At Leiden Greiner learnt a lesson that he would explore in his later theatre spaces: 'My conclusion is that thorough study and analysis of the older theatres would help us with the realisation of new ones.' On the plans and sections of Leiden he traced the oval which suggested 'a centre of the magnetic field in space', which became known more simply as 'Greiner's egg'. His young professional partner Martien van Goor summarised it thus: 'Actor and audience close together; Actor feels as if he is part of the auditorium; Audience members have visual contact with the actor and one another.' The Greiner approach was also summarised in the Dutch architectural

12.2 De Maagd *Theatre within deconsecrated church, Bergen op zoom 1990 over Greiner drawing of renovation at Enschede Schouwburg 1988. Both advised by TPC.*

magazine *Bouw* of November 1982 where he wrote that 'it does not interest me in the least **what** people say they want. What does interest me is **why** they want a thing.'

Another theatre was truly unique: *De Maagd* at Bergen op Zoom. This was a redundant Roman Catholic Church of 1829 transformed by Greiner into a theatre in 1990. I was invited to join Greiner's team. The aisle had eight pairs of columns in the nave less than 11 metres apart, which was just wide enough to insert a 650-seat theatre space with two sets of superimposed balconies subtly curved and stepped down to the stage. One pair of columns were removed for the main stage which extends upstage into the apse. In the side aisles the original huge stained-glass windows were celebrated and backlit. Everywhere one turns one knows that this **is** a theatre but **was** a church. In Chapter 14 some American theatres and movie palaces are mentioned which have become churches. This may be easier to achieve than the other way round. In 1991 Francis Reid reported in the *Architects' Journal* of July 1991:

> Church and theatre have always been much more closely related than most theologians and thespians across the ages have been prepared to acknowledge. Certainly, they declare a common purpose of spiritual uplift. With something of a tendency towards a surplus of churches and shortage of theatres, we may see an increase in conversion activity. In which case I nominate de Maagd as an indispensable reference.

At Enschede on the German border we refreshed a dull, cinema-like 900-seater from 1950. We added four boxes stepping down each side to the proscenium, not unlike what TPC had introduced for the 1983 rebuild at St Lawrence Centre, Toronto. Above the boxes at Enschede hang three stalactite lighting positions, a simplification of those pioneered by Pilbrow at the Olivier. Suspended over the stalls seating are two glittering and interlocked lighting bridges giving centrality to the theatre space as their predecessors do at Toronto.

In Den Haag, the centre of government in the Netherlands, I worked briefly on some improvements to *Der Koninklijke Schouwburg* (Theatre Royal) with Belgian architect Charles Vandenhove. This theatre had been constructed in 1804 and was entered through an elegant nobleman's palace built in 1766. Working on this theatre allowed me the rare pleasure of researching what had happened in 1910/11 when it had been the subject of a unique architectural competition that shortlisted the two most prolific theatre architectural firms in Europe: Matcham and Co. of London and Fellner and Helmer of Vienna. Both produced impressive proposals, neither of which was built. Shortly after the First World War, during which the Netherlands had been neutral in a conflict that had Britain and Austria on opposing sides, the city architect of Den Haag, J.J.Gort, carried out a more modest scheme. Curators of public collections in Den Haag helped, as did scholar Marlies van der Riet who shared my passion for finding out how it all did not happen. I contributed 'King Kong versus Godzilla: The Competition for the Royal Opera House at The Hague, 1910–1911' to *Frank Matcham & Co.*, a volume edited and published by David Wilmore in 2008. For my article there are seventeen illustrations, many in colour and of hitherto unpublished designs by both Matcham and Fellner and Helmer as well as by Gort, all of which were sourced from the *Haags Gemeentearchief*, the municipal archives.

Two historic theatres in East Berlin

In 1989 the Berlin Wall came down and the socialist east and capitalist west were joined at the hip. In June 1995, when driving across central Europe to serve on the international jury for the

Prague Quadrennial of Scenography and Theatre Architecture, my stop-off was in what had been East Berlin. I can date this precisely as on the first morning of my short visit I went along with 100,000 others to watch the final knot being tied on the wrapping of the Reichstag by artist Christo.

On my first visit to West Berlin twenty years earlier I had visited the soberly efficient *Deutsche Oper* as well as the gloriously original *Philharmonie*. On this second visit, to East Berlin, I encountered two famous historic theatres which had survived both the Nazi and communist regimes.

The first was the rococo *Komische Oper* where you must not be put off by the boring stone and glass box exterior added in 1966. The original interior, by Fellner and Helmer and holding 1,200, was built in 1892 and has that elusive quality of working equally well for the comic and for the tragic. Walter Felsenstein founded the opera company which bore the name of the theatre and was its *Intendant* from 1947 until his death in 1975. Harry Kupfer took over in 1981 and in 1986 directed a production of *The Marriage of Figaro* which critic Barry Millington said 'highlighted the social repression and chauvinism of the world depicted by Beaumarchais'. The conductor was Rolf Reuter, musical director of the *Komische Oper* from 1981 to 1993.

By sheer chance, on 24 June 1995 I witnessed a special performance of Kupfer's still fresh production of *Figaro* at the *Komische Oper* conducted by Reuter. I discovered that there had been a change in the meticulously planned repertoire. There were stickers on the posters outside announcing the change, something unheard of in efficiently managed German opera houses. There was a good reason: it was to be Reuter's farewell to the company. At the curtain calls, while on stage Reuter acknowledged the applause from a packed theatre, the leader of the pit orchestra moved quietly to the conductor's rostrum and raised his baton. The orchestra and the singers then reprised the happy ending of the Act Four sextet, directing it personally at Reuter.

The second was the *Theater am Schiffbauerdamm,* of similar size to the *Komische Oper* and built in the same year. This is where the Berliner Ensemble was founded in 1949 by Bertolt Brecht after his return from self-imposed exile. What strikes one immediately about this romantic theatre space is its theatricality, which is much more than mere background. When Brecht banished theatrical illusion he deliberately chose his theatres at home and on touring abroad for their theatricality. This was at the time when the British theatre establishment was waxing lyrical over Brecht, the prophet of a revolutionary theatre, while planning their own buildings which were relentlessly modernist with the notable exception of Joan Littlewood's Theatre Royal at Stratford East. Brecht's own theatre was decidedly not a concrete people's palace. Both Felsenstein and Brecht needed the clutter of theatricality to frame their rejection of theatrical illusion rather than austere modernism which too often lowers the temperature before the show has even started.

From Prague to Brazil

That summer I was on my way to Czechoslovakia, which had recently acquired, as its first president, the previously imprisoned playwright Václav Havel. On the suggestion of John Bury I was to be the first Briton to sit on the international jury of the 1995 Prague Quadrennial of Stage Design and Theatre Architecture. I soon realised that worldwide directors, playwrights, designers and performers needed something more than an auditorium with satisfactory sightlines, acceptable acoustics and functional stage equipment. With these priorities there would always be something missing. William Combe in the *Political Magazine* included a plate dated 1 February 1815 by Thomas Rowlandson, introducing his theatric tourist, Dr Syntax to the brand-new Theatre Royal Covent Garden of 200 years ago. Dr Syntax did not like it:

'I think,' says Syntax, looking round,
'It is not good this vast profound;
Too large to hear – too long to see –
Full of unmeaning symmetry;
And all, alas! too plainly show
How easy 'tis to form a row:
But where's the grand, the striking whole?
A theatre should have a soul.'

Today's theatric tourist learns as much from geography as from history. In 1995, at Prague, we the jury awarded the premier prize, the Golden Triga, to Brazil. A dozen men and women from a dozen countries took only fifteen minutes to come to this decision and then three hours to decide the six or so other awards. Brazilian designers and directors had worked in conventional theatres, both old and new, both big and small, as well as in found spaces that had not hitherto experienced performance. I needed to see those theatres in Brazil which I suspected as definitely having a soul.

Five years later I was invited to Brazil to speak at a theatre architecture conference held at São Paulo. My host was José Carlos Serroni, the modest doyen of Brazilian stage design. Modest because in Prague in 1995 he had been so certain that Brazil would not win that he had left the country before the prizegiving. At his conference I realised that São Paulo was the fourth great theatre city in the world after London, New York and Paris, and not least for the *Teatro Oficina* mentioned earlier. For a short post-conference tour José Carlos Serroni asked my wife and me to choose three theatres to visit anywhere in that vast country. We chose three historic theatres, those in Ouro Preto, Manaus and Fortaleza.

Ouro Preto is 500 kilometres from the coast and before the aeroplane was reached only by road through tropical jungle. It has the oldest surviving theatre in the Americas, built in 1770. Like its contemporary, the Theatre Royal in Bristol, it never closed for a long period but had been marginally modified as fashions changed. However, the narrowness of this gently curved auditorium, which holds 500 today, had probably been determined by the limits in length of spanning roof timbers easily available in Ouro Preto at the time. Like all Brazilian theatres built prior to the introduction of mechanical ventilation the tier fronts were spun delicately of wood or later of iron imported from Europe which allowed the air to circulate naturally.

Why Ouro Preto possessed a theatre as fine as this as early as 1770 is explained by the fact that it was then the largest city in the Americas. Its population was 80,000 in the late eighteenth century when that of New York City was scarcely 25,000. Ouro Preto, then called Vila Rica, was also the richest city in the Americas – in the eighteenth century 800 tons of gold were mined locally and shipped back to Portugal. Today in Ouro Preto there is scarcely a modern building. The streets and squares are irregularly terraced and there is a simple conservation by-law: you may do what you like to the interior of your house but for the carefully preserved plaster exterior you must choose from a palette of authorised authentic colours, preferably a different one from that of your neighbour. The theatre itself is not in the centre but on a low hill to take advantage of every available breeze in the hot humid air.

12.3 *Interiors of Ouro Preto theatre 1770 over Manaus Opera House 1897.*

Manaus lies 1,600 kilometres up the tidal Amazon. The Portuguese invented the tapping of rubber in the middle of the nineteenth century. The rubber boom, which lasted three decades, made Manaus one of the richest places on earth and as such it had to have an opera house. The *Teatro Amazonas* was proposed in 1881 and opened in 1897, one of the first theatres in the world to be lit entirely by electricity. Some will know it from Werner Herzog's movie *Fitzcarraldo*. In 1876, an Englishman smuggled some rubber tree seedlings out from Manaus to Malaya and there created a new British industry to undercut the Amazon Brazilian boom, which then faltered. The city's electrical generators proved too expensive to run and few performances took place in the *Teatro Amazonas* until its centenary in 1997. By then the economy of Manaus had partially recovered and the population had reached two million. The restored *Teatro Amazonas* now holds 700 in stalls and four horseshoe tiers. Short seasons of opera are presented regularly.

In the late nineteenth century European ocean-going cargo ships had steamed 1,500 kilometres up the tidal Amazon to Manaus to collect cargoes of rubber and coffee. They had brought upstream very different cargoes: for the *Teatro Amazonas* furnishings from France, marble and statues from Italy and ironwork from Scotland. The ironwork included the columns supporting the gilded galleries and the filigree tier fronts, all forged at George Smith's Sun Foundry in Glasgow. The grandeur of this 'temple sacred to opera' was admired by all the rich rubber barons. The streets around the opera house, like those around the best brothels, were finished in rubber so the clatter of carriages would not disturb the pleasures being enjoyed.

While Scottish ironwork was just one element in the sumptuous *Teatro Amazonas* the design of the *Teatro José de Alencar* at Fortaleza of 1910 had involved Scotland from the outset. Lieutenant Bernardo José de Mello, not an architect but 'an illustrious engineer' from Portugal, had studied the catalogues of another Glasgow Iron Foundry, that of Walter Macfarlane & Co., whose works covered ten acres. Hotels, railway stations and, on the Amazon, floating harbours arrived as flat packs by boat, often with a Scottish engineer to help assemble the bespoke ironwork structures. At Fortaleza, de Mello and a representative of Macfarlanes had chosen a style which was part art nouveau. It was also functional in detail: the gas feed for the house lighting rose up within the hollow iron supporting columns, each of which was proudly cast with the name Macfarlane & Co. What is remarkable about the *Teatro José de Alencar*, which holds 760 today, is the coherence of the style and the fact that this is a practical design for a humid climate where the average year-round temperature day and night is in the high 20s. Round the circle fronts are the names of Goethe, Shakespeare, Verdi, Wagner, Victor Hugo, Gluck and Brazil's own playwright, the eponymous José de Alencar. His theatre, which when I visited had just been beautifully restored for its ninetieth anniversary in 2000, is something of which Brazil is proud but which Scotland has forgotten.

Learning lessons in Australia

In 1971 I had shepherded Prospect to the biennial Adelaide Festival followed by visits to Sydney and Melbourne. We presented two plays in repertoire, *King Lear* and *Love's Labour's Lost*. Timothy West had already given his Lear at the Assembly Hall Edinburgh, at *Teatro la Fenice* in Venice and on tour in the UK. *Love's Labour's Lost* had been added and cross cast as Adelaide wanted two plays. The whole eight-month venture was to end at London's Aldwych as guests of

12.4 Theatro José de Alencar *Fortaleza 1910*.

the RSC. In Adelaide we played Her Majesty's, which had been built in 1913 but in 1930 had been given a cinema-like auditorium with a single balcony. There I learnt a useful lesson about how technical devices can interfere with live theatre. After a hard-to-hear first night West stated that for the second the management would have to choose between the noisy air conditioning and his Lear. The manager of the theatre agreed to switch off the air conditioning but said that at least half a dozen of the audience would faint and be carried out. He exaggerated – I counted only five. The next day workmen on the roof followed up my simple suggestion of running the extract fan at half speed. At the end of the run the theatre reintroduced the noisy high speed. In the press some complained of the interfering limeys who did not understand that air conditioning was a necessity for the humid Australian summers. Why were English actors so fussy? Others, who had arrived in Australia more recently, thanked us for taking a stand at the principal theatre in town where the rattle of the ventilation was ruining their pleasure.

After Adelaide we went to Sydney and played the Theatre Royal. This was already the third Theatre Royal, of which there had been those of 1827, 1875 and the 1921 version which was the one Prospect closed. The original site was then redeveloped and a fourth Theatre Royal, described in their own Wikipedia entry as being 'in a plain modernist style', opened in 1976 and closed for refurbishment in 2016.

Prospect finished its Australian tour at the 1876 Princess Theatre in Melbourne, where successive British drama companies had played from Laurence Olivier's Old Vic Company in 1948 onwards. The Princess had also staged the third production in the world of the musical *Camelot*, which ran for two years there and was designed by Australian stage designer John Truscott, who would go on to win two Oscars for the 1967 movie of *Camelot*. The relevance of Truscott is that the vast Melbourne Arts Centre was nearing completion in 1983 when I returned to give a paper at a conference on eighteenth-century studies. Trial concerts were being given in the 2,650-seat concert hall at the new Arts Centre. Next door the large lyric theatre for 2,000 was being fitted out. The architect, Roy Grounds, had started his design in the 1960s. Everything was to be in the modernist style and fashioned in impregnable concrete. But Grounds had died in 1981 and Truscott was appointed to 'decorate' the interior. Architectural tastes having changed, he was given free rein. The only constraint was that he could not remove elements already constructed but was allowed to decorate the concrete with colour, vibrantly textured by scenic artists, and introduce metallic finishes. Truscott added perforated brass balls and draped areas with shining steel mesh. The Melbourne Arts Centre became a friendly place. Truscott had wrapped in gaiety the inherent severity of brutalist concrete.

Re-examining Indian and Chinese indigenous theatre cultures

India and China are potentially the two biggest theatre countries in Asia. How they regard their ancient theatrical traditions and how they enlist international theatrical and architectural practices to serve their populations differ greatly. In India, Bollywood rules and most theatrical discussion and experiment is at a small scale. In China there is little discussion or experiment while every city with aspirations for 'world-class' status hires international starchitects to spend public money on eye-catching 2,000-seat theatres in which to entertain their hard-working citizens.

In 2003 I was invited to Mumbai in India by Atul Kumar, founder in 1993 of the Company Theatre, and by architect and author Himanshu Burte to a conference held at the renowned Prithvi Theatre, built in 1978. I had met them both in London and knew that the Prithvi had been modelled on the Young Vic by architect Ved Segan and client Jennifer Kapoor, who was the elder sister of English actor Felicity Kendal. The Prithvi has a thrust stage which Guthrie would have recognised.

A second All India Seminar on theatre spaces was held in March 2012 at Ninasam in Karnataka, a night's train journey north-west of Bangalore. It had been founded in 1947 and has become a centre for dramatists, students of film and, since 1985, a troupe of actors who tour to rural communities. One evening at the conference we enjoyed a production of Chekhov's *The Seagull* in Kannada, which is the language of Karnataka. At both conferences it was apparent that most of the theatrical energy in India came from much smaller performance spaces although the theatre itself at Ninasam was an exception, holding 700. Elsewhere and in contrast to China there is simply no public and little private money for large spaces. The most vivid expression of the unwillingness of any public authority to build a major theatre is illustrated by the sad story of the Indira Gandhi National Arts Centre in New Delhi, which never happened.

In 1987 American architect Ralph Lerner won an international competition for the Indira Gandhi National Centre for the Arts, held in parallel with an international theatre conference entitled *Concepts of Space Ancient and Modern*. The proceedings were published by IGNCA in 1991; 600 pages with sixty-four papers given by the sixty-seven delegates from all over the world. The only theatre architect of international stature present was Dutchman Onno Greiner, who stated his theories of the underlying geometry of good theatres. Otherwise, the contributions were mainly scholarly reflections on space, sacred and social as well as theatrical. For the concurrent competition there were 134 entries from thirty-seven countries. Fifty of these are reproduced in *Concepts and Responses: The International Competition for the Indira Gandhi National Centre for the Arts*. Many ideas but no action. Existing buildings in New Delhi were extended for libraries, galleries and administrative spaces for IGNCA but no single part of the winning design has ever been built.

One of Lerner's three main spaces had been inspired by India's only indigenous theatre form: the ancient *kuttampalams* of Kerala. These are temple theatres which are still in use. If you are not a Hindu you are unlikely to be allowed into the temple precincts where a few of these ancient free-standing theatres survive and in which performances of *kutiyattam* regularly take place. The more familiar *kathakali* with its similar fantastical make-up and costume is a pure dance form derived from the earlier *kutiyattam*. The latter, in which the actors and musicians also sing, dates back nearly 2,000 years. From the start female performers were allowed. The plays are long. In 2007 my wife and I spent three consecutive evenings in a small theatre space at Irinjalakuda in Kerala watching performances each lasting three hours. These added up to a small part only of the saga of *Shakuntala* by the Sanskrit poet Kalidasa, of which Goethe wrote that 'it contains the history of a development – the development of a flower into fruit, of earth into heaven, of matter into spirit'. Irinjalakuda is home to the secular training establishment for the arts of *kutiyattam* overseen by the Chakyar family, who are the hereditary exponents of this art. The evenings were created by guru Gopal Venu, whom I had met at the Mumbai conference. It was unforgettable but would have been even better had it taken place in a *kuttampalam*, ancient or modern, with square stage and audience on three sides. *Kuttambalams* in Kerala temples can be found at Haripad, built in 1769, and at Thrissur, similar in plan but slightly larger, which was built a century later in 1880. There are no new *kuttambalams* outside temple precincts, which was what Lerner had intended with his winning entry.

That was not the only spin-off from the Mumbai conference. In London in April 2012 Shakespeare's Globe opened a seven-week season of all thirty-seven plays in thirty-seven different languages. Kumar brought his Company Theatre production of *Twelfth Night* performed in Hindi, which they played without an interval in under two hours. Half of that London audience were Hindi speakers. Those of us who were not but knew the play were helped by the Indian company's mime techniques. Together we became one audience that warm spring evening and laughed a lot.

In the People's Republic of China architecturally striking and publicly funded 2,000-seat-plus lyric theatres provide musical entertainment which is unlikely to disturb the political peace.

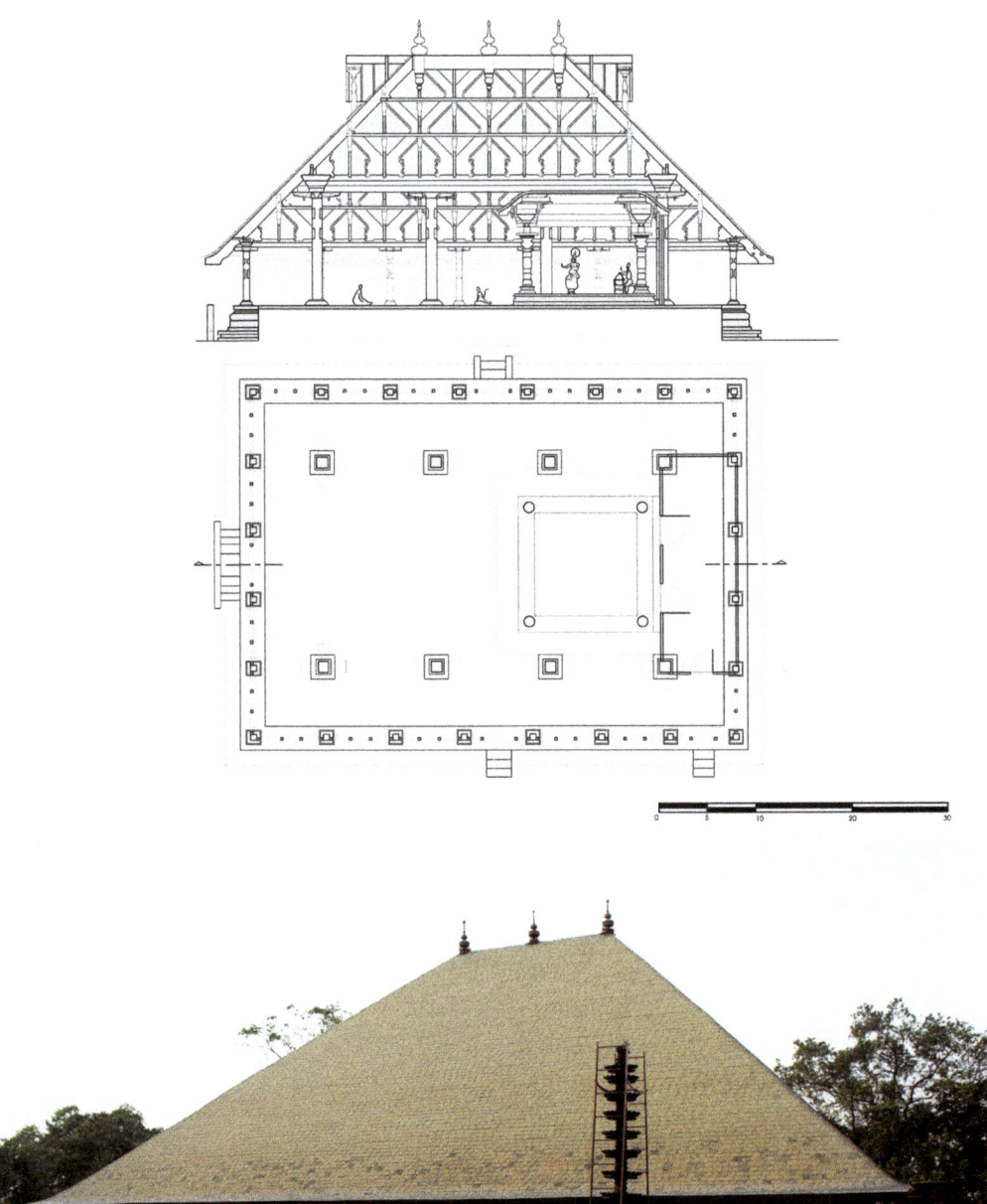

12.5 *Two temple* kuttampalams *in Kerala India at Haripad 1769 and at Thrissur 1880. Drawn and photographed by Gopika Jayasaree.*

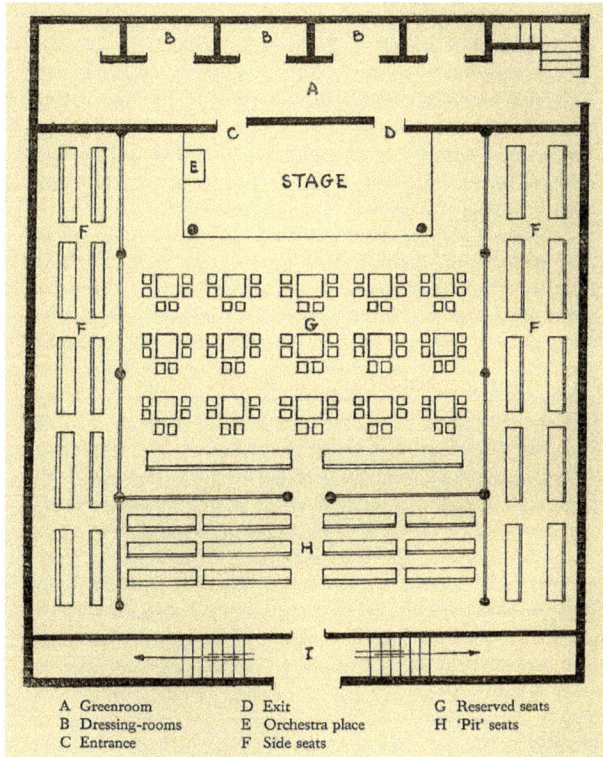

12.6 Zhengyici *Beijing, photo over plan of typical classical theatre drawn by Jack Chen.*

All these theatres, generally termed opera houses, are photogenic and are well documented on the internet. The National Centre for the Performing Arts in Beijing of 2007, designed by French airport architect Paul Andreu, is 'a semi-ellipsoidal titanium and glass shell' set in the middle of a lake under which audiences arrive and has three performance spaces: an opera house for 2,200, a concert hall for 1,800 or a third fully equipped theatre holding 1,000. The Guangzhou Opera House by Zaha Hadid opened in 2010: 1,800 theatregoers are held in the asymmetric auditorium described in the *Guardian* in February 2011 as 'a great grotto like a shark's mouth'.

In China very few old classical theatres survive. Elegant stone-built stages can still be found in private parks originally built for the delight of the ruling classes. The real theatres, the people's theatres in the strict meaning of that term, were of wood and were not unlike Elizabethan playhouses with a stage projecting into a yard where the audience sat, drank and talked. The square yard was often open to the sky and was surrounded by galleries in which the ladies sat.

Most of these did not survive the civil wars of the 1930s, the Japanese invasion and the decade-long Cultural Revolution from 1966 to 1976 when not only buildings were destroyed but plays were burnt and actors sent to work in the fields. In Beijing in the 1920s there had been at least twenty-two such theatres for a population then of only 850,000. This evidence comes from the cogent short history *The Chinese Theatre* by Jack Chen, published in London in 1949. Chen came from a French Creole/Chinese Trinidadian family and was both an artist journalist and a staunch communist until he left China for the USA during the Cultural Revolution.

Today in Beijing the few surviving old theatres include the relatively small *Zhengyici*, parts of which date back to the seventeenth century, which attracts both Chinese and foreign tourists. But 99 per cent of performances in all China of what the west termed Peking Opera now take place in those huge state-funded and well-amplified auditoriums facing western-style stages. The motives seem admirable at first sight: much larger audiences can experience the national heritage than ever could in the cramped old theatres. Yet it was in these smaller theatres that the ancient arts of Chinese theatre had been nurtured.

In Singapore in the early 1990s TPC was advising London-based architects Michael Wilford on what was to become the Esplanade Theatres on the Bay and which were opened in 2002. There were to be a 1,950-seat lyric theatre, a 1,800-seat concert hall and a 500-seat playhouse. My role was to come up with ideas for the last of these What sort of space would best serve the predominately Chinese culture? I also visited Manila and Kuala Lumpur to see shows and to talk with actors and academics. What we started to sketch for Singapore was a space which followed the scale and plan of the old Chinese theatres: a square courtyard but with only one side fixed and the other sides consisting of matching three-storey wagons, movable on-air pallets, to be occupied by audience or performers. In the centre there was to be a modular floor, sections of which could be raised to form a thrust stage or be lowered for variously distributed audiences, either seated or standing. This playhouse was cut because it would have been either too expensive or possibly politically dangerous.

The political background is relevant. From 1948 to 1960 British and Commonwealth troops had fought and defeated communist forces in the Malayan jungle. In 1965 Singapore became a state separate from Malaya. Its benevolent one-party centrist government had to act ruthlessly to avoid the communist coups as had happened in China and Vietnam. There is a clue that the abandonment of a playhouse in Singapore might have been partly political. The Wikipedia entry for charismatic playwright and left-wing political activist Kuo Pao Kun honours his theatrical achievements as well as mentioning his reinstatement after detention without trial in Changi jail from 1976 to 1981.This 'caused him to undergo a major re-evaluation and reflection of his perceptions and thoughts'. When I talked with him in London, soon after he had been handed back his passport, Kuo's voice took on an artificial tone when the government's role in the arts came up in conversation. He died in 2002 at the age of only sixty-three. This was the year that the Theatres on the Bay opened, lacking a playhouse.

Meanwhile, when planning the Esplanade, a meeting was arranged with the then pre-eminent female martial artist of the People's Republic of China who that week was playing the inadequate twentieth-century Victoria Hall in Singapore. We had a translator. I tried with difficulty and a sketch pad to get her views on traditional Chinese theatre buildings. Suddenly her face lit up: 'You mean the old theatres. They were everywhere. They were wonderful. They have destroyed them all.' This conversation took place fifteen years after the end of the Cultural Revolution.

Research offered some surprises. Chinese immigrants from mainland China in the late nineteenth century had brought their *wayangs* to Singapore to celebrate religious festivals. This name was used not only for puppet theatres but for the temporary stages of bamboo erected by itinerant companies of actors. The stages were about five feet off the ground and roofed. There was performed everything from Chinese opera to acrobatics. Audiences of up to about 500 would stand in front or sit inside galleries of bamboo. Curiously the stages were often built over water, both for religious reasons and because at the water's edge it was easier to find a pitch for a temporary structure. An image of a waterside bamboo theatre at night by a nineteenth-century European artist is included here. By the time we were planning the Esplanade the *wayang* had

12.7 *Oil painting by an unknown mid-19th-century Chinese artist of a waterside open-air performance.*

moved indoors in both Singapore and Hong Kong. Health and safety and the ambient noise of a modern city had made performance out of doors no longer feasible.

Twenty-five years later a more self-confident Singapore government did add a playhouse to the Esplanade Theatres on the Bay. This is a semi-flexible space but one which could have happened in any 'world-class' city anywhere.

13

2010–2020: Some new builds, two renovations – one at Stratford-upon-Avon and one in London – and diversions on in-the-round and the open air

The first two decades of this century

The 1920 start date for this century of theatre space makes sense because after the end of the war in 1918 the recovery in theatre building was slow, other than in the USA where the theatre building boom had never stopped. The end date of 2020 suddenly became significant because the Covid-19 pandemic arrived that year and almost all theatres worldwide closed for eighteen months.

Shortly before 2020, public money for new theatres was drying up after the recession of 2008. The new theatre spaces being created were generally small. Architects, stakeholders, government officials and leaders of the theatre profession put first the keeping going what was already there. But there were exceptions such as the glorious renovation of the Theatre Royal Drury Lane, occupying Britain's oldest theatre site, which was completed a year late in 2021. Lastly in this chapter there are three unique theatre spaces, each more than twenty-five years old, which surprisingly have not been replicated.

The first two reviewed here are medium-sized, seating around 400: the Everyman at Liverpool (2014) and the other at Chateau d' Hardelot near Boulogne (2016). There follow three larger ones that are each refreshingly different: the new Royal Shakespeare Theatre at Stratford-upon-Avon (2010), the Yard in Chicago (2017) and the Bridge in London (2017). The sixth is the aforesaid renovation of Drury Lane. The three innovative older successes consist of two in-the-round, the large Royal Exchange Manchester, which opened in 1976, the small Orange Tree in Richmond Surrey of 1991 and third the Regent's Park Open Air Theatre, holding 25 per cent more than the Olivier on a site which has been in regular use for drama since 1932 and today has an auditorium built in 1975 and gently renovated in 1999.

The Everyman Liverpool

This theatre, which won the Stirling Prize in 2011, is colourful. It has a near-fixed-form thrust stage space holding 400 to 450 depending on details of the arrangement. There is a

13.1 *Liverpool Everyman 2011. Architects Howarth Tompkins. Exterior over performance on thrust stage.*

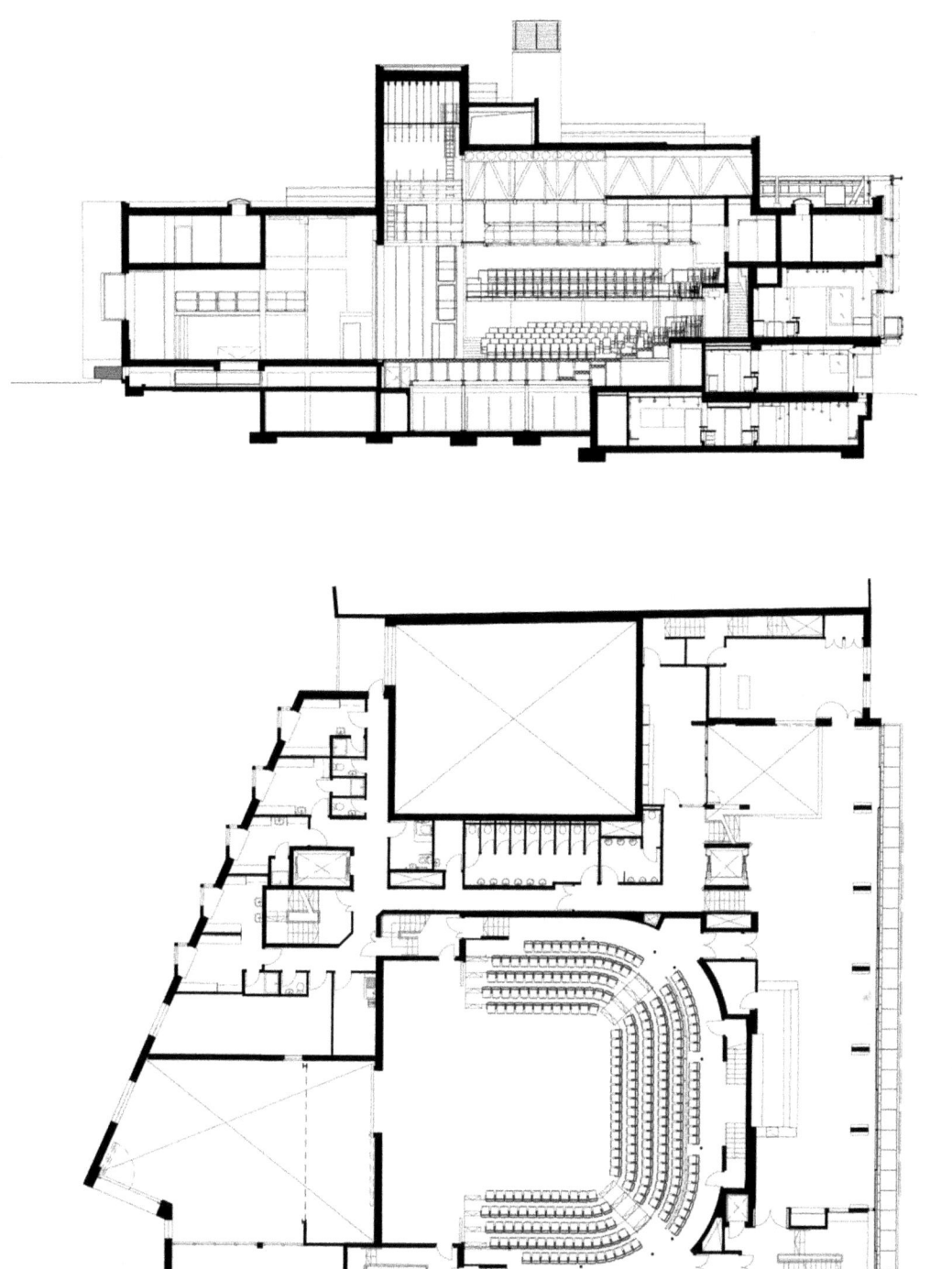

13.2 *Liverpool Everyman section over stalls level thrust without stage riser plan. Architects Haworth Tompkins.*

wrap-around gallery on three sides with two rows of seating. Below there are five stepped rows with the front row generally at stage level. On this arrangement there is no stage riser, which can create some sightline problems for viewing the downstage actor from all but the front couple of rows. That problem was succinctly stated by Swedish theatre design guru Per Simon Edström in his *Why Not Theaters Made For People?* published in 1990: 'If a naked ballet came on to the stage most of the audience would think that hair grew only on their heads.' However, at the Everyman, on all three sides of the playing area the rake of the lower level can be seamlessly extended forward by two further stepped rows which results in a stage riser of 600 mm. A further adjustment gives three rows below stage level in the centre block of seating plus, if wanted, a small orchestra pit. The result is a forestage and beyond a shallow scenic stage complete with fly tower suitable for panto or traditionally staged musicals.

The first Everyman had been created in 1964 in the Hope Hall of 1837, which had been first a Dissenters' chapel and then a cinema. A remodelling in 1977 was judged unsatisfactory. New funding was found and adjacent buildings were acquired. In 2011 the entire structure was demolished, but not before newly appointed architect Haworth Tompkins had captured its essence. The bricks from the old space, 25,000 of them, were carefully taken down and scrubbed to be reused in the new. That sense of continuity contributes to a coherent journey from the Hope Street entrance, above which 102 life-size images representing every man and every woman in Liverpool welcome you to walk through congenial public spaces to a warm auditorium.

A theatre in a wood: Chateau D' Hardelot in the Pas-de-Calais

This remarkable space offers the option of working with natural light. We are exhilarated by the blue sky above us at Epidaurus in Greece and at Shakespeare's Globe or at Regent's Park, both in London. This is also possible in a new indoor theatre at Chateau d' Hardelot standing in a wood near Boulogne-sur-Mer, France. The architect is Andrew Todd, a talented and quixotic English architect based in Paris. In 2013 Todd won a competition to devise an Elizabethan theatre at Chateau d' Hardelot which is a Norman castle, partially rebuilt in the nineteenth century in the Tudor style. The aim was to celebrate the *Entente Cordiale* between France and Great Britain signed in 1904. As luck would have it the theatre was inaugurated in June 2016 on the day after it was announced that Great Britain had decided, by referendum, to leave the European Union. Brexit then took four years to happen, which seems a long time until one remembers that for more than two centuries, from 1346 to 1558, the Pas-de-Calais had been part of England.

Todd has designed a totally modern timber theatre which consciously echoes the form but not the detail of the theatres of William Shakespeare. When Chorus in *Henry V* talks of 'the very casques / that did affright the air at Agincourt' he is referring to the battlefield just up the road from Hardelot. When Todd decided to make his 'unworthy scaffold' of wood he achieved just that as near as damn it, adding only some slim steel where necessary for load bearing. The result is at once minimalist and romantic. Todd was quoted by Rowan Moore in the *Observer* of 26 June 2016: 'Unlike many palaces of culture it is possible to put on a show in this building literally with nothing, using only natural light from the sun and natural ventilation, the breath

13.3 *Theatre at Chateau d'Hardelot, Pas-de-Calais. Architect Andrew Todd.*

of the surrounding forest.' For Todd the architecture of a theatre space should bring 'atmosphere, spirit . . . suggest, provoke, inspire, but not instruct nor demand'. The whole project can be seen as Todd's creation and his alone. At first there were disagreements between the local authority and successive artistic directors and the result at the time of writing was that there was no properly funded user to breathe life into this magic place. Yet a theatre space as good as that at Chateau d'Hardelot will surely find its Prospero. It may have more built-in potential than the average Elizabethan reiteration.

Stratford-upon-Avon: the third Memorial Theatre of 2011

Stratford-upon-Avon has already featured twice: in Chapter 3 for Elisabeth Scott's Memorial Theatre of 1932, the auditorium of which was demolished for the recent remodelling, and in Chapter 7 for the introduction of the 450-seat Swan Theatre. What follows is an account of the genesis of the third theatre space on the site. This took an interminable twenty years from 1991, when Adrian Noble was appointed to succeed Trevor Nunn as director, to 2010 and the opening of the rebuilt theatre by architect Rab Bennetts advised by theatre consultants Charcoalblue and to the taste of new RSC director Michael Boyd.

Usually, the wrong turnings for a new theatre are left out of any account of how a new theatre space happens. In the case of Stratford-upon-Avon the twists and turns may help to understand the roles of artistic directors and boards of governors as well as those of architects and their consultants. I had the misfortune to be involved for two years starting in late 2000. Things did go wrong.

The invitation to join the team at Stratford came as a surprise. My first meeting took place in December 2000 when I met with director Noble, architect Erick van Egeraat and project manager Jane Blackburn, whose main role was to keep the record. I was told this was to be a fresh start but later discovered that van Egeraat had been appointed nearly two years previous. I do not know in what archives you would find the files on the early days of this long-running RSC saga. The good thing was that unlike so many projects there seemed to be money: £50 million from government if the RSC could match this from private sources. The RSC were confident of that.

The National Heritage Lottery had been distributing funds nationally to arts building projects since 1994. At Stratford there had been studies by others before van Egeraat was appointed under new rules that had only recently been set out in the *Official Journal of the European Union*. This carefully delineated process had been endorsed by the Arts Council of Great Britain and the Royal Institute of British Architects. The idea was that the *OJEC* procedure would lead to a shortlist of architects from all over Europe to be interviewed by a panel made up of the client's representatives plus disinterested senior architects. It was thought such a process would be preferable to any kind of competition. Cronyism and cock-ups would be avoided, like those that bedevilled both the competition for the Shakespeare Memorial Theatre held in 1927 and the more recent aborted first competition for the Cardiff Opera House of 1995. For Stratford-upon-Avon's third Memorial Theatre this new procedure had resulted in the selection of a young Dutch architect, van Egeraat, who had neither built anything in Great Britain nor designed any theatre anywhere.

A couple of weeks after the first lunch of 2000 a two-day retreat was arranged in London, the first day just the four of us and on the second with the addition of a colleague of van Egeraat and, for the RSC, associate director Michael Attenborough, and administrator Chris Foy. Joining me from TPC were long-time colleague Jerry Godden and comparative newcomer Gavin Green, whom we had introduced to theatre design consultancy on projects such as the Lowry Centre. Green later joined Charcoalblue and thus was the only person to work on both the van Egeraat project which did not happen and the Bennetts one which did.

The start of the second day was taken up with a disagreement over Blackburn's one-page summary of the first day. She had written: 'The Elizabethan playhouse offers a physical representation of the cosmology of heaven, earth and hell which has dynamic connection to the text. This needs care, the architectural treatment of the space must support not dominate.' Van Egeraat objected. Garnier's opera house dominated and what was wrong with that? Noble disagreed, and if the minutes were to be altered as van Egeraat insisted then he, Noble, would want recorded his own feeling that 'not dominate' was an accurate account of his own position. Impasse. I recalled Richard Eyre saying that the problem of the Olivier was that the architecture 'intruded' on the job of the director. After more than an hour and a half's discussion it was agreed that the minute be changed to read: 'This needs care, the architectural treatment of the space should prepare and stimulate the audience, not intrude.' True, but at this rate the design of a new theatre space was going to take a very long time. Noble and van Egeraat, neither of whom had any experience of creating a new theatre building, had already spent a lot of time together looking at theatres all over Europe. They had visited theatres new and old but had not been able to see a show in any one of them such, or so they said, was the pressure of their itinerary.

Over the next few months there were more surprises. First the Barbican Theatre was to be abandoned by the RSC, so this was no longer to be a reference point. Second there was growing uncertainty backstairs at the RSC whether the iconoclast van Egeraat was the right man for the job.

The brief was solely the new main theatre. The Swan, where Noble wanted to introduce a scenic stage beyond the thrust, was not to be discussed. For the main theatre van Egeraat had the admirable aim of arranging the audience so that they grasped the actors. He showed sketches of steeply swooping and sparsely populated balconies curving in all planes. The rest of the design team doubted that this could be made to work. It needed a 1:1 part model of the said galleries, constructed in the RSC's spacious workshops, to convince the client that radical changes would be needed.

When the design team issued its feasibility study in October 2001 two options were shown for the 1,050-seat theatre, which Noble had stated was to have a flexible thrust in the summer and be convertible into an intimate proscenium stage in the winter for RSC musicals and for visiting companies. Neither van Egeraat's nor our solution satisfied both parts of the brief. We at TPC had explored three-storey towers moved on air pallets in the critical area where the fixed part of the auditorium ended so as to provide different options for the junction of audience space and acting area, whether thrust or end-stage. Guthrie would have quoted the Vivian Beaumont and suggested that the result would have been a proscenium theatre not as good as it should be and a thrust stage ditto. Greiner would have told the client that he was wanting the wrong thing. I blame myself for not grasping the nettle that it was the brief and not the tentative solutions that was the problem.

Meanwhile it transpired that hidden in the one of the client papers was the statement: 'As a result of exhaustive exploration during the Feasibility Study, the RSC is convinced that full

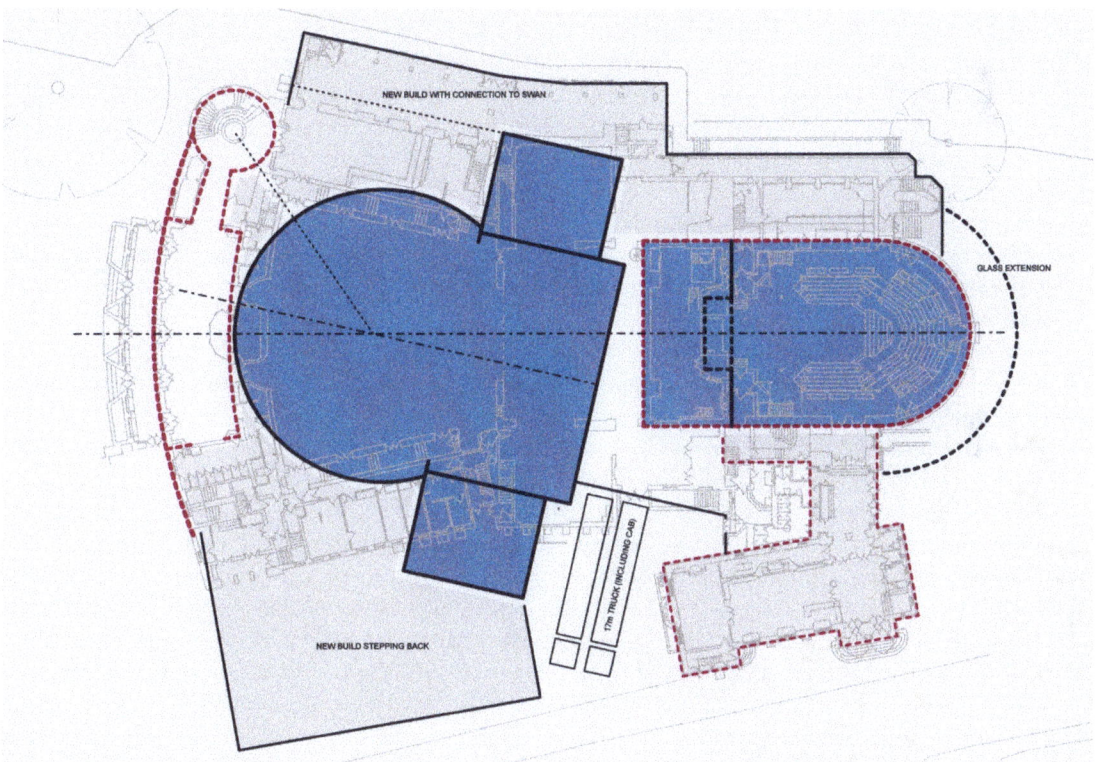

13.4 *Stratford-on-Avon Plan 'B' Theatre Projects Consultants 14 December 2001.*

demolition of the 1932 RST building is an unavoidable prerequisite to creating the new principal playhouse urgently needed to sustain its work in Stratford.' Had this been a ruse by van Egeraat and Noble to clear the decks for what opponents had already described in the press as 'the replacing of the existing Royal Shakespeare Theatre with a crowd-pleasing Shakespeare Village'? Or was it to allow generous space to service the scenic stages of both the new main theatre and a rejigged Swan? There is just the one small image of Egeraat's Shakespeare Village to be found in the RSC archives, the arguments for this strategy having been apparently wiped from the record. The drastic idea of clearing almost the whole site seemed to me as serious a matter as pursuing the impossible dream of providing a thrust stage for the summer season and a proscenium stage for the winter.

Accordingly, on 14 December 2001, Godden, Green and I presented to the planning sub-committee our Plan B. This shows that the new main theatre could be inserted on the site between the Swan at one end and the best bits of Scott's building which were the front facade, the foyer and the spiral grand stair. Contrary to what had been stated by Noble and van Egeraat we maintained that comprehensive demolition was avoidable. Building sub-committee chairman, architect Ian Ritchie, closed the meeting abruptly. Behind the scenes heads were banged together.

Noble resigned in 2002. The RSC and van Egeraat parted company. Michael Boyd was appointed director the following year from a shortlist of two, the other one being Greg Doran, who succeeded Boyd in 2012. Under Boyd the first design team was stood down. Administrator Foy resigned in 2003. Previous studies were torn up. Boyd's priority was to balance the RSC books on current account. He achieved this remarkably in only two years and the design process was then restarted with an entirely new team led by Rab Bennetts – the second fresh start. The result was the theatre which was completed in 2010.

The new team was given a simple brief for the main house. It was to be like the Swan ('the same only bigger') plus the scenic stage of the 1932 theatre, which was to be retained upstage of the new thrust. Boyd got exactly that, having earlier commissioned a temporary 1,000-seat theatre called The Courtyard up the road from the RST and designed by Ritchie which served as the main house from 2006 to 2009. This had a similar thrust stage to the Swan plus only a vestigial scenic stage beyond. Meanwhile designs were being prepared by Bennetts for the new main theatre space to be ingeniously shoehorned into the space occupied by the old Memorial Theatre auditorium.

Boyd stepped down in 2012 after only two full seasons in the new house. Doran had not played a significant role in the design of what Boyd had wanted. But it was Doran who had to make it work. Boyd and Doran did not approach the design of theatre space in the same way. Their differences can be guessed at by their attitudes post-2012 as to where the RSC should play in London. In 2011 Boyd had taken the RSC to play a season of his histories – first to the Roundhouse in London and second to the Armory in New York where he built a temporary demountable version of his Courtyard theatre. The American unions had agreed to this being built at Stratford and imported into the USA on the condition that after the end of the New York season it was taken back to Britain. Which it was. Boyd hoped that the RSC would find a site for it and that this would be the London theatre space where the RSC would henceforth play. Doran on the other hand preferred to return to the Barbican. Under Doran the RSC made a new arrangement for regular seasons at a theatre which had been specifically designed for the RSC – four artistic directors previous.

Bennetts' new main theatre at Stratford-upon-Avon comes close to completely satisfying both ear and eye. Individual microphones are used less often than at the Olivier, Lyttelton and

SOME NEW BUILDS, TWO RENOVATIONS AND DIVERSIONS 187

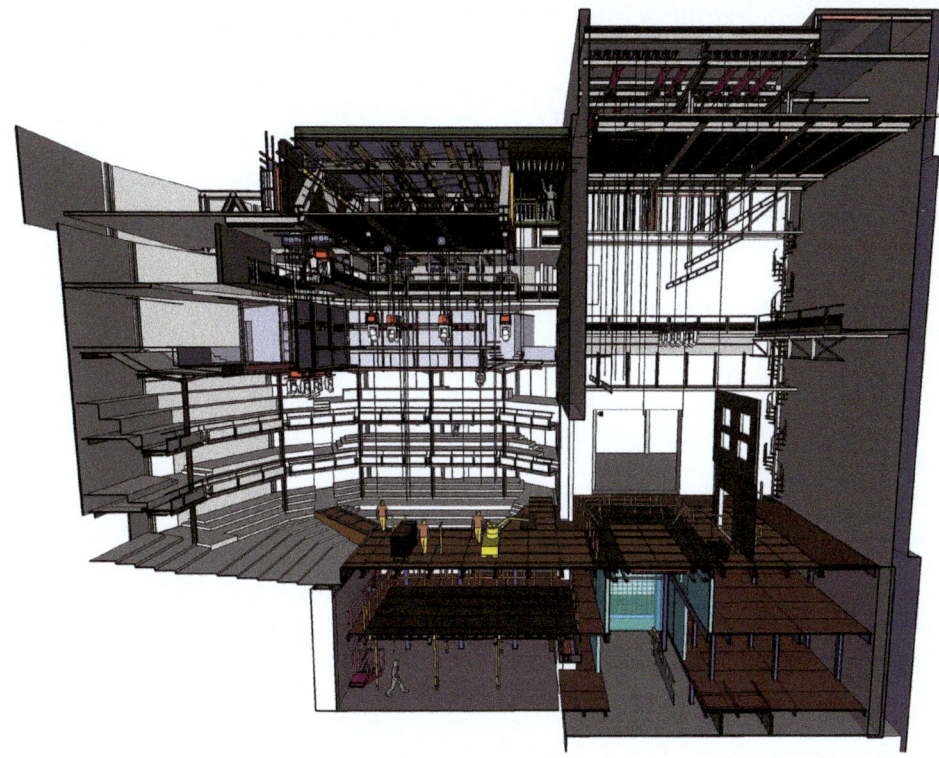

13.5 *Royal Shakespeare Theatre 2010. New stage and auditorium over stage cutaway. Architects Rab Bennetts Associates advised by Charcoalblue.*

Chichester theatres. The odd thing is the retention of the 1932 scenic stage in its entirety. This makes for difficult sightlines to actors performing within scenery set underneath the old fly tower. The director and designer can use only a shallow triangle at the front of the old scenic stage lest those in the side tiers near the proscenium opening lose too much of the action. At this critical point there is, as yet, no architectural device to complete 'the girdle of these walls'.

Theatre consultant Andy Hayles, founder of Charcoalblue, advised architect Bennetts who served the client in the persons of director Boyd and head of design Tom Piper. Additional facilities for spectacle were created above and below the new thrust stage. Wrote Hayles in the section dealing with the RSC in *The Guthrie Thrust Stage: A Living Legacy*, published by the ABTT for PQ 2011:

> Could we make the forest of Dunsinane appear from under stage, plant it on the thrust stage for the final scene in Macbeth and then fly it out from view? ... Could we mask the old proscenium and then fly out a backcloth or wall and reveal the whole depth of the old RSC stage – a hidden upstage room? ... Could we fly performers in from on high without them being seen beforehand from the yard; and could we bring a Roman Army up from way down below without them being seen from the highest, steepest sight line?

One may ask whether such technical ingenuity might have been better directed at what happens at the auditorium end of the thrust. In a mainstream Guthrie thrust theatre actors and properties can appear speedily up ramped vomitories reserved for actors only. At the new RST vomitories are absent though there is a diagonal pair of Kabuki *hanamichi* at stage level which link the forward corners of the thrust to the fourth row of the surrounding seats. Along these the arriving actor must either proceed in stately fashion or run. Vomitories had not been needed in the smaller Swan, but at the larger main RST they might have helped the pace of production. After all they could always have been covered over if not required for a particular show. Experience in Britain, other than at Sheffield where they work very well when needed, has not been good. At Chichester the vomitories are stepped not ramped and are shared with the arriving audience. At the Olivier the vomitories are far to the sides, which emphasises that this is more an end-stage than the thrust as Olivier himself had claimed it would be at the time of the fracas at Sheffield.

The continuing interest in open thrust stages was emphasised by the creation in 2021 of a temporary open-air 500-seat theatre space immediately downstream of the existing theatres. This was precisely aligned with the first Memorial Theatre auditorium which had become the shell for the Swan. No architect was involved. It was the result of purposeful collaboration between the workers of the RSC and the builder, rather as it would have been in Shakespeare's day. This did have actor-dedicated vomitories.

The 2010 Stratford building, incorporating delightful chunks of the earlier buildings of 1879 and 1932, is warm and welcoming from Bennetts's eye-catching tower through a brilliantly executed link, on the landward side rather than the river side, from the front entrances of 1932 right through to the Swan. This has allowed Scott's original vision for the riverside to be completed in a way that disposes of the much-quoted original insult that her building looked like a jam factory. In Chapter 4 the story was told that it was in 1950 that a thrust stage theatre space was first proposed for Stratford by Guthrie himself in conversation with the then director Anthony Quayle. Guthrie had suggested bulldozing Scott's theatre into the river. Instead, the main theatre space had been gradually improved as fashions changed and as resources allowed. But after all the ingenuity it was still no good. It took sixty years for Stratford to acquire the thrust stage which Guthrie had suggested to Quayle.

13.6 *RST Swan Theatre 1986 within 1879/1932 shell. Architect Michael Reardon. Over open-air theatre of 2020 with Swan shell in background.*

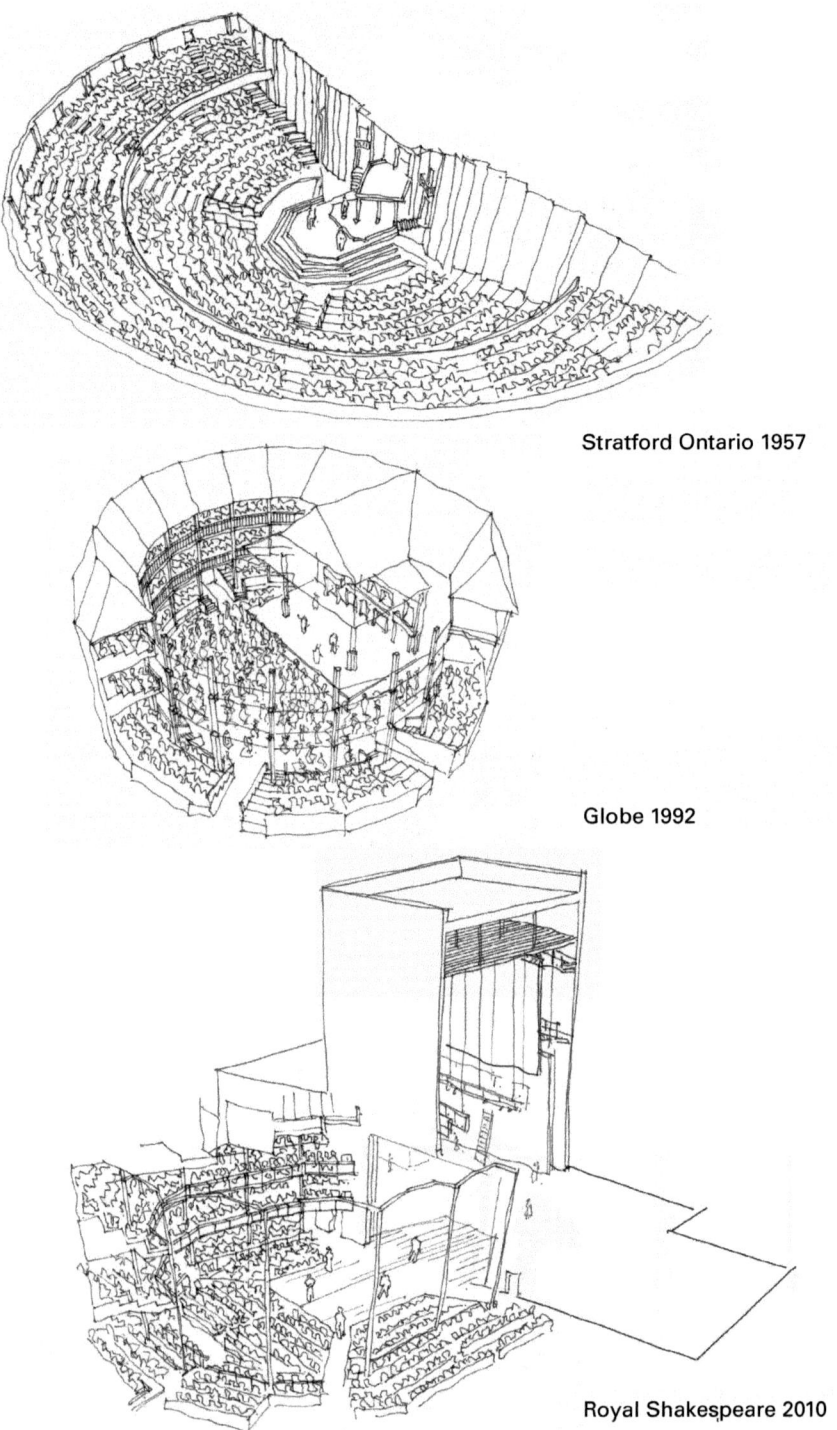

13.7 *Three Shakespearean theatres compared: Stratford Ontario 1957; Wanamaker's Globe 1997; RST revised 2010. Drawn by Gavin Green.*

Another comparison between different views of how different generations come up with different stages for Shakespeare is the trio of Stratford Ontario in 1957, Wanamaker's Globe of 1997 and Boyd's Stratford-upon-Avon of 2010, here all faithfully drawn by Gavin Green.

At 'Shakespeare's Globe' of 1997 on London's Bankside, where scholars will forever be rethinking the detail, Shakespeare will be reinterpreted by future generations but broadly within the context of an unchanging theatre space. But at what sort of new theatre will the balance between looking and listening be freshly explored, and not just for Shakespeare? Andrew Todd's low-tech Elizabethan theatre represents one approach. Another is the high-tech approach of the third theatre space for the Shakespeare Theatre Company in Chicago, the Yard, which holds up to 850, opened in 2017 and is the latest example of the flexibility of format that can be achieved by the comparatively recent air pallet.

High-tech in Chicago and its antecedents

Air caster technology arrived in the design of theatre space at the end of the 1970s. The new technology allowed two or three stagehands to move large pieces of scenery having raised them on cushions of compressed air. The use of air pallets for the reconfiguring of a theatre space is another thing altogether. The technology arrived too late for the opening of Bill Howell's theatre at Christ's Hospital School in 1975 where the four audience towers, which complete the courtyard, relied on boy power until air cushions were retro fitted much later. Next, in 1983 and 1993, two much larger schemes happened, in both of which TPC were involved, at the Derngate in Northampton seating up to 1,200 and at the slightly larger Cerritos, Southern California. In both, sections of the auditorium float on air pallets and are built into movable towers while the greater part of the audience is anchored in fixed tiers facing that flexible area where actors, singers or musicians interact with the audience. In two other theatre spaces there are no fixed elements whatsoever and all the audience are seated either in towers or in the centre of the space where, when the seats are cleared away, they can stand. In 1987 there came the 275-seat Telus Theatre at the Chan Centre, Vancouver Island, conceived by Canadian architects Bing Thom working with TPC and, thirty years later, the much larger Yard in Chicago.

There are now two major Shakespeare theatres on Navy Pier at Chicago. In 1999 founder Barbara Gaines had created two theatre spaces, the larger being the 500-seat Courtyard theatre, which is a Swan reconceived by TPC with a small scenic stage beyond its thrust. In 2017 she launched the Yard, conceived by Green and Hayles of Charcoalblue together with Chicago architects Adrian Smith and Gordon Gill. Nine three-storey towers, each the size of a London bus, can be moved into an infinite number of different layouts. The impermeable floor is dead level. Within each tower and fed from above or the sides are not only the power lines for stage lighting and sound systems but also a fire sprinkler system, which must be reconnected for all the arrangements. (This additional complexity is not required under either British or Canadian regulations.) In large horseshoe mode it is wide, 56 feet (17 metres), between facing galleries. Such width was driven by that part of the brief which called for a 50-feet-wide scenic opening for musicals. Two smaller thrust modes are available, one which measures between opposite towers 44 feet (13.4 metres) and an even smaller one, the size of the Swan, with an internal width of only 37 feet (11 metres). The *Chicago Tribune* wrote: 'Despite the flexibility of its design, its movable towers interlock in such a way as to feel permanent' while the *Sun Times* talked of its 'Elegant, industrial-style beauty'. The sketch design shows the intention while the photo of a curtain call of *Macbeth* in 2018 evokes the atmosphere of a full auditorium.

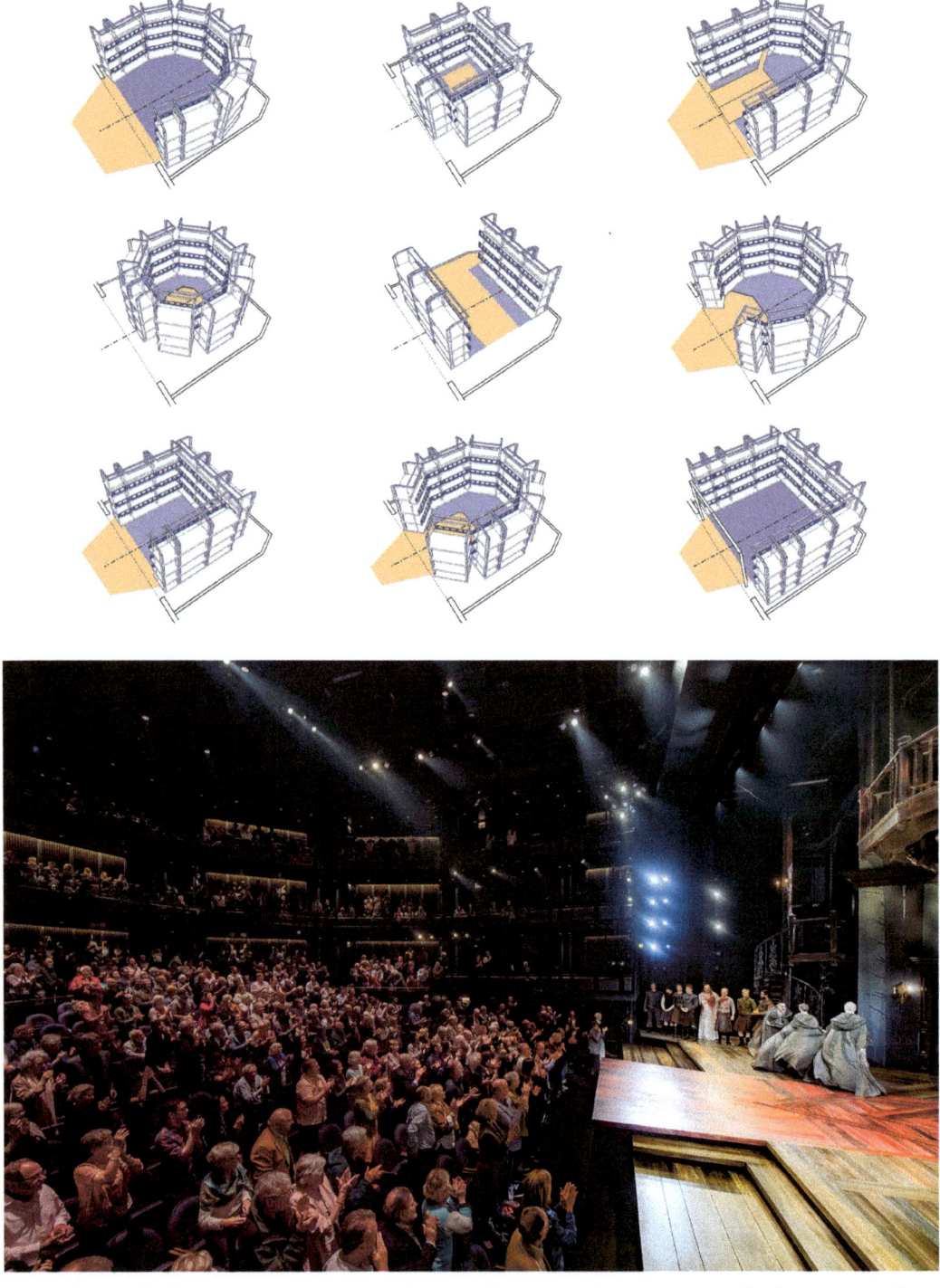

13.8 *The Yard, Chicago 2017 – concept drawing by Gavin Green over* Macbeth *curtain calls in opening season 2018.*

The plus, as in the much smaller Telus, is that the permutations are infinite, unlike those overengineered spaces where components that fly in or rise through the floor fit together only in a limited number of predetermined permutations. The downside at Chicago is that changing the more flexible format does take longer and requires more labour than originally anticipated. Here the compressed air skid technology involves sliding a limited number of air pallets under the corner of each tower, tower by tower, rather than having the air cushions integrated into every tower as had been the practice elsewhere. This was certainly cheaper to construct than equipping each tower with its own set of air cushions.

The Bridge Theatre on the River Thames

The Bridge Theatre of 2017 is downstream of the National Theatre and the Globe near to Tower Bridge. Here artistic director Nick Hytner and executive director Nick Starr, both late of the NT, created the first major commercial theatre in London to be built on a new site in seventy-five years. They chose as architects Haworth Tompkins, with whom they had worked on renovations to the NT. The near-impossible task was to fit 900-plus theatregoers into a rectangular space under a residential development already under construction. The space had a clear height of only 10.5 metres from basement floor to the underside of downstand steel beams which span the internal width of 22 metres. There was no easy access, just a standard goods access door at the rear which was 6.9 metres above basement floor level. The budget was tight because investors who put up the cash had to feel that a dividend could and would be paid in the not-too-distant future.

Tompkins's solution for the theatre space was a miracle of compression. With stage level set at 2.3 metres above pre-existing basement level there are three levels of encircling tiers with three rows of seats at each level. The space is lined with vertical caissons which are also vertical ducts containing both circulating air and cabling for stage lighting. The tiers are tied back to the caissons and cantilevered from torsion beams connected by pairs of columns each side of the gangways to the tier seating. Threaded between the downstand beams are the lighting bridges which, like everything else, had to be prefabricated and bolted together on site. The approach of building a structure that passes all its load down to the lowest level of a pre-existing space with minimal pinning to side walls for lateral stability is as old as the original Tricycle of 1980 or the Founders' Theatre of 2001, now the Tina Packer, in Lenox, Massachusetts. But the Bridge is structurally much more sophisticated.

The only snag is that to pack in 800 to 950 for some formats and also limit the three horizontal tiers on the three sides to three rows deep the central courtyard had to be wide. The internal width of this rectangular space is 16 metres, which is the same as that between the five tiers at the proscenium end of the 2,200-seat Royal Opera House Covent Garden. Width matters in theatre spaces with a strong axis front–back, which are generally used with the players positioned at the far end. Width and the volume of air in the middle does challenge some of the younger women's voices but generally the verdict for this welcoming theatre space must be never mind the width, feel the quality.

The foyer opens out onto lawns giving views of the Tower of London and Tower Bridge. Inside attractive and irregularly formed lighting pendants in the foyer/bar give a party feeling to a single uninterrupted space large enough to hold the big audience but not too large in which to lose a friend. The Bridge is both a fun place to visit as well as being functional in the broader sense of that word as championed in this book. Flexibility of staging is achieved not with

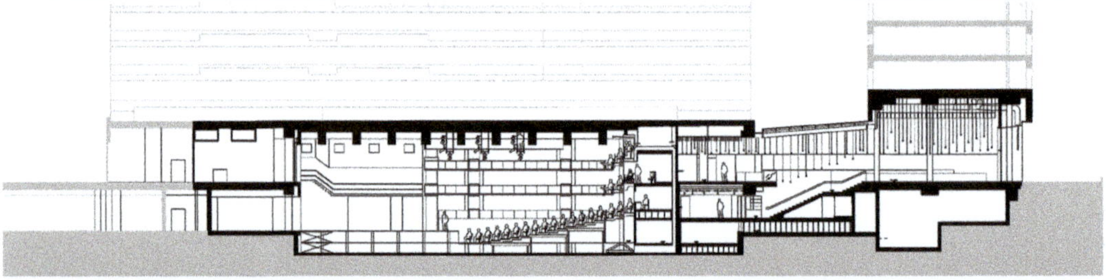

13.9 *The Bridge 2017 Architect Haworth Tompkins, Three full tiers over long section over promenade performance of* A Midsummer Night's Dream.

expensive but inherently inflexible mechanical gizmos beloved by many theatre consultants; rather the Bridge is a larger version of the empty-hole philosophy. It was never intended to be a repertoire house. Shows run for at least a couple of months. When a new show requires a different layout in the centre or at the stage end of the courtyard the riggers arrive with a mobile crane and rearrange the simple kit of columns supporting the modulated floor. By lunchtime on the second day the seats are being slotted into any new arrangement for the centre of the courtyard and the whole has been handed back to the Bridge's technical team. They can then get on with putting up the scenery and focusing the lighting. The only thing that has not yet happened at the Bridge is the introduction of a demountable architectural fourth wall for the courtyard. This would complete the yet-to-be fully-realised in-the-round option which would takes the capacity to over 1,000, which is what it is for promenade. Also, the side-angled components of such a fourth wall might be used to narrow the overwide end and thrust stage formats with something more cheerful than black drapes. An architect-designed solution will surely materialise when the money is found.

The Theatre Royal Drury Lane remodelled – once again

The Theatre Royal Drury Lane (TRDL) closed in January 2019 and reopened in late summer 2021. This is the fourth theatre on the site since 1663. The younger Theatre Royal Covent Garden of 1732 is essentially, from portico to proscenium, the work in 1858 of one architect, Edward Barry, while the 1812 TRDL was designed by Benjamin Dean Wyatt but has had its auditorium often and radically reshaped by others. Also, for over 300 years it has been a commercial undertaking. The site, though deep front to back, was restricted on the south side by a narrow alley which has now become an attractive top-lit coffee shop which on the south side opens onto a restaurant. This, like the rest of the front of house, will be open all day for the casual visitor who is to be welcomed as if to any five-star hotel. On the north is Samuel Beazley's elegant colonnade of 1831 which has been smartened with an overdue lick of paint.

Of the major surviving elements of Wyatt's TRDL theatre historian John Earl wrote in *The Theatres Trust Guide to British Theatres 1750-1950*: 'The great staircase, rotunda and saloon are important late Georgian monuments in their own right and unparalleled in any British theatre for their splendour and sense of occasion.' But the side entrance to the gallery was mean and the general circulation lamentable. Until now only a minority of theatregoers were routed through the incomparable Georgian spaces. Now the circulation is much clearer. Tompkins has brought all the audience through the three large front doors into the wide foyer and, once they have checked on their ticket whether they are to be seated on the King's side or on the Prince's side opposite, has guided them to take the left or right grand entrance doors to proceed on to the stalls or up one of the symmetrical grand stairs to the circles. The centre route leads directly to the rotunda. Here is Wyatt's lofty pantheon with statues in niches showing the great gods of British theatre. William Shakespeare occupies the focal point looking back *enfilade* to the portico. This was a place of wonder until a short-lived central connection with the stalls was inserted in 1911 by Max Pilditch, who dared to shift Shakespeare off the centreline. This unnecessary gloss on Wyatt was pointed out by David Wilmore, historical consultant to Haworth Tompkins. In 1922 the intrusion was replaced by a pair of stairs to take you down to much-needed lavatories in the basement with Shakespeare placed back at the focal point of the *enfilade*.

In the auditorium Tompkins, in conjunction with Roger Watts, leader of his design team, successfully added elegant takes to the finishes to a theatre space which had already appeared in

13.10 *Theatre Royal Drury Lane 2021. Renovation architect Haworth Tompkins. Photos of auditorium showing clumsy pre-2019 over the smoother 2021 revision.*

SOME NEW BUILDS, TWO RENOVATIONS AND DIVERSIONS

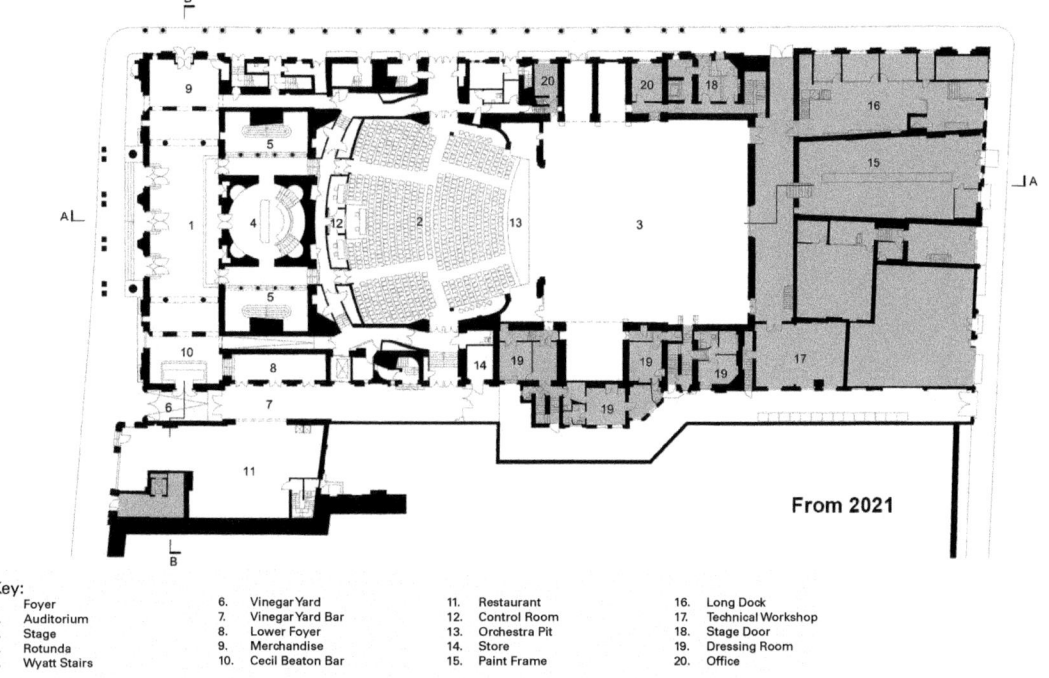

Key:
1. Foyer
2. Auditorium
3. Stage
4. Rotunda
5. Wyatt Stairs
6. Vinegar Yard
7. Vinegar Yard Bar
8. Lower Foyer
9. Merchandise
10. Cecil Beaton Bar
11. Restaurant
12. Control Room
13. Orchestra Pit
14. Store
15. Paint Frame
16. Long Dock
17. Technical Workshop
18. Stage Door
19. Dressing Room
20. Office

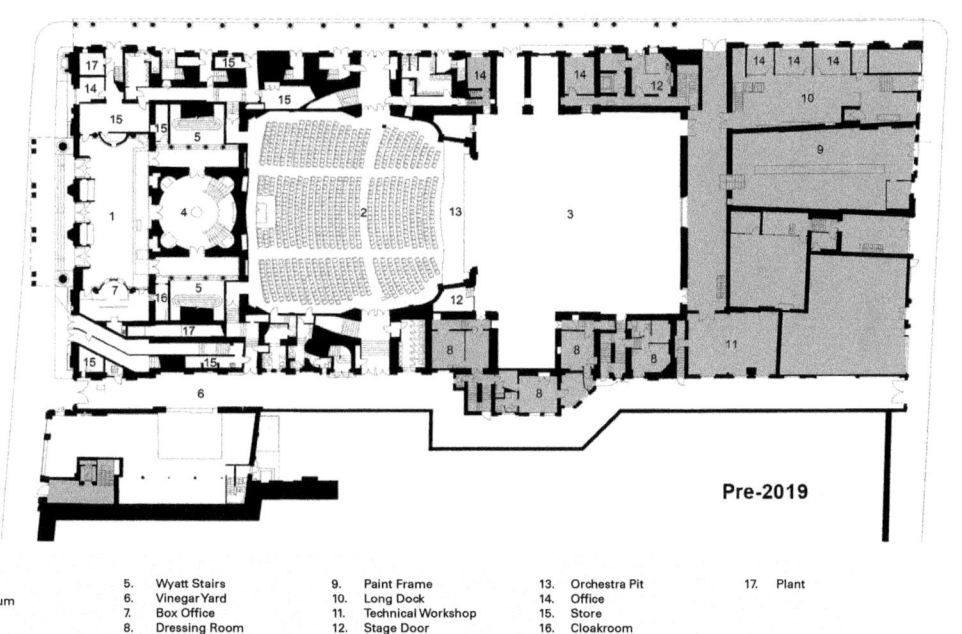

Key:
1. Foyer
2. Auditorium
3. Stage
4. Rotunda
5. Wyatt Stairs
6. Vinegar Yard
7. Box Office
8. Dressing Room
9. Paint Frame
10. Long Dock
11. Technical Workshop
12. Stage Door
13. Orchestra Pit
14. Office
15. Store
16. Cloakroom
17. Plant

13.11 *Theatre Royal Drury Lane: comparison of entrance level from 2021 over pre-2019.*

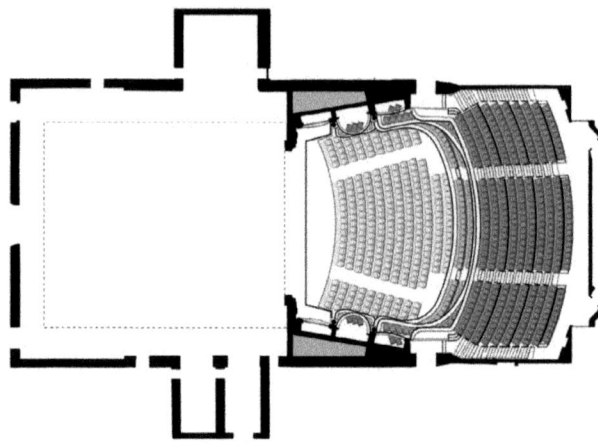

Drury Lane of 1812 with 1922 auditorium. Renovated 2021. Stalls and three tightly stacked circles. **Capacity 1,979**

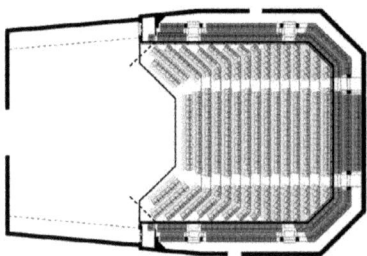

The Bridge of 2017. Flexible courtyard with three shallow tiers. **Capacity in end stage format 915**

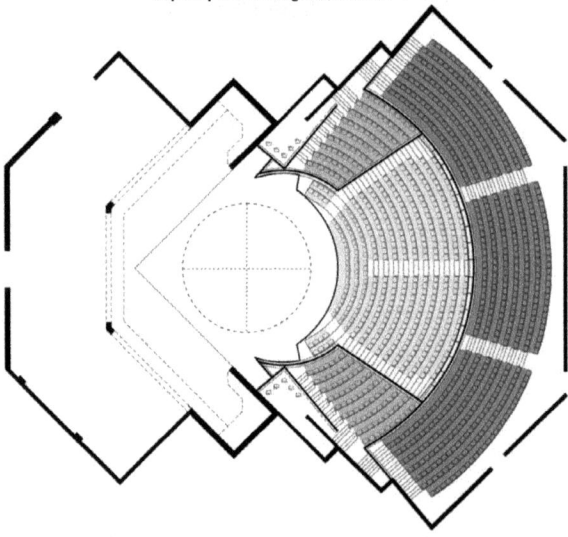

The Olivier at the National of 1976. Curved stage edge since 2003. One gallery and little overhang. **Capacity 1,150**

13.12 *Same-scale comparisons: Theatre Royal Drury Lane holding 1,979, The Bridge holding 915, Olivier holding 1,150.*

four distinct guises since 1812. They subtly adjusted the form by accelerating the transition from the two lower circles to the front of the stage where long runs of spectacular musicals are the custom and the show usually starts scenically on the audience side of the proscenium. The 1922 near-symmetrical arrangements of seven stepped boxes a side grouped around the King's box on the left and the Prince's on the right seemed interminable. Client Andrew Lloyd Webber also owned the London Palladium and knew how there Matcham had achieved intimacy for the whole by a more adroit junction of circle, boxes and stage than that achieved at Drury Lane a dozen years later by architects Emblin Walker, Edward Jones and Robert Cromie. (The latter had been the client's second choice after the sudden death of Matcham in May 1920). The Haworth Tompkins team have accentuated the positive by allowing the circles to enfold the outer boxes and to resolve themselves into the main architectural components that command the royal boxes. Adjustments elsewhere have led to the total capacity being reduced from around 2,250 to under 2,000 (1,979), the worst positions having been lost and legroom increased.

A strange decision has been taken within another surviving Georgian space. Designers other than the architect have placed a large bar centrally in the grand saloon, which is not movable like the similar-sized but better-scaled central one in the nearby Floral Hall at the Opera House. This may surprise those who had shared Earl's enthusiasms. Others will maintain that in an unsubsidised theatre he who pays the pipers may call first for bar profits, all day long if he or she so chooses. A movable bar in the grand saloon would have allowed occasional other activities to continue such as daytime concerts and theatre meetings. A smaller bar in the now much busier rotunda might reduce the overall take but would allow the easier movement of theatregoers and increase their enjoyment of this historic shrine to Shakespeare.

Meanwhile the stage and fly tower have been thoroughly reorganised and the rather seedy backstage areas spruced up. This revised TRDL will be both grander and more intimate, not least because the auditorium is so densely packed. Compare the density of Drury Lane with that of the Olivier, which has 850 fewer seats in an auditorium which occupies twice the plan area of TRDL.

In-the-round and open air: unique theatres that still surprise

The final large theatres are unusual, which allows some discussion of two unorthodox forms: in-the-round and in the open air. The Royal Exchange Manchester opened in 1976 and for coming on half a century has been one of Britain's most successful producing playhouses of any form. It is the only theatre-in-the-round with two galleries, which means the audience surrounds the actor on three levels. Prime mover Michael Elliott said that his actors should wear the theatre like a long scarf. It seats over 700, which gives it the biggest capacity of any major theatre-in-the-round in the English-speaking world. The form is uniquely seven-sided so that there is no obvious centreline.

The steel structure kisses the main floor of the listed old Royal Exchange where cotton futures were traded between 1874 and 1968, after which the Trading Hall became redundant. Its vast flat floor had been built to support many people but was not strong enough to take the point loads of a steel structure. Hence the new theatre could not stand on the floor. Instead, the whole is supported off the four main columns that hold up the hall's central dome. This solution emerged in discussions between the client and three leaders of the design team – architects Levitt

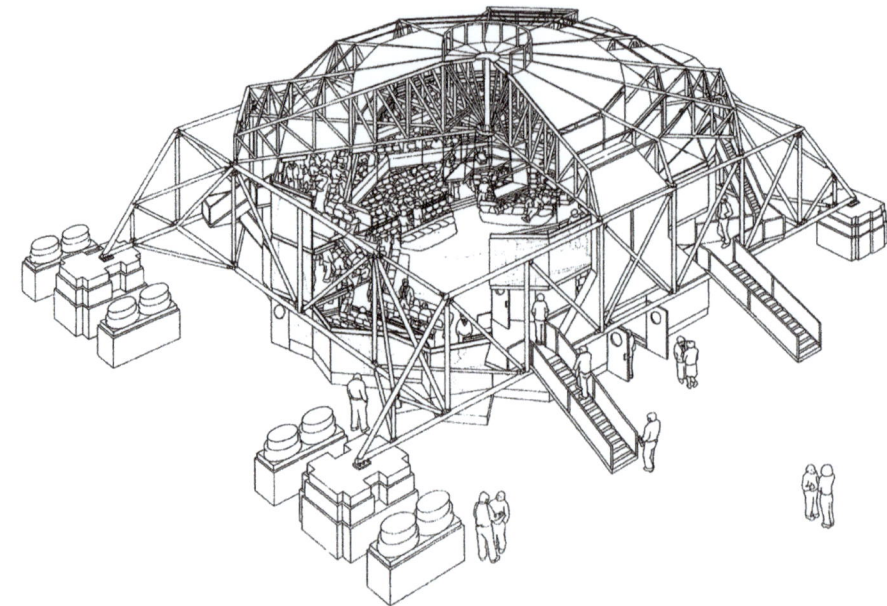

13.13 *Manchester Royal Exchange Theatre 1976. Architects Levitt Bernstein. Structure supported off pillars over curtain call for* Lord Arthur Savile's Crime *1982.*

Bernstein, engineers Ove Arup and stage designer Richard Negri. Negri had been the lead designer first of the 59 Theatre Company at the old Lyric Theatre Hammersmith and second of the new 69 Theatre Company, temporarily housed in the University Theatre Manchester, alongside director Elliott and stage and film director Caspar Wrede, who provided the intellectual ballast. Having heard of the vacant Royal Exchange in 1973 the trio installed a temporary scaffolding theatre for two seasons. They liked the place and had started to design something more permanent before they discovered that the main floor could not support what they wanted. The 69 Theatre Company was not dismayed and proceeded with what was from the outset a deeply poetic idea. Levitt Bernstein reported that 'the beginning for us was a small paper and wire model sitting in the middle of a table with Richard Negri striding round it talking about the form of a rose. How, we wondered, would we ever bring this man down to earth? Fortunately we never did.'

Neither the client trio nor architects Levitt Bernstein had conceived any new theatre space of any kind before the Royal Exchange. The single-mindedness of Elliott and his band of brothers, who managed to conceive and construct a steel-galleried space for 700 in under four years, was a refreshing contrast to the labyrinthine politics of getting the NT designed and built. Coincidentally the two opened within a few months of each other in 1976.

Manchester had in a sense been the home of theatre-in-the-round in Britain before the arrival of the 69 Theatre Company. Author, theatre space designer and chief apologist for theatre-in-the-round Stephen Joseph taught in the drama department of the University of Manchester from 1962 until his early death at the age of only forty-six. By then he had helped create many theatres-in-the-round including two of the three successive theatres at Scarborough. It was prolific playwright Alan Ayckbourn who opened the third of these in a converted Odeon cinema in 1996 and named it the Stephen Joseph Theatre.

Nearly all theatres-in-the-round in Britain are 'fit-ups' or 'found spaces' in that they exist in buildings built for another purpose. Almost all have stage and front rows of seating at the same floor level. The seating rows on all sides rise steeply enough for those further back to see the full figure of an actor standing close to the front row. There is a natural limit of around 400 to theatres where the seating rises in unbroken rows on all four sides. The latest Scarborough theatre, which was sized by Ayckbourn after much thought, holds just 404. It is the galleries at the Royal Exchange, tightly packed one above the other, which has allowed a capacity of 700. It can be intimate or epic.

A second and much smaller galleried theatre-in-the round: the Orange Tree

One of the smallest theatres-in-the-round in Britain is the only other with a gallery, the Orange Tree in the London borough of Richmond. This I designed for founding director Sam Walters, assisted by a team from TPC. Walters had started his company in 1971 in a small room over the Orange Tree pub across the road from where the second theatre was finally constructed. There eighty people were sat in-the-round on uncomfortable church pews. The brief for the new one was simple: double the capacity, preserve the intimacy and provide minimal facilities for company and public. There would rarely be more than eight or nine in the cast, I was told, and little or no scenery, just furniture.

13.14 *Orange Tree February 1991. Architects TPC. First preview of opening production of* All in the Wrong *by Arthur Murphy.*

After looking at many unsuitable buildings in Richmond we reverted to the derelict primary school opposite the Orange Tree pub. By then all that was left was the end wall of the school hall and the entrance to the schoolmaster's house, which gave us a characterful hexagonal entrance porch. Beyond that there was just enough space to accommodate, in addition to the galleried theatre space, a bar for the public, lavatories, three dressing rooms and a small admin office. The shell was built by the developer to our designs as part of a planning deal. Director and actor Richard Attenborough, who was a long-time Richmond resident, led the fundraising for the other half of the total cost. We opened in 1991. Walters, the founding director, ran it for forty-three years. He lived and breathed theatre-in-the-round. Walters was a hard act to follow but from 2014 his successor, Paul Miller, made the Orange Tree a slightly different sort of success despite having been warned by the Arts Council before he took the job that the theatre was to lose its annual grant.

The Orange Tree has a relatively small acting area. There is an asymmetric gallery with a single row of seats and below, at all four corners, entrances which are marked with pairs of supporting steel columns for the galleries clad in oak. Two of the four sides are a couple of feet higher than the other two. Asymmetry helps in making the space seem smaller and more intimate. Above is a complex roof structure which met two onerous challenges to sound insulation: supersonic Concorde preparing to land at Heathrow and English rugby supporters in the road between pub and theatre celebrating victory at nearby Twickenham.

The chief design influences were, once again, the Cottesloe, the Tricycle and the smaller Georgian playhouses. I was new to theatre-in-the-round but had a good introduction. My wife, Jan Carey, had acted regularly at the old Orange Tree followed by two seasons in-the-round at Scarborough in 1992 and 1995 before playing in the opening seasons at the new Orange Tree. That Scarborough connection also manifested itself when, soon after we opened, I was standing in the gallery at the Orange Tree with Ayckbourn, who said, 'I like it, Iain, but I could not work on such a small acting area.' Yet he did. Walters took his own productions to Scarborough and invited Ayckbourn to direct at the Orange Tree.

The other obvious influence was the Royal Exchange. If two galleries worked there for 700 surely a single gallery would work for my miniature theatre space. Both are intimate. Laughter comes more quickly in these galleried spaces than in some of the larger ones where the rows rise remorselessly like a football stadium, as they do at the Arena Stage, Washington DC, which holds 680. The balcony fronts also provide the whole of the Orange Tree with opportunities to form part of the scene, as they did for Walters's opening production in February 1991 which was of Arthur Murphy's 1761 comedy *All in The Wrong*.

The finest and biggest open-air theatre in Britain

Lastly in this chapter is the only large-scale open-air theatre in Britain. The Regent's Park Open Air Theatre in London normally plays a full summer season from mid-May to mid-September. Audiences average around 140,000 a season. In most years not more than 5 per cent of performances a season are lost to rain. In the autumn productions are toured and are frequently transferred to the West End. There is no public subsidy.

It all started in in 1932 with actor/director Robert Atkins, who set out deckchairs facing a grassy knoll in a quiet corner of Regent's Park. The repertoire at first was wholly Shakespearean. It reopened after the war, still with the deckchairs. Bankrupted in 1961, Regent's Park Open Air Theatre was rescued by actor-manager David Conville. In 1974 he found the funds to commission a fully raked permanent auditorium from architect Bill Howell, who had already designed the Young Vic and the school theatre at Christ's Hospital. Howell died tragically in a car accident in November 1974, which meant he did not live to see either his Christ's Hospital or Regent's Park completed. The latter opened in summer 1975.

Howell's fan-shaped auditorium holds over 1,250 in two banks of seating. The front nine rows descend shallowly from the cross gangway at bar and audience entrance level down to a movable feast of a stage riser, while the rear bank of eleven rows is in five facets and rises more steeply from that same entrance level. The whole is dished in section and is superbly focused on the tree-backed stage acting area which works equally well with a little or a lot of scenery. The width of the stage is variable simply by gradating the transition from nature to theatre.

The renovation of the winter of 1999/2000 was led by architect Tompkins working closely with the theatre staff led by actor-manager Ian Talbot, who ran the theatre from 1987 to 2007, and with my team from TPC with Andy Hayles on the technical side. As at the Royal Court I had been able to suggest a few architects that Conville, Talbot and I might interview. Tompkins got the job although at that point the Royal Court was still under construction. The introduction of a new entrance, new lavatories, revised catering and a discrete full-width technical bridge at the rear of the seating was simply done. The planting and picnic areas were given new life – not for nothing had the last leader of the GLC and first Mayor of London, Ken Livingstone, christened it 'the people's Glyndebourne'.

In 2008 Tim Sheader became artistic director, only the third in half a century. In a dozen pre-Covid seasons Sheader successfully completed the move from a company repertoire, with a Shakespearean emphasis, to consecutive runs of separately cast shows of Shakespeare, musicals and occasionally an opera. In addition there is always something for younger audiences. Howell's sophisticated fan-shaped auditorium plays a major role in making all this possible.

Into The Woods, 2010

Twelfth Night, 2014

Lord of the Flies, 2015

13.15 *Three productions at Regent's Park Open Air Theatre 2010–2015.*

Of late, smaller open-air theatres are springing up but, like theatres-in-the-round, they rarely seat more than 400. They may cost little to build but to make significant impacts on the communities they serve more of them need to have larger capacities. Which is why the Royal Exchange Manchester and Regent's Park Open Air Theatre are pointers to the future. The latter gets left out of books on theatre architecture because it hasn't got a roof. More is the pity. Should you be involved in creating a new larger theatre space they are both certainly worth a visit. Should you simply want a summer evening's picnic and a great show you will certainly get that at Regent's Park, where we are reminded that out of doors the gods can create a special magic that allows large audiences to be conscious both of each other and of their collective place in the universe. Reconnecting theatre with nature is going to be a priority for climate-conscious generations to come.

ACT FOUR

2021: The future

14

Unforeseen consequences of seventeenth-century plagues, of the arrival of the talkies and the more recent dangers of the pandemic and of 'virtual theatre'. Some central themes restated

Learning from the past

There are clues in the past to what sort of unforeseen consequences there could be to changes in the circumstances of how live theatre takes place. Theatre closures caused in the mid-seventeenth century first by plagues and soon after by the Puritans and those triggered at the end of the 1920s by the arrival of the talkies both had unforeseen consequences. The recent introduction of live transmission and streaming of stage productions both to art cinemas and to ever higher-resolution TV screens at home is as likely to have unforeseen consequences. Will the easy availability on screen of 'virtual theatre' of major productions from the likes of London's National Theatre or the New York Metropolitan Opera reduce both the touring of their own major productions and attendances for smaller companies at other lesser theatres and opera houses? Will it mean the rich in the big cities take part in live performances while those who live further away or are less well-off must make do with watching them on screen? When the Covid-19 pandemic, which periodically closed theatres worldwide from mid-2019 to late 2021, is finally tamed, might regular theatregoers conclude that it is safer, cheaper and easier to have 'live theatre' streamed to them at home?

Unforeseen consequence of the plagues and of the Puritans

In the early seventeenth century, when the plague peaked, the authorities closed the densely packed public theatres because these were among the most dangerous sources of contagion in London. The longest closure took place in 1603 and lasted more than a year. A whole year's closure seemed a long time until 1642, when all theatres were closed for eighteen years by Cromwell, ending only in the restoration of King Charles II in 1660. Within months the king granted two men, William Davenant and Thomas Killigrew, exclusive rights to present plays in London. Their new indoor theatres catered for smaller and richer audiences than had the old ones. There was a greater emphasis on spectacle. None of the audiences stood after 1642, which contrasts with Paris where the standing *parterre*, immediately in front of the stage, survived at the *Comédie Française* until 1782. The new London theatres were less densely packed than before the Commonwealth and hence made for a more sedate theatregoing experience for a more socially exclusive audience than the robust cross section of the public that had patronised the open-air playhouses in Shakespeare's day. The number of people going to theatre in London must have shrunk by three quarters. It would be more than a century before playhouses recovered their central role in society. Such were the unforeseen consequences of the seventeenth-century closures.

Unforeseen consequences of the arrival of the talkies

In the early 1920s in the USA silent moving pictures were considered a novel attraction which, as part of a live show, would help revitalise vaudeville. Vaudeville and burlesque were then the pre-eminent forms of live theatre, as were their British counterparts, music hall and variety. Over the previous decades film had emerged as a worldwide business, worldwide simply because there was no language barrier in silent movies. Silent film was presented in live theatres with live musical accompaniment. Then, suddenly, all changed with the arrival of the talkies, of which the first was *The Jazz Singer* of 1927.

About 20,000 movie palaces and theatres were built in the USA between 1925 and 1935. Most had well over 2,000 comfortable seats and were equipped with capacious stages with fly towers and large orchestra pits. Before *The Jazz Singer* vaudevillians performed on many of these stages, from which the flat screens for silent movies could be easily flown out. The orchestra pits of the grandest had been full of musicians, there to accompany both the silent movies and the live performers. The medium-size spaces had cinema organs and the smallest a lonely pianist. But all too soon live performers were redundant. Those who thought the talkies would be an extension of silent films found out how wrong they were. In no more than a generation three quarters of the live theatres in America either closed or went over exclusively to the talkies.

Apart from closures the major unforeseen consequence was the modern single-balcony theatres. Two architects led the move. First came John Eberson who in 1926 moved to New York in time to design early movie palaces. He described his 'atmospheric' auditoriums, often pitched in Moorish gardens under star-studded skies, as 'the most palatial homes of His Excellency – The American Citizen'. What were termed 'movie palaces' in the USA in Britain were more prosaically christened 'super-cinemas'. All had just the one balcony, a practice that almost immediately spread to the few new large live theatres then being built in any country.

Eberson had one major rival who also built both live theatres and movie palaces, Thomas Lamb, who had arrived from Dundee in Scotland. He built nearly 300 theatres and movie palaces, forty-seven of which were in New York City. In summer 1980 I visited some of these with the New York Conclave of the Theatre Historical Society, who were more interested in movie palaces than live theatres. It was many years before I realised exactly why the arrival of the movie palaces led directly to live theatres losing their second and third balconies, initially in North America and soon everywhere.

Eberson and Lamb had worked out how to achieve near-perfect sightlines, both in the horizontal and vertical planes, for viewing a cinema screen. Films would generally be in the 'Academy ratio' and hence the screens when 28 feet wide would be 20 feet high. The bottom edge would be about three feet above stage level and the top just underneath the proscenium arch. In a movie palace all the public must see the whole screen. This is different from the minimum sightline requirements in section for live theatres, where the audience focuses on the performers standing, sitting or dancing at stage level. Until 1928 a key ingredient in achieving intimacy in section for three or four-level theatres was the packing of the audience as tight as possible, gallery upon gallery, and tightly round the sides. The back rows of the audience at each level in a live theatre could see the performers on stage. The many who could not see the top half of a painted backcloth would simply be charged less. In a movie palace if they could not see the whole screen the public would not buy a ticket whatever the price.

In plan the fan of seating of a movie palace needed to be narrower than that of live theatres to ensure that all could have an undistorted view of the screen. In section the maximising of the number of seats in a large movie palace with acceptable sightlines could not be achieved on a tight city-centre site either with a single rake or with many levels but could with a single deep balcony, pitched at the right slope above a carefully raked stalls level so that all cinemagoers, above and below, could see the whole screen at an acceptable angle. Since new live theatres might have to switch to movies the architect had to give his client an auditorium where movies would work. Hence, one balcony and no seats at the sides from then on, despite live performers then and now preferring theatres with two or three wrap-around tiers of audience.

Those who believe that the new two-level theatres in the USA were the product of segregation, with whites below and blacks above, are mistaken because the whole audience in a movie palace enters together from the street. In British late-nineteenth-century theatres separated the social classes from street to seat. At the 1897 Her Majesty's the single square box office had four windows in four walls serving separate groups of audience, who were strictly segregated by what they could pay. In America such pre-talkies multi-level theatres lent themselves more easily to keeping the races apart in a way that the later single-balcony movie palaces did not because all entered from the street through the same entrance.

On Broadway there are only nine theatres left with more than one balcony, and they all date from before the arrival of the talkies. They are, in date order and with their current capacities shown: the Victory (1900) 499; the New Amsterdam (1903) 1,704; the Lyceum (1903) 922; the Belasco (1907) 923; the Cort (1912) 926; the Longacre (1912) 1,096; the Shubert (1912) 1,438; the Palace (1924) 1,701; and the St James (1927) 1,615. In London's West End and in Britain's major cities the older pre-1928 three- or four-level houses still outnumber the later ones with only the one balcony.

On that 1980 tour of NYC, I was also to wonder how many redundant movie palaces later found a new role as churches. We visited a Lamb flagship one-balcony movie palace of 1930, 'Lowe's at 175th Street', the style of which was described by the *New York Times* in 2007 as 'Byzantine-Romanesque-Indo-Hindu-Sino-Moorish-Persian-Eclectic-Rococo-Deco'. Across the East River in Queens at 165-11 Jamaica Avenue was the 1929 Valencia, which was an Eberson movie palace with 3,500 seats in the Spanish Colonial style. In 1977 it was donated to The Tabernacle of Prayer for All People. Our kindly guide explained to us the fifteen life-sized figures over the proscenium arch: 'The Pastor, he had a vision. And he sent for the sculptor and said unto him, "Clothe those naked bodies." And now you see these angels who watch over our prayers in this our Tabernacle to which you are now welcome. Alleluia.' But wings and plaster robes could not quite conceal the sassy poses of those MGM goddesses. You can find images of many such lavishly re-gilded and freshly consecrated movie palaces proudly pictured on the internet. They were built for the miracle of the movies and latterly became settings for the ecstasy of revivalism. On Broadway itself is the Times Square Church, designed by Lamb in 1930 as the Warner Bros. Hollywood Theatre. This became a church in 1989, having already been renamed the Mark Hellinger Theatre. It had staged many a Broadway musical including. Ralph Allen's hymn to burlesque, *Sugar Babies*. This was the show in which film star Mickey Rooney made his Broadway debut in 1979 and never missed a performance in a run of nearly three years. I tried and failed to bring the show to London. After a coast-to-coast tour and seasons in Australia, the show with Rooney topping the bill was finally brought by others to London in 1989 but to the wrong theatre, the streamlined Savoy rather than the down-to-earth Victoria Palace which had been home to the Crazy Gang from 1947 to 1964. The Victoria Palace was then more run-down saloon bar than the gilded cocktail lounge it became much later and hence would have suited the show better. Of *Sugar Babies* at the sophisticated Savoy, the *Times* critic Irving Wardle wrote that it came over as 'a fart in a drawing room'.

Early single-balcony live theatres in Britain include the Belgrade Coventry of 1959 and the Ashcroft Croydon of 1962. We had to wait until 1968 for a new theatre with more than one balcony, the innovative Forum Theatre Billingham, which is so different from the single-balcony Lyttelton of 1976, where the sightlines ensure that nobody in that shelf-like single balcony is aware of the audience below in the stalls and vice versa. At the Curve Leicester, built as late as 2008, one third of an audience of over 900 is marooned in a distant single balcony. The main auditorium of the new Factory, Manchester (overdue and over budget in 2022), has almost twice the capacity of the Curve but only the one balcony. Neither is intimate.

Simultaneous transmission to cinemas and to homes of live theatre performance

The closure of theatres during the Covid-19 pandemic led in the short term to the free streaming of screen versions of past live shows by a few companies such as the National Theatre of Great Britain. At first these had been single simultaneous transmissions to paying audiences in cinemas, hence the title *NTLive*. Live transmissions from theatres with an audience present had been started by farceur and actor-manager Brian Rix in May 1952, before the arrival of ITV or BBC 2 and therefore when there was but the one television channel. The first live transmission was of Act One of the army farce *Reluctant Heroes*, performed by Rix's company and broadcast live from the Whitehall Theatre (now the Trafalgar) in London. The film of this farce had already been made and the stage show was still playing after two years. The first free-to-view live transmission was in fact an hour-long trailer engineered by the BBC outside broadcasting department. The next day, queues formed at the box office and the show ran for a further year. Such live broadcasts did not survive for long when the novelty of being miraculously transported to London's glamorous but still black and white West End wore off.

Sixty years later as well as regular transmissions of *NTLive* in London, there were regular simulcasts of matinees from the Metropolitan Opera in New York and from some other major institutions. The first five productions transmitted by *NTLive* took place between June 2009 and June 2010, all live from the Olivier Theatre.

The expansion of NTLive

Fast forward to the tenth season of *NTLive* in 2019 and the figures are staggering. Total viewings in the cinema of *NTLive* 2018/19, the last season before the Covid-19 lockdown, exceeded a total of 800,000 in the UK alone. Add to that the overseas audience in 1,490 cinemas in sixty-five countries. The financial outcome is a surprise. In 2018/19 the income, including sponsorship by Sky Arts, amounted to £4.3 million and expenditure to £4.9 million, which surprisingly meant a not-to-be-repeated small loss. So the motive cannot have been profit but more the commendable urge to share with a wider audience publicly subsidised national productions.

NTLive presents two different sorts of show in two different ways. One is productions being played by the National Theatre Company on the South Bank and the other selected productions by other companies playing at other London theatres such as the Old Vic, the Bridge or some in the West End. In summer 2019 Phoebe Waller-Bridge's *Fleabag* played just thirty performances at Wyndham's but was also streamed under the banner of *NTLive* many times in that and the following year. A lot of money must have been made for all concerned.

The other difference was that, while *NTLive* started as being transmitted only live, there were soon added repeats christened *Encores*. As for fees, the National Theatre had a predetermined payment system for actors and creatives agreed with the unions which was a uniform ratio of the actor's individually negotiated weekly salary or performance fee. This formula allowed for repeats within a year and was then renegotiated. Some actors called this a pre-nup. Theoretically, each actor at the NT can turn down the offer of having his performance on stage transferred to the screen, but none to date has dared to do so.

In 2019 the NT announced a streaming service to schools and *bona fide* students called *The National Theatre Collection* which consisted of existing *NTLive* recordings from a library of thirty or so productions, each batch of which are licensed for a decade. The following year a fresh arrangement was announced whereby anyone in the UK could, for an annual subscription of £100, join *National Theatre at Home*. This allowed subscribers at home to have streamed to them at home past *NTLive* productions selected from a constantly revised library. British Actors' Equity ensured that the actors receive an appropriate share of profit. Each expansion of the *NTLive* service has seemed desirable at the time and the motives irreproachable. But one must ask whether there may not be unforeseen consequences.

Simulcasts from the Metropolitan Opera

At the New York Metropolitan Opera House, Saturday matinee performances had been broadcast live on radio regularly from 1931. In 2006 the then general manager of the Met, Peter Gelb, decided to take advantage of high-definition television technology and satellite broadcasting to offer 'simulcasts' on screen, generally of the same Saturday matinees. The first was in December that year and soon Met simulcasts were being watched in more than 2,000 cinemas in sixty-six countries, grossing more than $60 million per annum. This resulted in a sizeable profit for the Met after paying all royalties and fees to performers and staff.

In a press release at the time the Met stressed that 'the movie theatre environment and affordable ticket prices make these events something that the whole family can enjoy'. In the *Guardian* of 22 April 2007 critic Peter Conrad was hooked: 'Watching it in the cinema was like having not just the best seat at the Met but all the best seats simultaneously. Thirteen cameras alternated between the stage, the orchestra pit, the wings and even the fly tower.' When they met, Conrad told Gelb: 'I decided that seeing *The Barber of Seville* in Clapham was actually better than being at the Met.' 'Oh, no, that's bad,' he groaned. 'We must be doing too good a job!'

In 2020 there were over 700 full-length high-definition recordings of Met productions available on demand to subscribers to the Met Opera's streaming service for watching on their own big-screen televisions at home. Does the Met still tour? Wrote Conrad: 'The Met used to undertake a cumbrous tour of the hinterland each spring, shoehorning corpulent tenors on to trains and unloading them to sing in ill-equipped barns in Detroit or Atlanta. Today, electronics instantly bridge the oceans and the Met can universalise itself without leaving home.' Quality touring had long been in decline in North America and the same may be an unforeseen consequence in Great Britain of the always well-intentioned *NTLive*.

Performers wary of the inherent eavesdropping nature of 'virtual theatre'

The principal problem of transmitting from large theatres such as the Met and the NT is that performers need to project differently to a live audience in a large theatre space than to cameras using close-up. Perhaps this is what Peter Hall had in mind as early as 1973 when the verbal brief for the yet-to-be-designed Cottesloe, which came my way, included a flat-floor facility which was for the filming of productions brought down from the big theatres upstairs. Perhaps Hall presciently realised that this might remove the danger of filming 'stagey' acting, which may well be needed to reach a distant audience in a large auditorium but jars in close-up.

To some actors live transmission of a stage performance to a screen, whether in a cinema or at home, is at best a documentary record and at worst eavesdropping. Although short camera rehearsals over a single day will have taken place, actors may find it hard to recall which camera has been chosen for which shot. Zoë Wanamaker was quoted in the *Observer* of 7 June 2020: 'I did an *NTLive* of *The Cherry Orchard* [she played Ranyevskaya] and it was awful. You do not know who to play to – the audience or the camera. When theatre is filmed it becomes intangible, you can't feel it, you can't smell it, you can't breathe it – it does not have the same effect on your body.' Said Ralph Fiennes, after being recorded live playing the lead in *Antony and Cleopatra* in 2018 at the Olivier: 'I just froze. I did my worst show ever that night. I was so aware of the cameras.' Yet all the actors involved, including Wanamaker and Fiennes, did agree that these two productions be made available in the batch of productions licensed for study in *The National Theatre Collection*.

On 7 May 2020, the artistic director of the Guthrie Theatre Minneapolis, Joseph Haj, in a message to his audience on YouTube, explained why he did not believe that the future of live theatre lies in 'virtual theatre'. While acknowledging the need to keep in touch with audiences during the Covid-19 closures he asserted there would always be a fundamental difference:

> Watching actors perform on screen is engaging and entertaining and it is an art form in another sense and there is a name for it. That is what film is. That is what TV is. But I do not think that it is theatre. The very premise of theatre is gathering people together in a shared space to enjoy a shared experience . . . In 2017 a study found that patrons' hearts beat at the same time during a live theatre performance. This type of synchronicity has been linked to trust, to empathy, to friendship, to the removal of social barriers, commonalities that do not happen in the same way when we watch theatre virtually.

In the larger major theatres what might be acceptable to all parties would be to revert to the original principle: that the only kind of 'virtual theatre' that should be made available is the actual performance streamed live in real time with delays permitted only for inconvenient overseas time zones. Such was the original vision of both the NT and the Met.

A different approach to the future of 'virtual theatre' for small spaces?

The equipment for transmitting live performance is getting ever smaller and ever less intrusive. For the smaller companies in smaller theatres, more frequent transmissions can be justified not just because they always need the money but principally because in theatre spaces with a capacity of no more than 400 the actors' main objection, that it is almost impossible to pitch a performance to both an actual audience of 1,000 plus and for a camera in close-up, is partially removed. In smaller flexible theatre spaces the positions for remotely controlled cameras can more easily be adjusted for the production being recorded. In 2021 the Young Vic under Artistic Director Kwame Kwei-Armah introduced an original coda in their *Best Seat in The House* service whereby those watching at home can either choose themselves to cut between multiple cameras or else accept the 'Director's Cut' as in all other streaming systems. By spring 2021 this ingenious facility had been successfully offered on three productions.

Many leading performers will always have a visceral objection to the blurring of the arts of theatre and of performance to camera. But it is too early to guess whether there will be unforeseen consequences in the worlds of drama, dance and opera which will outweigh the obvious advantages to major companies based in the metropolises, social and financial, which thereby reach out to wider audiences. These are those who are too distant or too fearful of pandemics to attend the actual live theatre and so must resort to the push-a-button alternative.

Is the survival of art cinemas an allied issue?

Meanwhile, the survival of art cinemas that provide auditoriums for the simultaneous transmission of live performances cannot be taken for granted. They are under threat due to the growing practice of producers bypassing cinemas and making large profits by streaming the latest movies directly to subscribers at home. While they survive, local cinemas do provide social cohesion to communities where the high streets are dying because too many are finding it ever easier to shop online without leaving one's home. If it is so easy to access 'virtual theatre' at home at the flip of switch, it makes it important that both the smaller theatre spaces and the art cinemas stay open as lively local centres which are fun to visit. You laugh more sitting with others in an auditorium than on your sofa with family or friends eating their supper.

Is a further decline in touring going to be an unforeseen consequence of the virus?

Commercial managers in New York and London used to try out new productions immediately before opening on Broadway or in the West End, where the big money is made. For different reasons a new stage in a new town every Monday was how our Prospect Theatre Company

14.1 *King's Theatre Edinburgh 1906: male and female caryatids over three-quarter view of auditorium after renovation of 1985 and before that of 2024.*

lived in the sixties and seventies. Touring had been in decline for many reasons, such as the complex technology of popular musicals taking too long to set up for get-ins and get-outs over a single weekend. I date from a generation where if the management bought enough train tickets for actors and staff for a company travelling from town A to town B one could 'get out' after the Saturday evening performance, take the set and costumes down to the railway station in town A, load it into a special wagon, supplied gratis by the railway company, and unload it in town B early on Monday morning. Without this concession Prospect could not have afforded touring the large-cast classics to major theatres.

The introduction of 'virtual theatre' may turn out to trigger a further decline in touring. The smaller provincial subsidised companies may shortly be unable to afford the large casts needed for many of the classics. If the local theatre can once more afford to stage the syllabus Shakespeare, local schools may still prefer to view the NT production of the same play if that is available for free at the push of a button.

Panto and headliner comedian Ken Dodd suggests that the place can also be the thing

However, on a more cheerful note, there will always be one form of popular theatre that fills the larger theatres of Britain for a couple of months every year and which appeals to all ages and to every stratum of society. This is the Christmas pantomime, an enduring form of theatre unknown in most other countries. The popularity of panto – at least in Britain – offers hope that the best large theatres still have a role to play in the community.

For many Britons their first experience of live theatre has long been the Christmas panto, preferably in a late Victorian theatre with lots of ice cream and other families having a good time. We are whipped into a frenzy or hushed into silence by the consummate professionals who have us hooked. We yell 'behind you!' and take part in other weird ways. In some towns panto has died out, as have so many summer seasons at the end of the pier. But in others panto lives on. Go to Liverpool, York, Glasgow, Bristol or to the fine old theatres in London suburbs such as Richmond and Wimbledon. At Christmas, four generations of my family have attended the panto in Edinburgh at the King's. Unforgettable at the end of the last century were Jimmie Logan as Buttons and Stanley Baxter giving his Dame alternate years in Glasgow and Edinburgh.

More recently at the King's Edinburgh the trio of Allan Stewart as Dame, Andy Gray as Buttons and Grant Stott as villain co-starred in seventeen of the twenty-two pantos from 1998 to 2019. In the Christmas season 2019/20 they gave eighty-two performances to audiences, young and old, totalling 89,304. Multiply that over a seventeen-year reign and you find that they must have sold nearly one and half million seats – surely a show business record for any panto *ménage à trois*. (This trio was sadly brought to an end by Gray's death in 2021 from Covid-19). It was also a triumph for the King's itself, which, since the first Edinburgh Festival of 1947, has provided a setting as appropriate for Scottish panto as for Viennese Mozart. Those slightly louche caryatids each side of the proscenium smile their agreement while holding their masks in one hand and taking the weight of the boxes above with the other.

If the gags are familiar, we do not complain. Dame, cupping his hands to talk in a stage whisper to a wee boy down stage left with his parents parked up stage right: 'I'm goin' tae gie ye a magic panto token. Ye canna see it. But if ye put it under your pillow, in the mornin' there'll be a crisp ten-pound note.' Laugh. 'And if there isnae they dinna love you.' Much, much bigger laugh. That's panto.

For Britons not baptised in panto there was always top-of-the-bill comic Ken Dodd. In 2017 Dodd celebrated his ninetieth birthday and was still covering thousands of miles a year touring around England. Michael Billington wrote in *The Guardian* of 4 November 2017:

> I've been lucky enough in my lifetime to see two performers kissed with genius. One was Laurence Olivier, who could enthral an audience with his animalistic power and interpretative originality. The other is Ken Dodd, who has the capacity to take a roomful of strangers and, through a fusillade of verbal and visual gags that never lets up, induce in them a spirit of collective ecstasy.

Explained Dodd:

> You have to take on the audience. I reckon you have thirty seconds in which to build a bridge to them and structure the act so you start with the 'hello' gags, then the topicals, then the surreal stuff: 'What a day for Dame Nellie Melba to drop a choc ice down her tights and say, "How's that for a knickerbocker glory?"'

Courses for horses

Dodd is the most successful northern English comedian ever to make it down south. It was Billington who had recorded his early years in a slim volume published in 1977 and aptly titled *How Tickled I Am: A Celebration of Ken Dodd*. In 1965 Dodd had brought his own show for a record breaking forty-two-and-a-half-week run, at the London Palladium. Frank Matcham's masterpiece of 1910 is intimate and yet holds more than 2,300. All London came, from Prime Minister Harold Wilson to playwright John Osborne. But it was the space itself that played a central role in the success of Dodd, who was soon giving three performances on Saturdays to make it nine a week. Nowhere else in London could he have played to so many people for over 350 performances in a single year.

For other examples take the longest-running musicals in London's West End, though it must be said they were all at theatres with half the capacity of the Palladium. At Her Majesty's Theatre, built in 1897, *Phantom of the Opera* ran for thirty-four years continuously up to the pandemic closure of 2020. The only other musical to have had more performances and be still running at that time was *Les Misérables*, but to achieve that it had played, consecutively, at three different theatres: the Barbican for a sticky opening, the Palace Theatre of 1891 for nearly twenty years, and the Sondheim, formerly the Queen's, since 2004.

There are many more examples of where the theatre space itself has contributed to theatrical success: from 1963 to 1976 the battered Old Vic of 1871 was a congenial home for the new National Theatre Company, being more actor and audience friendly than either what went before – Chichester – or what followed – the Lyttelton and the Olivier. The place where theatre happens is so much more than a frame.

Future forecasts summarised

I may have been foolhardy to have titled Act Four '2021: The future'. How will this read in ten years' time? Yet I do believe that both recent technical developments in the theatre and the worldwide pandemic have already had consequences, some good and some bad, and will have further consequences unforeseen by many including those who provide public and private financial support for live theatre. Studying the grim events that took place after the plagues and the puritans of seventeeth-century Britain and post the arrival of the talkies world-wide at the end of the nineteen-twenties can help us prepare for the unexpected.

New work, meaning both new plays and new styles of productions, will continue to flourish in the many well designed smaller theatres spaces holding between 250 and 400 which have been created in theatre cities across the world. But how such achievement can reach wider audiences in the existing larger theatres has grown more difficult. The older commercial ones have been re-seated for fewer more comfortable theatregoers paying higher prices. There are not so many cheap seats. For those theatres in the big cities which once presented more plays than musicals it is now the other way round. The microphone is often everywhere for every performer in every show - both in Britain's grandest playhouses such as the Olivier and the Lyttleton and in the spectacular new big theatres recently built in 'world class' cities such as those in China.

Along with the microphones there have also arrived ever smaller cameras with which managements of great institutions such as the Metropolitan Opera New York or the National Theatre London can stream into your local cinema, or even to your home TV set, not just the opera or play actually being performed at that moment on their stages (as they did at first) but also, if you pay a subscription, the pick of past performances. This was a godsend during the pandemic when so many feared to congregate indoors. But performers in these big spaces do not know whether to play to the large live audience in front of them or to the hidden eavesdropping cameras. The unforeseen consequences could be serious. The classics in all languages almost always have large casts. Operas generally have a chorus. This makes it harder to pay for a tour unless this is generously and specifically subsidised. And why should the local theatre company present their own productions of the school syllabus Shakespeare, as was the custom in Britain, if the teacher can the press a button to show the class a star-studded recent production from NTLive? The megacity dweller will continue to see large cast plays and operas live but the rest of us may have to be content with 'virtual theatre'. Nevertheless, there will always be ever popular panto and rare larger-than-life performers like Ken Dodd who cannot be captured by the camera. *Mutatis mutandis* the same applies in other cultures.

Lastly a good thing is that the modernism prevalent in the mid twentieth century has turned out to be a blip on the architecture of the theatre space. It had been engendered by an incomplete functionalist philosophy which neglected the role of audience. In 1994 Marcus Binney in *Glyndebourne: Building a Vision*, talking of 1990 and the start of design for the new Glyndebourne theatre space, quoted George Christie: 'It was Mackintosh who convinced that the horseshoe was the best shape. It happened remarkably quickly. We all felt that intimacy would be most easily achieved with the people in the audience wrapped around like wallpaper. That's something that neither the fan shape nor the shoebox does.' Attitudes to theatre space had changed in the previous twenty years. The functionalist forms and the brutalist styles of the Olivier fan and of the Lyttleton shoebox were being rejected. By 2021 more of the newer designers of theatre spaces have rediscovered the fun in functionalism.

The author at his desk at TPC in 1984 shortly after the remodelling of the auditorium of the theatre in the St Lawrence Centre, Toronto at the invitation of an old friend from Oxford Playhouse days, director Eddie Gilbert. This was the first job in North America completed by Theatre Projects Consultants. The poster for On the Razzle *by Tom Stoppard celebrates Gilbert's opening production.*

BIBLIOGRAPHIES

Select books cited

Amery, Colin, Marcus Binney and Rosy Runciman (1994). *Glyndebourne: Building a Vision*. London: Thames and Hudson.
Appia, Adolphe (1927). 'Art is an Attitude'. In: Walter René Fuerst and Samuel J. Hume, eds, *Twentieth-Century Stage Decoration*. London.
Atkins, Eileen (2021). *'Will She Do?' Act One of a Life on Stage*. London: Virago.
Barron, Michael (1993). *Auditorium Acoustics and Architectural Design*. 1st edn. London: E. & F.N. Spon.
Barron, Michael (2009). *Auditorium Acoustics and Architectural Design*. 2nd edn. London: Routledge.
Baugh, Christopher (2013). *Theatre, Performance and Technology*. 2nd edn. Basingstoke: Palgrave Macmillan.
Baur-Heinhold, Margarete (1967). *Baroque Theatre*. London: Thames and Hudson.
Beauman, Sally (1982). *The Royal Shakespeare Company: A History of Ten Decades*. Oxford: Oxford University Press.
Beerbohm, Max (1924 [1954]). *Around Theatres*. New York: Simon and Schuster.
Bel Geddes, Norman (1932). *Horizons*. Boston, MA: Little, Brown and Company.
Billington, Michael (1977). *How Tickled I Am: A Celebration of Ken Dodd*. London: Elm Tree Books.
Brook, Peter (1968). *The Empty Space*. London: Atheneum.
Calder, Barnabas (2016). *Raw Concrete: The Beauty of Brutalism*. London: William Heinemann.
Carson, L. (1912). *The Stage Guide and Directory*. London: The Stage.
Cave, Richard (1980). *Terence Gray and the Cambridge Festival Theatre*. Cambridge: Chadwyck-Healey.
Chen, Jack (1949). *The Chinese Theatre*. London: D. Dobson.
Cornwell, Paul (2004). *Only by Failure: The Many Faces of the Impossible Life of Terence Gray*. Cambridge: Salt Publishing.
Craig, Edward Gordon, ed. (1908–1929). *The Mask: A Monthly Journal of the Art of the Theatre*. Florence, Italy: Edward Gordon Craig.
Craig, Edward Gordon (1930). *Henry Irving*. New York: Longmans, Green and Co.
Dillon, Patrick (2015). *Concrete Reality. Denys Lasdun and the National Theatre*. London: National Theatre.
Earl, John and Michael Sell, eds (2000). *The Theatres Trust Guide to British Theatres 1750–1950: A Gazetteer*. London: A&C Black.
Edström, Per Simon (1990). *Why Not Theaters Made for People?* Värmdö, Sweden: Arena Theater Institute Foundation.
Eyre, Richard (2003). *National Service: Diary of a Decade at the National Theatre*. London: Bloomsbury.
The Festival Theatre Review (1926–1933). Cambridge: Festival Theatre.
George, Colin and Tedd George (2021). *Stirring Up Sheffield: An Insider's Account of the Battle to Build the Crucible Theatre*. London: Wordville.
Gibson, Charles Dana (1896). *Pictures of People*. 1st edn. New York: Life Publishing Co.

Gibson, Charles Dana (1901). *Pictures of People*. 2nd edn. London: John Lane.
Glasstone, Victor (1975). *Victorian and Edwardian Theatres*. London: Thames and Hudson.
Granville-Barker, Harley (1922). *The Exemplary Theatre*. London: Chatto and Windus.
Grice, Elizabeth (1977). *Rogues and Vagabonds: Or, The Actor's Road to Respectability*. Lavenham: Terence Dalton.
Grover, Razia, ed. (1992). *Concepts and Responses: International Architectural Design Competition for the Indira Gandhi National Centre for the Arts, New Delhi*. New Delhi: Indira Gandhi National Centre for the Arts.
Guthrie, Tyrone (1960). *A Life in the Theatre*. London: Hamish Hamilton.
Hall, Peter (1993). *Making an Exhibition of Myself*. London: Sinclair Stevenson.
Holden, Michael (1971). *The Stage Guide*. London: Carson and Comerford with the Association of British Theatre Technicians.
Izenour, George C. (1977). *Theater Design*. New Haven, CT: Yale University Press.
Joseph, Stephen, ed. (1964). *Actor and Architect*. Manchester: Manchester University Press.
Küller, Rikard, ed. (1975). *Architectural Psychology: Proceedings of the Lund Conference*. Lund: Studentlitteratur AB.
Leacroft, Richard (1973). *The Development of the English Playhouse*. Ithaca, NY: Cornell University Press.
Leacroft, Richard and Helen Leacroft (1984). *Theatre and Playhouse: An Illustrated Survey of Theatre Building from Ancient Greece to the Present Day*. London: Methuen Drama.
Lewis, Peter (1990). *The National: A Dream Made Concrete*. London: Methuen Drama.
Mackintosh, Iain (wrote catalogue and was curator) (1975). *NT: The Georgian Playhouse, Actors, Artists, Audiences and Architecture, 1730–1830*. London: Hayward Gallery.
Mackintosh, Iain (1977). 'Scene Individable or Poem Unlimited'. In: Colin Amery, ed., *The National Theatre – The Architectural Review Guide*. Oxford: The Architectural Press.
Mackintosh, Iain (1979). *Pit, Boxes and Gallery: The Story of the Theatre Royal, Bury St Edmunds 1819 to 1976*. London: National Trust.
Mackintosh, Iain (1993). *Architecture, Actor and Audience*. London: Routledge.
Mackintosh, Iain (2008). 'King Kong versus Godzilla: The Competition for the Royal Opera House at The Hague, 1910–1911'. In: David Wilmore, ed., *Frank Matcham & Co*. Dacre, UK: Theatreshire Books, pp.142–177.
Mackintosh, Iain, ed. (2011). *The Guthrie Thrust Stage: A Living Legacy*. London: Association of British Theatre Technicians.
Mackintosh, Iain and Michael Sell, eds (1982). *Curtains!!! or A New Life for Old Theatres*. Eastbourne: John Offord Publications.
Marshall, Norman (1947). *The Other Theatre*. London: John Lehmann.
Marshall, Norman (2nd edition 1962). *The Producer and the Play*. London: Macdonald & Co.
Maugham, Somerset (1955). 'Introduction'. In: Raymond Mander and Joe Mitchenson, *The Artist and the Theatre*. London: William Heinemann.
Mulryne, Ronnie and Margaret Shewring (1989). *This Golden Round*. Stratford-upon-Avon: Mulryne and Shewring Ltd.
Mulryne, Ronnie and Margaret Shewring (1995). *Making Space for Theatre: British Architecture and Theatre Since 1958*. Stratford-upon-Avon: Mulryne and Shewring Ltd.
Pilbrow, Richard (2023). *The Untold Story of the National Theatre*. London.
Quayle, Anthony (1990). *A Time to Speak*. London: Barrie and Jenkins.
Ridge, Harold (2nd edition 1930). *Stage Lighting*. Cambridge: W. Heffer & Sons Ltd.
Sachs, Edwin O. (1896–1898). *Modern Opera Houses and Theatres*. 3 vols. New York: Benjamin Blom.
Saunders, George (1790). *A Treatise on Theatres*. London.
Schubert, Hannelore (1971). *The Modern Theatre: Architecture, Stage Design, Lighting*. London: Pall Mall Press.
Southern, Richard (1948). *The Georgian Playhouse*. London: Pleiades Books.

Todd, Andrew and Jean-Guy Lecat (2003). *The Open Circle: Peter Brook's Theatre Environments.* London: Faber & Faber.

Tolmie, A.W. (1946). *The Stage Guide (Revised Edition).* London: Carson & Comerford.

Vatsyayan, Kapila, ed. (1991). *Concepts of Space: Ancient and Modern* [conference proceedings]. New Delhi: Indira Gandhi National Centre for the Arts/Abhinav Publications.

Winston, James, edited by Iain Mackintosh with Marcus Risdell (2008). *The Theatric Tourist: A Facsimile of the First and Only Edition of 1805 Preceded by a Facsimile of the Original Prospectus.* London: The Society for Theatre Research and The British Library.

Periodicals cited

Select articles either referred to in the text or suggested for further reading from publications or available online only. Presented in idiosyncratic format.

Anonymous (1965). 'The National Theatre Plan – and How it Evolved', *The Sunday Times* (21 February).
Appia, Adolphe (1908). 'Notes sur le théâtre', *La vie musicale* April issue.
Atkinson, Brooks (1974). 'The Theatre is not the Thing', *New York Times* (31 October).
Avery, Bryan (1992). 'Beauty is in the Eye of the Beholder', *The Architectural Review*.
Beacham, Richard C. (1988). '"Brothers in Suffering and Joy": the Appia–Craig Correspondence', *New Theatre Quarterly* (August) 4.15: 268–288.
Bevan, Robert (2019). 'Grange Park Opera: A look inside the company's new Surrey home', *Evening Standard* (6 June).
Billington, Michael (2017). 'Ken Dodd at 90: the rib-tickling genius is still crazy after all these years', *The Guardian* (4 November).
Conrad, Peter (2007). 'Opera from New York in your home town? Easy. Just go to the pictures', *The Observer* (22 April).
Elliott, Michael (1972). 'A Theatre Director's View of the Crucible', *The Architectural Review* (February).
Elliott, Michael (1973). 'On Not Building for Posterity', *TABS* (June) 31.2: 41–44.
Evers, A. (1982). 'De toekomst van de architect', *Bouw* (13 November) 23, 48–49.
Foster, Tim (2005). 'The Sage, Gateshead', *Sightline* (Winter) 28:4: 8–12.
Glancey, Jonathan (2011). 'Move over, Sydney: Zaha Hadid's Guangzhou Opera House', *The Guardian* (28 February).
Guthrie Theater (2020). *A Message From Artistic Director Joseph Haj* (YouTube 7 May 2020). Or consult Guthrie Theater Archive.
Hall, Peter (1973). 'The Studio. Third Auditorium of the National Theatre' [internal correspondence]. 28 February.
Hatherley, Owen (2016). 'Strange, Angry Objects', *London Review of Books* (17 November).
Higgins, Charlotte (2005). 'Back-row Blogger on . . . Sage Gateshead', *The Guardian* (27 October).
Kellaway, Kate (2020). 'Zoë Wanamaker: "I hate communicating virtually. Honestly, the palaver"', *The Observer* (7 June).
Küller, Rikard (1977). 'Psycho-Physiological Conditions in Theatre Construction', edited by James F. Arnott and others. Papers prepared in advance for *Theatre Space* International Federation for Theatre Research World Congress, Munich, 18–25 September, 158–80. Munich: Prestel-Verlag.
London Weekend Television (1975). *Aquarius*, season 9, episode 1 [television broadcast in which Peter Hall interviews Denys Lasdun at Epidaurus].
Mackintosh, Iain (1973). 'Inigo Jones – Theatre Architect', *TABS* (September) 31.3: 99–105.
Mackintosh, Iain (1977). 'Newest and Oldest Theatres of Germany', *ABTT Sightline* (Spring) 11.1.
Mackintosh, Iain (1978). 'Old and New: The Rejection of the Fan-Shaped Auditorium and the Reinstatement of the Courtyard Form', *Theatre Design and Technology* (the Journal of the United States Institute of Theatre Technology) and edited version in *Theatre Research International*, Oxford University Press, 1978.
Mackintosh, Iain (1982), 'Britain's Sleeping Beauties', *Observer Colour Magazine* (28 February). Research by Christopher Brereton, John Earl, Victor Glasstone, Iain Mackintosh and other members of the *Curtains!!!* team. Of the sample of eleven sleeping beauties two had only recently been restored to full theatrical use, five were subsequently, one private one was then fully restored, three now have a flat floor laid over the stalls in use for popular music and in 2022 only two are still judged by the Theatres Trust as being 'Theatres at Risk'. All this sample are now protected by being listed Grade II* or Grade II.
Mackintosh, Iain (1984). 'Rediscovering the Courtyard', *The Architectural Review* (April), 64–71.

Mackintosh, Iain (1990). 'Out of the Packing Case, The Dunfermline Opera House moves to Florida', *ABTT Sightline* (July) 24.3.
Mackintosh, Iain (1994). 'The Last of the Empire' from *Theatre Scotland Issue 10 August 1994*.
Mackintosh, Iain (2000). 'Coming Full Circle', *Glyndebourne Festival Programme Book*, 113–117.
Moore, Rowan (2015). 'The 10 Best Theatres', *The Guardian* (11 December).
Moore, Rowan (2016). 'Elizabethan Theatre, Chateau d'Hardelot Review – a great view from the circle', *The Guardian* (26 June).
Moore, Rowan (2019). 'Nevill Holt Opera Review – a quiet kind of drama', *The Guardian* (13 January).
Reid, Francis (1984). 'Theatre of Change', *Architects' Journal* (6 June) 179: 24–27.
Vidal, Felipe (2017). '"Bacantes" [*The Bacchae*] in the Best Theater in the World', *The Theatre Times* (25 February). Available online: https://thetheatretimes.com/bacantes-bacchae-best-theatre-world.
Weiss, Hedy (2017). 'Chicago Shakespeare's opens Yard with twitchy "Toad"', *Chicago Sun Times* (20 September).
Wilson, Richard (2017). 'Bonfire in Merrie England', *The London Review of Books* (4 May).

Further reading

Association of British Theatre Technicians (2023). *Theatre buildings: a design guide.* London: Routledge.
Beacham, Richard (1987). *Adolphe Appia: Artist and Visionary of the Modern Theatre.* London: Routledge.
Binney, Marcus and Rosy Runciman (1994). *Glyndebourne: Building a Vision.* London: Thames and Hudson.
Bo Bardi, Lina, Edson Elito and Jose Celso Martinez Correa (1999). *Teatro Oficina, São Paulo, Brasil 1980–1984.* Lisbon, Portugal: Editorial Blau Insituto Lina Bo e PM Bardi.
Breton, Gaille (1989). *Theatre/Theaters.* Paris: Editions du Moniteur.
Brock, Susan and Marian J. Pringle (1984). *The Shakespeare Memorial Theatre 1919–1945.* Cambridge and Teanock, NJ: Chadwyck-Healey.
Burman, Alasdair G. (1995). *Theatros do Brasil /Theatres of Brazil.* São Bernardo do Campo: Mercedes Benz do Brasil.
Burte, Himanshu (2008). *Space for Engagement: The Indian Art Place and a Habitational Approach to Architecture.* Kolkata: Seagull Books.
Edström, Per (2010). *Theater, Theatre, Theatre, Teatr and Teatro, Told and Retold.* Varmdo, Sweden: Arena Theatre Institute.
Evershed-Martin, Leslie (1971). *The Impossible Theatre.* Chichester: Phillimore & Co.
Ferraz, Marcelo Carvalho (1996). *Lina Bo Bardi* (2nd edn.). São Paulo, Brazil: Instituto Lina Bo Bardi and PM Bardi.
Fair, Alistair (2018). *Architectural History of Britain's New Theatres, 1945–1985.* Oxford: Oxford University Press.
Fair, Alistair (2019). *Play On: Contemporary Theatre Architecture in Britain.* London: Lund Humphries.
Gascoigne, Bamber (1994). *World Theatre: An Illustrated History.* London: Thames and Hudson.
Gurr, Andrew (2004). *Playgoing in Shakespeare's London* (3rd edn.). Cambridge: Cambridge University Press.
Gurr, Andrew with Orrell, John (1989). *Rebuilding Shakespeare's Globe*, London: Weidenfield and Nicolson.
Hardin, Terri (1999). *Theatres and Opera Houses: Masterpieces of Architecture.* New York, Robert M Tod.
Hartnell, Phyllis (1968). *A Concise History of the Theatre.* London: Thames and Hudson.
Henderson, Mary C. (1973). *The City and the Theatre: The History of New York Playhouses: A 235-year Journey from Bowling Green to Times Square.* Clifton, NJ: James T. White & Company.
Henderson, Mary C. (1986). *Theater in America: 200 Years of Plays, Players and Productions.* New York: Harry N. Abrams, Inc.
Joliffe, John (1999). *Glyndebourne: An Operatic Miracle.* London: John Murray.
Joseph, Stephen (1963). *The Story of the Playhouse in England.* London: Barrie & Rockcliff.
Joseph, Stephen (1968). *New Theatre Forms.* London: Sir Isaac Pitman & Sons.
Mielziner, Jo (1970). *The Shape of Our Theatre.* New York: Clarkson N. Potter, Inc.
Pennick, Nigel (1980). *Sacred Geometry.* Wellingborough: Turnstone Press Limited.
Rees, Terence (1978). *Theatre Lighting in the Age of Ga*s. London: The Society for Theatre Research.
Rowell, Kenneth (1968). *Stage Design.* London: Studio Vista.
Sell, Michael (2020). *The Matcham Directory.* Torquay: The Frank Matcham Society.
Serroni, J.C. (2002). *Teatros da Brasil.* São Paulo, Brazil: Editors Senac.
Southern, Richard (1962). *Seven Ages of the Theatre.* London: Faber and Faber.
Staples, David (2021). *Modern Theatres 1950–2020.* London: Routledge.
Todd, Andrew (2016). *Common Sense: Building a World to Share.* Montreal: Rightangle International.

Wickham, Glynne (1972). *Early English Stages 1300 to 1660: Volume Two: 1570 to 1660 Part II*. London: Routledge and Kegan Paul.
Wiles, David (2003). *A Short History of Western Performance Space*. Cambridge: Cambridge University Press.

ACKNOWLEDGEMENTS

Author's thanks

I thank first Sir Richard Eyre for his generous foreword and then all who have helped me prepare this text and images for publication: for picture research and editing Vicky Simon and Fran Birch; for textual advice Richard Pilbrow, Sir James Dunbar-Nasmith and Professor Christopher Baugh; for IT guidance my son Fred Mackintosh; for help with the indices and works cited Kelli Zezulka; and those architectural partnerships and individuals for the granting of rights in images they owned and the pleasure of working with them in the past. These include: Spencer de Grey and Jason Flanagan of Foster + Partners; Tim Foster of Wilson Foster Architects; Onno Greiner and Martien van Goor of GGH Architecten; Steve Tompkins of Haworth Tompkins; Graham Law, Sir James Dunbar-Nasmith and Colin Ross of LDN Architects; Graham Gund of the Gund Partnership Boston; Axel Burrough of Levitt Bernstein Architects; George Marsh of Payette Boston; and Robin Snell both when he was working for Michael Hopkins and later with his own practice. I thank all whom I enjoyed working with at Theatre Projects Consultants for thirty years from 1973. However, there are four who need special thanks for sourcing some of the best images of our projects: architect Mark Stroomer, who has been with Theatre Projects Consultants since 1992 and is now Director of the London office, and his office manager Sophie Oskys and earlier two young architects who were introduced to theatre in our office, Anne Minors and Gavin Green before they became partners in their own theatre consultancies. For this book they have contributed their own series of drawings, some of which started life in *The Guthrie Thrust Stage: A Living Legacy* which I edited on behalf of the Association of British Theatre Technicians for the Prague Quadrennial 2011. I must also thank Fran Birch and Vicky Simon, my picture editors, who helped source the images and create the composites to allow for instant comparisons.

    The role of the client in the design process varies in different projects from the small schemes, where the user client calls the shots and finds the funds, to the much larger state and civic projects beset with committees, which take much longer and are all too frequently opened by artistic leaders quite different from those who had been involved at the outset when critical design decisions were being made. In contrast the most rewarding for all involved was the new Glyndebourne opera house of 1994 where the client Sir George Christie, accompanied only by his general manager Anthony Whitworth-Jones, eschewed committees and instead assembled a few experts, including acoustician Derek Sugden, stage designer John Bury and myself plus my principal technical colleague at Theatre Projects Consultants Alan Russell, in a small team led by Christie's chosen architect Sir Michael Hopkins with his wife and professional partner Patty. We met fortnightly for some months and soon set the design for a fresh and affordable theatre. This was a process which government bodies would take many years to achieve, often with less satisfactory results.

I must also thank the actors and the small permanent staff of the homeless theatre company Prospect which I had co-founded in 1961 with the invaluable assistance of Oxford Playhouse manager Elizabeth Sweeting and show business lawyer Laurence Harbottle. Principal colleagues in Prospect's halcyon days were Richard Cottrell and Toby Robertson. On the road I learnt that the architecture of theatre space is much more than a frame for the production when discovering those spaces that served actors and audience better than others on tour in Britain and across the globe, in London's West End and in wonderful venues that had not been created for the drama such as the Assembly Hall in Edinburgh and the *Teatro La Fenice* in Venice.

Permissions for images

The author and publisher gratefully acknowledge the permission granted to reproduce the copyright material in this book. The word 'courtesy' denotes there was no charge.

Every effort has been made to trace copyright holders and to obtain their permission for the use of copyright material. The publisher apologises for any errors or omissions in the below list and would be grateful if notified of any corrections that should be incorporated in future reprints or editions of this book.

1.1. Overlay of Old Vic over Olivier courtesy of Vicky Simon from sources. 1.2. Courtesy of John Earl Collection. 2.1. Courtesy of Theatresearch. 2.2. Courtesy Richard and Helen Leacroft Collection at the V&A. 3.1. Courtesy Richard and Helen Leacroft Collection at the V&A. 3.2. Photo Scott & Wilkinson from *Stage Lighting,* Harold Ridge (1928) over drawing courtesy Vicky Simon sources *The Theatric Tourist,* James Winston (1808) and *Rogues and Vagabonds*, Elizabeth Grice (1977). 3.3 and 3.4. From *Stage Lighting,* Harold Ridge (1928). 3.5. Courtesy Richard and Helen Leacroft Collection at the V&A. 4.1. Courtesy Richard and Helen Leacroft Collection at the V&A. 4.2. Top: Courtesy Festival Theatre, Stratford Ontario. Photographer not known. Bottom: Courtesy Guthrie Theater. Photo Marty Nordstrum. 4.3. Drawings courtesy Anne Minors. Commissioned by ABTT 2011. 4.4. Photo courtesy Philip Vile. 4.5. Courtesy the Young Vic. Photo Leon Puplett. 5.1. Courtesy Shakespeare's Globe. Photo John Tramper. 5.2. Drawings courtesy Jon Greenfield architect. 6.1. Lasdun Collection / RIBA archives. 6.2. Top: Lasdun Collection / RIBA archives. Bottom: Simon Turner / Alamy Stock photo. 6.3. Drawing by Onno Greiner 1959. Courtesy GGH Architecten. 6.4. Courtesy copyright LDN Architects. 6.5. Top: Courtesy University of Bristol Theatre Collection. Bottom: Courtesy designer Elizabeth Bury. 6.6. Photo Clive Barda / ArenaPAL. 7.1. Drawings courtesy Theatre Projects Consultants. 7.2. Photo courtesy Michael Mayhew. 7.3. Photo courtesy of The Wilde Theatre, Bracknell, architect Levitt Bernstein. 7.4. Photos courtesy Trudie Lee. 7.5. Photo courtesy and copyright the Steve Rosenthal Collection of Commissioned Work at Historic New England. Architect Graham Gund Partnership Boston. 7.6. Drawing and photo courtesy Tim Foster architect. 7.7. Author's own overlay on supposed plan by Inigo Jones – see also 7.8. 7.8. Courtesy Provost and Fellows of Worcester College, Oxford. 7.9. Courtesy Shakespeare's Globe. Photo Pete Le May. 7.10. Top: Drawing courtesy Theatre Projects Consultants. Bottom: Photo Richard Bryant courtesy Foster + Partners. 8.1. Top: Tricycle photo courtesy Steve Stephens. Bottom: Photo courtesy Georgian Theatre Royal Richmond photographer not known. 8.2. *Teatro Oficina* by architects Lina Bo Bardi and Edson Elito, photo courtesy Jennifer Glass Studio. 8.3. Top: Royal Court section courtesy Haworth Tompkins architect for renovation 2000. Bottom: Photo Stephen Cummiskey. 8.4. Tina Packer Playhouse drawing and ESTO photo by Peter Mauss courtesy Payette Architects. 8.5. Photo courtesy Jean-Guy Lecat. 8.6. Drawing courtesy

Jean-Guy Lecat. 8.7. Photo courtesy Jean-Guy Lecat. 9.1. Lawrence Batley Theatre auditorium 1994 designed by Kirklees Council Architects and Theatre Projects Consultants within existing building. Photo courtesy Peter Rourke. 9.2. Photos courtesy Peter Vile. Architect for auditorium renovation 2012 Andrzej Blonski. Architect for 2018 whole building renovation Haworth Tompkins. 9.3. Top: 1906 photo photographer not known. Bottom: Photo Peter Cook. 9.4. Wilkins' 1819 geometry courtesy Levitt Bernstein Architects of the 2007 renovation. 9.5. Top: Photo Graeme Peacock. Bottom: Photo Sally Ann Norman. 9.6. Photo courtesy Steve Stephens. 10.1. Photos of the Asolo / Dunfermline. Top: Wayne Eastep / Getty Images. Bottom: Courtesy James Dunbar-Nasmith. 10.2. Photo courtesy Steve Stephens. 10.3. Photo Clive Barda / ArenaPAL. 10.4. Photo courtesy and copyright LDN Architects. 11.1. Courtesy Theatre Projects Consultants: Their concept design July 1990 for the new Glyndebourne. 11.2. Geometry concept sketch courtesy Theatre Projects Consultants April 1990. 11.3. Top: Photo Sam Stephenson / ArenaPAL. Bottom: Glyndebourne Productions Ltd / Arena PAL. 11.4. Photo Matthew Williams-Ellis. 11.5. New Garsington Opera 2011 courtesy architects Robin Snell and Partners. Top: Photo Dennis Gilbert. Bottom: Photo Richard Davies. 11.6. New Garsington Opera 2011. Sketch courtesy Robin Snell and Partners architects. 11.7. Top: Original design and illustration for Grange Park Opera courtesy Tim Ronalds Architects. Bottom: As built by others courtesy Grange Park Opera photo Richard Lewisohn. 11.8. Photo Nigel Young courtesy Foster + Partners. 11.9. Photo courtesy Christopher Hagelund. Architects Snøhetta. 12.1. Photo Frank Greiner De Tamboer Hoogeven courtesy GGH Architecten. 12.2. Top: Photo Sybolt Voeten De Maagd Bergen-op-Zoom. Bottom: Drawing Onno Greiner. Both: Courtesy GGH Architecten. 12.3. Photos Puppin Fotografos. Courtesy and copyright José Carlos Serroni. 12.4. Photo Puppin Fotografos. Courtesy and copyright José Carlos Serroni. 12.5. Drawings and photos courtesy Gopika Jayasree. 12.6. Top: Felix Stennson / Stock Alamy Photo. Bottom: Drawing by Jack Chen. 12.7. Private Collection. Image in public domain. 13.1. Photos courtesy and copyright Philip Vile. Architects Haworth Tompkins. 13.2. Drawings courtesy Haworth Tompkins 13.3. Architect Andrew Todd. Photo Martin Argyroglo. 13.4. Drawing courtesy Theatre Projects Consultants. 13.5. RST Top: Photo Peter Cook. Bottom: Drawing courtesy Charcoalblue. Architects Rab Bennetts Associates. 13.6. Top: Martin Charles / RIBA Archive. Bottom: Photo Pete Le May courtesy RSC. 13.7. Drawing courtesy Gavin Green of Charcoalblue. 13.8. The Yard Chicago. Top: Drawing courtesy Charcoalblue. Bottom: Courtesy Chicago Shakespeare Theater, photo Vito Palmisano. 13.9. Photo courtesy Philip Vile over section courtesy Haworth Tompkins over photo Manuel Harlan / ArenaPAL. 13.10. Both photos courtesy Philip Vile. 13.11. Drawings courtesy Haworth Tompkins architects for 2021 renovation. 13.12. Drawings courtesy Haworth Tompkins architects for The Bridge 2017 and 2021 renovation Theatre Royal Drury Lane. 13.13. Manchester Royal Exchange. Top: Line Drawing by Andrew Holmes courtesy Levitt Bernstein. Bottom: 1982 'curtain call' photographer not known. 13.14. Photo courtesy Steve Stephens. 13.15. Regent's Park Open Air Theatre. Photos top and bottom courtesy David Jensen, middle courtesy Nik Dudley. 14.1. Photos of King's Theatre Edinburgh courtesy Mike Hume Historic Theatre Photography. Final photo by Iain Mackintosh.

THEATRE INDEX

All theatres/venues are in the UK unless otherwise indicated. The spelling of 'theatre' has been standardised throughout for UK and US theatres. European theatres retain their original spelling.

Page numbers in italics refer to illustrations.

Abbey Theatre, Dublin 34
Aldwych Theatre, London 11, 15, 76, 170
Almeida Theatre, London xii, 117
Ancient Theatre of Epidaurus, Epidaurus, Greece 69–71, *70*, 182
Art Theatre, Moscow, Russia 54, 58
Arts Theatre, Cambridge 11, 30
Ashcroft Theatre, Croydon, London 212
Asolo Theatre, Sarasota, FL, USA (recreation of auditorium of Opera House, Dunfermline) 134, 136–7, 230
Assembly Hall, Edinburgh 11, 40–2, *41*, 44, *45*, 46–7, 49–50–1, 118, 139, 170, 229

Badisches Staatstheater, Karlsruhe, Germany 54, 76
BAM Harvey Theatre, Brooklyn, NY, USA (previously Majestic Theatre) 112–14
Barbican Theatre, London 15, 57–79, *75*, 77, 184, 186, 218
Battersea Arts Centre, London 124
Bavarian *Nationaltheater*, Munich, Germany 8, 53
Belgrade Theatre, Coventry 212
Birmingham Repertory Theatre, Birmingham 57, 100
Bouffes du Nord, Paris, France 8, 12, *111*, *113*, 112–15
Bridge Theatre, London xi, 101, 193–5
Bristol Old Vic (also known as Theatre Royal Bristol) 10, 121–4

Castle Terrace Opera House, Edinburgh, unbuilt 138–41
Chateau d' Hardelot, Boulogne, France 179, 182–3, *183*
Chichester Festival Theatre, Chichester 46, *47*

Christ's Hospital Theatre, Horsham 89–90, 100, 191, 203
Citizens Theatre, Glasgow 138
Company Theatre, near Mumbai, India 172–3
Cottesloe Theatre, London (now the Dorfman Theatre) xi, 1, 12, 50, 60, 74, 83–91, *84*, 102, 105, 115–16, 147, 202, 214
Courtyard Theatre, Stratford-upon-Avon 186
Crucible Theatre, Sheffield *45*, 46, 48–50, 65, 68
Curve Theatre, Leicester 212
Cuvilliés Theater, Munich, Germany 53, 128

Der Koninklijke Schouwburg, Den Haag, the Netherlands 166
Dominion Theatre, London 143
Donmar Warehouse, London 117
Dorfman Theatre, London (part of the NT; previously the Cottesloe Theatre) xi, 60, 86, 89–90
Dutch National Opera, Amsterdam, the Netherlands (Het Musiektheater in Dutch) 117

Eden Court Theatre, Inverness 12, 72, *73*, 76, 139
Edinburgh Playhouse, Edinburgh 140
Elgin Theatre, Toronto, Ontario, Canada 142
Empire Theatre, Edinburgh (in 1994 rebuilt as the Festival Theatre) 134, 138–43, *142*
Esplanade Theatres on the Bay, Singapore 176–8
Everyman Theatre, Liverpool xii, 158, 179–82

Factory Theatre, Manchester 212
Festival Theatre, Cambridge 24, 27–39, *65*
Festival Theatre, Edinburgh (present theatre of 1994, when renamed Festival, retains from previous Empire of 1928 only the auditorium) 118, 134, 138–43

Festival Theatre, Stratford, Ontario, Canada 19, 43
Festspielhaus Bayreuth, Bayreuth, Germany xi, 7, 17, 38, 53, 141
Fortune Theatre, London 50
Forum Theatre, Billingham 72, 212
Founders' Theatre, Lenox, MA, USA (now renamed the Tina Packer Playhouse) *109*, 112, 193
Freie Volksbühne, Berlin, Germany 53–4

Gainsborough Studios, London 107
Garrick Theatre, London 13, 119
Garsington Opera, near High Wycombe (previous theatre was near Oxford) 152–8
Georgian Theatre Royal, Richmond, North Yorkshire 11, 85, 88, *104*, 121–8, 139
Glyndebourne Opera House, Lewes xi, 63, 78, 87, 118, 139, 114–62, 219
Grand Theatre and Opera House, Leeds (original full name) 130
Grange Festival Opera, Alresford, Hampshire 157
Grange Park Opera, West Horsley *156*, 157
Granville Theatre, London 15, 119
Guangzhou Opera House, Guangzhou, China 176
Guthrie Theatre, Minneapolis, MN, USA 43, 44, *45*, 47, 214

Her Majesty's Theatre, London 211, 218
Het Muziektheater, Amsterdam, the Netherlands (same as Dutch National Opera) 158–9
Hungarian State Opera House, Budapest, Hungary 54

Indira Gandhi National Arts Centre, New Delhi, India (subject of competition but never built) 173

Kammerspiele, Munich, Germany 53
Kiln Theatre, London (replaced the Tricycle on same site) 105
King's Theatre, Edinburgh 11, 130, 134, 139–40, 144, *216*, 217, 230
Komische Oper, Berlin, Germany 167
Kunstler Arts Theatre, Munich, Germany *37*, 38

La Fenice Opera House, Venice, Italy 11, 170, 229
Lawrence Batley Theatre, Huddersfield 117–8
Lincoln Center, New York, NY, USA 47, 115, 138
London Coliseum, London 57, 62, 159

Longborough Festival Opera, Longborough *152*
Lowry Theatre, Salford, Greater Manchester (part of the Lowry Centre) 90, 184
Lyceum Theatre, Edinburgh (also known as Royal Lyceum) 11, 14, 42, 132, 138–40
Lyceum Theatre, London 23, 115–16, 119, 130
Lyric Theatre, Hammersmith, London 119, *136*, 137, 201
Lyttleton Theatre, London (part of the National Theatre) 219

Majestic Theatre, Brooklyn, NY, USA (now the BAM Harvey Theatre) 112–15
Markgräfliches Opernhaus, Bayreuth, Germany 53
Mark Hellinger Theatre, New York, NY, USA (previously Warner Bros. Hollywood Theatre; since 1989 the Times Square Church) 212
Martha Cohen Theatre, Calgary, Alberta, Canada 90, *92*
Melbourne Arts Centre, Melbourne, Australia 172
Mercury Theatre, London 76
Mermaid Theatre, London 11, *95*
Metropolitan Opera, New York, NY, USA 150, 159, 209, 212–14, 219

National Centre for the Performing Arts, Beijing, China 176
National Theatre, London [contains the Olivier, Lyttleton and Dorfman (Cottesloe) Theatres] xi, 1, 7, 12, 14–16, 21, 27–39, 49–50, 53, 57–9, 64–5, 68–9, 71–2, 74, 78–9, 83, 85, 91, 137, 139, 150, *198*, 209, 212, 219
National Theater, Munich, Germany 8, 53
Nevill Holt Opera, Market Harborough 158
New Theatre, Cambridge (demolished in 1956) 30
New Wolsey Theatre, Ipswich 57
Nottingham Playhouse, Nottingham 121, 131, 133

Old Vic Theatre, London 6, 7, 12, 14, 40, *57*–8, 68, 87, 164, 213, 218
Olivier Theatre, London (part of the National Theatre) 1, 6, 7–9, 12, 16, 30, 39, *45*, 46, 49, 55, 57–79, 83, 86–7, 105, 145, 166, 179, 184, 186, 188, *198*, 199, 212, 218–19
Opera House, Buxton 23
Opera House, Cardiff 57, 110, 184
Opera House, Dallas, TX, USA 144, 154, 158, *159*, 160–1
Opera House, Dunfermline [auditorium recreated in Sarasota, FL (USA)] 134, *135*, 136–8, 142

Opera House, Helsinki, Finland 140
Opera House, Manchester 12
Opera House, Oslo, Norway (Operahuset in Norwegian) 160, *161*, 162
Opera House, Tunbridge Wells 120, 144
Orange Tree Theatre, Richmond, London 179, 201, *202*, 202–3
Oxford Playhouse, Oxford 11, 32, 102, *220*, 228

Palace Theatre, London 211, 218
Palais Garnier, Paris, France 17, 54
Phoenix Theatre, London 30
Piccadilly Theatre, London 11, 54
Polonsky Theatre, Brooklyn, NY, USA (also known as Theatre for a New Audience) 89–90
Princess Theatre, Melbourne, Australia 172
Prithvi Theatre, Mumbai, India 172
Public Theatre, Pittsburgh, PA, USA 102

Quays Theatre, Salford, Greater Manchester (part of the Lowry Centre) 90

Radio City Music Hall, New York, NY, USA 62
Regent's Park Open Air Theatre, London 179, 182, 203, *204*, 205
Royal Exchange Theatre, Manchester 14, 90, 107, 179, 199, *200*, 201, 203, 205
Royal Opera House, Covent Garden, London 62, 89, 115, 130, 148, 152, 193
Royal Shakespeare Theatre, Stratford-upon-Avon (also known as Shakespeare Memorial Theatre in successive versions of 1879, 1932 and 2010) 30, 32, 57, 179, 184, 186, *187*, 190

Sadler's Wells, London 38, 64–5
Sage Gateshead, Gateshead (concert venue with two auditoriums and education venue) 93, 98, *99*, 161
Sam Wanamaker Playhouse, London (referred to as the Inigo Jones Theatre during design) 93–8, 126
Shakespeare Memorial Theatre, Stratford-upon-Avon (later the Royal Shakespeare Theatre) 30, 32, 57, 179, 184, 186, 187, 190
Shakespeare's Globe, London (reconstruction of 1997) 8–9, 44, 54–7, 89, 95, 97, *97*, 126, 173, 182, *190*, 191, 193
Shaw Festival Theatre, Niagara, Ontario, Canada 102
Sondheim Theatre, London (formerly the Queen's Theatre) 218
Stadthalle, Biberach an der Riß, Germany 164

St James's Theatre, London 119
St Lawrence Centre, Toronto, Ontario, Canada 102, 166, *220*
Swan Theatre, Stratford-upon-Avon (part of Royal Shakespeare Theatre) 39, 100, 103, 183, 185–6, 188, *189*, 191

Teatro Amazonas, Manaus, Brazil 170
Teatro José de Alencar, Fortaleza, Brazil 170
Teatro Municipal, Ouro Preto, Brazil 168, *169*
Teatro Oficina, São Paulo, Brazil 105–7, 168
Telus Theatre, Vancouver, British Columbia, Canada (part of Chan Centre for the Performing Arts) 191, 193
Theater am Schiffbauerdamm, Berlin, Germany 167
Theater De Bonkelaar, Sliedrecht, the Netherlands 164
Theater De Flint, Amersfoort, the Netherlands 164
Theater De Maagd, Bergen op Zoom, the Netherlands *165*, 166
Theater De Tamboer, Hoogeveen, the Netherlands *163*, 164
Theatr Clwyd, Mold, Wales 57, 119
Théâtre de Vieux-Colombier, Paris, France 21–3
Theatre Royal Brighton, Brighton 11
Theatre Royal Bury St Edmunds, Bury St Edmunds 27, 121–8
Theatre Royal Covent Garden, London 10, 12, 168, 195
Theatre Royal Drury Lane, London 10, 62, 179, 195–9
Theatre Royal Glasgow, Glasgow 140
Theatre Royal Newcastle, Newcastle 11, 121, 128–33
Theatre Royal Nottingham, Nottingham 120–1, 128–33
Theatre Royal Sydney, Sydney, Australia 172
Theatre Royal York, York 122
Tina Packer Playhouse, Lenox, MA, USA (previously named the Founders' Theatre) *109*, 112, 193
Traverse Theatre, Edinburgh 139
Tricycle Theatre, London (rebuilt and renamed Kiln Theatre) 50, 103–5, 112, 193, 202
Twentse Schouwburg, Enschede, the Netherlands *165*, 166
Tyne Theatre and Opera House, Newcastle 130

University Theatre, Warwick 76

Vanbrugh Theatre (RADA), London 93–8

Vivien Beaumont Theatre, New York, NY, USA (part of Lincoln Center) 46–8, 63, 65, 102, 115, 185

War Memorial Theatre, San Francisco, CA, USA 150
Warner Bros. Hollywood Theatre, New York, NY, USA (later the Mark Hellinger Theatre) 212
Whitehall Theatre, London (now the Trafalgar Theatre) 212

Wilde Theatre, Bracknell 90, *91*
Wimbledon Theatre, London 39, 217
Winspear Opera House, Dallas, TX, USA 160
Winter Garden Theatre, Toronto, Ontario, Canada 142

Yard Theatre, Chicago, IL, USA (part of Chicago Shakespeare Theatre) 179, 191, *192*
Young Vic Theatre, London 15, 49–51, 89, 172, 203, 215

PERSON INDEX

Page numbers in italics refer to illustrations.

Agrippa, Heinrich Cornelius (1486–1535), German polymath 98

Albery, Bronson (1881–1971), Theatre owner and producer. Knighted 1949 39

Albery, Donald (1914–1988), Owner of theatres inherited from Bronson. New (now Noel Coward), Wyndham's and Piccadilly. Knighted 1977 11, 39

Amery, Colin (1944–2018), Architectural scholar. Editor of *The National Theatre, the ARCHITECTURAL REVIEW Guide* 58, 61, 71

Andreu, Paul (b.1938), French architect. National Grand Theatre of China Beijing 2007 176

Appia, Adolphe (1862–1928), Swiss theatre designer and pioneer of stage lighting 17–24, 35

Ariosto, Ludovico (1474–1533), Italian poet, author of *Orlando Furioso* 86

Arlen, Stephen (1913–1972), Administrator of Sadler's Wells Opera 1976–1972 65

Aslet, Clive (b.1955), Architectural critic 137

Atkins, Eileen (b.1934), Actor. Appointed dame in 2001 11, 126

Atkins, Robert (1886–1972), Actor–manager who founded Regent's Park Theatre 203

Atkinson, Brooks (1894–1984), American drama critic 5

Attenborough, Michael (b.1950), Director. Associate director, RSC 184

Attenborough, Richard (1923–2014), Film and stage director and actor. Knighted 1976. Ennobled 1993 202

Audi, Pierre (b.1957), Opera and theatre director. Founder of Almeida Theatre 1979. Artistic director of the Dutch National Opera 1988–2018 117

Avery, Bryan (1944–2017), Architect. Vanbrugh Theatre RADA 2001 93, 95, 97

Ayckbourn, Alan (b.1939), Playwright. Scarborough from 1957. Knighted 1977 201–3

Baker, George (1934–2011), Stage, film and television actor. Actor–manager of Candida Plays from 1965 126

Barnes, Jason (b.1947), Production manager, Cottesloe 1977–2009 85, 89, 115

Barrie, James (1880–1987), Dramatist. Works include Peter Pan 36

Barron, Michael (b.1945), Acoustician and author *Auditorium Acoustics and Architectural Design* (1998 and 2009) 63, 144–51

Barry, Edward (1830–1880), Architect. Royal Opera House Covent Garden 1858 148, 195

Bart, Lionel (1930–1999), British writer and composer of musicals 8

Barton, Anne (1933–2013), American–English Shakespearean scholar. Married John Barton 1969 100

Barton, John (1928–2018), Shakespearean director and scholar. Invited to join the RSC in 1961 and was still involved forty years later 100

Batzner, Helmut (1928–2010), Principal architect, Baadisches Staatstheater, Karlsruhe 1975 54

Baugh, Christopher (b.1944), Theatre scholar and scenographer 5–6, 48, 133

Baxter, Stanley (b.1926), Scottish stage and television actor. Pantomime dame 217

Beaumont, Binkie (1908–1973), Hugh Beaumont. British theatre producer. Co-founder of H M Tennent 1936 11

Beazley, Samuel (1786–1851), Architect. Lyceum Theatre 1834 126, 130, 195

Beerbohm, Max (1872–1956), Theatre critic and author 13

Bel Geddes, Norman (1893–1958), American industrial and film and designer. Designed influential unbuilt theatres 24

Bennetts, Rab (b.1953), Architect. Co-founder of Bennetts Associates. Hampstead Theatre 2003, Royal Shakespeare Theatre 2010 183–8

Besch, Anthony (1924–2002), Opera director and arts consultant 74

Betjeman, John (1906–1984), Poet Laureate. Writer and broadcaster. Knighted 1969 16

Billington, Michael (b.1939), *Guardian* theatre critic 1971–2019 64, 105, 218

Bing, Rudolf (1902–1997), Austrian opera manager Glyndebourne 1934. First director of the Edinburgh Festival 1947. Director of Metropolitan Opera New York 1950–1972. Knighted 1971 144

Binney, Marcus (b.1944), British architectural historian. Chairman of SAVE Britain's Heritage. Co-author with Rosy Runciman of *GLYNDEBOURNE Building a Vision* 145, 147, 219

Blonski, Andrzej (b.1942), London-based architect. Own practice formerly worked with Peter Moro 121, *123*, 124

Bo Bardi, Lina (1914–1992), Italian architect, emigrated to Brazil in 1946 105

Bornemann, Fritz (1912–2007), German modernist architect. Deutsche Oper Berlin 1962, Frei Volksbuhne Berlin 1963 53

Bourchier, Arthur (1863–1927), Actor–manager 13

Boxer, Mark (1931–1988), 'Marc', British political cartoonist

Boyd, Michael (b.1955), Artistic director, RSC 2003–2012 74

Brecht, Bertolt (1898–1956), Playwright and theatre director. Founder, Berliner Ensemble 1949 xii, 167

Brereton, Christopher (1941–1992), Architect and author 120

Brett, Richard (1938–2014), Head engineer, TPC 1967–1985 62, 87, 89, 154

Bridges-Adams, William (1889–1965), Director, Stratford-upon-Avon 1919–1934 36

Bridie, James (1988–1951), Scottish dramatist 40

Britten, Benjamin (1913–1976), Composer. Co-founder, Aldeburgh Festival 1948. Ennobled 1976 144

Brook, Peter (1925–2022), Theatre and film director. Bouffes du Nord Paris 1974–2011 7–8, 65, 103, 111–15

Bryden, William (1942–1922), Known as Bill Bryden. Theatre director and NT associate 68, 73, 86, 115–16

Burte, Himanshu (b.1967), Indian architect and author. Associate Professor Centre for Urban Science and Engineering, Indian Institute of Technology Bombay 172

Bury, Elizabeth (b.1941), Design partner and widow of John Bury 75, 78, 133, 145

Bury, John (1925–2000), Designer. Theatre workshop. RSC head of design 1963–1968 and NT 1973–1988. Designer at Glyndebourne 1974–1994 12, 15, 61, 71, 76–8, 83, 86–7, 90, 100, 133, 145–7, 150, 167

Busch, Fritz (1890–1951), German conductor. Founding musical director, Glyndebourne 1934 144

Calatrava, Santiago (b.1952), Spanish/Swiss artist and engineer turned architect 162

Carey, Jan (b.1941), Actor and wife of Iain Mackintosh 202

Casson, Lewis (1875–1969), Actor. Married to Sybil Thorndike. Knighted 1945 39

Celso, Zé (b.1937), Brazilian theatre director. Co-founder of Teatro Oficina 105–6

Chen, Jack (1908–1995), Son of Eugene. Author of *The Chinese Theatre* 1949 *175*, 176

Chesterton, A K (1899–1973), Drama critic for the *Stratford-on-Avon Herald* 36, 38

Chesterton, G K (1874–1936), Author, poet and dramatist 36, 38

Chesterton, Maurice (1882–1962), Architect. Employed Elisabeth Scott 36, 38

Christie, George (1934–2014), Son of John Christie and director of Glyndebourne 1963–2014. Knighted 1984 87, 144, 151, 219

Christie, John (1882–1962), Founder of Glyndebourne Opera 144–52, 157

Christo (1935–2020), Artist of large-scale environmental installations 167

Clarke, John (1946–2017), British quantity surveyor of performing arts buildings 59

Clough, Arthur (1819–1861), English poet 61

Coffey, Denise (1936–2022), Actor 134

Conville, David (1929–2018), Actor–manager, Regent's Park Open Air Theatre 1962–1987 203

Copeau, Jacques (1879–1949), French theatre director, actor and producer; founder of the Vieux Colombier 21–3

Cottrell, Richard (b.1936), One of Prospect trio with Toby Robertson and Iain Mackintosh 1966–1969. Co-founder and director of Cambridge Theatre 1969–1972. Director BOV 1975–1980. Emigrated to Australia 1984. Translator of Russian and French plays 11–12, 122

Coward, Noel (1899–1973), Playwright, director and actor. Knighted 1969 113, 126

Cowell, Richard (b.1944), Acoustician. Sound Research Laboratories and Arup Acoustics 63

Craig, Edward Gordon (1872–1964), Designer, author and theatre historian 21–4, 34–6

Cremer, Lothar (1905–1990), Acoustician. Berlin Philharmonie 1963 162

Crosby, Theo (1925–1994), Architect Shakespeare's Globe 55, 95

Crowley, Graham (b. 1950), General manager Royal Court Theatre during renovation completing 2000 107

Cumberland, Richard (1732–1811), Playwright and essayist 10

Daldry, Stephen (b.1960), Stage and film director. Artistic director, Royal Court Theatre 1989–2002 107, 110

Dam, Cees (b.1963), Dutch architect 158

Davenant, William (1606–1668), Poet and playwright 210

de Grey, Spencer (b.1944), Architect. Partner in Foster and Partners 98, 160

de Valois, Ninette (1898–2001), Dancer, choreographer and director. Appointed Dame 1951 30

Devine, George (1910–1966), Theatre director. First artistic director of the English Stage Company 1956 65, 110

Dexter, John (1925–1990), Theatre, opera and film director 65

Dickie, Brian (b.1941), General administrator of Glyndebourne 1981–1988 145

Dixon, Jack (1936–2020), Reopened the 1867 Tyne Theatre and Opera House Newcastle in the 1970s 130

Dodd, Ken (1927–2018), Comedian 120, 132, 217–19

Donnellan, Declan (b.1953), Director. Co-founder, Cheek by Jowl 1981 11–12

Doran, Greg (b.1958), Director, RSC from 2013 78, 186

Dowling, Joe (b.1948), Director of the Guthrie Theatre in Minneapolis 1995–2015 44

Dudley, William (b.1947), Known as Bill Dudley. Theatre designer best known for much work at NT 1978–2002 62, 86, 115–16

Dunbar, Alexander (1930–2012), Known as Sandy. First director of North-Eastern Association for the Arts (later Northern Arts). Director Scottish Arts Council 1971–1980 139–40

Dunbar-Nasmith, Sir James (b.1927), Architect. Co-founder, LDN Architects. Deputy chairman, Edinburgh Festival 1981–1985. Knighted 1996 12, 72, 134, 136–7, 139–42

Dunlop, Frank (b.1927), Stage director. Founder, Pop Theatre Company and Young Vic 49, 65, 89, 131, 141

Earl, John (b.1928), Theatre historian 120, 122, 195

Eberson, John (1875–1954), American theatre architect 210–11

Ebert, Carl (1887–1980), Director of productions, Glyndebourne 1934–1959 144

Eddison, Robert (1908–1991), Actor 119

Edgeworth, Jane, Head of British Council drama and music department 11

Edström, Per Simon (b.1929), Swedish playwright, author and theatre director 182

Elliott, Michael (1931–1984), Theatre and television director. Co-founder, Theatre 69 and Manchester Royal Exchange 14–15, 49, 65, 73, 199, 201

Emden, Walter (1847–1918), Architect 121, 130

Essert, Bob (b.1956), Acoustician. Co-founder with architect and wife Anne Minors of Sound Space Vision 98, 147, 154, 158, 160

Evershed-Martin, Leslie (1903–1991), Founder of Chichester Festival Theatre 1962 46, 48

Eyre, Richard (b.1943), Stage, TV and film director. Director of the National Theatre 1987–1997. Knighted 1997 xi–xii, 7, 61, 63, 71, 89, 184

Fair, Alistair (b. 1982) Architectural historian and author. Joined University of Edinburgh in 2013 becoming Reader in 2020

Farrah, Abd'Elkader (1926–2005), Resident associate designer of the RSC 1961–1991 100

Felsenstein, Walter (1901–1975), Founder, Komische Oper 1947 167

Ferraby, Clare (b.1938), Theatre interior designer 132

Field, Anthony (1928–2014), 28 years as finance director of the Arts Council of Great Britain then 20 years as vice-chairman of Theatre Projects 116

Fiennes, Ralph (b.1962), Actor and director 107, 214

Finney, Albert (1936–2019), Actor 7, 68

Flanagan, Jason (b.1967), Architect. Co-founder, Flanagan Lawrence Architects 98

Fleming, Tom (1927–2010), Actor and director 42

Flower, Archibald (1865–1950), Of the Flower family of brewers. Chairman of the Shakespeare Memorial Theatre. Three times Mayor of Stratford-upon-Avon. Knighted 1930 36, 38

Foley, Mark (b.1950), Architect. Refurbished Almeida Theatre 2003 117

Garrick, David (1717–1779), Playwright. Actor-manager Drury Lane 1747–1776 10

Gascoigne, Bamber (1935–2022), Television presenter and author 157

Gaskill, Bill (1930–2016), Theatre director. Artistic director of the Royal Court Theatre 1965–1972 65

Gehry, Frank (b.1929). Canadian–American architect. Guggenheim Museum Bilbao 1997 and Disney Concert Hall Los Angeles 2003 161

Gelb, Peter (b.1953), General manager, Metropolitan Opera New York from 2006 213–14

George, Colin (1929–2016), First artistic director of the Crucible Theatre Sheffield 46, 48–9, 65

Getty, Mark (b.1960), Co-founder and chairman of Getty Images 154–5, 157

Gielgud, John (1904–2000), Actor and theatre director. Knighted 1953 51, 91, 115

Gilbert, Eddie (b.1937), Theatre director in UK, US and Canada. Director of Manitoba, St Lawrence and Pittsburgh theatres 102–3, *220*

Glasstone, Victor (d.2013), Author and Photographer *Victorian and Edwardian Theatres* 1975 120

Godden, Jerry (b.1945), Theatre consultant. TPC 1976–2012 107, 184, 186

Goodman, Arnold (1919–1995), Leading showbiz lawyer. Chairman of ACGB. First chairman of the Theatres Trust. Ennobled 1965 119

Granville-Barker, Harley (1877–1946), English actor, director, playwright, manager, critic and theorist 36, 72, 110

Gray, Andy (1959–2021), Actor and panto legend 217

Gray, Terence (1895–1986), Founder of Cambridge Festival Theatre 1926. Retired 1933 to become a Buddhist and breed racehorses 27, *28*, 30–6

Green, Gavin (b.1973), Architect. Co-founder in 2004 of Charcoalblue. Head of design. Before that, eight years at TPC 184, 186, *190*, 191, *192*

Greenfield, Jon (b.1959), Theatre architect. Project architect, Shakespeare's Globe before and after death of Theo Crosby *55*, 57

Greiner, Onno (1924–2010), Dutch architect of theatres, cultural centres and psychiatric centres *70*, 163–6, 173, 185

Gropius, Walter (1883–1969), Director of the Bauhaus. Arrived Britain 1934, USA 1937 24, 60

Grounds, Roy (1905–1981), Modern Australian architect. National Arts Centre Melbourne completed after his death. Knighted 1969 172

Gunter, John (1938–2016), Film and stage designer 61

Guthrie, Thomas (1803–1873), Scottish cleric. Grandfather of Tyrone Guthrie 42

Guthrie, Tyrone (1900–1971), Theatre director. Founder of Stratford Festival of Canada and Guthrie Theatre in Minneapolis 9, 11, 15, 20, 30, 32, 40–52, 65, 102, 112, 115, 131, 172, 185, 188

Hadid, Zaha (1950–2016), British–Iraqi architect, artist and designer. Appointed Dame 2016 176

Haitink, Bernard (b.1929), Dutch conductor. Music director, Glyndebourne 1978–1988 145

Hall, Peter (1980–2017), Theatre and opera director. Director, RSC 1960–1968 and NT 1973–1988 Knighted 1977 7, 12, 14–15, 30, 36, 65, 68–71, 73, 76, 78, 83, 86, 89, 116, 133, 145, 214

Hallifax, Michael (1919–2008), Company manager at Royal Court, RSC and NT 71

Ham, Roderick (1925–2017), Architect. Theatres in Leatherhead 1969, Derby 1975 and Ipswich 1979 57

Harbottle, Laurence (1924–2015), Lawyer specialising in the entertainment industry 11, 229

Harris, Rob (b.1954), Acoustician and theatre consultant. Arup Acoustics 1983–2015. Rob Harris Design 2015–2020 150, 160

Harrison, Tony (b.1937), Yorkshire poet and playwright 69, 71, 115

Havel, Vaclav (1936–2011), Czech politician and playwright. President of Czechoslovakia then Czech Republic 1989–2003 61, 167

Hayles, Andy (b.1967). Theatre consultant. Lighting designer. Founder in 2004 of Charcoalblue. Managing partner. Before that, eight years at TPC 188, 191, 203

Herbert, Jocelyn (1917–2003), Theatre stage designer 65, 67, 68, 71, 73

Higgott, Gordon (b.1953), Architectural historian 97

Hodges, C. Walter (1909–2004), Artist, Elizabethan historian and stage designer 55

Holloway, Baliol (1883–1967), Stage and film actor 36

Holzbauer, Wilhelm (1930–1986), Austrian modernist architect. Lead architect, Amsterdam Opera House 1986 158

Hopkins, Michael (b.1935), Architect. Founder and director of Hopkins Architects xi, 145, 147–8, 150–1

Hopkins, Patty (b.1942), Architect. Founder and director of Hopkins Architects 150

Howell, Bill (1922–1974), Architect. Young Vic 1970 and Christ's Hospital Theatre 1974 50, 89–90, 100, 191, 203

Howell, Mark, Theatre historian specialising in Georgian playhouses 124

Humphreys, Henry (died 1974), Acoustician 63

Hunt, Hugh (1911–1993), Theatre director and scholar 39

Ingrams, Leonard (1941–2005), Founder and chairman of first Garsington Opera 1989 154, 158

Irving, Henry (1838–1905), Theatre actor–manager. Knighted 1895 21, 23

Izenour, George (1912–2007), Engineer. Theatre designer and author 19–21

Jaques-Dalcroze, Émile (1865–1950), Swiss composer, musician and choreographer 18, 76

Jenkins, Hugh (1908–2004), British Labour politician. First director of Theatres Trust 119

Jones, Inigo (1573–1652), Architect and theatre designer 93–8

Joseph, Stephen (1921–1967), Theatre director and pioneer of theatre-in-the-round 15, 46, 201

Kani, Wasfi (b.1956), Founder of Pimlico Opera and Grange Park Opera 157–8

Kapoor, Jennifer (1934–1984), Actor. Founder of the Prithvi Theatre 172

Kemp, Robert (1908–1967), Scottish Playwright 40–2

Kendal, Felicity (b.1946), Stage and television actor. Sister to Jennifer Kapoor 172

Kenny, Sean (1929–1973), Irish theatre and film designer, lighting designer and director 8, 46, 65, 76, 122

Kent, Jonathan (b.1946), Theatre and opera director. Joint director with Ian McDiarmid of the Almeida 1990–2002 107, 117

Kent, Nicolas (b.1945), Artistic director of Tricycle Theatre 1984–2012, 103, 105

Killigrew, Thomas (1612–1683), Playwright and theatre manager of the first Theatre Royal Drury Lane 210

Kuller, Rikard (1938–2009), Environmental psychologist and author of *Architectural Psychology* 1975 20

Kumar, Atul (b.1968), Founder, the Company Theatre Mumbai 1993 172–3

Kun, Kuo Pao (1939–2002), Singaporean playwright and left-wing political activist 176

Kupfer, Harry (1935–2019), German opera director and academic 167

Lamb, Thomas (1871–1942), Scottish-born American theatre architect 210–12

Langham, Michael (1919–2011), Director. Followed Guthrie at Stratford Ontario and at Minneapolis 44

Lasdun, Denys (1914–2001), Modernist architect. Notable concrete buildings include Royal College of Physicians and University of East Anglia. NT his only theatre. Knighted 1976 7, 15–16, 21, 24, 38, 49, 54, 59–73, 78, 83, 87

Law, Graham (1924–1996), Architect. Co-founder, LDN architects. Pitlochry Theatre 1981 and Eden Court Theatre Inverness 1976 12, 72, 134, 139–42

Le Corbusier (1887–1965), Swiss–French architect, designer and writer 69

Leacroft, Richard (1914–1986), Architect, stage designer, illustrator and author of books including *The Development of the English Playhouse* 1973 and *THEATRE AND PLAYHOUSE An Illustrated Survey of Theatre Buildings from Ancient Greece to the Present Day* 1984 22, 27, 28, 38, 41, 121, 124, 127

Leigh, Vivien (1913–1967), Theatre and film actor. Married to Laurence Olivier 1940–1960 119

Lerner, Ralph (1949–2011), Professor of architecture, Princeton University 173

Lewenstein, Oscar (1917–1997), Producer. Co-founder of English Stage Company at the Royal Court Theatre 1954 110

Lichtenstein, Harvey (1929–2017), American arts administrator. President, Brooklyn Academy of Music 112–14

Littlewood, Joan (1942–2002), Theatre director. Founder of Theatre Workshop at Stratford East 1953 78, 167

Livingstone, Ken (b.1945), Labour Politician. Leader of the GLC. Mayor of London 203

Lloyd Webber, Andrew (b.1948), Composer, producer and owner of theatres including the London Palladium, the Gillian Lynne Theatre (formerly the New London) and the Theatre Royal Drury Lane. Knighted 1992. Ennobled 1997 199

Longman, Peter (b.1946), Director of The Theatres Trust 2000–2016 120

Lubetkin, Berthold (1901–1990), Georgian-British architect 60

Lutyens, Edward (1869–1944), Architect 39

McDiarmid, Ian (b.1944), Actor and joint director of Almeida 1990–2002 117

McElfatrick, J. B. (1828–1906), American theatre architect 113

McElfatrick, W. M. (1854–1923), American Theatre architect. Son of J. B. McElfatrick 113

McKellen, Ian (b.1939), Film and theatre actor. Knighted 1991 11, 30, 100

Mackintosh, Hugh Ross (1870–1936), Scottish cleric. Theologian. Moderator of the General Assembly of the Church of Scotland 1932. Grandfather of Iain Mackintosh, author of this book 42

Mander, Raymond (1911–1983), Theatre historian. Co-founder of Mander and Mitchenson Theatre Collection 21

Marlowe, Christopher (1564–1593), Playwright and poet 11, 30, 88

Marsh, George (b.1957), Architect. Payette Architects Boston from 1980. Theatres for Gordon College Wenham and Shakespeare & Co 112

Marshall, Norman (1901–1980), Theatre director, producer and author 23, 32, 34–6, 39, 64–5, 75

Maugham, Somerset (1874–1965), Novelist and playwright 21

May, Val (1927–2012), Director of Nottingham Playhouse 1957–1961, BOV 1961–1975 and Yvonne Arnaud Theatre 1975–1992 121–2, 124

Mielziner, Jo (1901–1976), American set and lighting designer 47

Mildmay, Audrey (1900–1953), Canadian soprano. Wife of John Christie 144

Miller, Paul (b.1968), Second artistic director of the Orange Tree Theatre, London 2014–2022 121, 202

Minors, Anne (b.1955), Architect. Theatre consultant. TPC 1984–1995. Co-founder with acoustician and husband Bob Essert of Sound Space Vision which followed on from Anne Minors Performance Consultants 147, 158

Mitchenson, Joe (1911–1992), Theatre historian. Co-founder of Mander and Mitchenson Theatre Collection 21

Moiseiwitsch, Tanya (1914–2003), Set designer and collaborator with Tyrone Guthrie 40, 44, 47–8, 65

Moore, Rowan, Architecture critic for the *Guardian* 106–7, 158, 182

Morley, Christopher (b.1937), Theatre stage designer 100

Moro, Peter (1911–1989), Architect. Theatres include Nottingham Playhouse 1964 and Theatre Royal Plymouth 1982 121–2, 124, 133

Morris, Tom (b.1964), Theatre director. Director of BOV from 2009 124

Mortimer, John, QC (1923–2009), Barrister, playwright author. Chairman Royal Court 1990–2000. Knighted 1998 110

Moya, Hidalgo (1920–1994), Architect. With Philip Powell designed Chichester Festival Theatre 1962 46

Negri, Richard (1927–1999), Theatre designer and director 201
Negus, Anthony (b.1946), Opera conductor 152
Neville, John (1925–2011), Theatre and film actor 131
Noble, Adrian (b.1950), Theatre director. Artistic director of the RSC 1991–2003 78, 100, 183–6
Nouvel, Jean (b.1945), French architect. Theatres include second Guthrie Theater Minneapolis 2006 and new 1993 theatre space within the old 1831 Lyon Opera, now renamed the Opera Nouvel 44
Nunn, Trevor (b.1940), Theatre director. Artistic director of the RSC 1968–1986 and NT 1997–2003. Knighted 2002 30, 38, 63, 100, 183

Obolensky, Chloe (b.1942), Worked with Peter Brook as designer for twenty years 113
Olivier, Laurence (1907–1989), Theatre and film actor and director. Director, NT 1963–1973. Knighted 1947. Ennobled 1970 7, 39–40, 49, 51, 53, 63–5, 68, 72–3, 119, 172, 188, 218
O'Neill, Eugene (1888–1953), American playwright and Nobel Laureate 110
Ormerod, Nick (b.1951), Theatre set and costume designer; co-founder of Cheek by Jowl 11
O'Rorke, Brian (1901–1974), New Zealand architect and interior designer 38–9
Orrell, John (1934–2003), Author and theatre historian 95

Packer, Tina (b.1938), Director and founder, Shakespeare & Company in Lenox, MA 1978 110
Phipps, C.J. (1835–1897), Theatre architect 14–15, 121–2, 130–2, 139
Pilbrow, Richard (b.1933), Lighting designer and theatre consultant. Founder, Theatre Projects 1957. Building committee then technical consultant for NT 11–12, 14, 39, 62–5, 68, 83, 87, 90, 116, 166
Porter, Andrew (1928–2015), Music opera scholar and critic for the *Observer* 118
Powell, Philip (1921–2003), Architect. With Hidalgo Moya designed Chichester Festival Theatre 1962 46, 74

Quayle, Anthony (1913–1989), Stage and film actor. Artistic director, Stratford-upon-Avon 1948–1955. Knighted 1985 40, 51–2, 188

Rambert, Marie (1888–1982), Dancer. Choreographer. Founder, Ballet Rambert 1926. Appointed dame 1962 76
Rapson, Ralph (1914–2008), American architect of Guthrie Minneapolis 1963 44
Reardon, Michael (b.1934), Architect. Swan 1986. Historical buildings specialist 100, *189*
Reid, Francis (1931–2016), Lighting designer, author and lecturer 90, 166
Relph, Simon (1940–2016), Film producer. Technical director, NT at opening 87
Reuter, Rolf (1926–2007), Musical director, Komische Oper 1981–1993 167
Ritchie, Ian (b.1947), Architect. RSC temporary (2006–2010), Courtyard Theatre 2006–2010 186
Rix, Brian (1924–2016), Farceur. Actor–manager, Whitehall Theatre 1950–1966. Knighted 1986. Ennobled 1992 212
Robertson, Toby (1928–2012), Stage and TV director. Artistic director, Prospect Theatre Company 1964–1980. Artistic director, Theatr Clwyd, North Wales 1985–1992 11–12, 30, 54, 124, 127
Ronalds, Tim (b.1950), Architect. Theatres include refurbishment of Hackney Empire and Wilton's Music Hall *156*, 157
Ronconi, Luca (1933–2015), Italian actor, theatre director and opera director 86
Rooney, Mickey (1920–2014), American film and stage actor. Star of *Sugar Babies* 212
Ross, Colin (1947–2018), Architect. Partner LDN architect working on all their theatres 141–3
Ross, David (b.1965), Founder, Nevill Holt Opera 158
Rubasingham, Indhu, Director of Kiln Theatre, London since 2012 105
Russell, Alan (1943–2021), Theatre consultant. TPC 1970–2010 83, 147, 150
Rylance, Mark (b.1960), Stage and film actor. First actor–manager, Shakespeare's Globe 1995–2005. Knighted 2017 57
Rylands, George (1902–1999), Known as Dadie. Shakespearean scholar. Fellow King's College 1927–1999. Chairman, Cambridge Arts Theatre 1946–1982 30

Saarinen, Eero (1910–1961), Finnish–American architect. Vivian Beaumont Theatre 1965 47

Scharoun, Hans (1893–1972), German architect. Berlin Philharmonie 1963 162

Scott, Elisabeth (1898–1972), Architect. Shakespeare Memorial Theatre 1932 36, 38, 183, 186, 188

Sell, Michael (b.1937), Author and theatre historian 120, 122

Serroni, José Carlos (b.1950), Leading Brazilian stage designer. Known universally simply as Serroni 105, 168

Shaktman, Ben (b.1937), Co-founder, Pittsburgh Public Theatre. Artistic director 1975–1982 102

Shaw, George Bernard (1856–1950), Irish playwright 18, 110

Sheader, Tim (b.1971), Artistic director, Regent's Park Open Air Theatre from 2008 203

Shorter, Eric (1930–2018), *Daily Telegraph* theatre critic 103

Snell, Robin (b.1968), Architect. Project architect for Michael Hopkins at Glyndebourne. Co-founder, Robin Snell and Partners. New Garsington Opera Pavilion 2011 148, 150, *153*, 154–5, 157

Southern, Richard (1903–1989), Theatre designer and author. Co-founder, Society for Theatre Research 1948. Associated with Bristol University drama department 1951–1969 39, 46, *55*, *75*, 76, 121, 124, 126

Staples, David (b.1951), Theatre consultant. TPC 1974–2018. Director from 1979 136

Stewart, Allan (b.1950), Actor. Panto dame 217

Stott, Grant (b.1967), Actor. Broadcaster. Panto villain 217

Sugden, Derek (1924–2017), Structural engineer and acoustician. Co-founder of Arup Acoustics, part of Arup group 1963 23, 139, 145, 147–8

Sweeting, Elizabeth (1914–1999), Arts administrator. General manager, Oxford Playhouse 1956–1976. Co-founder, Prospect Theatre Company 1961 11, 127

Talbot, Ian (b.1942), Artistic director, Regent's Park Open Air Theatre 1987–2007 203

Tams, John (b.1949), Singer and songwriter. The Mysteries 1977–1985 115

Terry, Ellen (1847–1928), Actor. Leading lady to Henry Irving 1878–1902. Appointed Dame 1925 21, 23, 35

Tessenow, Heinrich (1876–1950), German architect. Planner of the Hellerau community 1909 18

Thom, Ron (1923–1986), Canadian architect. Theatres include Niagara-on-the-Lake 102

Thompson, Nick (b.1935), Theatre architect. First was Sheffield Crucible Theatre for Renton Howard Wood Levin 1971 48, 132

Todd, Andrew (b.1968), English architect living in France 182–3, 191

Tompkins, Steve (b.1959), Theatre architect. Many theatres new and old including Royal Court London 2000, Everyman Liverpool 2014, The Bridge 2017 and TRDL 2021 xi, 89–90, 107–110, 124, 193, 195, 203

Truscott, John (1936–1993), Australian stage designer 172

Ustinov, Peter (1921–2004), Actor, writer and filmmaker. Knighted 1990 131

van Egeraat, Erick (b.1956), Dutch architect 184–6

van Goor, Martien (b.1944), Dutch architect. Partner of Onno Greiner 164

Venu, Gopal (b.1945), Indian expert in Kuttiyatam 173

von Fischer, Karl (1782–1820), Neo-classical Bavarian architect 8

Wagner, Richard (1813–1883), German composer. Director of his Bayreuth Festspielhaus 1876–1882 xi, 7, 17–24, 38, 53, 144, 152, 170

Wagner, Wieland (1917–1966), Stage designer. Grandson of Richard Wagner. Co-director with brother Wolfgang of Bayreuth 1951–1966 18

Wagner, Wolfgang (1919–2010), Opera director. Grandson of Richard Wagner. Sole director of Bayreuth 1966–2008 18

Walters, Sam (b.1939), Founder and director of the Orange Tree Theatre, Richmond, London 1971–2014 201–3

Wanamaker, Sam (1919–1993), American actor and director. Led recreation of Shakespeare's Globe reconstruction 1997 54–5, 95, 97, 126, *190*, 191

Wanamaker, Zoe (b.1949), Actor. Daughter of Sam Wanamaker 214

Warre, Michael (1922–1987), Theatre consultant. Stage designer 72